D0847440

Australia 1944–45
VICTORY IN THE PACIFIC

The years 1944 and 1945 were pivotal in the development of Australia's approach to strategy during the Second World War and beyond. While the main battlefront of the Pacific War had moved further north, Australian air, land and sea forces continued to make a significant contribution to the Allied campaign and towards achieving Australia's strategic interests and objectives. In New Guinea, Australian operations secured territories and released men from service, while in Borneo a highly successful campaign was clouded by uncertain motives and questionable strategy.

Australia 1944–45: Victory in the Pacific examines this complex and fascinating period, which has been largely under-represented in Australian military history. Peter Dean leads a team of internationally regarded military historians in assessing Australian, Allied and Japanese strategies, the conduct of the campaigns in the Southwest Pacific Area and Australia's significant role in achieving victory.

Thoroughly researched and generously illustrated, *Australia 1944–45* is the compelling final instalment in Peter Dean's Pacific War series.

Peter J. Dean is an Associate Dean in the College of Asia-Pacific and a Senior Fellow at the Strategic and Defence Studies Centre, at the Australian National University. He is a member of the editorial board of the *Australian Army Journal* and the journal *Global War Studies* and a Managing Editor of the journal *Security Challenges*.

ALSO PUBLISHED BY CAMBRIDGE UNIVERSITY PRESS

Peter J. Dean *Australia 1942: In the Shadow of War*

Peter J. Dean *Australia 1943: The Liberation of New Guinea*

AUSTRALIA
1944–45

VICTORY IN THE PACIFIC

Edited by

PETER J. DEAN

CAMBRIDGE
UNIVERSITY PRESS

CAMBRIDGE
UNIVERSITY PRESS

477 Williamstown Road, Port Melbourne, VIC 3207, Australia

Cambridge University Press is part of the University of Cambridge.

It furthers the University's mission by disseminating knowledge in the pursuit of education, learning and research at the highest international levels of excellence.

www.cambridge.org
Information on this title: www.cambridge.org/9781107083462

© Cambridge University Press 2016

First published 2016

Cover designed by Anne-Marie Reeves
Typeset by Integra Software Services Pvt Ltd
Printed in China by C & C Offset Printing Co. Ltd

A catalogue record for this publication is available from the British Library

A Cataloguing-in-Publication entry is available from the catalogue of the National Library of Australia at www.nla.gov.au

ISBN 978-1-107-08346-2 Hardback

For Jessica

FOREWORD

The year 2015 is a momentous one for remembering Australia's military history. Few Australian citizens would be unaware of the 100th anniversary of the landings at Gallipoli. This milestone represents one of the most significant commemorations to take place in Australia's history. One of the reasons that this anniversary is so significant is that it honours the experience of the members of the Australian and New Zealand Army Corps who landed at Gallipoli over 100 years ago. The Anzac Centenary is a time to 'reflect upon the service and sacrifice of *all* those who have worn our nation's uniform – past and present', and as Chairman of the Anzac Centenary Advisory Board I am committed to ensuring all Australians gain an understanding of 'our military history and its enduring impacts on the Australia of today'.[1]

Besides the centenary of the landing at Gallipoli, another significant day of remembrance for Australia in 2015 is 15 August. On this date we will commemorate the 70th anniversary of Victory in the Pacific (VP) Day. This date honours Japan's acceptance of the Allied demand for unconditional surrender, and for our country it meant that the Second World War was finally over. It was a day when the Prime Minister, Ben Chifley, noted that Australians should 'remember those whose lives were given [so] that we may enjoy this glorious moment and may look forward to a peace which they have won for us'.[2] The announcement was met with scenes of jubilation, and crowds of Australians spontaneously gathered in cities and towns to celebrate.

The Second World War would have a lasting effect on generations of people around the globe. I was born in the immediate aftermath of the war in Scotland and grew up as part of the generation that lived with its legacy and with immediate family who were directly affected by the experience of war. My family, like so many across the Commonwealth and around the globe, had its members serving in the various theatres of the war.

My father served in the Royal Air Force and was shot down at Handzame in West Flanders, Belgium, on 20 September 1943, spending the rest of the war as a prisoner of war. While Belgium is a long way from the ravages of the Pacific War, his time as a prisoner of war was part of an experience shared by thousands of other British, Australian, New Zealand, Canadian and other Commonwealth air crew that remind us of the truly global nature of this conflict. On the very day that he was shot down, Australia's military forces were in action around the globe; thousands of air crew were undertaking missions in the skies over Europe and New Guinea, while the 7th and 9th Australian Divisions consolidated their position after taking the strategically important town of Lae.

This was a time when Australia's military contribution had shifted firmly to the Pacific theatre. In the previous year war had come to our doorstep, and it changed our nation forever. From this period to the end of the Pacific War it would be a long, difficult and at times tortuous road to victory. In reading through *Australia 1944–45: Victory in the Pacific*, what is striking is the magnitude of Australia's war effort at this time and the lasting impact it has had on this great nation. By 1944 Australia had already been at war for five years, and unlike the First World War the war in the Pacific demanded a 'total' war effort: conflict had come to the homeland. This war changed Australia in innumerable ways, including major structural changes to the economy, as well as profound changes to society, Australian culture and our nation's engagement with the region.

This period and this book are also about war fighting. While Australia's military effort would be overtaken in size and scope by our larger Allied partner, the United States, the final year of the war would see some of the largest operations that the Australian military has ever undertaken. While many of these battles and campaigns remain controversial, the commitment of Australia's service men and women, their tactical prowess and their fortitude remains undiminished.

During the period of 1944–45, the pressures, stresses and strains of war were evident at every level of command and organisation. With 41 years' of service in the Australian Defence Forces, having held command and leadership positions and having served in Indonesia, Singapore, Papua New Guinea and across the region, I have a deep sense of respect and empathy for the experiences that the personnel of Australia's Army, Navy and Air Force endured in the lead up to Victory.

From a military perspective what stands out is the sheer scale and complexity of operations in which the Australians were involved. As Professor David Horner notes in chapter 1, in July 1945 the Australian Army had six infantry divisions in action at the one time, more than any other month of the war. For the Royal Australian Air Force the war in the Pacific was the first time that integrated formations of the Air Force had seen service; it would also organise, deploy and operate its own Tactical Air Force during 1944–45.[3] For the Royal Australian Navy this was the pinnacle of its war effort. It had been there from the very beginning of the war; from 'the dark days in the Mediterranean, at Dakar, in the Middle

East ... [through] the Indian Ocean, the ABDA Area, the South-West Pacific, the Mediterranean again, on to the shores of Japan up to the last day of the war'. The Navy was continually on operations side by side with its British and American 'companions, in the exercise of that sea power which decided the issue of the conflict'.[4]

The 'sea power' that Herman Gill refers to was above all achieved through the exercises of combined, joint and coalition operations at the very cutting edge of technology and doctrine in a continuous cycle of learning and adaptation. For Australia 1945 represents the high point of tactical and operational proficiency of Australia's military forces in the Second World War. This period also represents a time when our strategic leaders carved out particular 'Australian' objectives, in response to the recognition of a set of unique Australian strategic interests, separate from those of the British Empire and our other coalition partners.

During the war in the Pacific, 1942 saw most of the major turning points, including the halting of the Japanese advance, the Allied seizure of the initiative and the movement of the Allied forces over to an offensive posture. The first tentative steps to victory were to be taken in 1943, and in 1944–45 the war in the Pacific came to its climatic conclusion. The year 2015 marks the 70th anniversary of the completion of the campaigns in New Guinea, Bougainville, Borneo and the Philippines.

More Australians saw service in the Second World War than in any other war Australia has fought. It is important that we take the opportunity of this Centenary year to honour the service and sacrifice of all those who have worn our nation's uniform, including the 39,000 who made the supreme sacrifice during the Second World War, the vast majority fighting the Japanese. In this significant commemoration it is important that Australians pause to reflect on the significance of the role that Australia's men and women played in the Pacific War to protect our nation and our freedoms.

Lest we forget.

Air Chief Marshal Sir Angus Houston
AK, AC, AFC (Ret'd)
Chair of the Anzac Centenary Advisory Board

Notes

1   Message from the Chair of the Anzac Centenary Advisory Board Air Chief Marshal Angus Houston, AC, AFC (Ret'd), 'Anzac Centenary Advisory Board', www.anzaccentenary.gov.au/anzac_centenary/advisory_board.htm.

2   Ben Chifley, address to the nation, 15 August 1945.

3   George Odgers, *Air War against Japan 1943–1945*, Australian War Memorial, Canberra, 1957, p. 499.
4   G. Herman Gill, *Royal Australian Navy, 1942–1945*, Australian War Memorial, Canberra, 1968, p. 705.

Contents

MAPS AND CHART

FIGURES AND TABLE

Table

Contributors

Joan Beaumont is Professor of History at the Strategic and Defence Studies Centre at the Australian National University. She is an internationally recognised historian of Australia in the two world wars, Australian defence and foreign policy, the history of prisoners of war and the memory and heritage of war. Her publications include the critically acclaimed *Broken Nation: Australians and the Great War* (2013), which was joint winner of the 2014 Prime Minister's Literary Award (Australian History), winner of the 2014 NSW Premier's Prize (Australian History), winner of the 2014 Queensland Literary Award for History and was shortlisted for the 2014 WA Premier's Prize (non-fiction) and the 2014 Council for the Humanities, Arts and Social Sciences Prize for a Book.

John Blaxland is a Senior Fellow at the Strategic and Defence Studies Centre at the Australian National University who writes about military history, intelligence and security and Asia-Pacific affairs. His publications include *The Australian Army from Whitlam to Howard* (2014), *Strategic Cousins* (2006), *Revisiting Counterinsurgency* (2006), *Information Era Manoeuvre* (2002), *Signals* (1999) and *Organising an Army* (1989). In 2014 he was selected to receive a Minerva Research Initiative grant for a project entitled 'Thailand's Military, the USA and China: Understanding How the Thai Military Perceives the Great Powers and Implications for the US Rebalance'. He is also the author of the second volume and co-author of the third volume of the three-volume official history of the Australian Security Intelligence Organisation (forthcoming) and editor of *Timor Intervention* (forthcoming).

Rhys Crawley is a historian with an honours degree in history from the University of Wollongong and a PhD from the University of New South Wales. In 2007 he was selected as an annual summer scholar at the Australian War Memorial. He is the principal researcher and co-author of the multi-volume *Official History of the Australian Security Intelligence Organisation* (ASIO), and is a co-author of volume 1 of the *Official*

History of Peacekeeping, Humanitarian and Post-Cold War Operations. The author of *Climax at Gallipoli: The Failure of the August Offensive*, he researches, teaches, and writes on aspects of Australian military, logistic, security, and intelligence history.

Peter J. Dean (Editor) is an Associate Dean in the College of Asia-Pacific and a Senior Fellow at the Strategic and Defence Studies Centre, at the Australian National University. He is the author or editor of numerous works including *Architect of Victory: The Military Career of Lieutenant General Sir Frank Horton Berryman* (2011), *Australia 1942: In the Shadow of War* (2012), *Australia 1943: The Liberation of New Guinea* (2013) *and Australia's Defence: Towards a New Era* (2014). He is a member of the editorial board of the *Australian Army Journal* and the journal *Global War Studies* and Managing Editor of the journal *Security Challenges.*

Lachlan Grant is a Historian in the Military History Section at the Australian War Memorial. Previously he worked as a Lecturer at Monash University, where he completed a PhD in 2010 and MA in 2005. He has published widely on Australian experiences of the Second World War in Europe, Asia and the Pacific, and on the prisoner-of-war experience. Lachlan's first book, *Australian Soldiers in Asia-Pacific in World War II*, was published in 2014. He is also a Visiting Fellow at the Strategic and Defence Studies Centre at the Australian National University.

Tony Hastings is a PhD candidate at the University of New South Wales, Canberra. His thesis is on the Borneo campaign of 1945. He had a long career as a journalist, news editor and senior executive at the Australian Broadcasting Corporation. Before that, he co-authored *Espirit De Corps: The History of the Victorian Scottish Regiment and 5th Infantry Battalion.* He holds a BA (Hons) and MA from the University of Melbourne.

Kevin Holzimmer is Research Professor and Adjunct Professor of History at the US Air Force Research Institute. He is the author of a biography of the commander of the Sixth US Army under General of the Army Douglas MacArthur, entitled *General Walter Krueger: Unsung Hero of the Pacific War.* In addition to completing a study of the current international security environment in the Asia-Pacific region, he is currently writing *MacArthur's Lieutenants: The Campaign in the Southwest Pacific Area, 1939–45.*

David Horner AM is Professor of Australian Defence History in the Strategic and Defence Studies Centre at the Australian National University. He is the author or editor of over 30 books on Australian military history, strategy and defence including *High Command* (1982), *Blamey: The Commander-in-Chief* (1998), *Strategic Command, General Sir John Wilton and Australia's Asian Wars* (2005) and the *Australian Military History for Dummies* (2011). In 2004, David was appointed the Official Historian of Australian Peacekeeping, Humanitarian and Post–Cold War Operations. He is the General Editor of this six-volume series and is writing two of the volumes, the first of which, entitled *Australia and the 'New World Order'*, was published in 2011. In 2009, David was appointed Official Historian for the Australian Security Intelligence Organisation.

Karl James is a Senior Historian at the Australian War Memorial, Canberra, and completed his PhD at the University of Wollongong. He has worked on several exhibitions and was the curator for the Memorial's special anniversary exhibition, 'Rats of Tobruk, 1941' on display during 2011. Karl's first book, *The Hard Slog: Australians in the Bougainville Campaign, 1944–45*, was published by Cambridge University Press in 2012. He is also a Visiting Fellow at the Strategic and Defence Studies Centre at the Australian National University.

Mark Johnston is Head of History at Scotch College, Melbourne. He is the author of nine books about the Second World War, including *Whispering Death: Australian Airmen in the Pacific War* (2011), *Anzacs in the Middle East* (2013) and histories of the 6th, 7th and 9th Australian Divisions.

Daniel Marston is Professor of Military Studies at the Strategic and Defence Studies Centre at the Australian National University. He is Principal of the Military and Defence Studies Program at the Australian Command and Staff College in Canberra and previously held the Ike Skelton Distinguished Chair of the Art of War at the US Army Command and General Staff College and advised the United States Marine Corps and the British Army in Iraq and Afghanistan, between 2006–14. His research focuses on how armies learn and reform. His first book *Phoenix from the Ashes,* an in-depth assessment of how the British/Indian Army turned defeat into victory in the Burma campaign of the Second World War, won the Field Marshal Templer Medal Book Prize in 2003.

Michael McKernan has written extensively in the area of Australian social history, in particular charting the effects of war on Australian society. He was a senior lecturer in History at the University of New South Wales, during which time he researched and wrote books including *The Australian People and the Great War*, and *All In! Fighting the War at Home* and *This War Never Ends: Australian Prisoners of War Come Home*. Now working as a consultant historian, Michael McKernan is the author or editor of more than a dozen books and was selected and described the top twenty military leaders of the twentieth century for the 'This Living Century' supplement in the Australian.

Michael Molkentin has a PhD in History from the University of New South Wales, Canberra. He is the author of three books, the latest being *Australia and the War in the Air*, Volume 1 of *The Centenary History of Australia and the Great War* (Oxford University Press, 2014).

Ian Pfennigwerth previously spent 35 years in the Royal Australian Navy. He researches, writes and promotes Australian naval history, and is the Editor of *Journal of Australian Naval History*. He is the author of *A Man of Intelligence, The Australian Cruiser, Perth, 1939–1942* and *Tiger Territory: The Untold Story of the Royal Australian Navy in Southeast Asia from 1948–1971*.

Garth Pratten is a Lecturer in the Strategic and Defence Studies Centre. He has had a varied career having worked for the Australian Army's Training Command, the Australian War Memorial and the Royal Military Academy, Sandhurst. Dr Pratten was a member of the research staff for the *Official History of Australia's Involvement in Southeast Asian Conflicts* and is currently contributing to the *Official History of Australian Peacekeeping and Post-Cold War Operations*. In 2010, while working for the British Ministry of Defence, Dr Pratten was deployed to Afghanistan as part of the team compiling the war diary for the International Security Assistance Force's Regional Command South. He is the author of *Australian Battalion Commanders in the Second World War*, published by Cambridge University Press in 2010.

Mr Hiroyuki Shindo is a Senior Researcher at the Centre for Military History of the National Institute for Defence Studies in Japan. He has an LLB from Kyoto University, a LLM from Kobe University and is a graduate of the Ohio State University PhD coursework program. His special areas of interest are Japanese military strategy and operations during the

Second World War and United States–Japan diplomatic and military relations in the 1930s.

Peter Stanley is a Research Professor at the Australian Centre for the Study of Armed Conflict and Society at the University of New South Wales, Canberra. Before that he was the inaugural Head of the National Museum of Australia's Research Centre (2007–13), and before that Principal Historian at the Australian War Memorial, where he worked from 1980 to 2007. Peter has published 27 books in Australian and British military-social history, most recently *Die in Battle, Do not Despair, the Indians on Gallipoli, 1915*, the first book on the subject. He has recently specialised in the Great War, and his books include *Quinn's Post, Anzac, Gallipoli, Men of Mont St Quentin, Digger Smith and Australia's Great War* and *Lost Boys of Anzac*. His book *Bad Characters: Sex, Crime, Mutiny, Murder and the Australian Imperial Force* was jointly awarded the Prime Minister's Prize for Australian History in 2011. He was recently elected a Fellow of the Australian Academy of the Humanities.

ACKNOWLEDGEMENTS

This is the third and final book in a rather accidental trilogy on Australia in the Pacific War. The first book in the series *Australia 1942: In the Shadow of War* (2012) developed out of a conference of a similar name run by Marcus Fielding and Andrew Kilsby of Military History and Heritage Victoria in mid-2011. In an effort to honour the excellent work done in the academic papers presented to this conference I volunteered to put them together as a book. The wonderful success that this book received both commercially and critically, as well as my personal interest in the major campaign that followed led to *Australia 1943: The Liberation of New Guinea* (2013). Soon after the completion of the manuscript for that book, Cambridge University Press enquired about *Australia 1944*, and in order to round out a series we decided that, due to the nature of Australia's war effort after 1943, a third book on 1944–45 would do nicely. While this book would naturally be a little larger, covering a few more chapters, like the previous other two it does not intend to be a comprehensive coverage of the period 1944–45. The extra room did, however, allow me to join the hands of a few sections covered in *Australia 1942* and add in a few more thematic chapters to round out some areas of focus in all three books.

As with the previous books the work here is a combined effort of a large group of historians. Again they have been a fine group to work with and in particular I want to acknowledge David Horner, Karl James, Ian Pfenningwerth, Mark Johnston and Hiroyuki Shindo who have contributed chapters to all three books. Kevin Holzimmer, Garth Pratten and Lachlan Grant have delivered for a second time in this volume, with Garth generously completing two chapters. I am also very grateful to the other contributors to this volume who all generously gave their time, effort, energy and expertise. On a personal note I decided to co-write two of the chapters in this book with Kevin Holzimmer and Rhys Crawley, both of whom were wonderfully easy to work with and definitely increased the quality of my contribution.

The production of this text would not have been possible without the support of a broad range of people and institutions. My work at the Strategic and Defence Studies Centre at the Australian National University continues to be enhanced by the fabulous colleagues that I have there, of particular note is the ongoing support from David Horner and Brendan Taylor. Jenny Sheehan and Kay Dancey at the College of Asia and the Pacific Cartography Unit once again did a fabulous job with the maps. The Australian War Memorial again supported the book, by providing images from its collection. Part of this project was completed at the Center for Australian, New Zealand and Pacific Studies in the School of Foreign Service at Georgetown University in Washington, D.C. A note of thanks must go out to the Head of Center, Alan Tidwell, who generously hosted me for six months and provided wonderful support to me during my time in DC – Hoya Saxa! No book can be completed without a publisher. This is my fourth book with Cambridge University Press and their ongoing support for my work has been terrific. As such I would also like to offer special thanks to Vilija Stephens, Isabella Mead, Lily Keil, Jodie Fitzsimmons and the rest of the team at Cambridge University Press.

Finally I would not have been able to complete this project without the encouragement, patience, guidance and support of my family – Sarah, Flynn and Jessica. During the production of this book, while we managed to avoid moving house again (well, at least not permanently), we did move to another country, the United States, for six months and moved twice internally while there. For this and all of the other support, I simply can't say thank you enough.

Canberra and Washington, DC,
2014–15

Abbreviations

ABG	Australian Beach Group
Adm	Admiral
Adv LHQ	Advanced Headquarters Allied Land Forces
AIF	Australian Imperial Force
AITM	Army in India Training Memoranda
AMF	Australian Military Forces
ARP	Air raid precautions
ASIS	Australian Secret Intelligence Service
ATC	Amphibious Training Command
AWM	Australian War Memorial
BBCAU	British Borneo Civil Affairs Unit
Bde	Brigade
Bn	Battalion
Brig	Brigadier
C-in-C	Commander-in-Chief
CO	Commanding officer
COIC	Combined Operations Intelligence Centre
CORONET	Code name for planned allied invasion of Honshu, Japan
CoS	Chief of Staff
COS	Combined Operations Section
Coy	Company
DCGS	Deputy Chief of the General Staff (Australian Army)
Div	Division
DMI	Director of Military Intelligence (Australian Army)
ESB	Engineering Special (Amphibious) Brigade
FELO	Far Eastern Liaison Office
FFR	Frontier Force Regiment
Forland	Forward Echelon of Blamey's Advance LHQ based at GHQ
FRUMEL	Fleet Radio Unit, Melbourne
FRUPAC	Fleet Radio Unit, Pacific (Station HYPO)

Fwd	Forward
GHQ	General Headquarters
GOC	General Officer Commanding (Australian Division)
GOC-in-C	General Officer-in-Command (Australian Corps or Army)
ICRC	International Committee of the Red Cross
IGB	Independent Garrison Battalion (Imperial Japanese Army)
IMB	Independent Mixed Brigade (Imperial Japanese Army)
IMR	Independent Mixed Regiment (Imperial Japanese Army)
JOOTS	Joint Overseas Operational Training School
MLG	Military Landing Group
MTP	Military Training Pamphlet
NARA	US National Archives and Records Administration
NGF	New Guinea Force (Corps, later Army level command based at Port Moresby)
NoA	North-of-Australia (*Gō-hoku*)
OLYMPIC	Code name for planned Allied invasion of Kyushu, Japan
RAA	Royal Australian Artillery
RAAF	Royal Australian Air Force
RAF	Royal Air Force
RAN	Royal Australian Navy
RANVR	Royal Australian Navy Volunteer Reserve
RENO	GHQ SWPA Plan for the advance to the Philippines
SEA	Southern Expeditionary Army (Imperial Japanese Army)
SOA	Special Operations Australia
SOPAC	South Pacific Area (US Navy Command under Adm Halsey)
SRD	Services Reconnaissance Department
SWPA	Southwest Pacific Area
TAF	Tactical Air Force
US	United States
USASOS	US Army Services of Supply
VP	Victory in the Pacific

MILITARY SYMBOLS ON MAPS

FUNCTION SYMBOLS

⊓	headquarters
⊠	infantry
▭	armour
◹	anti-tank artillery
⊡	artillery
⬭	defensive position
王	Japanese Naval Infantry
✚	Airfield

STRENGTH INDICATORS

.	section
…	platoon/troop
I	company/squadron
II	battalion
III	regiment
x	brigade
xx	division
xxx	corps
(+)	reinforced
(−)	Sub-unit(s) detached

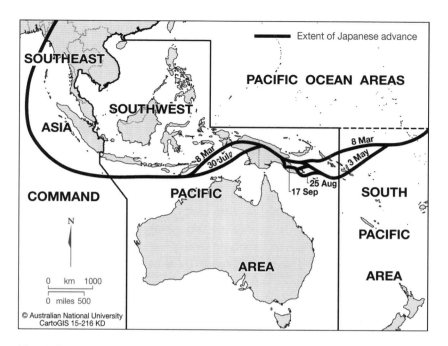

Map 1: Southwest Pacific Area

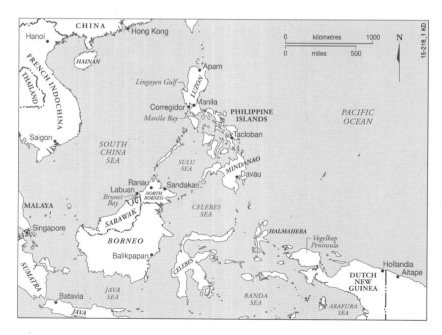

Map 2: Hanoi to Aitape

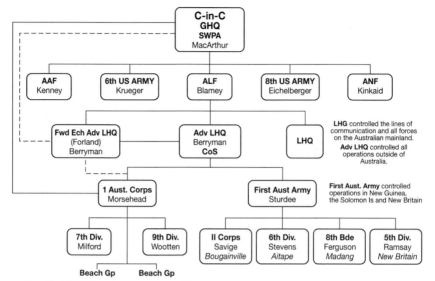

Chart 1: Command diagram

C-in-C
GHQ
SWPA
MacArthur

| AAF | 6th US ARMY | ALF | 8th US ARMY | ANF |
| Kenney | Krueger | Blamey | Eichelberger | Kinkaid |

Fwd Ech Adv LHQ
(Forland)
Berryman

Adv LHQ
Berryman
CoS

LHQ

LHG controlled the lines of
communication and all forces
on the Australian mainland.
Adv LHQ controlled all
operations outside of
Australia.

1 Aust. Corps
Morsehead

First Aust Army
Sturdee

First Aust. Army controlled
operations in New Guinea,
the Solomon Is and New Britain

7th Div.	9th Div.	II Corps	6th Div.	8th Bde	5th Div.
Milford	Wootten	Savige	Stevens	Ferguson	Ramsay
		Bougainville	*Aitape*	*Madang*	*New Britain*

Beach Gp   Beach Gp

From March 1945 **1 Aust. Corps** operated under **GHQ** with
Adv LHQ to undertake administrative arrangements and
Fwd Ech Adv LHQ to liaise with **GHQ** on Operational matters.

INTRODUCTION

This book is a sibling of two previous works: *Australia 1942: In the Shadow of War* and *Australia 1943: The Liberation of New Guinea*. While following a similar theme and approach, both of the two previous books had a different focus. *Australia 1942* was centred on Australia's first traumatic year of the Pacific War, from the fall of Singapore to the victory in Papua in January 1943. It discussed the battles of 1942 that were fought in the air and sea approaches to the Australian continent and in the islands of the archipelago to Australia's north. That book not only placed these events in their strategic context but also more broadly addressed the major reforms and issues that occurred in Australian politics, the economy and in the relationship Australia had with Japan in the lead up to the war. It did so in order to provide a broad overview of the changes that Australia underwent as a result of the onset of the Pacific War.

Australia 1943 had a somewhat narrower focus. That book focused heavily on Australia's role in the Southwest Pacific Area (SWPA) during 1943, including its strategic challenges and the broader context of US and Allied strategy. *Australia 1943* was much more centred on military operations and strategy. The broader context was provided by an examination of Allied and Japanese strategy in the Pacific as well as the operations undertaken by US forces in the South Pacific Area (SOPAC) and the SWPA. It focused on the decisive campaign that occurred in New Guinea between January 1943 and April 1944. That narrower approach did not seek to deny the critical importance of the home front. Rather it was a reflection of the fact that many of the major policy and social reforms in Australia's war effort occurred in 1942, and that 1943 was a year of execution and implementation.

For *Australia 1944–45: Victory in the Pacific*, the focus has shifted again. This time the approach is designed to bring together the themes from the first two books. It once again focuses on strategy and operations, but also revisits the home front and shows how the period of 1942–43 relates to 1944–45. As such this book includes a number of chapters that go beyond the strict confines of the period 1944–45 in order to provide depth of understanding to the operations of this period and also to cover material that had only been touched on briefly, or indirectly, in the first two volumes. While no book is capable of providing full coverage of all areas of Australia's wartime experience, all three books have attempted to provide coverage of key areas, themes and military operations within the context of major developments in Australia within the context of US and Japanese strategy and operations.

One of the major factors for this wider aperture, in comparison to *Australia 1943,* is so as to include a number of more thematic chapters. These chapters tie the home front sections of *Australia 1942* to the period of 1943–45 to round out this story. Also included are chapters on some key developments in military affairs such as jungle warfare and Australian and Allied intelligence activities, special operations and amphibious warfare. These chapters trace these elements of military art all the way through from 1942 until the end of the war and place them in their Allied rather than just Australian context in order to better understand Australia's role and approach.

Australia 1944–45 covers the period when the main battlefront of the war moved even further north and away from Australia, and when US primacy in the SWPA had become cemented. This work focuses on the Australian operations in the 'bypassed' areas of New Guinea and the surrounding islands and the strategically dubious campaign in Borneo. The New Guinea operations were fought principally to secure Australian mandated territories, clear up Japanese outposts in order to free Australian troops for participation in the planned invasion of Japan in 1945–46 and in order to release men from the military to support the war economy, which played a major role in both the Australian and Allied war effort in 1944–45. Despite this rationale in that most horrible of military terms, and one that is often completely at odds in relation to the intensity and nature of the fighting, the Australian operations in New Guinea during 1944–45 are often described as 'mopping up'. The operations in Borneo, while tactically and operationally highly successful were undertaken for uncertain strategic reasons. In fact despite the military personnel in the New Guinea operations feeling left behind and marginalised, their role was more significant to the longer term aims of Australia's war strategy than the operations in Borneo, especially if, as believed at the time, the war would continue into 1946–47 and an invasion of Japan was required.

Like the campaign that immediately preceded this period, the major Australian operations in the Pacific theatre in 1944 and 1945 are neither well known nor well understood. They are also somewhat controversial. In particular the question of the necessity (or not) of the Australian operations in New Guinea and Borneo is often asked in the history of this period, as well as whether or not, as British historian Max Hastings controversially claimed in 2007, Australia was 'bludging' in relation to its commitment to the war. These controversies were at the forefront of the minds of most of the historians who wrote chapters in this book. For different reasons, the historians in this book hold that both of these implications are mistaken. In order not to subject the reader to a deluge of counter claims, rebuttal of the tag of 'unnecessary war' in New Guinea and of 'bludging' has been largely contained in the first chapter of this book, written by Australia's pre-eminent military historian, David Horner. However, the power and enduring nature of these claims means that they are addressed directly and or indirectly in different ways throughout this book.

Such claims like those made by Max Hastings and Peter Charlton must be viewed within the context of the Australian contribution to the Allied war effort in 1944–45, Australia's strategic policy, Australia's role and position vis-à-vis the US and broader Allied strategy as well as the command structure and the personalities of senior commanders in the theatre during the period under examination. While rebutting these claims is not the principle driving force of this book, its organisation and layout is designed (as per the previous books) to provide such context to Australia's role in the great Allied effort to defeat Japan. Ultimately, as the chapters in this book will attest, given its requirement to support the Allied war effort both operationally and economically Australia was far from 'bludging', especially when reflecting upon how Australia's strategic approach was influenced by the character of the Allied coalition.

In addition while Australian air, land and naval forces may not have been concentrated together in the main operations against the Japanese during this period it was nonetheless an exceptionally important period for Australian strategy. As Stephan Frühling has noted, this period saw the 'first instance of a new, distinctly Australian approach to strategy in a coalition context in which Australia contributed to achieve a specific Australian – as opposed to shared Empire – interest[s] ... From [then] on Australia [has] paid increasing attention to achieving its own, specifically Australian objectives when making contributions in a larger coalition context'.[1]

In order to establish the importance of this period and these campaigns to Australia's military history the authors of this book will cover a range of key issues and events. In order to cover the scope and length of time of this volume the book has been divided into five parts: Strategy; Australia at War; Green Armour and Special Operations; The Naval and Air War; The New Guinea Campaign; and The Borneo Campaign.

Of paramount importance to directing Australia's war effort was the consideration of matters of policy and strategy. In part 1, David Horner AM, Peter J. Dean and Kevin Holzimmer, and Hiroyuki Shindo outline the challenges for Allied and Japanese strategy at the national and military strategy levels. These chapters provide the foundation for understanding the development of Australia's military operations in 1944 and 1945.

Part 2 comprises chapters on two very important aspects of the Australian experience of war: the ordeal of Australian prisoners of war in the Pacific War and the experience of the Australian home front. In chapter 4 Joan Beaumont outlines the broad experience of the Australian prisoners of war and delves into some new and unique insights from the period of 1944–45. In chapter 5 Michael Molkentin draws together the threads of the Australian experience on the home front from where the relevant chapters in *Australia 1942* left off. He investigates the extent of government control over the Australian war economy and society through an analysis of manpower, rationing, censorship, and the political impact of Australia's 'total war' effort.

Part 3 delves into two important thematic areas that cut across the whole period of 1942–45, but reached their principle significance in the final two years of the war. In chapter 6 Daniel Marston investigates the nature of fighting the 'jungle war', especially the process of learning and adaptation. In chapter 7 John Blaxland outlines the critical role that intelligence played in the Allied success in the SWPA. He outlines the broad ranging intelligence network established in the SWPA, focusing on the critical role of Australia in this Allied effort through the period of 1942–45.

In part 4 chapters 8 and 9 cover the naval and air aspects of the period 1944–45, focusing on the RAN and the RAAF. As a maritime theatre of war, air and naval power in the SWPA were critical to the Allied success, these chapters outline the continued hard work and high tempo of operations of the RAN and the RAAF and assess their contribution and importance to Australian strategy and the Allied war effort in the Pacific War.

Part 5 and part 6 cover Australia's major combat operations during 1944–45. In part 5 Lachlan Grant and Karl James detail the major commitment Australia made to operations in New Guinea, covering not only the tactical actions but also broader strategic issues as well as the experience of the soldiers in these campaigns. In part 6 Rhys Crawley and Peter Dean start off by providing another of the thematic chapters covering the training and logistics aspect of amphibious warfare in the period of 1942–45 that were critical for the Australians to develop in order to undertake the highly complex assault landings in Borneo in 1945. This final part then details the three Oboe operations. Tony Hastings and Peter Stanley undertake a critical assessment of the landing at Tarakan, while in the final two chapters Garth Pratten undertakes a close analysis of the performance of the 9th Division at Brunei-Labuan and the 7th Division at Balikpapan.

Balikpapan was to prove to be the last major Allied landing of the Pacific War; soon afterwards the dropping of the atomic bombs would end the war with Japan. As for all countries involved, the war would have a lasting impact on Australia. To sum up this book and the trilogy, one of Australia's leading authorities on the Second World War, Michael McKernan, provides an afterword that addresses the legacy of the war in the Pacific for Australia – a conflict that saw, for the first and only time, direct attacks on Australian soil by a foreign power and the country geared up for total war. It was a war that redefined our role in the Asia-Pacific region, reshaped our relationship with the United States, and changed the political, economic and social makeup of the country.

Note

1   Stephan Frühling, 'Australian Strategy and Strategic Policy' in Peter Dean, Stephan Frühling and Brendan Taylor, *Australia's Defence: Towards a New Era*, MUP, Melbourne, 2014, p. 189.

PART | **I**

S T R A T E G Y

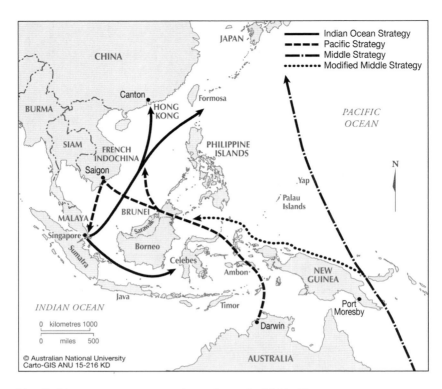

Map 3: Alternative strategy options, Australia 1944–45

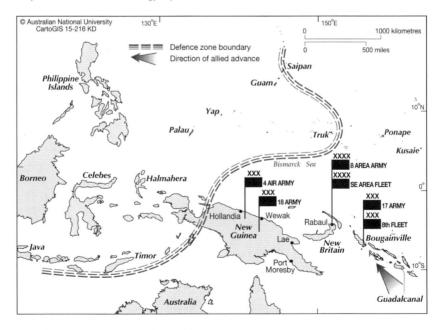

Map 4: Japan National Defence Zone

Advancing National Interests: Deciding Australia's War Strategy, 1944–45

David Horner

Australia's war effort during the last two years of the Second World War has been the subject of considerable criticism, much of it ill-informed. Some historians have claimed that the operations in Bougainville and New Guinea were part of an 'unnecessary war'.[1] The British historian Sir Max Hastings went further when he claimed that 'as the war advanced, grateful as were the Allies for Australia's huge contribution towards feeding their soldiers, there was sourness about the limited contribution by this country of seven million people'. According to Hastings, the Australians were 'bludging'; he has claimed, for example, that the government cut the Army's size by 22 per cent because of the 'unpopularity of military service'.[2]

These claims are a distortion of what actually happened. The deployment of five Australian divisions during the 1943 offensives was hardly a 'limited contribution'. And in July 1945 Australia had more infantry divisions (six of its seven) in action at one time than in any other month of the war. Hastings was, however, right in one respect: in the last year of the war, the Commander-in-Chief (C-in C) of the Southwest Pacific Area (SWPA), General Douglas MacArthur, sidelined Australia's troops into campaigns that could not affect the outcome of the war.

While it is important to examine views such as these, it is equally important to ask other questions. Why and how did Australia change its war strategy for 1944 and 1945? What were the alternatives? Were Australia's national interests advanced? Did Australia have the most appropriate machinery for determining its war strategy? What roles were played by the key individuals? The answers might help place Australia's war effort in a broader historical context and also provide some guidance for latter-day strategic decision-makers. In considering these issues it is important to remember that that strategy is not just about the deployment of forces, but also about the allocation of resources.

Australian War Strategy, 1942–43

Australia's war strategy in 1944–45 was built upon the strategy of earlier years. Australia's pre-war defence policy was based on imperial defence, and, as an outcome of this policy, in 1939 and 1940 Australian naval, land and air forces were deployed overseas to serve under British Commanders-in-Chief. After the outbreak of war with Japan and the entry of the United States in December 1941, Allied higher direction of the war was assumed by US President Franklin Roosevelt and British Prime Minister Winston Churchill. Australia had little influence over their deliberations. Allied commanders-in-chief – all US or British officers – were appointed to command operations in the various theatres of war, and in April 1942 the US General MacArthur (who had commanded US forces in the Philippines) was appointed C-in-C of the SWPA, which included Australia and the islands to the north.

With Australia under threat of invasion, Prime Minister John Curtin placed Australia's forces under MacArthur's command. Curtin also looked to MacArthur for advice on strategic matters. As MacArthur told Curtin, 'we two, you and I, will see this thing through together … You take care of the rear and I will handle the front'.[3] The deployment of Australian forces within the SWPA was in MacArthur's hands, but in the emergency of 1942 Curtin had little choice but to accept this abrogation of Australian sovereignty.

Australia's war strategy in 1942 was relatively simple. Australia needed to raise and sustain as large an Army as possible to resist a possible Japanese invasion. Curtin also needed to persuade Roosevelt and Churchill to send resources to help defend Australia and to mount a counteroffensive against the Japanese. Unfortunately for Australia, Roosevelt and Churchill had agreed on a policy of 'beating Hitler first', thus relegating the Pacific theatre to secondary importance. With little capacity to influence Roosevelt and

Figure 1.1: The Prime Minister, John Curtin, with General Douglas MacArthur, Canberra, 18 March 1944. (Australian War Memorial 072967)

Churchill, Curtin found a ready ally in MacArthur, who wanted to return to the Philippines, and applied his own pressure to the US Joint Chiefs of Staff to reinforce his theatre.

Australia's war strategy at this time was determined by three interrelated bodies. The first was the War Cabinet, which was chaired by Curtin (who was also Minister for Defence) and included seven other senior ministers. The chiefs of staff of the three Australian armed services attended as advisers. Sir Frederick Shedden, Secretary to the Department of Defence, was secretary to the War Cabinet. The second body was the Advisory War Council, which was also chaired by Curtin and included four War Cabinet ministers and four members of the federal opposition. Again, the chiefs of staff attended, and Shedden was the secretary. The Advisory War Council operated until the end of the war, but had less influence after the federal election of September 1943. The third, and perhaps most important body in the higher direction of the war, was the Prime Minister's War conference, which consisted of Curtin, MacArthur, Shedden and any other ministers or advisers invited by Curtin. General Sir Thomas Blamey, C-in-C of the Australian Army, attended the War Cabinet when invited, but crucially was not a member of the Prime Minister's War conference.

Curtin, MacArthur, Shedden and Blamey were the key figures in deciding Australian strategy. Conscientious and determined, Curtin had little experience in military matters. MacArthur, a clever and experienced political general, carried much prestige, but for personal as well as US national reasons, wanted to lead his forces back to the Philippines. Shedden had devoted his life to defence policy and administration; he had served in the Department of Defence since 1910, becoming its secretary in 1937. As Secretary of the War Cabinet and the Advisory War Council and as a member of the Prime Minister's War conference he was Curtin's chief Australian adviser on strategic and defence matters. Blamey was Australia's most senior and experienced military officer, and he insisted on having direct access to the Prime Minister. His advice could not be ignored lightly.

In the Allied command structure of the SWPA, Blamey was Commander of the Allied Land Forces (in addition to his role as C-in-C of the Australian Army), in recognition that the Australian Army formed the largest part of MacArthur's ground forces. The Australian Army carried the heaviest burden in the fighting in Papua in 1942 and in the New Guinea offensives of 1943.

WAR CABINET DECISION, 1 OCTOBER 1943

The foundation for Australia's war strategy in the last two years of the war was set by the War Cabinet on 1 October 1943, and there were several reasons why it needed to consider a new war strategy. Facing the threat of possible invasion in early 1942, Australia had raised an Army of some 13 divisions (including the 8th Division which had gone into captivity at Singapore and the islands), but after the heavy casualties in Papua the Army was beginning to face shortages in manpower. Similarly, the government had ordered the manufacture of large qualities of weapons and ammunition, but by early 1943 there was a surplus in production.

The strategic situation had also changed substantially. Between July 1942 and January 1943 SWPA forces had halted and turned back the Japanese advance in Papua. Then in June 1943 MacArthur advised Curtin that 'the threat of invasion of Australia had been removed'.[4] There would now be less imperative to maintain large forces in Australia. Meanwhile in June SWPA forces began a major offensive in New Guinea, which included the Australian amphibious landings at Lae and Finschhafen and the advance into the Ramu Valley in September.

Against this background, at its meeting in Canberra on 1 October the War Cabinet considered a 25-page report prepared by Shedden, which reviewed 'the nature, extent, and balance of the war effort in the light of the manpower position'.[5] Blamey and the Chief of the General Staff, Lieutenant General John Northcott, were present for the first part of the meeting. After a discussion lasting five and a half hours the War Cabinet agreed that by June 1944 20,000 men should be released from the armed services, 10,000 men should be released from munitions and aircraft industries and the monthly intake into the services should be fixed at 5000 men and women. But apart from stabilising the Royal Australian Air Force (RAAF) at its 'present strength' in Australia at 48 squadrons, there was no commitment to reducing substantially the forces fighting in the SWPA. The War Cabinet affirmed two key principles:

(a) It is of vital importance to the future of Australia and her status at the peace table in regard to the settlement in the Pacific that her military effort should be concentrated as far as possible in the Pacific and that it should be on a scale to guarantee her an effective voice in the peace settlement.

(b) If necessary, the extent of this effort should be maintained at the expense of commitments in other theatres . . .[6]

The political and economic official historians Hasluck, Butlin and Schedvin criticised the way this policy was formulated as well as the policy itself, complaining that the government did not allocate resources adequately: the War Cabinet 'had ducked choosing between clear-cut alternatives'.[7] While this criticism has some validity it fails to take into account the difficulty the government faced dealing with the arrangement whereby the employment of Australian forces was determined by General MacArthur. MacArthur had advised Shedden in May and Curtin in June that Australia should provide a striking force of three divisions. Although Blamey knew that MacArthur was already making plans to reduce the Australian offensive role, he too believed that Australia should maintain a substantial military commitment, warning Curtin that 'any reduction in the strength of the striking force below three divisions [would] greatly weaken Australia's place in determining the future' and that such a reduction was 'most undesirable in the national interest'.[8]

However much there might have been an air of expediency in the government's decision, we can now see that it was a major turning point in the history of Australian strategic and defence policy. In the First World War, Australia deployed forces overseas to help the Empire to win the war. Similarly, at the beginning of the Second World War Australia sent forces overseas to help the Imperial war effort in the European theatre. Forces were also deployed to Malaya, the Netherlands East Indies and New Guinea to help ensure the security of Australia, culminating in the Papuan and New Guinea campaigns of 1942 and 1943.

After 1944, however, Australian forces were deployed for purely political purposes – to guarantee a voice in the peace settlement. This does not mean that the Australian government was wrong to maintain forces on operations, but the harsh fact is that if Australian forces had conducted no more offensive operations after 1944 there would have been no change in the outcome of the war. Further, over the next 70 years Australia deployed forces to seven more wars for political purposes. Again, if Australia had not contributed forces there would have been no change to the outcome, and again this does not necessarily mean that these commitments were wrong or that in some way they did not contribute to Australian security. This broader view underlines the importance of the decision of October 1943.

Securing Allied Agreement

Having decided on its course of action, the government needed to obtain concurrence from the British and US governments, and as the first step on 8 October Curtin cabled an outline of the decision to Churchill, seeking his reaction. Meanwhile, the government was waiting on further advice from MacArthur as to how he was planning to use the Australian forces. In turn, MacArthur was waiting on the outcome of a meeting of Churchill, Roosevelt and the Combined Chiefs of Staff in Cairo in late November. In the short term, however, it was clear that the Australian Army would have little offensive role in the coming operations. The Army had deployed five divisions during the New Guinea offensives, and these were progressively withdrawn to Australia for rest and retraining. US forces would take over the SWPA offensive as it moved along the north coast of New Guinea.

By this time, Curtin and the Minister for External Affairs, Bert Evatt, were becoming increasingly wary of US intentions, fearing that they wished either to seize bases or secure commercial advantages in the Pacific. On 27 September 1943 Blamey had told Curtin that the operations in New Britain would be by US forces 'to strengthen a claim to retain New Britain in the post war settlement'.[9] In the view of the later controversy over the 1944–45 Bougainville operations, it is pertinent to note that on 22 November 1943 Curtin reminded MacArthur that Australia had a mandate from the League of Nations over Australian New Guinea and Bougainville and that Australia 'therefore has a special interest in the employment of its own forces in the operations for the ejectment of the enemy from territory under its administration'.[10] To balance US influence, Curtin was anxious to see an increase in British influence in the area, and he intended proposing a plan for increased Commonwealth cooperation when he attended a conference of Commonwealth prime ministers in London in May 1944.

Curtin was deeply offended that Churchill had not replied to his cable outlining the decision of October, and annoyed that Australia was excluded from the discussion about Pacific strategy in Cairo. On 15 December he learned that the Combined Chiefs had agreed to maintain offensives in the Pacific, but the details had not yet been decided. Reacting to this feeling of exclusion, in January Evatt met with his New Zealand counterpart in Canberra and proposed a regional organisation to be called the South Seas Regional Commission. They saw a need to take a strong part in the administration of the island colonies and, in collaboration with other allies, to establish bases and major defence installations in the islands. The Anzac Pact, as it was called, upset the British and antagonised the Americans, but indicated a desire to take a more independent line.

Eventually, on 14 March 1944, more than three months after the conclusion of the Cairo conference, Churchill informed Curtin that the British were considering establishing a base in Australia. MacArthur had already been told that he was to lead an advance towards the Philippines, and it was expected that Britain would despatch a fleet and eventually troops to the SWPA. MacArthur could now develop his plans, and on 17 March at a meeting in Canberra he told Curtin that the spearhead of his advance would be three Australian Imperial Force (AIF) divisions and a US paratroop division. MacArthur had not been completely honest with Curtin, for his outline plan for the capture of the Philippines actually made no mention of Australian units.

On 5 April 1944 Curtin, Shedden and Blamey set sail from Sydney on the US naval transport USS *Lurline* to visit the United States and Britain. Curtin's primary aims were to win approval for his modifications to the Australian war effort, and to establish guidelines for Commonwealth cooperation. Blamey had slightly different aims. Unlike Curtin, he was convinced that MacArthur was going to exclude the Australians from the coming operations, and he was therefore thinking of an Australian and British offensive from Darwin into the Netherlands East Indies. Such an offensive would complement British plans to establish a base in Australia.

When the Prime Minister's party arrived in London on 29 April they learned that the British were indeed contemplating an advance from Darwin to Ambon and Borneo and on to Indo-China (the so-called Middle Strategy). Curtin was happy to have British forces based in Australia, but was unwilling to change the command arrangements already established with MacArthur. While Blamey argued strongly for the new campaign, which he imagined he might lead, Curtin concentrated on obtaining British endorsement for the reallocation of the Australian war effort. Eventually, on 27 May, after a month of discussion, Churchill agreed to the reallocation and also that the British military mission, then arriving in Australia, be integrated with Australian staff for possible future operations. He had taken no interest in Curtin's plans for Commonwealth cooperation.

Churchill agreed that since Australia was 'in a sphere of American strategic responsibility', Australia's war effort should be discussed in Washington. Therefore on 2 June, on his return journey, Curtin outlined his proposals to the Combined Chiefs of Staff in Washington. He explained that Australia would maintain six divisions for active operations. The Royal Australian Navy (RAN) was to stay at its present strength; the RAAF was to be maintained at its present strength of 54 squadrons; food for Britain (including India) was to be exported on the 1944 scale; and Australia was to review other aspects of the war effort to see if production could be increased. The Combined Chiefs immediately referred these proposals to MacArthur, who replied that he considered that Australia's war effort should be determined by Australia. MacArthur had, of course, previously discussed the proposals with Curtin. The Combined Chiefs therefore approved the proposals.

The question remains, however, whether Curtin really needed to seek Allied agreement to the shape and size of Australia's war effort when Australia had not been involved in the Cairo or any of the other Allied conferences. Certainly it was better to persuade Churchill to return certain Australian ships, men and aircraft to Australia than to demand their release, but the episode illustrates Australia's lack of confidence in framing and pursuing its own strategic policy.

AUSTRALIANS FOR THE PHILIPPINES

On 26 June, the day that their ship arrived in Brisbane from the United States, Curtin and Shedden met with MacArthur, who said he was disturbed to learn that the AIF divisions would not be battle-worthy until after the Philippines campaign. Although he had originally contemplated using the AIF divisions in his advance to the Philippines, 'he did not now intend using them until later on, when he proposed to attack Borneo and the Netherlands East Indies'. MacArthur strongly opposed any plan that would affect the boundaries of his command and stated that if any additional Australian or British forces became available they should be allotted to him. Curtin was concerned at MacArthur's statement that the Australian divisions would take time to become battle-worthy. He was anxious that Australian forces should be involved in the Philippines, but told MacArthur that since they had been assigned to him, 'their use was a matter for decision by him'.[11]

In further talks with Shedden, MacArthur said that he had already had discussions with Blamey, who had flown back from the United States earlier, and he was convinced that Blamey wanted to be commander-in-chief of the new British–Australian command. MacArthur said that Blamey's position as Commander of the Allied Land Forces 'had now become a fiction' and that he 'intended to take personal charge of the operations against the Philippines'. Since the Australians might be withdrawn from his command, he had instructed his chief of staff, Major General Richard Sutherland, to plan on using only US forces in future operations. MacArthur thought that Blamey was holding back the Australian troops for the new command as well as to command all the Australian defence forces.[12] Through his over-enthusiastic advocacy of the use of Commonwealth forces on a separate axis, Blamey had provided MacArthur with a ready-made excuse for not using Australian troops in the Philippines.

Worried by MacArthur's claim that Australian troops could not be ready for the Philippines, Curtin wrote to Blamey asking when his major formations could be ready for operations. Blamey replied on 11 July that the 6th Division was 'available at short notice if necessary', the 7th Division would be available in November and the 9th Division in October.[13] On the face of it, there seemed no reason why all three divisions should not have been available for the first operations in the Philippines, scheduled for November.

MacArthur's intentions soon became clear when, on 12 July, he issued a directive that Australian forces were to assume 'responsibility for the continued neutralisation of the Japanese' in the Bougainville area by 1 October 1944 and in Australian New Guinea, including New Britain, by 1 November. In the advance to the Philippines MacArthur contemplated employing one AIF division in November 1944 and another in January 1945.[14] Blamey objected to the deployment of the AIF divisions separately, rather than as a corps, but MacArthur would not budge. Then, when Blamey developed a plan to relieve the US divisions in the New

Guinea–Bougainville area with a total of seven Australian brigades, MacArthur said such forces were 'totally inadequate'.[15] Instead, on 2 August MacArthur directed Blamey to deploy a minimum of 12 brigades. To find the additional five brigades Blamey was required to use the 6th Division, thus reducing his striking force to the 7th and 9th Divisions, and making it even less likely that the AIF could be used in the Philippines. Blamey questioned MacArthur's motives in this matter, believing that the US general was holding out the possibility of using the Australians in the Philippines so that they would not be used in the Middle Strategy, without ever intending to do so. But Curtin and Shedden's confidence in Blamey had declined and they would not support him.

On 31 August MacArthur issued a formal directive for the Philippines landings, to begin in southern Mindanao on 15 November. For the Australians, MacArthur had concocted a plan for landing a corps of two divisions at Aparri on the north coast of Luzon on 31 January 1945. In early September 1944 Churchill, Roosevelt and their Chiefs of Staff gathered at Quebec to consider future operations in the Pacific. Churchill offered the British Main Fleet for operations in the Pacific, and Roosevelt immediately accepted. Blamey's hopes for a separate British Commonwealth offensive were dashed. During the conference the Combined Chiefs also agreed to an accelerated timetable by which MacArthur's forces would invade Leyte Island in the Philippines the following month, thereby decreasing the chances of Australian involvement in the Philippines.

When Curtin and Shedden met MacArthur in Canberra on 30 September, MacArthur said that the Australian divisions would be involved in two groups of operations. The first would be garrison duties in Bougainville, New Britain and New Guinea. The second would be the operations undertaken by the 7th and 9th Divisions in Borneo and Java, not in the Philippines. Curtin offered no comment, and thereby gave tacit approval to this employment of Australian troops.

This was MacArthur's last meeting with Curtin, and after he left Australia two weeks later he never returned. He landed with his troops on Leyte on 20 October and made his headquarters there. In the final event no Australians (except for an airfield construction unit) were employed in the Philippines, but it was not until February 1945 that MacArthur completely dismissed the possibility of their being used. Curtin had not been willing to apply pressure to MacArthur, even when he found that MacArthur's claim that the Australians were not ready was false. Perhaps Curtin was blinded by his loyalty to MacArthur, or perhaps he was happy for Australian lives to be spared.

REALLOCATING MANPOWER

Work on implementing Australia's new war effort plan began as soon as Curtin and Shedden arrived in Canberra after their overseas visit, and on 5 July the War Cabinet instructed the Defence Committee (senior military and civilian officials) to report on manpower requirements for the services. From Blamey's comments while overseas Curtin understood that the Army would be able to release 50,000 and eventually 90,000 men. However, the Defence Committee now recommended no net reduction in total enlistments. At the same time, the War Commitments Committee estimated a need for 78,602 men in high priority industries by the end of 1944, with a shortfall of at least 39,000 men between labour requirements and supply.

Faced with this impasse, on 2 August Curtin directed Blamey to investigate a way of releasing 50,000 men from the Army. Blamey replied that 50,000 would be a 'severe blow' and suggested 20,000 or 25,000.[16] The remainder could be released by the RAAF. The Chief of the Air Staff had to admit that a reduction in air force personnel would not greatly impair RAAF operations, and Curtin therefore directed that the Army was to release 30,000 men and the RAAF 15,000 men. Of these 45,000 men, 20,000 were to be released by 31 December and 25,000 by 30 June 1945.

Over the next two months Blamey linked strategic policy directly to the manpower problem, advising Curtin that further reductions would 'greatly reduce the status of Australia and our voice later in important matters of policy'.[17] Blamey said that MacArthur had directed him to employ additional forces in New Guinea but if he lost manpower he would have 'grave misgivings as to the maintenance of our offensive forces in the event of protracted operations in 1945'.[18]

When on 18 October the War Cabinet ordered the Defence Committee to report on a proposal to release a further 40,000 men from the services as soon as possible, Blamey again protested strongly. He pointed out that in the coming months all six divisions and one armoured brigade would be in action overseas. If he was ordered to reduce his force by 40,000 he would need to advise the government that it should:

> inform General MacArthur that the Australian Army cannot be maintained at the strength allotted and that it will be necessary to reduce the expeditionary force from one Army corps of two divisions and essential services to one division. This will bring the Australian expeditionary forces to approximately the same dimensions as that of New Zealand.[19]

Curtin replied that so far no direction that an additional 40,000 be released had been given. Blamey had won the argument, but Shedden believed that Blamey had been less than honest, recalling that while overseas Blamey had told the Combined Chiefs that 'the reduction to 6 divisions would progressively release some 90,000 men'.[20] Shedden thought that Curtin had given way because he was unwell, and indeed on 3 November Curtin was admitted to hospital with an apparent heart attack.

During these debates Curtin had also faced demands from the Chief of Naval Staff, Vice Admiral Sir Guy Royle, who said that Britain could provide an aircraft carrier, one or two cruisers and six destroyers if Australia could man them. Royle linked his claim to the government's policy of providing a force that would give Australia 'an effective voice in the peace settlement'. As he put it: 'Ships steaming and fighting side by side with those of the British Forces will be highly tangible evidence of our active participation in the war to the very end'.[21]

The manpower required was not large; the carrier required 1500 men and the cruisers 350 each, but there were other considerations. MacArthur told Curtin that the proposal was too late to be of value in the present war, and if the ships remained in Australia after the war they would be out of date. Curtin therefore rejected the proposal.

There was much truth in Royle's assertion that the RAAF strength was out of proportion to that of the Navy and the Army. In the SWPA MacArthur had sidelined much of the RAAF, and many of its aircraft were unsuited to frontline operations. On 1 July 1944, however, there were approximately 14,000 RAAF personnel in the United Kingdom, of whom 12,400 were aircrew. Yet there was no RAAF bomber group within Bomber Command where most Australians were operating, so Australia received little recognition. As the official historian, John Herington, observed, 'few Australians (except air gunners) who arrived [in the United Kingdom] after the launching of OVERLORD reached combat units, and some who had arrived earlier still lacked active employment at the end of the war'.[22]

Of course the Australian government had no way of determining whether its forces in Europe were vitally necessary, but it is certain that they did not contribute to the government's declared aim of giving Australia status at the peace table in the Pacific. Curtin pressed the Chief of the Air Staff, Air Vice-Marshal George Jones, to reduce Australia's contribution to Bomber Command, but Jones claimed that to do so would result in heavier casualties among the remaining forces.[23] On 31 December 1944 there were 34,520 personnel in the Navy, 411,321 in the Army and 179,544 in the Air Force.

A ROLE FOR THE AIF

By October 1944 the Allies were closing the ring around Japan and it seemed likely that Australian forces would be excluded from the main offensives. The government thought it important that Australia maintain an active role in the operations, but its exact nature depended to a large extent on MacArthur. The negotiations with MacArthur over a role for the AIF divisions were to highlight the limitations on Australian strategic decision-making.

Responding to MacArthur's directive to relieve the US divisions in New Guinea, New Britain and Bougainville, Blamey ordered the First Army of four divisions to undertake this task, and they began taking over in October. This left the 1st Australian Corps (7th and 9th AIF Divisions) at MacArthur's disposal. The RAAF was to support the Australian forces while the RAN squadron operated under MacArthur's naval commander. The government had been unable to withdraw its commitment to the air forces in Britain, but arranged for its naval units operating under British command in the Indian Ocean to return to Australian waters.

Four months later, in February 1945, little had changed with regard to the Australians. Although US forces were engaged in large-scale operations in Luzon, the 1st Corps had been out of action for almost a year and Blamey observed that 'a feeling that we are being side-tracked is growing strong throughout the country'. Urged by Blamey and Shedden, on 15 February Curtin told MacArthur that there was 'considerable public criticism of the inactivity' of the Australian forces, and said that it was 'a matter of vital importance to the future of Australia and her status at the peace table ... that her military effort should be concentrated as far as possible in the Pacific and that it should be on a scale to guarantee her an effective voice in the peace settlement'.[24]

Meanwhile, Blamey learned that MacArthur was planning to use the 6th, 7th and 9th Divisions to undertake operations in Borneo, culminating in an attack on Java. This would involve withdrawing the 6th Division from operations at Aitape in New Guinea. Blamey knew that the Chief of Staff of the US Army, General George Marshall, had told MacArthur 'that operations in Borneo would have little immediate effect on the war against Japan', and Blamey deferred any plans to use the 6th Division until they had been considered by the government.[25]

Eventually, on 5 March MacArthur replied to Curtin, saying that he would be using the 7th and 9th Divisions in North Borneo, and was leaving open the possibility of using the 6th Division in Java. On 13 and

14 March Blamey visited MacArthur in Manila where he pointed out that while US forces were being retained in the southern Philippines to clear out the Japanese, MacArthur was wishing to withdraw Australian forces from New Guinea. MacArthur argued that he intended to use the Philippines as a base for the invasion of Japan, but Blamey said that if the Australians were withdrawn from New Guinea they would need to return later to complete their task.

On Blamey's advice, Curtin withheld the 6th Division from MacArthur, thereby disrupting MacArthur's plans to capture Java. As MacArthur's biographer, D. Clayton James, has noted, 'it was most fortunate for the lives of the soldiers of the Australian I Corps' that MacArthur did not get 'his way on the Java plan, for that two division invasion could have produced the most tragic blood-bath of the Pacific War'.[26] On 1 May a brigade of the 9th Division landed at Tarakan off the northeast coast of Borneo, and the remainder of the division landed at Brunei on 10 June. While the operations were successful, neither of them shortened the war.

UNNECESSARY OPERATIONS

Two other issues – the First Army's role in New Guinea and Bougainville, and the Balikpapan operation – illustrate the government's difficulty in deciding its strategy in the last months of the war. By April 1945 the First Army's operations were being criticised in Parliament and the press as wasting Australian lives. There were also claims that the forces were insufficiently equipped. When, on 17 April, Curtin sought MacArthur's views, the General replied that the local commanders had considerable freedom of action as to the methods employed. Blamey, however, advised Curtin that he had discussed the campaigns with MacArthur who had allocated the necessary landing craft for the 6th Division's operations. 'It is therefore a proper claim that these operations meet with General MacArthur's approval.'[27]

According to Shedden, Curtin was 'somewhat concerned about the reservations which appeared to be indicated in' MacArthur's reply, and wanted to discuss the matter personally, but he again fell ill, and with the Deputy Prime Minister, Frank Forde, and Evatt overseas, the Treasurer, Ben Chifley, became acting Prime Minister. On 7 May Chifley asked Blamey to attend a War Cabinet meeting to give the government 'fuller information in regard to your plans for the future use of the Australian Forces'. The same day, Chifley wrote to MacArthur that he assumed that the 6th Division's operations met with his approval. Blamey took issue with the view that the operations should not have been undertaken, advising Chifley that: 'Any commander, who is prepared to remain with superior forces, equipped to a degree greatly superior to that of the enemy, and who does not bring him to battle rapidly, is deserving of censure'. Replying on 20 May MacArthur said that although the operations were 'unnecessary and wasteful of lives and resources', it was a matter for the Australian commanders.[28]

By this time, Blamey had serious doubts about the 7th Division's landing at Balikpapan, in southeast Borneo, ordered by MacArthur and scheduled for 1 July. On 16 May he advised the government that if the 7th Division were to land at Balikpapan then Australia would be committed to a 'very large garrison', and he recommended withdrawing the division from the operation.[29]

Chifley and the acting Defence Minister, Jack Beasley, immediately put Blamey's suggestion to MacArthur, who replied promptly that the Borneo campaign had been ordered by the Joint Chiefs of Staff. To withdraw the 7th Division 'would disorganise completely not only the immediate campaign but also the strategic plan of the Joint Chiefs of Staff'. If the Australian government contemplated withdrawing the division MacArthur said he would make representations to Washington and London.[30]

MacArthur's blunt reply was hardly honest. The Joint Chiefs had reluctantly agreed to the Balikpapan operation only because MacArthur had advised that not to carry it out would 'produce grave repercussions with the Australian government and people'.[31] Now the Australians were being told that it had to be carried out because the Joint Chiefs had ordered it. It is hard to see how the operation's cancellation would have disorganised completely 'the strategic plan of the Joint Chiefs'.

Shedden received MacArthur's signal in Canberra in the morning of Sunday 20 May. As he recalled later, the ministers were 'scattered in various parts of the Commonwealth', but he consulted Curtin in hospital. In his 'last administrative act relating to the war', Curtin 'had no hesitation in approving the reply' drafted by Shedden. Shedden then read it to Chifley and Beasley by phone and despatched a signal to MacArthur that the government had 'no hesitation in agreeing to the use of the 7th Division as planned'.[32]

On 22 May Blamey attended a War Cabinet meeting, chaired by Chifley, to consider Australian operations.[33] Questioned closely about the First Army's operations and administrative problems in them, Blamey said, 'MacArthur was in complete agreement with his plans for operations'. He did not consider the enemy forces were 'strategically impotent' as stated by MacArthur, since they were still operating as organised forces with adequate supplies. The War Cabinet minute did not formally approve Blamey's policy, but Shedden later told Chifley that 'so far as the general question of strategy is concerned it is considered that General Blamey had made a very sound case in justification of the operations which he has been carrying out'.[34]

The War Cabinet then turned to the proposed landing by the 7th Division at Balikpapan, and Chifley noted that in a letter on 19 April Blamey had agreed to the operation. Blamey replied that he had agreed with the landings at Tarakan and Brunei, but not at Balikpapan, which was 'a derelict Dutch oilfield'. He added that MacArthur had hoped to go as far south as Java, but the Joint Chiefs had permitted him only to go to Balikpapan and, he suspected, only so long as US troops were not used. Blamey explained that five Australian divisions were on operations, and if the sixth was to be used there would be no 'flexibility' left. He wanted to be able to release from the Army men who had been serving for four or five years.

Beasley asked Blamey to consider the government's position; it did not want 'disharmony' with MacArthur, and it would be difficult for the government to 'pull out' of the operation. Blamey pointed out that, with the end of the war in Europe, Australia would have twice as many men on operations in proportion to its population as any other country and he feared some would be left on garrison duty in the Netherlands East Indies. Balikpapan was 'unimportant and should not be undertaken'. (Neither he nor the government had any idea that the war was to end, after the dropping of the atomic bombs on Japan, in August.) Finally Shedden, who obviously had a stake in the decision made two days earlier, said Chifley had had no alternative but to send his approval to MacArthur, since to do otherwise would have meant repudiating its earlier commitment.

There was nothing more Blamey could do about Balikpapan, but the government's approval of the First Army's operations seemed lukewarm. Blamey's appreciation was scrutinised again at the Advisory War Council on 6 June, and Sir Earle Page of the opposition thought Blamey's strategy was 'not justified'. Eventually, the Council agreed to Blamey's objectives, but by this time he was back in New Guinea and was not informed of the outcome until 31 July.

Chifley was deeply disturbed at MacArthur's letter of 20 May which had stated that the government was in error in construing the provision of landing craft as approval of the 6th Division's operation, but he did not know quite what to do. Eventually, on 21 July (after the death of Curtin and when Chifley had become Prime Minister), Chifley wrote to MacArthur and reminded him that as commander-in-chief he was responsible for the operation of the forces assigned to him. Australia's only right was to withhold forces, and the government had assumed that 'even within the limits of discretion allowed to subordinate commanders, their plans would be subject to your broad approval'. He regretted that the government was 'greatly embarrassed by your reply. It has publicly defended the wisdom of these operations'.[35] This was the strongest letter written by an Australian Prime Minister to MacArthur, but the general never deigned to reply.

The operations by the Australians in Borneo differed from those in New Guinea and Bougainville in at least one respect. The Borneo operations had been proposed by MacArthur and were conducted for strategic purposes of doubtful merit. By contrast, the New Guinea and Bougainville operations were not supported by MacArthur, but were conducted for Australian strategic and political purposes. The controversy over the operations was a telling commentary on the shortcomings of Australian strategic decision-making.

The controversy also says much about the key players. MacArthur put US national interests, as well as his own, ahead of Australia's. Curtin found it easier to accept MacArthur's advice than to challenge it, and as he became ill he lacked the drive to maintain a grip on Australian war strategy. Blamey wanted to advance Australia's interests, but was distrusted by MacArthur, Curtin and Shedden, who believed Blamey was advancing his own cause. Shedden, capable and clear thinking, worked to articulate and promote the government's policy but, like Curtin, deferred to MacArthur.

The events of 1944 and 1945 had required the Australian government to ask a number of important questions about the use of Australian forces. Once the direct threat to Australia was removed, and after the Americans took over the main offensive, what should have been the guiding principle for the employment of Australian forces? To what extent should the government have left the employment of the AIF in the hands of Douglas MacArthur? And what about the aircrews in Britain? While the government recognised that it needed to keep troops fighting in the Pacific, it ducked the harder questions. As a junior partner in a coalition war, the Australians government's options were limited, but there is no evidence that it worked hard to find alternatives. There were many lessons for the future.

FURTHER READING

Paul Hasluck, *The Government and the People, 1942–1945*, Australian War Memorial, Canberra, 1970.

David Horner, *High Command: Australia and Allied Strategy 1939–1945*, Australian War Memorial, Canberra, and George Allen & Unwin, Sydney, 1982.

David Horner, *Blamey: The Commander-in-Chief*, Allen & Unwin, Sydney, 1998.

David Horner, *Defence Supremo: Sir Frederick Shedden and the Making of Australian Defence Policy*, Allen & Unwin, Sydney, 2000.

Notes

1   Peter Charlton, *The Unnecessary War: Island Campaigns of the South West Pacific 1944–45*, Macmillan, Melbourne, 1983.

2   Max Hastings, *Nemesis: The Battle of Japan, 1944–45*, HarperPress, London, 2007, pp. 364, 366.

3   Douglas MacArthur, *Reminiscences*, McGraw-Hill, New York, 1964, p. 151.

4   'Minutes of Prime Minister's War Conference', Sydney, 7 June 1943, NAA: A5954, 2/5.

5   'A review of the nature, extent, and balance of the war effort in the light of the manpower position', 30 September 1943, NAA: A9240, 1/6.

6   Minutes of War Cabinet Meeting, Canberra, 1 October 1943, NAA: A5954, 809/2.

7   Hasluck, *The Government and the People 1942–1945*, pp. 301–2; S. J. Butlin and C. B. Schedvin, *War Economy 1942–1945*, Australian War Memorial, Canberra, 1977, p. 365.

8   'Minutes of Prime Minister's War Conference', Canberra, 27 September 1943, NAA: A5954, 4/2.

9   'Minutes of Prime Minister's War Conference', Canberra, 27 September 1943, NAA: A5954, 4/2.

10 Letter, Curtin to MacArthur, 22 November 1943, AWM: 3DRL6643, 2/5.1.

11 'Notes of Discussions with Commander-in-Chief . . . 26 and 27 June 1944', NAA: A5954, 3/10.

12 'Notes of Discussions with Commander-in-Chief . . . 27 June 1944', NAA: A5954, 3/10.

13 Letter, Blamey to Curtin, 11 July 1944, AWM: 3DRL6643, 2/23.11.

14 Letter, MacArthur to Blamey, 12 July 1944, AWM: 3DRL6643, 2/23.11.

15 Notes of an interview with General MacArthur, 1 August 1944, UK National Archives: CAB 127/33.

16 'Notes of Conference between the Prime Minister and the Commander-in-Chief, Australian Military Forces', Melbourne, 2 August 1944, NAA: A2680, 17/1944 Part 1.

17 Letter, Blamey to Curtin, 11 August 1944, AWM: 3DRL6643, 2/23.1.

18 Letter, Blamey to Curtin, 15 September 1944, AWM: 3DRL6643, 2/23.1

19 Letter, Blamey to Curtin, 27 October 1944, AWM: 3DRL6643, 2/23.1

20 Shedden manuscript, Book 4, chapter 48, p. 4.

21 War Cabinet Minute, 3 May 1944, NAA: A5954, 305/8.

22 John Herington, *Air Power Over Europe 1944–1945*, Australian War Memorial, Canberra, 1963, p. 285.

23 Interview, Air Marshal Sir George Jones to author, 24 January 1979.

24 Letter, Blamey to Berryman, AWM: 3DRL6643, 2/43.68; letter, Curtin to MacArthur, AWM: 3DRL6643, 2/23.11.

25 Letter, Berryman to Blamey, 10 February 1945, AWM: Berryman papers, PR84/370.

26 D. Clayton James, *The Years of MacArthur Volume II, 1941–1945*, Houghton Mifflin Company, Boston, 1975, pp. 716–17.

27 Letter, Blamey to Curtin, 19 April 1945, AWM: 3DRL6643, 23.11.

28 Letters, Chifley to Blamey, 7 May 1945, and Blamey to Chifley, 18 May 1945, both in AWM: 3DRL6643, 2/23.11; letter, MacArthur to Chifley, 20 May 1945, NARA: RG200, Sutherland Papers, Correspondence with Australian government.

29 Letter, Blamey to Fraser, 16 May 1945, AWM: 3DRL6643, 2/23.11.

30 Letter, MacArthur to Chifley, 20 May 1945, NAA: A5954, 570/2.

31 Signal, MacArthur to Marshall, 12 April 1945, NARA: RG 218, CCS 381, Pacific Ocean Area (6–10–43) Section 11.

32 Signal, Shedden to MacArthur, 21 July 1945, NAA: A5954, 1133/2; and teleprinter message Chifley to MacArthur, 20 May 1945, NAA: A5954, 570/2.

33 The following paragraphs are based on: Minutes of War Cabinet Meeting, Canberra, 22 May 1945, NAA: A5954/46, 811/1; Shedden notebook, NAA: A5954/2, 733/2; and Quealy notebook, NAA: A92401/1, set 1, volume 9.

34 Notes on W. C. Agendum No. 209/1945, 22 May 1945, NAA: A5954, 570/3.

35 Letter, Chifley to MacArthur, 21 July 1945, NARA: RG200, correspondence with Australian government.

CHAPTER 2

THE SOUTHWEST PACIFIC AREA: MILITARY STRATEGY AND OPERATIONS, 1944−45

Peter J. Dean and Kevin Holzimmer

On Thursday 7 October 1943 two senior officers, one Australian and one American, held meetings in their respective headquarters. Even though some 2000 kilometres of the Coral Sea separated them, they were linked by a common cause and a common role. They were both senior operations officers of their respective headquarters in the Southwest Pacific Area (SWPA). US Brigadier-General Stephen Chamberlin was the senior operations officer for General Douglas MacArthur, the theatre Commander-in-Chief (C-in-C). The Australian Major-General Frank Berryman was the Deputy Chief of the General Staff responsible to the C-in-C General Sir Thomas Blamey, while concurrently also holding down the position of senior staff officer of New Guinea Force (NGF), the Australian Army formation fighting the Japanese in New Guinea.

On the morning of 7 October, Berryman sat in a tropical bungalow in Port Moresby, Papua, that served as the headquarters of NGF. Across from him sat Lieutenant-General Iven Mackay, or 'Mister Chips', as he was known, whom Blamey had installed as the General Officer-in-Command (GOC-in-C) New Guinea Force six weeks earlier. With them was Lieutenant-General Leslie Morshead, the 'hero of Tobruk and El Alamein' and commander of II Australian Corps.

Despite the fact that the three men had served together in the Australian Army for decades, had a close rapport and a high degree of mutual respect for one another, the atmosphere was tense. Morshead was about to fly out to relieve Lieutenant-General Edmund Herring of his command. Herring was the commander of I Corps, whose troops were in the frontline in the Markham Valley and Huon Peninsula fighting the Japanese. Berryman had held reservations over Herring's suitability for his command for some months and in September, after Herring had mishandled relations with the Americans, lost 'grip' of his operations and openly criticised Mackay, Berryman advised Blamey that he lad lost all confidence in him.[1] He told Blamey that he did not think that Herring was 'tough enough mentally' for the job. Major-General Vasey, General Officer Commanding (GOC) of the 7th Australian Division in Herring's Corps was even more frank. He recorded that Herring's 'trouble is a lack of decision occasioned by a lack of knowledge and combined with wishful thinking and optimism'. He is 'incapable of training a staff ... [and] good deal of our recent problems are his doing ... Ned is a nice man but the army is not the place for those people'.[2]

The three men discussed the matter at hand and reviewed the I Corps' situation. Berryman reminded Morshead that Herring remained close to Blamey and that the decision to relieve him was being coached in the terms of a regular relief of his headquarters. Blamey had wanted it to appear as if this was a routine transfer of command in line with his philosophy of the rotation of senior officers operating in tropical conditions. As such Herring was going to 'host' Morshead for a week in order for a smooth transition, but Berryman harboured doubts. It was obvious that Herring was being replaced, and it was more likely than not that Herring would be on the first plane back to Port Moresby.

While Berryman discussed the sacking of Herring at Port Moresby, Chamberlin's routine was altogether different. Back in Brisbane at the AMP building that housed MacArthur's General Headquarters (GHQ), the staff were enmeshed in their usual hive of activity. Chamberlin was busy putting the final touches on a briefing memo to the C-in-C in pre-paration for his meeting with Admiral 'Bull' Halsey, the C-in-C of the neighbouring South Pacific Area (SOPAC). While Berryman was down in the weeds dealing with current operations with the Japanese in New Guinea at the theatre headquarters, Chamberlin had been thinking about the next big steps in the war in the SWPA. It was obvious that Halsey's command, which fell under MacArthur's strategic 'direction', would soon become a backwater. The decision had been made to isolate rather than attack the Japanese fortress in Rabaul, and within a month the

US Navy's Central Pacific Command would strike its first major blow in its march across the Pacific at Tarawa in the Gilbert Islands. The next phase of MacArthur's strategy to re-take the Philippines was about to unfold.

Chamberlin and his staff had laboured long and hard on MacArthur's planned drive to the Philippines. The first draft of the plan, codenamed RENO, had been finished in early 1943 just after the Japanese were defeated in Papua. MacArthur's determination to secure the Philippine archipelago was a personal obsession relating to the US defeat in 1941–42 and his personal commitment that he would 'return'. Control of the archipelago would also allow him to cut off the Japanese Home Islands from the Netherlands East Indies, Malaya and Indo-China. As it stated in MacArthur's official record of the war:

> whoever controlled the air and naval bases in the Philippine Islands logically controlled the main artery of supply to Japan's factories. If this artery were severed, Japan's resources would soon dry up, and her ability to maintain her war potential against the advancing Allies would deteriorate to the point where her main bases would become vulnerable to capture.[3]

By now Chamberlin and his staff were on the third iteration of RENO and serious decisions would soon have to be made in order to facilitate the plan. In particular Chamberlin was concern about the allocation of forces for the operation, the allotment of tasks and command arrangements. While Chamberlin was keen to progress his planning MacArthur was hamstrung by a lack of a directive from the US Joint Chiefs of Staff. As such Chamberlin had planned for the initial phase of RENO, the final push for the isolation of Rabaul, to be undertaken under the current command relationships. Thereafter he argued that with there being only one line of operation to the Philippines in the SWPA, along the north coast of New Guinea, SOPAC would have reached its culminating point as an operational theatre and thus its forces should be merged with the SWPA under MacArthur's command.[4]

While all this was logical to GHQ, the major concern for Chamberlin was the flow-on effects such moves would have on the command relationship within the SWPA. Specifically, he questioned how he should manage the uneasy coalition that had existed between Australia and the United States since the creation of the SWPA in early 1942. For Chamberlin the answer was clear; the combined US forces from the SWPA and SOPAC would form an 'exclusively' American force designed for the 'offensive' prosecution of the war. Thus it

would appear that it was now the 'proper time to separate the elements of other nationalities from this force and allot to them the static
defensive role, or to divide the general area of the SWPA into areas
along national lines'. Chamberlin's plan would mean a complete reorganisation of the SWPA with the Americans forging ahead to the
Philippines and the Australians garrisoning the lines of communication
and clearing up pockets of the Japanese cut off in the advance.[5]

Meanwhile back in Port Moresby things had not played out as planned.
Morshead's plane had taken off but soon returned, unable to break the
formidable weather at the top of the Owen Stanley Range. His flight the
following morning was successful, but, as suspected, 'Morshead got out of
the plane at Dobodura and Ned [Herring] got in – no hand-over'.[6] Herring
was back in Port Moresby for lunch and complaining about the US navy.[7]
Berryman, however, had more important things to do than taking
Herring's mind off his worries. On this day he released New Guinea
Force Operational Instruction No. 96A 'Role of the I Aust Corps consequence to the capture of BINOCULAR [Lae]'. In this document he laid out
the strategic and operational reality for the Australian forces in New
Guinea. Specifically, he noted that in two days time the SWPA Allied Air
Forces bomber effort would be diverted to assist the operations of SOPAC.
From 1 November Allied Naval Forces would start to relinquish their
support for the operations at Lae and Finschhafen, and by the end of the
month they would switch over their support completely to the US landing
on the west coast of New Britain at Cape Gloucester. The Australian role
was to focus on the developments of ports and airfields to support the US
advance.[8]

Berryman's orders and Chamberlin's memo signified that a critical
moment had arrived in the SWPA; October 1943 represented a key turning point for the US–Australian coalition. As David Horner has noted the
manpower strain on the Australians was acute, and it was clear that they
could not play the same role in the theatre that they had in 1942 and most
of 1943. Australian forces would continue to play a substantial role in
New Guinea in the following months, but as Berryman's operational
instruction and Chamberlin's forward planning demonstrated, in
October the centre of gravity in the SWPA's operations had clearly started
to swing away from the Australians. By the time of the capture of Madang
in April 1944, closing down the Australian campaign for New Guinea, US
dominance in the theatre had been cemented, and it was clear that there
was to be no role for the Australian Army in the drive to the Philippine
archipelago.

MacArthur's Approach to the Philippines

Before US ascendency in the SWPA came about, however, there were many tough decisions to be made and even tougher fighting, both of which lay just over the horizon. MacArthur's RENO III plan called for the isolation of Rabaul by capturing Hansa Bay in New Guinea, and Kavieng in New Ireland, beginning on 1 February 1944 and the Admiralty Islands by 1 April 1944. MacArthur's forces would then follow up these moves by further attacks on New Guinea which would eventually end in the Vogelkop Peninsula by 1 October 1944. MacArthur's plan even included an assault on Mindanao by 1 February 1945, despite not having the US Joint Chiefs of Staff approval for any such move into the Philippines.

To the contrary, the Joint Chiefs of Staff designed a twin drive during 1944. In addition to MacArthur's drive through New Guinea, and New Ireland, they also saw Admiral Chester A. Nimitz punching through Japanese defences in the Central Pacific, specifically to reach the Marianas so that the new B-29 Superfortresses – with its 2500-kilometre range – could strike the Japanese Home Islands. The Joint Chiefs of Staff believed that a twin-drive strategy would have the benefit of being mutually supporting. Although they had decided on a strategy that included both the SWPA and the Central Pacific, the US Navy's portion of the offensive was considered the most important. This route was easier to support and supply, as it was more direct.[9]

Nimitz's timetable for his offensive roughly resembled MacArthur's. He would move into the eastern and central Marshalls by the end of January 1944, then strike the Japanese stronghold of Truk in late March. In May his forces would move into the western Marshalls, invade the Palau Islands in August and enter the Marianas by 1 November.[10] Just when it seemed MacArthur would watch the US Navy take the lead while he took a supporting role, a series of events gave the SWPA commander the impetus he felt he needed to accelerate his own offensive up the northern coast of New Guinea. The first involved a number of intercepted Japanese messages that indicated that they intended to reinforce their defensive positions in the Admiralties, New Ireland, Hansa Bay and Wewak.[11]

The second set of incidents involved Lieutenant-General George C. Kenney's Fifth US Air Force. Throughout the first half of February, Kenney's planes had been targeting Japanese positions in the Admiralties and New Ireland. His pilots reported that the Japanese had evacuated one of the Admiralty Islands, Los Negros, on which the Japanese had built Momote airfield. Kenney – excited by the reports of his pilots – concluded that Los Negros was 'ripe for the picking'.[12]

Armed with this new intelligence, Kenney went to see MacArthur on 24 February and suggested that a 'reconnaissance in force' be sent to the island to investigate the situation. MacArthur recognised that a weakly defended Los Negros would provide him the perfect opportunity to put some much-needed speed in SWPA offensive operations to match the pace of the navy. Later that day, MacArthur ordered his US ground commander Lieutenant General Walter Krueger to prepare to conduct a reconnaissance in force of Los Negros in the vicinity of the Momote airstrip in five days, the 29 February. MacArthur then ordered the 1st Cavalry Division to follow the reconnaissance and secure the two main islands of the Admiralties: Manus and Los Negros. The 1st Cavalry Division began its landing on 2 March and secured it seven days later.

Kenney's news and Krueger's actions to secure the Admiralties a full month ahead of schedule provided MacArthur the perfect opportunity to further accelerate operations in the SWPA and keep pace – if not move faster – than the navy. On 5 March, he proposed a revised RENO plan. RENO IV scrapped the planned assault against Hansa Bay. Not only was it strongly defended, now that the Admiralties were firmly in his hands, Hansa Bay had lost its significance. Instead, MacArthur advocated a direct jump to Hollandia and Aitape. Once Hollandia and Aitape were secure, MacArthur wanted to press forward to islands in the Arafura Sea, the Vogelkop Peninsula, Halmahera and finally an assault on the Philippines itself.

Although the Joint Chiefs of Staff had not decided whether the Philippine Islands would be liberated, the members approved MacArthur's plan. Thus began a whirlwind campaign up the northern coast of New Guinea. The first was a 640 kilometres jump in mid-April to capture Hollandia, a Japanese air base that possessed few ground defences. Nevertheless, the distance alone involved innumerable difficulties. But MacArthur made sure that the Japanese believed the Americans were going to land at Wewak through an extensive deception campaign. In addition, Kenney's planes pounded Hollandia, virtually crushing Japanese air power in New Guinea. Everything went according to plan as Lieutenant-General Robert L. Eichelberger's I Corps landed virtually unopposed at the two landing sites at Hollandia, while Brigadier-General Jens A. Doe landed at the lightly defended town of Aitape, which the Americans wanted for an airstrip to aid the assault on Hollandia. By

28 April both of Hollandia's airstrips were in US hands as the Japanese defenders melted into the jungle. This bold move to occupy Hollandia cost the Japanese dearly, cutting off three Japanese divisions that protected the Wewak–Hansa Bay area.

Following the Hollandia operation came a succession of movements up the northern coast of New Guinea: Wakde Island and Sarmi (18 May), Biak Island (27 May), Noemfoor (2 July), and Sansapor on the Vogelkop Peninsula. Hollandia marked the beginning of the campaign by Krueger's forces to hit the Japanese at their weak points while avoiding their large strongholds. When the Americans ended their role in the campaign in New Guinea on 31 August, over 100,000 Japanese were trapped there, between dangerous jungle on one side and the ocean on the other.

Role of the AMF in 1944

At the end of October 1943 the Australian command arrangements in NGF changed again. Mackay left to take up the post of High Commissioner in India and Morshead was promoted from corps to army command and took over NGF. Berryman replaced Morshead at I Australian Corps, which was renamed II Australian Corps with the change of command. It would take another five months for the Australian campaign in New Guinea to come to a close. By April 1944 the Australians had totally defeated the Japanese 51st and 20th Divisions in New Guinea and by then the areas around Lae and the Finschhafen–Langemak Bay–Dreger Harbour areas had been transformed into a massive sea and air base from which the US would launch its major subsequent amphibious assaults against Hollandia and Aitape.[13]

Command Arrangements, Southwest Pacific Area, 1944–45

As the campaign was closed most of II Australian Corps staff and the majority of the Australian formations, including the 7th and 9th Australian Divisions, returned to the Atherton Tableland in northern Queensland to rest, recuperate, absorb replacements and undertake training. Lieutenant-General Stanley Savige and his staff were brought in to take over NGF (reduced to a corps headquarters), and the role of defending the conquests in northeastern New Guinea and developing the bases and airfields fell to the 5th Australian (Militia) Division. It would also mean that this was the smallest number of Australia troops in New Guinea than at any time since the start of the Kokoda campaign in July 1942.[14]

At the time of the return of the Australian Imperial Force (AIF) divisions to Australia, the future role of the Australian Army remained uncertain. As Berryman returned his corps headquarters to Australia, he learned of Advanced Land HQ (Adv LHQ) plans to base the corps in Darwin to seize the islands in the Arafura Sea. However he would soon learn from MacArthur's GHQ that these operations were 'contingent one only and will be governed by the results of the big [US Navy] operations through the central Pacific'.[15] While the troops recovered from their ordeals in New Guinea the future of the Army's operations remained in limbo.

As discussed in chapter 1 the Australian government had committed to MacArthur 'a force of three infantry divisions, an armoured brigade, garrison forces, forty-eight RAAF squadrons' and the maintenance of the Navy at its then strength for operations during 1944–45. Of these formations the 6th Division AIF would be available for operations by mid-year, the 9th Division, which was given priority on reinforcements from the reduced manpower pool, would be ready for operations later in the year and the 7th Division when manpower constraints allowed. Blamey assessed that the 3rd, 5th and 11th Divisions, made up of militia units, would also be available for service outside of Australia in the mandated territories.[16] The question was what would the focus of this force be?

The future of Australia's military effort would be decided by four separate factors: the complex dynamics between the major powers at their conference in Cairo (Sextant) in December 1943; the Pacific War conference between the senior officers of the SWPA, SOPAC and the Central Pacific Commands at Pearl Harbor on 27 and 28 January 1944; MacArthur's position as to the use of Australian troops; and the wishes of the Australian government. So while Curtin and Blamey travelled to the United Kingdom and the United States early in 1944, the RAAF would continue to support Australian troops in New Guinea and the RAN would also support the US operations in their march towards the Philippines, while the Australian Army undertook garrison duties in New Guinea with only very limited offensive activity towards Alexishafen from Madang.[17]

With Blamey's return to Australia he started preparations for a Commonwealth Army to be based in Darwin to re-take Singapore.[18] In order to pull together his plan, Berryman was relieved of his corps command and put in charge of a planning cell to develop this proposal which would mean that a new Pacific theatre would be opened, and that Australia would be a partner with Britain and New Zealand in the reconquest of the Pacific. It would mean an enlargement of Australia's prestige, such as Australia could not hope for as the junior, very junior member of an American–Australian Relationship.[19]

Blamey's plan was audacious, but it had little chance of success and it fell apart completely when the British cut a new deal that would see their Pacific fleet operate with Nimitz in the Central Pacific.[20] The major consequence of Blamey's Singapore plan was a widening of his rift with MacArthur and the power imbalanced in this relationship shifted further in MacArthur's favour when he received permission from the US Joint Chiefs for the assault on the Philippines in June and confirmation of the assault on Luzon in late July.[21] This decision meant a reorganisation of forces and a large injection of US formations into the SWPA. But in order to develop his plan and conduct the requisite operations MacArthur needed to form a new US army (the Eighth). To do so he had to release the six US divisions currently tied up garrisoning Torokina, Aitape and New Britain.[22]

Now in a position to push harder with the Australians, on 12 July 1943 MacArthur directed them to relieve the US forces in the South Pacific and in the island bases encircling Rabaul,[23] and Berryman oversaw arrangements for the transfer of forces at a conference with GHQ on 29 October 1944.[24] These troops would be known as the First Australian Army, with headquarters in Port Moresby (replacing NGF), while the I Australian Corps (Morshead), less the 6th Division AIF which was allocated to First Australian Army, would be available for operations with the Americans in the Philippines.

MacArthur, the Joint Chiefs of Staff and the Debate over the Philippines

The road to the Philippines, however, was not straight or fast. In fact there was a time when the Joint Chiefs of Staff favoured not an assault on Leyte or Luzon but on Formosa. Everyone agreed that the United States had to wrest control over the vast strategic triangle of Formosa, Luzon and mainland China, which acted as a throughway for Japan's resources from the south. MacArthur was convinced that a push into the Philippines was not only the most strategically sound course of action but that the United States also had a moral imperative to liberate the island nation. Others, most notably Fleet Admiral Ernest J. King (Chief of Naval Operations and Commander-in-Chief, United States Fleet), believed that Formosa provided the best position to control the flow of resources due to its proximity to the Chinese mainland.

The military debates over which island possessed the most promise were influenced by inter-service rivalries. The Formosa invasion would be led by Nimitz, while MacArthur would lead the Philippine option. The only suitable solution for the US Army and Navy involved having their own service commander lead the way. The events of mid-September 1944 would solve this strategic dilemma.

Until then MacArthur's RENO IV plans had an assault on Mindanao on 15 November. Due to the speed is his advance to the Vogelkop area, MacArthur revised his timetable and reported that he could jump from his position in Morotai (which Krueger's forces had attacked on 15 September), skipping over Mindanao and make a landing on Leyte on 20 October. This was not only a jump further into the Philippines but was also a month ahead of his previous estimates. MacArthur then informed the Joint Chiefs of Staff that he could make the jump from Leyte to Luzon on 20 December.[25]

In the meantime, the military logic of taking Formosa was slowly losing ground. According to various staff studies Nimitz's assault on Formosa would be 77,000 to 200,000 service troops short of those required for the task. By the end of September, almost all of the military evidence pointed to an invasion of Luzon rather than Formosa.[26] Despite King's continued objections, the Joint Chiefs of Staff instructed MacArthur on 2 October to prepare for an invasion of Leyte on 20 October.

THE ASSAULT ON LEYTE

Until the Leyte campaign, most of the battles across New Guinea – with the exception of Hollandia – were ones of regiments, not divisions or corps. Leyte would change all of that. For Leyte, Krueger's Sixth Army would have over 200,000 men divided into four divisions and two corps; it would be a massive and complex invasion, in part because of the terrain of Leyte. The island stretches to about 185 kilometres in length and varies in width from 24 to 69 kilometres. A chain of rugged mountains dominates the centre of the island.

Krueger's plan included first securing the entrance to Leyte Gulf by seizing three small islands. The second phase was the main landing, with the XXIV Corps landing in between the towns of Tanauan and Dulag, while the X Corps landed near Tacloban. Phase three envisioned the breakout of the two corps by the X Corps moving north along the coast of Carigara Bay and then

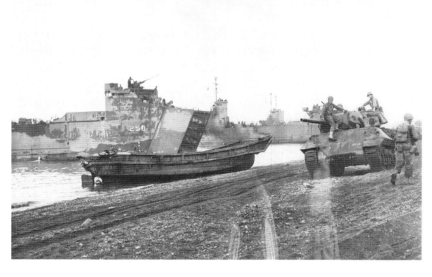

Figure 2.1: A Japanese barge against a background of US ships, Ormoc
Bay, Leyte, Philippines, 14 December 1944. (Australian War Memorial 017903)

swinging south toward Ormoc on the western side of the island. Meanwhile
the XXIV Corps would swing south to Abyuog then move west to Baybay.
Upon arriving at Baybay, the corps was to drive north and link up with the X
Corps at Ormoc. The last phase of the plan – now that the Japanese garrison
was encircled – was to secure the island.

The first two phases of the operation went well, with the two corps landing
with little loss of life. The third phase saw some difficulty as the X Corps ran
into well-entrenched, recently arrived Japanese defenders on their way to
Carigara on mountainous terrain that Krueger's men called Breakneck Ridge.
It took over 20 days of hard fighting to push the Japanese out of their
defences. After the battle of Breakneck Ridge, the X Corps was on the
move again along Highway Two toward Ormoc. Meanwhile the XXIV
Corps moved through the rain-soaked central Leyte region along Highway
One toward Baybay. The two wings of Krueger's pincer movement met near
Ormoc on 21 December. After securing the last remaining port city of note –
Palompon – Leyte was finally in US hands. However there remained approximately 15,000 Japanese troops still holding out, a task MacArthur assigned
to the Eighth US Army on 25 December, as Krueger's Sixth US Army was
allocated to the invasion of Luzon scheduled for 9 January 1945.

THE I AUSTRALIAN CORPS AND THE PHILIPPINES

In September 1944 MacArthur's GHQ decamped and moved from Brisbane to Hollandia in Dutch New Guinea. In response Blamey formed a Forward Echelon of Adv LHQ (Forland), under Berryman's commander, whom he had made Chief of Staff (CoS) of Adv LHQ in July. This meant that Blamey now had three headquarter elements: Forland to liaise with GHQ; LHQ in Melbourne for training and support in Australia; and Adv LHQ at St Lucia, Brisbane, to control operations outside Australia.[27] At Forland Berryman was to 'assist [GHQ] in the preparation of plans for future operations of the Australian Forces abroad',[28] and the HQ would spend the majority of its time working with GHQ on the use of the AIF Corps. It opened for operations at Hollandia on 7 September 1944.

At this point in time the major consideration for the use of I Australian Corps in the Philippines was Operation Love II. The plan called for an amphibious assault on the northern shore of the central Philippine island of Luzon near the town of Aparri to seize and develop its airstrip for the US Marine Air Corps, to provide for a naval base for US patrol torpedo boats and to capture the airfield at Tuguegarao and then to secure Balete Pass.[29] The operation to capture Aparri gave the Australians an important yet supporting role, and considerable work was put into developing a plan between Forland and headquarters I Australian Corps for its implementation. But the plan was cancelled in late September after the US Joint Chiefs of Staff allocated fleet carriers to support MacArthur's landing at Luzon, negating the need for the airfield and port at Aparri.[30]

This move left the Australians in limbo. During September 1944 GHQ had indicated to Forland that the corps might be used at either Sarangani in the Philippines or for an assault on Borneo. As September drifted into October and November, GHQ put forward proposals to use the corps or its divisions independently in Mindanao, at Davao,[31] and then as part of the follow-on forces for the main assault at Lingayen Gulf. As November became December MacArthur met with Blamey and Berryman and told them that he intended using the corps to clear up Luzon after the initial American assault. By mid-December 1944 it was becoming clear that, despite MacArthur's assurances to Curtin,[32] the AIF would not be used in operations in the Philippines unless the campaign dragged on longer than MacArthur anticipated.

At the time of the US Sixth Army's landing on Luzon on 9 January 1945, the I Australian Corps remained without a firm commitment for its use. MacArthur was, however, adamant that the troops remain in theatre and under his command and he refused to release them for operations elsewhere. While it was not given an operational role, the Australian corps was fulfilling a critical role for MacArthur, as his only uncommitted theatre reserve.[33] The final crunch came in early February 1945 when Berryman told Blamey that 'the AIF is not likely to be employed in the Philippines'.[34] However it took another month before MacArthur wrote to Curtin outlining the reasons why. He laid most of the blame at Blamey's feet, especially as the Australian C-in-C had insisted that the AIF Corps fight together as a national command, thereby, he claimed, ruling out a number of plans GHQ had developed to use the 7th and 9th Divisions in separate operations under direct American command. Thus the Australians had missed out on what Berryman saw as the 'decisive battle' of the Pacific War,[35] and MacArthur's intentions for the AIF now turned to Borneo.[36]

First Australian Army Operations

While the role of the AIF Corps remained uncertain, the First Australian Army undertook what was to become one of most controversial campaigns in Australian history. Despite its tag as an 'unnecessary campaign' the strategy behind the First Army's operations was sound. What is critical is that they are understood both in the context of Australian government policy, the manpower problems of the Army, and the fact that the war was expected to go on well into 1946 and possibly even 1947.

First Army's role was to 'destroy the enemy where this can be done with relatively light casualties so as to free our territory and liberate the native population and thereby progressively reduce our commitments and free personnel from the army'.[37] In addition it cannot be overlooked that this campaign was being fought on Australian sovereign territory that was occupied by a foreign country that had posed a direct threat to Australia's security.

From a purely military perspective the completion of their objectives was critical to the developments of Blamey's strategy for 1945 and for forward planning into 1946–47. The manpower crisis meant that Adv LHQ had to plan for a reduction in the size of the Army in 1946 that would affect the role of the Army's operations. Significantly, the successful prosecution of limited offensives by First Army in New Guinea and Bougainville to reduce the size of the Japanese garrisons would result in a much smaller containing force. In turn this would mean that troops could be released in 1946 in order to maintain the Australian economic contribution to the wider war effort, which was especially critical to MacArthur's forces operating further north. In addition the reduction of the Japanese forces around Wewak in New Guinea would allow the 6th Division to move forward in 1946 to form part of the AIF Corps that was allocated for the invasion of Japan.[38]

As noted in chapter 1 the operations in the First Army were undertaken with the support of GHQ and with the (albeit delayed) sanction of the Australian government. Blamey's strategy had been developed in an effort to ensure that the Australian Army was reduced in 1946–47 in line with the government's direction while concurrently maintaining an AIF strike force of sufficient strength to participate in major operations to secure victory in the Pacific – namely the invasion of Japan. Only through this approach would Blamey be able to meet the government's policy of maintaining a military effort that would guarantee Australia's 'status at the peace table'. Significantly, by June 1945 the First Army had shown some considerable success in achieving their objectives, and as a result Adv LHQ was able to plan with confidence for the transfer of the 6th Division to the AIF strike force for the invasion of Japan, for the reduction of the AMF by 30,000 men and the garrisoning of the First Army to be reduced to as little as three to five brigades.[39]

THE ASSAULT ON LUZON AND THE LIBERATION OF THE PHILIPPINES

Seventeen days separated General Walter Krueger from taking his Sixth US Army to finish the major phase of combat operations in Leyte to invading Luzon, the most strategically significant of the Philippine islands. The Japanese had over 260,000 men committed to the defence of Luzon, but as they lacked the ability to manoeuvre, thanks to the decimation of both Japanese sea and air power, the Japanese commander decided to fight a war of attrition with the Americans by retreating to three large and dispersed mountain strongholds.

In order to defeat this force, MacArthur, like he had on Leyte, marshalled four divisions and organised into two corps, the I and XIV. These two corps would land abreast on the northeast side of Luzon at Lingayen Gulf, their goal the Philippine capital of Manila, approximately 100 miles to the south. The plan was simple. While the XIV Corps would spearhead the dash to Manila, the I Corps would protect its left flank. 'The basic tactical principle of American offensive operations on Luzon', Krueger noted, 'was the use of overwhelming material strength to crush the enemy with a minimum loss of American manpower'.[40]

While there was little initial opposition to the Sixth Army landing on that 9 January morning, logistical problems caused men and material to get caught up in heavy traffic congestion on the beachhead. In addition, I Corps was taking Japanese artillery fire on its left flank from one of the mountain strongholds. These two major factors made Krueger halt his offensive south-ward and await the arrival of the two follow-on divisions that had been planned to land shortly after 9 January to reinforce Krueger's army. Once these two divisions arrived, he would have the forces to hold the bridgehead and protect the left flank of the XIV Corps for its offensive to Manila.

MacArthur, however, had other thoughts about the way operations were going in Luzon. On 12 January he arrived at Krueger's command post with the idea of badgering his subordinate to continue southward without waiting for the additional two divisions. It was 'the only time I ever saw the two of them when they had cross words,' Brigadier-General Clyde D. Eddleman, a member of Krueger's staff, noted. Krueger defended his actions, and it is a testament to MacArthur's respect for Krueger that the SWPA commander did not override his subordinate. 'The old man stuck to his guns', Eddleman remembered, 'but he didn't feel to[o] good' about it.[41]

While Krueger did not have the strength to take Manila, he wanted to maintain the momentum of his army by taking Clark Airfield, an important objective since its runways were superior to those hastily built near the landing at Lingayen Gulf. By 23 January Krueger's soldiers reached the northeastern runway of Clark, but the Japanese were putting up tough resistance, forcing Krueger to turn his corps 90 degrees to face west toward the airfield. Over several days, soldiers of the Sixth Army faced tough and resilient Japanese defences that took carefully planned US combined tank and infantry attacks to overcome. The whole area was in Krueger's hands by 29 January.[42]

By this time, Sixth Army had the extra division it so desperately needed, and on 1 February the anticipated movement to liberate Manila had begun. By largely bypassing enemy resistance, the XIV Corp reached the capital's suburbs in two days and began rooting out the 17,000 defenders. The battles evolved into a slugging match that lasted a month and destroyed large sections of the city and killed approximately 100,000 Filipinos. According to Ronald Spector only the city of Warsaw incurred greater damage during the Second World War.[43]

With Manila taken, Krueger turned toward clearing out the main pockets of Japanese resistance still on the island, specifically around Lingayen Gulf and Manila. At the same time, MacArthur sent his Eighth US Army under the command of Eichelberger to liberate the rest of the Philippine Islands. This was an unfortunate decision, as the Japanese had many tens of thousands of soldiers willing to fight for virtually every piece of ground no matter how strategically insignificant. MacArthur felt this so important that he even transferred three divisions away from the Sixth Army to the Eighth, severely crippling the ability of Krueger's army to finish its operations. 'MacArthur', D. Clayton James argues, would have been wiser to have used the Eighth Army primarily to expedite the reconquest of Luzon, for few bases set up in the central and southern islands proved of value later and the beleaguered enemy garrisons south of Luzon were so isolated that they posed no threat to MacArthur's lines of communication or his future moves.[44]

Thus, while he acted boldly in leap-frogging around Japanese garrisons on New Guinea, he unfortunately abandoned this concept of operations once he reached the Philippines. Thus, in early February, while the fight for the Philippines was still raging, MacArthur was looking at moving in three different directions. The first was towards central and southern Philippine Islands; the second was southward towards Borneo, Java, and the rest of the East Indies; and the third – which would be the toughest challenge of all – the invasion of the Japanese Home Islands.

Oboe Operations: The Road to Nowhere

By the time MacArthur finally informed Curtin that the Australians would not participate in the liberation of the Philippines, Morshead's corps had been out of the frontline for almost a year. The only other plan that the Australians had been actively considered for was the liberation of Borneo. The original plan for this operation called for the use of all three AIF divisions in landings at Tarakan, Balikpapan and Banjermasin in Borneo, and one in Java at Soerabaja (Oboe 1–4) set for 1 July 1945.[45] This was subsequently expanded to include a second landing in the Netherland East Indies and another at Brunei Bay (Oboe 5 and 6). Planning had been underway concurrently with the Philippine operations since September 1944, and with the absence of Australian troops in the Philippines and the success of the Luzon operations GHQ informed Forland that the 9th Division would be used against Brunei Bay and Balikpapan and the 7th Division against Tarakan.[46]

The problem that now arose was that the war in the Pacific had moved on rapidly, especially in the Central Pacific, and the strategic rationale for the operations against Borneo had lapsed. Claims were made that the capture of Brunei would provide for a base for the British Pacific Fleet, but the British Admiralty rejected this. It was also argued that the Dutch oil fields in Brunei were of immense importance to the both the Japanese and Allied war efforts, but in reality they were already cut off from the Japanese Home Islands, and when in Allied hands it would take months, if not years, to get them operational again. The operation clearly lacked strategic value to everyone but MacArthur.

Figure 2.2: Amphibious landing, Balikpapan, Borneo, 1 July 1945. (Australian War Memorial 128283)

The Australians were not blind to these developments. Berryman wrote to Blamey on 10 February 1945 and argued that the 'operations in BORNEO would have little immediate impact on the war against Japan'.[47] Furthermore, in addition to the lack of a strategic rationale the operational and tactical reasons for the landings were unsound. The only reason for taking Tarakan was to support the operation against Balikpapan, but the airfields on the island would not be ready in time for the scheduled follow-on landing. Balikpapan was only ever envisaged in the original Oboe plans as a staging base to launch the final assault against Java, but by June 1945 the Australians were well aware that MacArthur had ruled out this final operation.[48] With this decision Balikpapan represented a road to nowhere.

Blamey raised these concerns with both MacArthur and the Australian government, in particular over the Balikpapan operation. However MacArthur countered by playing a duplicitous hand, telling the Prime Minister, John Curtin, that the US Joint Chiefs of Staff demanded the operations go ahead. At the same time he told the Joint Chiefs of Staff that the Australian government demanded that, for political reasons, they go ahead.[49] The government found itself in a position where it believed it could not say no to MacArthur and its major coalition partner, even if the rationale for those operations remained weak.

Balikpapan operation was thus undertaken on 1 July by Major-General 'Teddy' Milford's 7th Division. It was to be the largest Australian amphibious operation of the war and the last Allied landing of the Second World War. It faced determined Japanese resistance for the next three weeks as the Australians advanced inland and fighting continued until the end of the war, and cost 229 Australians lives with a further 634 wounded.[50] It was an exceptionally high price to pay for an operation that had absolutely no strategic or operational purpose.

MacArthur's Plan for the Invasion of Japan

Unlike the Balikpapan operation, the next major operation would prove to be of the utmost significance – the invasion of the Home Islands of Japan. The first target was the southernmost island, Kyushu. Other Japanese territories or Japanese-held locations (such as in China) were quickly dismissed.[51] It was unlike the Americans to attack the enemy any other place than the heart of its power. The invasion of Kyushu (Operation OLYMPIC) would next lead to landings on the Kanto Plain of Honshu (Operation CORONET). Five hundred and sixty kilometres from Okinawa, Kyushu held great promise for MacArthur and Nimitz. It would unite the long twin drives of the SWPA and Central Pacific campaigns. Furthermore, the forces involved in landing on Kyushu – it was hoped – might persuade the Japanese leadership to finally surrender.[52] Finally, in the absence of surrender, American occupation of Kyushu would allow for air, land and sea bases for the assault on Honshu.

The forces available for OLYMPIC were staggering. Twenty-two battleships, 27 heavy and light aircraft carriers, 36 escort carriers, 50 cruisers, and 458 destroyers and destroyer escorts, and 2458 other ships – including landing craft – prepared to descend upon Kyushu, over 3000 ships in all.[53] While the Navy was in charge of the amphibious landing, Krueger would be at the lead of the over 323,000 combat troops whose responsibility it was to secure the southern end of the island. Divided into four corps, the American V Amphibious Corps would land south of Kushikino with the 3rd, 4th, and 5th Marine Divisions. The XI Corps – comprised of the 1st Cavalry, the Americal, and the 43rd Divisions – would land in Ariake Bay, while the I Corps would land the 25th, 33rd, and 41st Divisions on the eastern side of Kyushu at Miyazaki. Lastly, the IX Corps with its 98th and 81st Divisions acted as Sixth Army reserve. These landings formed the first phase of a three-phase plan. Krueger designated Phase Two to clear territory for the construction of airfields, while Phase Three included the destruction of the final Japanese defenders in the southern portion of Kyushu.

The Sixth Army would not face an easy task, as each of the three landing sites would greet the invasion troops with unique challenges. Perhaps the easiest landing would be the I Corps. The Miyazaki landing made defending the beaches difficult and would have prevented easy movement of inland Japanese units towards the American landings without being on the receiving end of US naval and air attacks. The landscape behind the landing beaches of the V Amphibious Corps produced great challenges. There were several tiers of high ground from which the Japanese could rain down murderous fire on the Marines. Fortunately, the Marines would have faced only a token force of two battalions defending the sector. Finally, troops of the XI Corps would have had their own unique set of problems, as their landing site was flanked by towering hills, offset by the potential of more manoeuvre space than either of the other corps once it had moved inland.[54]

If the battle had played out, the Americans would have faced a most difficult task. The Japanese planned to fix the invaders with their units placed near the landing sites, while more mobile units from inland would mobilise within 10 days of the invasion and attempt to destroy the enemy in their beachhead positions. Although the Japanese faced critical shortages of raw materials and ammunition, and their army units lacked mobility, they would have fought a fanatical and potent defence of Kyushu.[55]

The invasion plans for the invasion of Honshu had not progressed as far as those plans for Kyushu. Nevertheless, two armies – the First and the Eighth – would land nineteen divisions, including two armoured divisions from the European Theatre, against the Kanto Plain for Operation CORONET. The First Army was designated to clear the defences around Tokyo Bay and then move through a natural corridor in order to capture Tokyo. At the same time, the Eighth Army would land on the beaches of Sagami Bay, clear the Miura Peninsula, capture the Yokosuka naval base, and then move to positions north of Tokyo. Once in these positions, both armies would then assault Tokyo itself.[56]

US intelligence analysts determined that the greatest Japanese air and naval threat would be to Operation OLYMPIC. The Japanese – it was assumed – were preparing their utmost to stop the Americans in Kyushu. Whatever air and naval assets, including suicide units, that remained for the defence of Honshu would be destroyed quickly.[57]

The evidence suggests that apart from the invasion of Kyushu and Honshu, US planners gave no serious consideration for what would happen if the Japanese continued to fight even after successful completion of the two operations. The Japanese still possessed about 2 million men on the Asian mainland, and strong Japanese forces would still occupy portions of Honshu and Kyushu. The US Joint Chiefs of Staff, however, believed that the invasion plan would cripple Tokyo's ability to govern and resign the leadership to the fact that any more resistance would be futile.[58] Whether or not occupation of southern Kyushu or even the Kanto Plain would have precipitated Japanese surrender will of course never be known, and discussion of this topic has been superseded by the decision to use two atomic bombs and the role they played in the cessation of the Second World War in the Pacific.

FURTHER READING

Peter J. Dean, *The Architect of Victory: The Military Career of Lieutenant-General Sir Frank Horton Berryman*, Cambridge University Press, Melbourne, 2011.

M. Hamlin Cannon, *Leyte: The Return to the Philippines*, Office of the Chief of Military History, Department of the Army, Washington, DC, 1954.

Kevin Holzimmer, *General Walter Krueger: Unsung Hero of the Pacific War*, University Press of Kansas, Kansas, 2007.

David Horner, *High Command: Australia's Struggle for an Independent War Strategy, 1939–1945*, Allen & Unwin, St Leonards, 1992.

David Horner, *Blamey: The commander in Chief*, Allen & Unwin, St Leonards, 1998.

Gavin Long, *The Final Campaigns*, Australian War Memorial, Canberra, 1963.

Robert Ross Smith, *Triumph in the Philippines*, Office of the Chief of Military History, Deptartment of the Army, Washington, DC, 1963

Stephen R. Taaffe, *MacArthur's Jungle War: The 1944 New Guinea Campaign*, University Press of Kansas, Kansas, 1998.

Notes

1   Berryman Diary, 1 September and 1 October 1943, AWM PR 84/370.

2   David Horner, *General Vasey's War*, Melbourne University Press, Carlton, 1992, pp. 260, 285.

3   Douglas MacArthur, *General MacArthur Reports*, Center of Military History, US Army, Washington, DC, 1966, p. 168.

4   Memo Chamberlin to Sutherland, October 1943, RG407 GHQ1-3.2 SWPA G-3 Journal September–October 1943, Box 601, US National Archives and Record Administration (NARA), pp. 2–3.

5 Memo Chamberlin to Sutherland, 7 October 1943, RG407 GHQ1-3.2 SWPA G-3 Journal September–October 1943 Box 601, NARA, pp. 4–5.
6 Berryman, interview, AWM 93 50/2/23/331.
7 Berryman, diary, 8 October 1943, AWM PR84/370.
8 New Guinea Force Operational Instruction No. 96A, RG407 GHQ1-3.2 SWPA G-3 Journal, September–October 1943, Box 601, NARA.
9 Robert Ross Smith, *Approach to the Philippines*, Office of the Chief of Military History, Washington, DC, 1953, p. 5.
10 Ibid., p. 6.
11 Edward J. Drea, *MacArthur's ULTRA: Codebreaking and the War against Japan, 1942–1945*, University Press of Kansas, Kansas, 1990, pp. 96–97.
12 George C. Kenney, *General Kenney Reports: A Personal History of the Pacific War*, Office of Air Force History, Washington, DC, 1987, p. 359.
13 John Coates, *An Atlas of Australia's Wars*, Oxford University Press, Oxford, Melbourne, 2001, p. 252.
14 Horner, *High Command*, Allen & Unwin, Sydney, 1981, p. 302.
15 Berryman, diary, 18 April 1944, AWM PR84/370.
16 Operations of the First Australian Army in Mandated Territory of New Guinea, August 1944, Blamey Papers, 2/45.
17 David Dexter, *The New Guinea Offensives*, AWM, Canberra, 1961, p. 807.
18 'The Basing of UK Forces in Australia', Part 1, p. 3, Berryman Papers, item 29.
19 John Hetherington, *Blamey*, AWM, Canberra, 1973, p. 213.
20 C. Baxter, 'In Pursuit of a Pacific Strategy', *Diplomacy and Statecraft*, vol. 15, 2004, p. 256.
21 M. Hamlin Cannon, *Leyte: The Return to the Philippines*, pp. 5–6.
22 Gavin Long, *The Final Campaigns*, AWM, Canberra, 1963, p. 19.
23 Operations of the First Australian Army in Mandated Territory of New Guinea, August 1944, AWM Blamey Papers, 2/45.
24 Conference on Relief of US Forces by Australian Forces in New Guinea, New Britain and Northern Solomons, 29 October 1944, RG-3, Papers of R.K. Sutherland, MacArthur Memorial Archives.
25 Robert Ross Smith, 'Luzon versus Formosa (1944)', in Kent Robert Greenfield (ed), *Command Decisions*, Harcourt, Brace and Company, New York, 1959, pp. 370.
26 Ibid., pp. 367–8.
27 Berryman, diary, 28 August 1944, AWM PR84/370.
28 Long, *The Final Campaigns*, p. 24.

29 Appreciation of the Situation by GSO I (Ops) Plans, 28 August 1944, Blamey Papers, 2/45.
30 Berryman to Blamey, 14 September 1944, Blamey Papers 2/139.
31 Berryman to Blamey, 16 October 1944, Blamey Papers 2/139.
32 Note of Conversation between MacArthur, Curtin and Shedden, 15 March 1944, DFAT Historical Documents online <www.dfat.gov.au/historical/index.html>
33 Long, *The Final Campaigns*, p. 29.
34 Berryman to Blamey, 8 February 1945, Blamey Papers, 2/139.
35 Berryman, diary, 3 April 1945, AWM PR84/370.
36 MacArthur to Curtin, 5 March 1945 as quoted in Long, *The Final Campaigns*, pp. 45–46.
37 Appreciation on Operations of the AMF in New Guinea, New Britain and the Solomon Islands, 18 May 1945, Blamey Papers, item 2/17.
38 Berryman to Lumsden, 24 December 1944, Berryman Papers, item 12.
39 Daily Journal of Fwd Ech LHQ (Forland) May–June 1945, 20 May 1945, AWM 52 1/2/3/16.
40 Krueger, *From Down to Nippon*, pp. 214–15.
41 Oral interview with General Clyde D. Eddleman by Lowell G. Smith and Murray G. Swindler, Interview #2, Section 2, 28 January 1975, pp. 32–33, US Army Military History Institute, Carlisle Barracks, PA.
42 Sixth Army, 'Sixth Army on Luzon,' Sections I–IV, Section I: 'Lingayen to Manila', p. 5, 106–0.3, Box 2405, National Archives and Records Administration, College Park, MY.
43 Ronald H. Spector, *Eagle Against the Sun: The American War with Japan*, The Free Press, New York, 1985, p. 524.
44 D. Clayton James, 'MacArthur's Lapses from an Envelopment Strategy in 1945,' *Parameters,* vol. X, no. 2, p. 30.
45 Berryman to Blamey, 24 September 1944 and 13 February 1945, Blamey Papers 2/139.
46 Long, *The Final Campaigns*, p. 29.
47 Berryman to Blamey, 10 February 1945, Blamey Papers 2/139.
48 Horner, *Inside the War Cabinet*, p. 183.
49 Ibid., p. 186.
50 Grey, *A Military History of Australia*, p. 186.
51 John Ray Skates, *The Invasion of Japan: Alternative to the Bomb*, University of South Carolina Press, Columbia, SC, 1994, p. 148.
52 Ibid.
53 Ibid., p. 167.

54 Ibid., pp. 188–91.
55 Edward J. Drea, *In the Service of the Emperor: Essays on the Imperial Japanese Army*, University of Nebraska Press, Lincoln, 1998, pp. 145–153.
56 Skates, *Invasion of Japan*, pp. 203–07.
57 Ibid., p. 211.
58 Ibid., pp. 211, 214.

CHAPTER 3

HOLDING ON TO THE FINISH: THE JAPANESE ARMY IN THE SOUTH AND SOUTHWEST PACIFIC, 1944–45

Hiroyuki Shindo

During the late spring and summer of 1944, the Allies penetrated the perimeter of the Japanese 'Absolute National Defence Zone', which was the line of defence that the Imperial Japanese Army and Navy had determined must absolutely be held for the Japanese Empire's survival. The Allies landed at Hollandia and in the Marianas, two distant parts of the perimeter. Thereafter, the Japanese continued to retreat in New Guinea and in the Central Pacific, before both axes of retreat converged in the Philippines. In 1945, the fighting moved on towards the Japanese Home Islands, but Rabaul was neutralised, while ground combat continued in New Guinea, Bougainville, Borneo, and elsewhere in the South Pacific and Southeast Asia.

This chapter reviews the Japanese Army's strategy and operations from late 1943 through the end of the war in New Guinea, the North-of-Australia (Gō-hoku; NoA) Area, Bougainville and Borneo. These were the areas of the war in which Australia's forces fought major battles during 1944–45. This overview of Japan's strategic and operational decisions will help the reader to better understand the experience of the Australian armed forces in the Pacific during the final years of the war.

The Japanese Army and Navy referred to the various regions in the Pacific Ocean with their own terms. The South Pacific Area included the Southeast Area and the NoA Area. The Southeast Area included Rabaul and the Bismarck Islands, the Solomon Islands and Eastern New Guinea – literally New Guinea east of approximately 140 degrees longitude (approximate to British New Guinea and Papua). Western New Guinea was New Guinea west of 140 degrees longitude, and the islands around the Banda Sea, including the Aru, Kai, Tanimbar, Timor and Molucca Islands, the area around the Flores Sea, the Lesser Sundas, and Celebes (approximate to Dutch New Guinea). The NoA Area included northwest New Guinea, and the areas around the Banda and Flores Seas. Western New Guinea therefore encompassed the NoA Area. The Central Pacific Area included the Caroline, Marshall, Mariana and Gilbert Islands, as well as Wake, Marcus, Nauru and Ocean Islands.[1] Finally, the Southwest Area, which was a more loosely used term, referred to the southwest corner of the Japanese Empire at its height, and included India, Burma, Malaya, the Netherlands East Indies, Indochina and Thailand.

THE 'NEW OPERATIONS GUIDANCE POLICY' (ABSOLUTE NATIONAL DEFENSE ZONE CONCEPT)

On 15 September 1943 the Imperial Japanese Army and Navy adopted a new operations guidance policy based on a defensive strategy. This strategy was unofficially labelled the Absolute National Defense Zone concept, and called for Japan's main defensive line vis-à-vis the Americans to be redrawn to encompass an area which would be more logistically sustainable. The new line extended from the Kuriles in the north and encompassed the Bonin Islands, Marianas, Truk and the Western Carolines, and Western New Guinea, before curving westward to include the Sunda and Banda Straits. Japanese forces which were eastwards of that line would be left in place and buy time by fighting 'holding operations' (*jikyū-sakusen*), while air, ground and naval forces were built up behind the main defensive line. This build up was to be completed by the summer of 1944, at which time a massive counteroffensive was to be launched against the enemy, which would regain Japan the initiative in the war.

The new operations guidance policy was incorporated into a wider national policy by an Imperial General Headquarters–Government Liaison conference on 25 September, and further approved by an Imperial conference held on 30 September. A new Army–Navy Central

Agreement was also adopted on 30 September, which spelled out the exact roles each service had under the new strategy.[2]

Strengthening the North-of-Australia Area Command Structure and Infrastructure

In accordance with the new operations guidance policy, the Imperial Japanese Army had to strengthen its capabilities in NoA, not only for defensive purposes, but also to enable NoA to become a springboard for the planned counteroffensive into the Central Pacific.[3] In the summer of 1943, NoA was defended by the XIX Army, which was under the command of Southern Expeditionary Army (SEA, with headquarters in Singapore) and consisted of the 5th and 48th Divisions. SEA's main concern from mid-1943 was the possibility of an Allied offensive from the west. The Army General Staff was concerned that the Axis capitulation in North Africa in May and Italy's surrender in early September might allow the British to send a major fleet from the Mediterranean to spearhead an offensive in the Indian Ocean area, possibly together with a US fleet. SEA's first priority therefore was to shore up its defences along the Bay of Bengal. In addition, SEA was also busy with its preparations for the upcoming Imphal operation, which eventually became a three-division attack into India in early 1944.

Earlier in 1943 the General Staff had considered relieving SEA of the burden of defending NoA by extending Eighth Area Army's area of responsibility westward to include NoA. Eighth Area Army was then responsible for operations in Eastern New Guinea and the Solomon Islands. As part of this plan, the headquarters of Eighth Area Army would be relocated from Rabaul to Western New Guinea or Halmahera. This idea was abandoned when General Hitoshi Imamura, Commander-in-Chief of Eighth Area Army, opposed it. Imamura felt a relocation of Eighth Area Army headquarters so far to the rear would only make it more difficult for him to command XVII and XVIII Armies in the Solomon Islands and New Guinea, respectively.[4]

The General Staff therefore decided to establish new Area Army and Army commands in NoA. In addition to strengthening the Imperial Japanese Army in NoA, the bureaucratic problems which had been growing between Eighth Area Army and SEA over the development of the infrastructure and logistics of NoA would be eased by the establishment of the new commands. SEA had been responsible for establishing the air, naval and ground bases and supporting infrastructure in NoA. However, it was increasingly likely that Eighth Area Army would use these bases in the near future, since it seemed only a matter of time before XVIII Army was pushed back into Western New Guinea. Since Eighth Area Army was not under SEA command, SEA and Eighth Area Army had to coordinate with each other regarding the development of these bases and lines of communication. Furthermore, after XVIII Army had retreated into Western New Guinea, Eighth Area Army would have to coordinate with SEA regarding XVIII Army's logistics, which would have to be managed by SEA. The General Staff, therefore, felt that the establishment of a new area army command in NoA which was directly subordinate to SEA would simplify those administrative processes.[5]

Instead of creating new commands from scratch, the General Staff transferred the staffs of Second Area Army headquarters and II Army headquarters from Manchuria to NoA. Second Area Army was initially directly attached to the General Staff, and consisted of II Army and XIX Army. Second Area Army headquarters was located in Halmahera, while II Army headquarters was placed in Manokwari. Both commands were activated on 1 December 1943. II Army initially consisted only of the 36th Division, while XIX Army had the 5th and 48th Divisions under its command, and was shortly scheduled to receive the 46th Division from the Home Islands. In addition, II Army was scheduled to receive the 3rd Division from the China Expeditionary Army, and one more division was scheduled to be sent to Halmahera, to act as an Imperial General Headquarters reserve. Second Area Army was ordered to secure Western New Guinea, and the Aru, Kai, Tanimbar, Timor, and Lesser Sunda Islands, and to construct bases, stockpile supplies, and otherwise prepare the area for use as a staging area for the planned counteroffensive in 1944.[6]

As the new command setup was being organised, the General Staff could not disregard the possibility of an Allied offensive from the Port Darwin area into the Banda Sea. It therefore arranged for the 46th Division to be deployed on Flores Island, even though the 5th and 48th Divisions were already stationed around the Banda Sea. The General Staff felt that XVIII Army could still hold off the enemy for a while in Western New Guinea and chose to use the 46th Division to reinforce the southeastern defences of NoA rather than to deploy it on the Vogelkop Peninsula.[7]

As for Western New Guinea, the General Staff, 2nd Area Army and II Army debated where to locate II Army's left flank. The General Staff wanted the 224th Regiment of the 36th Division deployed as far forward as Hollandia, which had become a vital air base and port for the Japanese forces in New Guinea. Hollandia was virtually undefended in fall of 1943, since XVIII Army's 41st Division had moved forward to Madang to secure the rear of the Japanese forces fighting at Finschhafen. Second Area Army and II Army, on the other hand, while initially agreeing with the General Staff, came to share the 36th Division's opinion that the 224th should be deployed no farther eastwards than Sarmi. Since the 36th Division would also have to defend Biak Island and the area around Geelvink Bay, which were more than 320 kilometres west of Hollandia, sending the 224th to Hollandia would result in a tactically unacceptable dispersion of the division. The General Staff ultimately relented, and ordered the 224th to Sarmi.[8] To fill in the void at Hollandia, the General Staff ordered the 6th South Seas Detachment to proceed to Hollandia instead of Palau on 19 January 1944. This force arrived in Hollandia on 4 March, but numbered only 240 men, since approximately 1000 men, including the detachment commander, had been lost en route to submarine attacks.[9]

As Second Area Army attempted to make preparations for the 1944 counteroffensive, it encountered two major problems. First, the Imperial Japanese Army alone had to construct over 100 new airfields in less than a year in Western New Guinea in order to enable the build up of air power along the perimeter of the Absolute National Defense Zone, which was a key prerequisite for the decisive counteroffensive planned for 1944. However, it was immediately evident that the Imperial Japanese Army lacked the manpower within NoA for such an ambitious construction plan. The Army could not mobilise enough airfield construction battalions, even if it stripped every other theatre of them, and the local population was not large enough to provide adequate labour either. Having no other option, Second Area Army ordered its combat troops to assist in the construction work. This greatly interfered with their combat training and created additional manpower problems for the Area Army as it prepared to defend the vast NoA area with the limited forces allocated to it.[10]

Next, the build up for the 1944 counteroffensive required the stockpiling of enormous volumes of supplies in NoA. In mid-November 1943 Second Area Army calculated that 600,000 tons of shipping per month for the next four months would be required for this build up of materiel.[11] However, this extra shipping capacity was unavailable because Japanese losses of shipping to enemy air and submarine attacks had been increasing at an alarming rate. During the 10 months from September 1943 and June 1944, the Japanese lost a total of approximately 2.3 million tons of shipping. In the four months from November 1943 through February 1944 alone, nearly 1.4 million tons were lost, including over 500,000 tons in February, which was a monthly record. This loss rate was far beyond the 800,000 tons the Japanese had expected to lose annually in their pre-war calculations, and affected not only the transport of raw materials from Southeast Asia to the Home Islands, but also the transfer of troops and supplies to areas around the Pacific.[12] The General Staff, therefore, decided to give priority in February and March 1944 to the transport of men and supplies to the Central Pacific, which had become a critical area with the onset of the US campaigns against the Gilbert and Marshall Islands. Second Area Army was therefore alerted by the General Staff on 13 February 1944 that the majority of shipments of supplies for the NoA area would be cancelled in February and March. In fact, shipments to Second Area Army decreased by only a third during this period, but this still delayed the build up of forces and supplies in NoA.[13] Second Area Army received only two thirds of its scheduled troop reinforcements by the end of June, and the remaining portion did not arrive until July and beyond. Furthermore, Second Area Army could stockpile only three or four months' worth of supplies by the end of June, which was also far behind schedule.[14]

REINFORCEMENT OF GROUND FORCES IN NoA

The General Staff had been taking steps to reinforce the Southwest Area before the new operations guidance policy was adopted. By the summer of 1943, the 36th Division had been ordered to Western New Guinea, where it would join the 5th and 48th Divisions in XIX Army. Other divisions were ordered to other areas in the Southwest Area as well, such as Malaya and Sumatra[15].

Following the adoption of the new operations guidance policy, the General Staff stepped up this effort by arranging for four more divisions to be sent to NoA. The 46th Division, a recently mobilised division, was sent to NoA from the Home Islands. Two regiments reached Sumbawa Island in the Lesser Sundas by December 1943, but the 145th Regiment, the last of the 46th's three regiments, could not reach NoA because of the lack of shipping. The 145th was sent to Iwo Jima instead where it was destroyed in March 1945.

The General Staff also arranged for the 3rd, 32nd and 35th Divisions to be transferred from China to NoA, but ultimately none of these formations played a meaningful role in subsequent battles. Even though the 3rd

Division had been ordered on 14 October to send an advance element to NoA, the General Staff and China Expeditionary Army changed their minds and retained the rest of 3rd Division in China, in order to employ it in Operation 'Ichi-go', a major offensive which involved 350,000 men, launched in spring 1944, with the major objective of capturing air bases used by the US Army Air Force in China.[16] Instead of the 3rd Division, the General Staff ordered the 14th Division from the Kwangtung Army to redeploy to NoA. The 14th was one of the first divisions to be transferred from the Kwangtung Army to the Pacific, but it was ordered to Saipan instead of NoA and further diverted to the Palau Islands. No division was sent to Second Area Army as a replacement for the 14th.[17]

The movement of 32nd and 35th Divisions to NoA was delayed, but they were en route by April 1944. However, both suffered serious casualties from submarine attacks during their transit south. The 32nd Division lost 2572 men of its 210th Regiment and other units when its convoy underwent a submarine attack off the northwest coast of Luzon on 26 April.[18] The convoys carrying the 32nd and 35th Divisions rendezvoused and sailed together through the Sulu Sea into the Celebes Sea, where on 6 May they were attacked by submarines. Three ships were sunk, and although over 7000 of the approximately 8500 men on board were rescued, the two divisions lost most of the artillery, vehicles, horses and heavy equipment. As a result, when the convoy arrived at Halmahera on 8 May, 32nd Division effectively consisted of only two regiments, while 35th Division had the strength of only four battalions.[19]

Even at this late date, the General Staff still intended to send the remnants of 35th Division to Manokwari and Sorong. However, on 9 May the General Staff reduced the area on New Guinea which 'absolutely had to be held' to Sorong, the western tip of the island. The General Staff cancelled the deployment of the 35th Division to New Guinea, and it remained in Halmahera together with the 32nd Division.[20]

The effort to reinforce ground forces in NoA was thus largely unsuccessful. This was largely because the General Staff gave priority to the force and shipping requirements of the Central Pacific. From October 1943 through to the end of January 1944, the General Staff sent approximately 40 Imperial Japanese Army infantry and artillery battalions to the Central Pacific, primarily the Marshalls and Eastern Carolines (Ponape, the Mortlocks and Kusaie).[21] The Japanese defeat in the Marshalls campaign and the disastrous US carrier air raids on Truk and Saipan in February 1944 exposed the extreme vulnerability of the main defensive line through the Bonins, Marianas and Truk, and the General Staff sent an additional 30 battalions to the Marianas and Western Carolines (Enderby, Woleai, Yap and the Palau Islands) by the end of May 1944.[22] The General Staff had to delay the shipment of men and supplies to NoA in order to secure the shipping capacity required to send these reinforcements to the Central Pacific.

The General Staff's obsession with its China operations also delayed the reinforcement of NoA. The General Staff did not lack a sense of urgency about the Central and South Pacific. Rather, due in part to the historical Army–Navy rivalry, the General Staff was not completely informed about the significance of the Navy's losses since Midway, and generally accepted the Naval General Staff's assurances that it could hold off the Americans in the Pacific for a year, as the new operations guidance policy mandated. The Army General Staff therefore felt it could afford to proceeded with its planning for operations in China.[23]

XVIII ARMY'S HOLDING OPERATIONS IN NEW GUINEA

Eighth Area Army's operations did not markedly change even after the new policy was adopted, especially since in New Guinea, the Area Army and XVIII Army had their hands full simply trying to maintain XVIII Army in the field.[24] On 7 October, General Imamura ordered that all units were to defend in place. By prohibiting any withdrawals, he intended to fight a strategic defence in depth. Imamura was fully aware that this meant that none of his forces would survive, as each was assaulted in turn by the enemy, but he accepted this as unavoidable and believed that this was the only way Eighth Area Army could carry out its holding mission. He also felt he had no other option, since his forces were in too poor a condition to stage a fighting withdrawal. Furthermore, the Army and Navy combined did not have the extra shipping capacity to withdraw the approximately 100,000 men stationed around Rabaul. However, with such a sizeable force Eighth Area Army believed that it could sustain itself in Rabaul for a considerable time, without suffering the fate of 'another Guadalcanal'. It should be noted that the 'no withdrawal' order was applied literally only to the forces around Rabaul and on Bougainville. The Area Army thought that operational withdrawals by XVIII Army in New Guinea were acceptable since it had the option of pulling back into NoA as an intact fighting force.[25]

In fact, from September 1943 through April 1944, XVIII Army withdrew steadily. Through the end of 1943, its primary mission was to secure the area around Sio, thereby enabling the Japanese to control the Vitiaz and Dampier Straits. The battles on the Sattelberg Heights took place during this time.[26] Following the US landings at Cape Merkus (Arawe) on New Britain on 15 December, and at Saidor on 2 January 1944, XVIII Army changed its objective to the securing of the area Madang – Hansa – Wewak. While the 41st Division held Madang, the 51st and 20th Divisions retreated towards Wewak and Hansa, respectively.

XVIII Army had to shift its defensive focus even farther to the west when US forces began their assault on the Admiralties at the end of February with landings on Los Negros Island. The loss of the Admiralties exposed the area between Madang and Wewak to enemy air power and a possible amphibious assault. XVIII Army now focused on holding the area between Wewak and Hollandia.[27]

Communications were physically severed between Eighth Area Army headquarters in Rabaul and XVIII Army, along with IV Air Army, with the loss of the Admiralties. Since Eighth Area Army could no longer exercise effective command over these two Armies, on 14 March 1944 the General Staff transferred XVIII Army and IV Air Army to Second Area Army command, effective March 25. XVIII Army was now ordered to defend IV Air Army's main air bases at Hollandia, as well as the airfields at Wewak and Aitape.[28]

The loss of the Admiralties had larger strategic repercussions as well. Their loss meant that for all practical purposes Rabaul had been isolated.[29] US control of the Admiralties also meant that the Japanese had lost control over the Vitiaz and Dampier Straits, which opened the southern Pacific Ocean to the Americans and raised the possibility of a US advance on the Philippines from the southeast. In addition, the southern flank of the vital Japanese naval base at Truk and the rest of the Carolines were thereafter exposed.[30]

Eighth Area Army's new mission after the isolation of Rabaul was spelled out on 14 March, when the General Staff ordered it to 'hold the area around Rabaul as long as possible, in cooperation with the Imperial Japanese Navy, and using available forces, thereby facilitating operations from the NoA area through the Central Pacific area'.[31]

As XVIII Army continued withdrawing towards Wewak, the Americans leapfrogged it and landed at Hollandia and Aitape on 22 April. The bulk of XVIII Army was then still east of Hansa. Hollandia, which was a major port and air base for XVIII Army, was defended by few combat troops, although there were approximately 14,600 Imperial Japanese Army flight and ground crew and administrative staff, along with some Army personnel.[32] On 26 March, Second Area Army had estimated that the Allies were most likely to assault Hansa next, and possibly the west bank of the Sepik River, in June at the earliest. The actual US assault on Hollandia, therefore, came much earlier and much farther to XVIII Army's rear than was expected.[33]

Second Area Army immediately ordered XVIII Army to expedite its westward march and counterattack at Aitape and Hollandia. On 29 April, Lieutenant General Hatazo Adachi, commander of XVIII Army, ordered his forces to attack the Americans at Aitape. Although XVIII Army numbered approximately 55,000 men, its three divisions were only at 30 to 80 per cent strength, excluding sick and wounded. XVIII Army's actual strength was the equivalent of one-and-a-half divisions. Adachi fully realised that there was little hope for XVIII Army winning the battle. There was no strategic and operational rationale for an attack, but he decided to attack anyway. He strongly felt that XVIII Army could not stand by idly, using its weakened condition as an excuse, when Japanese forces elsewhere were fighting desperately against the enemy under similarly unfavourable conditions. He also believed a 'holding operation' near Wewak would be morally impermissible, even though enough rations had been stockpiled around Wewak by then to support XVIII Army for a considerable time. Adachi also hoped that any attack on Hollandia and Aitape from the east might ease the pressure that US forces there could bring to bear upon the 36th Division and other Second Army forces farther to the west.[34]

The General Staff was concerned that XVIII Army might be totally destroyed and attempted to create an opening for Adachi to call off his attack. It placed XVIII Army under direct General Staff command on 20 June, and released XVIII Army from Second Area Army's mission of 'holding Western New Guinea'. Adachi reaffirmed the operation anyway. The attack finally began on 10 July, led by the 20th Division and backed up by the 41st Division. The attacking force totalled 35,000 men, albeit with many sick and wounded. After suffering 13,000 killed, Adachi terminated the offensive on 4 August. The survivors began a long and painful withdrawal to Wewak. These men, along with the remnants of the 51st Division and other units, totalling approximately 20,000 men, consolidated their defensive positions around Wewak. XVIII Army thereafter focused on attaining self-sufficiency in food, albeit at a minimum level of sustenance.[35] By mid-December, XVIII Army had barely established itself around Wewak when they came under attack by Australian ground forces, which gradually compressed XVIII Army in an eight-month long campaign that ended only with the conclusion of the war.[36]

The unexpected thrust by the US to Hollandia raised concerns within the General Staff that Allied air power could threaten the entire Geelvink Bay – Vogelkop Peninsula area. After the Naval General Staff announced on 28 April that it was no longer confident about successfully defending Biak against any US assault, the Army General Staff on 2 May redefined the area which Second Area Army absolutely had to hold to Geelvink Bay, Manokwari, Sorong and Halmahera, and effectively abandoned Aitape, Hollandia and Sarmi. This decision left the 36th Division, which by then was fighting the latest US assault near Wakde Island and Sarmi, and XVIII Army to fend for themselves as best as they could.[37]

On 9 May, the Army General Staff further reduced the area to be absolutely held to Sorong and Halmahera. During a conference held on 8 May, the Naval General Staff had said it was not confident about sending large transports to Manokwari or Sorong because of the loss of local naval and air superiority. General Hideki Tojo, Chief of the Army General Staff, therefore decided to abandon the plan to send the 35th Division to the Vogelkop Peninsula.

This decision to pull II Army's front in New Guinea back to Sorong meant that the Imperial Japanese Army had effectively withdrawn from New Guinea. Japan's official war history argues that the holding of Sorong, which itself had no strategic value, was an effort by the Army to save face. If the Army held Waigeo, Waisai and Batanta Islands, which all lay just offshore of Sorong, and which were considered to be part of Western New Guinea, then it could claim that it still held Western New Guinea and that the Absolute National Defense Zone was still intact, since Western New Guinea was a section of the Absolute National Defense Zone's perimeter.[38]

The Imperial Japanese Army thus strategically abandoned New Guinea. However, much hard fighting would continue on New Guinea, at Biak, and near Wewak and Sarmi.

XVII ARMY'S HOLDING OPERATIONS ON BOUGAINVILLE

Meanwhile, on Bougainville, XVII Army had been fighting the Americans at Empress Augusta Bay since 1 November 1943. The Japanese immediately counterattacked during November on land, at sea and in a series of air raids. Not only did these efforts fail to dislodge the Americans, but the Combined Fleet's carrier air forces suffered heavy losses, which prevented them from playing any meaningful role in the US campaigns in the Gilberts and Marshalls which followed.

Following the failure of these initial counterattacks, XVII Army immediately planned another counterattack, scheduled for 22 November, this time with four battalions from the 6th Division. Eighth Area Army overruled this plan, not only because of the danger of enemy landings elsewhere on Bougainville, but also because Eighth Area Army felt that the opportunity to counterattack the Americans before they could consolidate their beachhead had passed. Eighth Area Army, therefore, ordered XVII Army only to make preparations for the time being for a renewed attack on the US perimeter at Torokina.[39]

Early in 1944, Eighth Area Army finally agreed to a renewed counteroffensive by XVII Army, and XVII Army issued its orders to the 6th Division on 11 February. The Second Battle of Torokina, as the Japanese called it, finally commenced on 8 March. None of the commanders involved were under any illusion that this attack could push the Americans off Bougainville. XVII Army knew by 6 March that the 6th Division's counterattack would receive no air support, because all of the remaining Imperial Japanese Navy air forces in Rabaul had been transferred during February to Truk, whose air forces had been severely weakened in mid-February by US carrier planes.[40] The rationale and timing of the counterattack was determined by the availability of rations, which were expected to last only until the end of March 1944, even at less than standard issue.[41] By attacking while rations were still available, Eighth Area Army and XVII Army hoped that the Japanese forces could fight to their fullest capabilities. Furthermore, Bougainville's line of communication to Rabaul had been severed by the capture of the Green Islands by the Americans in mid-February. This clearly meant that the supply situation on Bougainville could only worsen.[42]

The attack began on 8 March. After suffering heavy losses in over two weeks of fighting, Lieutenant General Haruyoshi Hyakutake, XVII Army commander, ordered the 6th Division and the other forces involved to cease attacking on 27 March and to prepare to withdraw. Out of 9548 men who had directly taken part in the offensive, over 2700 were killed in action or wounded. Including the casualties suffered by other units of the 6th Division, the Second Battle for Torokina cost the Japanese approximately 5400 dead and 7100 wounded.[43]

For the remainder of 1944, the Japanese on Bougainville were preoccupied mainly with survival. They began to grow sweet potatoes, which eventually became the staple of the Bougainville diet. The combat troops who had survived the Second Battle of Torokina were especially hard hit by the lack of food, as they had to recover from the exhaustion of battle even as they waited for their crops to ripen, which took three months. While some of the units were able to harvest their crops from as early as October, others had to wait until January or February 1945. During this time, exhaustion, malnutrition and disease accounted for far greater numbers of dead than battle casualties. As of 10 December 1944, Eighth Area Army reported that the Japanese on Bougainville numbered 23,053 men, down from approximately 40,000 at the end of March, when the Torokina offensive was called off. Most of the roughly 17,000 deaths came from non-battle related causes. As many as 6341 men were reported as having died between August and December 10. In the case of the 6th Division, deaths peaked in October.

XVII Army also faced major problems with declining morale and discipline during this period. In a desperate effort to improve the morale of his forces, Lieutenant General Masatane Kanda, commander of the 6th Division, promoted the strengthening of religious beliefs. Kanda hoped to go beyond the superficiality of the so-called 'spiritual education' which the men had been subjected to and 'instill something that would truly appeal to each man's soul'. There was a more practical side to this as well. Kanda promoted the use of faith healing as a means of overcoming the dismal lack of medical supplies. He admitted this distressed his doctors, but felt that 'if we said to our patients that "there is nothing we can do, because we have no medicine", the patients' outlook would only become more negative. So, the doctors themselves had to believe that they will heal their patients without fail when coming into contact with them'.[44]

During this time, XVII Army on Bougainville was roughly grouped into three areas. The largest was on the south end of the island, around Erventa, where the 6th Division and XVII Army headquarters were located, along with the 45th Regiment at Kieta. In the centre of the island, mostly on the eastern side near Numa Numa, was the 38th Independent Mixed Brigade, which had been formed in July 1944 from the 17th Division's 53rd and 81st Regiments, and other assorted units. Finally, on the northern end of the island were parts of the 38th Brigade, the 4th South Seas Garrison Force and other naval security units.

The relatively quiet military situation for XVII Army changed with the arrival of the Australians in November 1944. For various reasons (see chapters 1 and 11), the Australians pursued a much more active policy than the Americans had after the Second Battle of Torokina, and intense fighting developed with XVII Army.

Despite its poor condition, XVII Army was still under orders to take aggressive action when possible. On 7 February 1945, 8th Area Army reaffirmed this by ordering XVII Army as follows:

1. In light of the military situation, which has put the Empire's fate at stake, the mission and plan of the Area Army is for each man to kill ten of the enemy, and for the entire Area Army to die in an 'honorable suicide' (*gyokusai*), thereby destroying the enemy's manpower, and also facilitating the execution of operations everywhere.
2. XVII Army's commander shall, in accordance with the guidelines given below, endeavour to establish a state of local self-sufficiency and to increase the Army's combat strength, while concurrently actively conducting operations within logistically supportable limits, thereby contributing to the Empire's overall military operations.
   (1) The common and consistent basic mission of the officers and men of the Area Army shall be for each to kill ten of the enemy, thereby destroying his combat strength.
   (2) Enemy attacks shall be boldly counterattacked and destroyed. XVII Army's mission does not include the securing of territory.
   (3) Men and officers who are capable of combat, other than scouts, messengers, raiding attack forces, and roving forces, shall resolutely abstain from withdrawing, and their battleground shall be their place of death.
   (4) Treatment of battle wounded shall be done by medics advancing to the front. Aiding of wounded comrades is not permitted. Wounded persons retreating from the front shall be court-martialled.

Imamura gave this order because he could not bear to have XVII Army, which was still a substantial force, stand in place and do nothing as the Empire went down in defeat. Imamura desired that XVII Army should fight to the fullest since his men had the opportunity to actually engage the enemy. He also hoped that XVII Army could make a contribution, however small, to Japan's overall military situation and operations elsewhere.[45]

In accordance with the spirit of this order Kanda, who had replaced Hyakutake as XVII Army commander when the latter was incapacitated by a stroke, ordered the 6th Division in March 1945 to attack the Australians advancing from Mosigetta to the Puriata River. By then, XVII Army's food situation had improved somewhat, with one month's worth of half-rations for 2000 men stockpiled as a reserve. The diet was still deficient in fats and proteins, and even units in relatively good condition reported that 25 to 30 per cent of their men were sick. In addition, the standard complement of weapons was not available, although nobody was unarmed. The high humidity meant that many of the weapons that were available were in poor condition, while some munitions had been rendered useless.[46]

This attack was the last major Japanese offensive on Bougainville, and lasted from late March to April 1945. The 6th Division determined that the enemy had suffered substantial casualties. Friendly losses, however, came to nearly a thousand men, including many senior officers. In addition, many automatic weapons had been lost, and Kanda feared the attack had revealed weaknesses in anti-tank weaponry and an inability to penetrate barbed wire defences.[47]

By this time, XVII Army had determined that the last stand on Bougainville would be made around Erventa. XVII Army ordered 6th Division to keep resisting the Australian advance southwards along the Buin Road, because the Japanese positions at Erventa would come within artillery range of the Australians if they were allowed to cross the Mivo River.[48]

In order to expedite the preparation of Erventa's defences, XVII Army coordinated its efforts with local Imperial Japanese Navy forces.[49] XVII Army was evidently dissatisfied, however, with the Navy's cooperation. When Lieutenant-General Yoshimura and Lieutenant-Colonel Matsuo returned from Bougainville to Tokyo in late April and reported to Lieutenant-General Shuichi Miyazaki, chief of the General Staff's Operations Bureau, Miyazaki was 'moved beyond bounds', and recorded Yoshimura's report as follows:[50] '6th Division is at a quarter of its strength. 25,000 men have died since the Second Battle of Torokina in spring of 1944, and current strengths on Bougainville are 20,000 Army, including 9000 in the 6th Division, and 10,000 Navy. Seventy per cent of the shells for the mountain artillery are duds, no howitzer ammunition has been received for two years, and the 6th Division has the strength of a regiment, similar to the situation in the Russo-Japanese War. A message of encouragement from Tokyo is unnecessary.' In addition, the two passed along a message from Hyakutake, who remarked that there was 'no help from Providence, a defensive approach is not good, and all efforts should be made to produce aircraft for an offense. Rabaul is coercing us to commit an honourable suicide. Suicides and deaths from illness should be treated as "killed in action"'. Finally, Miyazaki recorded the following scathing comments on the Navy.

> They have a tendency to overrate things which have no strength.
> The higher commands have no ability to command, and nobody is supervising the execution of actions.
> Preparations are very poor.

There is no sense of responsibility, and no spirit of fighting to the finish.
Forces are scattered, and committed piecemeal.
The Naval Landing Forces are completely useless.

In late April, XVII Army issued guidelines for the final battle. Along with the usual exhortations for each man to kill 10 of the enemy, the guidelines called for the main defensive perimeter to be completed by the end of August. 'Brief and daring' attacks were to be the favoured tactical method. The perimeter was to run along the line Buin–Tsurikoiru–Tsurutai–Tonolei Harbor. Priority was given to the defence of the main roads in this area. The defence would consist of individual strongholds, which would enable a defence in depth. If the situation permitted, the main body of XVII Army would fight the enemy outside the main perimeter. Meanwhile, the 6th Division was ordered to delay the enemy advance as long as possible. Depending on how the situation developed, the main body of the 38th Independent Mixed Brigade was to be redeployed from Numa Numa to Erventa.[51]

In order to assemble the necessary manpower to defend the Erventa perimeter, XVII Army headquarters, quartermaster units, arsenals and field hospitals were reorganised through May as two infantry battalions and eleven infantry companies. Each battalion and company carried on with their previous functions as well. Each company numbered between 50 and 100 men, and not all of these units were fully armed.

In order to enable the 6th Division to concentrate on contesting the southward advance of the Australians, the Erventa garrison was put under direct XVII Army command. In addition, the 45th Regiment at Kieta and other units on the Shortland and Fauro Islands were recalled and placed under XVII Army command.[52]

XVII Army's self-sufficiency in food had improved to the point where the Erventa garrison could supply itself with the meagre amount of 2 kilograms of sweet potatoes per person daily. They also had enough to supply rice and sweet potatoes to the 6th Division, and as the 6th Division continued to fall back it had to rely more and more on the Erventa garrison for its supply of food. As a result, the Erventa garrison had to cut back on its own rations until it was down to 1 kilogram of sweet potatoes per person daily.[53]

XVII Army ordered the preparation of defences along Erventa's perimeter to be completed by the end of August, because it assumed the 6th Division could hold the Taitai area until the end of July. When the 6th Division had to retreat from Taitai earlier than anticipated, XVII Army called for preparations in the key areas of the perimeter to be completed by early July, and the entire perimeter to be generally completed by the end of July.

As they prepared for the defence of Erventa, the Japanese were well aware of their shortcomings. Japanese anti-tank defences had been ineffective, Japanese rifles were deemed to be inferior in jungle combat to the enemy's automatic rifles and the few light machine guns available were cumbersome and hard to transport. Grenades were the most useful weapon, but then were only available in insufficient numbers. In addition, the high humidity had ruined ammunition stocks. For example, thousands of 70mm rounds for the Type 92 Battalion Gun had to be discarded, along with volumes of rifle ammunition, because they had been exposed too long to the pervasive humidity. To rectify this situation, Kanda arranged for Lieutenant Hiroshi Iimura, a company commander with the 6th Field Artillery Regiment on Fauro Island and who was known to have a certain talent with weapons and ammunition, to be recalled and put in charge of fixing these problems. Iimura devised the use of land mines as anti-tank weapons and converted rifles into grenade launchers. He also came up with a method of recycling cloth sacks from field hospitals to shield 70mm shells from the humidity. These efforts resolved many of the XVII Army's problems with weaponry. Kanda tried to award Iimura with a letter of commendation, but under Army regulations such letters could not be awarded if the deserving action took place in rear areas, which was Iimura's case. Kanda appealed to Eighth Area Army for an exception to be made, but the war ended before Eighth Area Army made a decision.[54] The fighting on Bougainville itself ended as well before the Australians reached the Erventa perimeter.

DEFENCE OF THE PHILIPPINES OR SINGAPORE: BORNEO'S ROLES

After the Japanese had occupied Borneo early in 1942 during the 'Southern Operations' which initiated the war, Borneo had been a backwater within Japanese strategy and had 'not been given a second glance, in terms of operational significance, until early summer 1944'.[55] From 1944 through 1945, however, Borneo came to play an increasingly important albeit peripheral role within the overall context of Japanese strategy in the area.

Under Japanese occupation, the Imperial Japanese Army was responsible for the military administration of British Borneo, while the Imperial Japanese Navy occupied Dutch Borneo. On 20 April 1942, the Imperial Japanese Army established the Borneo Defence Force (BDF), consisting mainly of the 4th Independent Mixed Regiment (IMR).[56] On 5 September, the 4th IMR was dissolved and reorganised as the 40th and 41st Independent Garrison Battalions (IGB). Each consisted of a headquarters element and four companies and was put under BDF command on 26 September.[57]

The Japanese garrison on Borneo basically remained unchanged until late summer 1944. From March 1943 to March 1944, Borneo was defended only by one battalion since the 41st IGB was temporarily sent to Thailand. This seemed an acceptable risk, since Borneo's location deep within the entire area occupied by the Japanese made it seemingly safe from a full scale amphibious assault. In fact, the Japanese believed until 1943 that Borneo was safe from even surprise hit-and-run raids by the enemy.[58]

Sometime in December 1943 or early the next year, the Army General Staff concluded that all of Japan's forces in the Southern Area, from NoA to Burma, should be placed under the unified command of SEA, in order to facilitate preparations for a decisive counteroffensive against the Americans.[59] Second Area Army (II and XIX Armies), in charge of NoA, was now placed under SEA command. Seventh Area Army was newly activated and given charge of XVI Army (responsible for Java), XXV Army (Sumatra), XXIX Army (Malaya), and BDF.[60] SEA's mission from spring 1944 was to secure and maintain the stability of the Andamans, Ecobar Islands, Malaya, Sumatra, Java, Borneo, NoA, Burma, Thailand, Indochina and the Philippines, counterattacking and defeating any enemy attacks on those areas. The General Staff also directed SEA to carry out offensive counter air campaigns over India, China, Australia and New Guinea as necessary.[61]

As the Marianas loomed as the next enemy objective, the Army General Staff increasingly felt the need to reinforce the Philippines and NoA. From around May 1944, the strengthening of Borneo's defences also became a more pressing issue, within the wider context of the defence of the Philippines. In mid-May, the BDF Chief of Staff warned that the enemy would likely use the northeast corner of Borneo as a supporting base for an assault of the Philippines. As a result, the 56th Independent Mixed Brigade (IMB) was mobilised in the Home Islands and assigned to BDF on 19 June. The 56th IMB consisted of six infantry battalions, plus artillery, engineers and signals units, for a total of 1783 men of which 997 were infantry. The actual deployment of this brigade took time, however, since its mobilisation was delayed. The first three battalions departed for Borneo only in mid-July.

The construction of Army air force bases on Borneo also became an issue as the General Staff began to prepare for the defence of the Philippines. The lack of manpower to construct the airfields was a problem as it was in NoA, since Army construction battalions were tied down elsewhere, and Borneo's local population was insufficient to permit the conscription of sufficient numbers of native labourers. The construction of airfields was further complicated by the fact that Borneo still lay within Seventh Area Army's jurisdiction. Seventh Area Army's primary mission was the defence of Singapore, and it was still primarily concerned with a threat from the west, whereas BDF was increasingly more concerned with a threat from the east as it attempted to construct air bases as part of SEA's preparations for the defence of the Philippines. Even as plans were made to construct 11 Army airfields on Borneo, these problems remained unsolved.

In July, BDF estimated that enemy forces in New Guinea would probably assault the northwestern tip of New Guinea or the Palau Islands in August, after which they might assault the Philippines. In addition, two divisions might possibly attack Celebes, and an attack on the Sulu Islands and northern Borneo was likely to occur in January 1945 or later. BDF duly revised its plans and decided to make its main defensive effort in northern Borneo. The airfields under construction were to be completed by early 1945, in anticipation of enemy air operations staged from the Celebes Sea area. BDF and Seventh Area Army differed, however, regarding the placement of the 56th IMB. BDF wanted to concentrate the brigade around Sandakan, facing the Sulu Sea, whereas Seventh Area Army wanted to station a substantial portion of the brigade around Jesselton and Brunei on the west coast. Seventh Area Army felt Borneo's west coast might be used as a base to support an attack on Singapore and was concerned that Borneo's geography would hinder any movement of troops from the east coast to the west. BDF ultimately won this argument, and the bulk of 56th IMB was deployed in northeast Borneo.[62]

Around this time, SEA began to consider the transfer of BDF to XIV Army (which later became Fourteenth Area Army) command. This would facilitate BDF's role in the defence of the Philippines, which was XIV Army's principal mission. Furthermore, both the General Staff and SEA believed that by transferring the responsibility for Borneo to XIV Army, Seventh Area Army could focus more on its mission of defending Singapore from an attack from the west.[63] On the other hand, BDF's supply line would continue running through Singapore, since XIV Army had its hands full supporting itself and did not have the excess capability to handle BDF's logistics.[64]

Similar problems arose concerning Borneo's airfields. Borneo was under III Air Army's jurisdiction, which in turn was under Seventh Area Army command. III Air Army's primary mission was the defence of Singapore, Malaya and Sumatra. If Borneo's airfields were to play a role in the defence of the Philippines, however, placing Borneo under IV Air Army's jurisdiction made better operational sense, since IV Air Army was responsible for the air defence of the Philippines.

This issue was resolved in late August, when the line of demarcation between III and IV Air Armies was shifted westward and IV Air Army was assigned operational use of Borneo's airfields. The important naval anchorage at Tawi Tawi was also shifted from XIV Army's area to BDF, which facilitated BDF's preparations for its defence. BDF was transferred from Seventh Area Army to SEA, effective 10 September. At the same time, BDF was allotted the 25th IMR from the Home Islands, along with two machine-gun battalions. BDF was now able to more readily coordinate its defensive preparations with XIV Army, and to better prepare for a possible American-Australian assault on Borneo.

At this time, BDF consisted of 11 battalions (the 40th and 41st IGBs, six battalions in the 56th IMB and three in the 25th IMR). However, as of 10 September, most of these units had yet to arrive in Borneo, since 56th IMB was still en route, and 25th IMR had yet to depart Japan. One battalion of the 56th IMB finally arrived in Tawau on 15 September. The General Staff expedited the movement of 25th IMR by arranging for it to sail from Japan on the battleships *Fuso* and *Yamashiro*.[65] As a result, the 25th IMR completed its deployment to Borneo by late September. However, 56th IMB did not complete its movement to Borneo until mid-November.[66]

On 18 September, BDF was upgraded to XXXVII Army and placed directly under SEA's command. Its IGBs were upgraded to standard infantry battalions, and XXXVII Army commander Lieutenant-General Masataka Yamawaki was promoted to full general.[67]

On 23 October, the General Staff expanded XXXVII Army's area of responsibility to include Southern Borneo, which had been the responsibility of the Imperial Japanese Navy, and assigned the 71st IMB from the Home Islands for its defence.[68] The onset of the battle of the Philippines greatly interfered with the transfer of the 71st to Borneo, however, and only two battalions managed to get as far as Kuching by spring 1945.[69]

After the Absolute National Defense Zone concept had been invalidated by the Japanese defeat in the Marianas campaign, the Imperial Japanese Army and Imperial Japanese Navy adopted a new operations guidance policy on 21 July 1944, which once again sought a decisive campaign. The new operations plans based upon this policy were the 'Sho' Plans, numbers one through four. The 'Sho-1' Plan dealt with an American offensive against the Philippine Islands and was activated in October 1944, when the Americans began their Leyte operation.

The de facto loss of the Philippines meant that SEA's maritime line of communication to the Home Islands was all but severed. On 27 January 1945, the Army General Staff ordered SEA to henceforth 'strictly follow a policy of supplying and fighting for yourself, without counting on any material reinforcements from the Home Islands'. Its mission now was to secure the territory still under its control and to defeat any enemy offensive within that territory, thereby interfering with an enemy drive towards the Home Islands or mainland China.[70]

Any role Borneo could play in the defence of the Philippines diminished with the Japanese setbacks on Leyte and Luzon, and the General Staff and SEA once again began to place more value on Borneo's role in the defence of Singapore. Near the end of 1944, XXXVII Army estimated that the Australians probably intended to assault the northern coastline of Borneo, in particular the area around Brunei, and then secure the west coast in order to establish the eastern flank of a campaign aimed at Singapore.[71] SEA concurred, and ordered XXXVII Army to give priority to defending the west coast. XXXVII Army accordingly ordered three out of the five battalions at Tawau to redeploy to Brunei and also ordered both battalions stationed on Tawi Tawi, and two out of the three at Sandakan, to head for the west coast. The transfers from Tawau and Sandakan began in late January, but involved gruelling marches of 320 to 640 kilometres through mountainous jungle, and were hampered by poor weather and the lack of rations, in addition to the general lack of an east–west road network in Borneo. The first units arrived in Jesselton around the end of February, but only about half of the force which set out managed to reach the west coast before the Australians began their assault of Borneo.[72]

Meanwhile, General Yamawaki had been replaced by Lieutenant-General Masao Baba on 26 December 1944. On 17 May 1945, XXXVII Army reverted to Seventh Area Army command, effective 20 May. SEA felt the US landings in the Sulu Islands in early April, and the Australian landings at Tarakan on 1 May, were the first steps of an offensive aimed at securing advance bases for an assault on Singapore. SEA therefore returned XXXVII Army to Seventh Area Army's command, in order to integrate XXXVII Army more effectively in Singapore's outer line of defence. On 24 May, Seventh Area Army ordered XXXVII Army to strengthen the defences of

Figure 3.1: Suspected Japanese war criminals guarded by troops of New Guinea Infantry Batallion, Rabaul, New Britain, 5 December 1945. (Australian War Memorial 099240)

western Borneo as soon as possible, while securing Borneo's airfields as long as possible and, in the worst case, to prevent the enemy from using Brunei Bay and areas in western Borneo as bases.

In addition to the transfer of various units to the west coast, one battalion each from Tawau and Tarakan was ordered to South Borneo. These redeployments took place in two phases, in early February and early March, and were assisted by the Imperial Japanese Navy. As a result, one battalion each was on station at Balikpapan, Tarakan and Banjarmasin by the time the Australians began landing.[73]

In a final effort to shore up the defences of western Borneo, Seventh Area Army ordered the 396th Independent Infantry Battalion from Banjarmasin to Kuching on 30 May. The battalion could not make a direct overland move to Kuching, but rather had to be ferried to Jakarta first, after which it was shipped to Billiton Island, then to Pontianak. In any event, only half of the battalion had arrived as far as Pontianak by August. In addition, XXXVII Army also ordered half a battalion to proceed from Mili to Kuching, but this force was still en route when the war ended in mid-August.[74]

By this time, the Australians had long since began their offensive against Borneo, starting with landings at Tarakan on 1 May, followed by landings at Labuan on 8 June, Brunei two days later and at Balikpapan on 1 July. The defenders at Tarakan and Balikpapan were gradually pushed back into the mountains. The defenders of Labuan were wiped out, and the forces around Brunei were in the process of redeploying towards the prepared defences near Savon when the war ended. In particular, the Japanese on the western side of Borneo were weakened by their arduous trek across the island, and handicapped further by repeated redeployments after they arrived, which limited their knowledge of the ground on which they ultimately had to fight.[75]

CONCLUSION

The Imperial Japanese Army's strategy and operations with respect to its ground forces during 1944–45 in the areas where the Japanese Army and Australian forces fought were reviewed in this chapter. These areas were New Guinea, Bougainville and Borneo. NoA was also a prominent area in Japan's strategy of September 1943 but never completely fulfilled the role envisaged for it. When viewed from Japan's perspective, these operations had only limited strategic significance on the war but should not be overlooked, considering the sizeable number of men on both sides who fought and suffered and died in them towards the end of the war.

FURTHER READING

Eric Bergerud, *Touched with Fire: The Land War in the South Pacific*, Penguin Books, New York, 1996.

David Dexter, *The New Guinea Offensives*, Australian War Memorial, Canberra, 1961.

Edward J. Drea, *MacArthur's Ultra: Codebreaking and the War against Japan, 1942–1945*, University Press of Kansas, Kansas, 1992.

Bruce Gamble, *Target Rabaul: The Allied Siege of Japan's Most Infamous Stronghold, March 1943-August 1945*, Zenith Press, Minneapolis, 2013.

Ooi Keat Gin, *The Japanese Occupation of Borneo, 1941–1945*, Routledge, New York, 2011.

Karl James, *The Hard Slog: Australians in the Bougainville Campaign, 1944–45*, Cambridge University Press, Melbourne, 2012.

Gavin Long, *The Final Campaigns*, Australian War Memorial, Canberra, 1963.

John Miller, Jr., *United States Army in World War II, The War in the Pacific: Cartwheel: the Reduction of Rabaul*. Center of Military History, United States Army, Washington, DC, 1959.

Henry I. Shaw and Douglas T. Kane, *History of U.S. Marine Corps Operations in World War II, Volume II: Isolation of Rabaul*, United States Marine Corps, Washington, D.C., 1963.

Robert Ross Smith, *United States Army in World War II, The War in the Pacific: The Approach to the Philippines*, Center of Military History, United States Army, Washington, D.C., 1984.

Stephen Taffe, *MacArthur's Jungle War: the 1944 New Guinea Campaign*, University Press of Kansas, Kansas, 1998.

Notes

1   Appendix to IGHQ Army Section Directive No. 1652. Bōeichō Bōei Kenshūsho Senshishitsu (ed.), *Dai-honei Rikugunbu (7) Shōwa 18 nen 12 gatsu made* (Army Section, Imperial General Headquarters, vol. 7: Until December 1943), Tokyo, 1968, p. 287. The terms 'Army General Staff' and 'IGHQ Army Section' are virtually interchangeable, and the former shall be used in this chapter, except when 'IGHQ Army Section' is used in a formal role. For the relationship between the IGHQ Army and Navy Sections and the Army and Naval General Staffs, see Hiroyuki Shindo, 'The Japanese Army's Search for a New South Pacific Strategy, 1943,' in Peter Dean (ed.), *Australia 1943: The Liberation of New Guinea*, Cambridge University Press, 2014, p. 85, fn5.

2   *Dai-honei Rikugunbu (7)*, pp. 185–94. Takushiro Hattori, *Dai-tōa Sensō Zenshi* (Complete History of the Great East Asia War), Hara Shobo, Tokyo, 1965, p. 498.

3   Hattori, *Dai-tōa Sensō Zenshi*, p. 500.

4   *Dai-honei Rikugunbu (7)*, pp. 91–2. Kumao Imoto, *Dai-tōa Sensō Sakusen Nisshi* (Operations Diary of the Great East Asia War) (Tokyo: Fuyo Shobo, 1998), p. 489. Reprint of Kumao Imoto, *Sakusen Nisshi de tsuzuru Dai- tōa Sensō* (The Great East Asia War as written in an Operations Diary), Fuyo Shobo, Tokyo, 1979.

5   *Dai-honei Rikugunbu (7)*, p. 97.

6   Ibid., pp. 456–7.

7   Ibid., pp. 459–60.

8   Ibid., pp. 487–91

9   *Dai-honei Rikugunbu (8)*, p. 235.

10   *Dai-honei Rikugunbu (7)*, pp. 310–5.

11   Hattori, *Dai-tōa Sensō Zenshi*, p. 501.

12   Imoto, *Sakusen Nisshi*, pp. 493–5.

13   Op. cit. *Dai-honei Rikugunbu (8)*, p. 130.

14   Ibid., p. 227.

15   Hattori, *Dai-tōa Sensō Zenshi*, pp. 500–1.

16 *Dai-honei Rikugunbu (8)*, pp. 30, 37–8.
17 Ibid., p. 52. *Dai-honei Rikugunbu (7)*, p. 579.
18 *Dai-honei Rikugunbu (8)*, p. 355.
19 Ibid., pp. 422–3.
20 Ibid., pp. 426–7.
21 Hattori, *Dai-tōa Sensō Zenshi*, pp. 501–2.
22 Imoto, *Sakusen Nisshi*, p. 493.
23 Ibid., pp. 498–500.
24 Shindo, 'Japanese Army's Search', p. 73.
25 *Dai-honei Rikugunbu (7)*, pp. 395–7.
26 Hattori, *Dai-tōa Sensō Zenshi*, p. 514.
27 *Dai-honei Rikugunbu (8)*, p. 212.
28 Ibid., p. 232. Imoto, *Sakusen Nisshi*, pp. 524–5.
29 *Dai-honei Rikugunbu (8)*, pp. 219–20. Hattori, *Dai-tōa Sensō Zenshi*, p. 521.
30 *Dai-honei Rikugunbu (8)*, p. 211.
31 IGHQ Army Section Order 964. *Dai-honei Rikugunbu (8)*, p. 219.
32 Hattori, *Dai-tōa Sensō Zenshi*, p. 545.
33 *Dai-honei Rikugunbu (8)*, p. 242.
34 Imoto, *Sakusen Nisshi*, p. 535. Hattori, *Dai-tōa Sensō Zenshi*, p. 555.
35 Ibid., pp. 558–9.
36 Ibid., p. 1000.
37 *Dai-honei Rikugunbu (8)*, pp. 370–1.
38 Ibid., pp. 426–7.
39 Hattori, *Dai-tōa Sensō Zenshi*, p. 512.
40 *Rikugun Sakusen (4)*, p. 479.
41 Bōeichō Bōei Kenshūsho Senshishitsu (ed.), *Minami Taiheiyō Rikugun Sakusen (4) Finschafen, Tuluvu, Tarokina* (Army Operations in the South Pacific (4) Finschafen, Cape Gloucester, Torokina), Asagumo Shinbunsha, Tokyo, 1972, p. 478.
42 Hattori, *Dai-tōa Sensō Zenshi*, p. 522.
43 *Rikugun Sakusen (4)*, pp. 526–9.
44 Bōeichō Bōei Kenshūsho Senshishitsu (ed.), *Minami Taiheiyō Rikugun Sakusen (5) Aitape, Puriaka, Rabaul* (Army Operations in the South Pacific (5) Aitape, Puriata, Rabaul), Asagumo Shinbunsha, Tokyo, 1975, pp. 227–8.
45 *Rikugun Sakusen (5)*, pp. 240–1. Hattori, *Dai-tōa Sensō Zenshi*, p. 1004.
46 *Rikugun Sakusen (5)*, p. 241.
47 Ibid., pp. 241–2, 254.
48 Ibid., pp. 254–5.
49 Ibid., p. 272.

50   Entry of April 30, 1945. Gunjishi Gakkai (Military History Society of Japan) (ed.) *Dai-honei Rikugunbu Sakusen-buchō Miyazaki Shūichi Chujō Nisshi* (Diary of Lieutenant-General Shuichi Miyazaki, Operations Bureau Chief, IGHQ Army Section) (Kinseisha, 2003), pp. 127–8. General Yoshimura's first name is not given but this was probably Masayoshi Yoshimura, who was promoted to Lieutenant-General on 30 April and who had been attached to XVII Army since July 1944, and who became chief of the Imperial Japanese Army's Ship Training Department on 7 May 1945. There is also no indication how the two returned from Bougainville. This author believes submarines were used for at least part of the trip, but could find no documentation to prove it.

51   *Rikugun Sakusen (5)*, p. 272.

52   Ibid., p. 274.

53   Ibid., pp. 275–6.

54   Ibid., pp. 276–7.

55   Hattori, *Dai-tōa Sensō Zenshi*, p. 788.

56   Bōeichō Bōei Kenshūsho Senshishitsu (ed.), *Nansei-hōmen Rikugun Sakusen: Malay, Ran-in no Bōei* (Southwest Area Army Operations: Defense of Malaya and Netherlands East Indies) (Asagumo Shinbunsha, 1976), pp. 7–8.

57   Ibid., pp. 30, 53.

58   Ibid., p. 99.

59   Hattori, *Dai-tōa Sensō Zenshi*, p. 524,

60   IGHQ Army Section Order No. 977, dated 27 March 1944, Hattori, *Dai-tōa Sensō Zenshi*, p. 530.

61   IGHQ Army Section Order No. 978, dated 27 March 1944, Hattori, *Dai-tōa Sensō Zenshi*, p. 531.

62   *Nansei hōmen*, pp. 236–8.

63   Ibid., p. 281.

64   Ibid., pp. 239–40.

65   Ibid., pp. 279–82.

66   Ibid., p. 302.

67   Ibid., p. 283.

68   Ibid., p. 302.

69   Ibid., p. 354.

70   Hattori, *Dai-tōa Sensō Zenshi*, pp. 789–90.

71   *Nansei hōmen*, p. 355.

72   Ibid., p. 355. Hattori, *Dai-tōa Sensō Zenshi*, p. 792.

73   *Nansei hōmen*, p. 355.

74   Ibid., pp. 396–7.

75   Hattori, *Dai-tōa Sensō Zenshi*, p. 999.

PART | 2

AUSTRALIA AT WAR

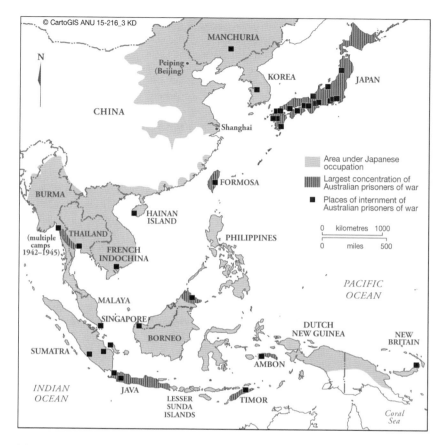

Map 5: Japanese occupation

CHAPTER 4

THE LONG SILENCE: AUSTRALIAN PRISONERS OF THE JAPANESE

Joan Beaumont

In retrospect, there is an air of inevitability about the Allied victory in the Pacific War. Even for those not inclined to economic determinism, there is inexorable logic about the application of the United States' prodigious military power, industrial production and technological expertise. No doubt many Australians living through the war sensed this by early 1944. Not only had the Japanese thrust southwards been halted, but US forces had also launched their island-hopping campaign that would lead ultimately to the doorstep of Japan. However, Tarawa was a long way from Tokyo, and no one could predict in 1944–45 how long the war would last and precisely when it would end.

This was a particular agony for the families of those who had been taken prisoner of war in the Asia-Pacific region. Very little had been heard of these men and women since the Japanese forces overwhelmed Hong Kong, Malaya, Singapore, the Netherlands East Indies and New Britain in late 1941 and early 1942. The Japanese authorities had consistently failed to provide the affected Allied governments (notably Australia, Canada, the Netherlands, the United Kingdom and the United States) with detailed nominal rolls of the units they had captured. Nor would they allow the International Committee of the Red Cross (ICRC) to access camps south of Hong Kong, where the vast majority of Australians were thought to be interned. Many Australian personnel had, in effect, disappeared behind a wall of silence.

However, it was known from the unofficial information that leaked out from Japanese-occupied territories from late 1943 that the Japanese were not observing the 1929 *Geneva Convention Relative to the Treatment of Prisoners of War*. Though not formally a party to this convention, they had promised to abide by its regulations *mutatis mutandi*. Yet the stories leaking out told of forced labour, malnutrition, disease and high death rates in camps south of Hong Kong. Only in north Asia, where the Japanese allowed the ICRC delegates to visit prisoner-of-war camps, was the treatment of prisoners known to be reasonable, at least by the standards of the local countries.

The options available to the Australian government in responding to this emerging disaster were limited, given Japanese obstructionism. Working in collaboration with the Australian Red Cross Society, the ICRC and other Allied governments, Australia pressed the Japanese for fuller information about prisoners of war, and contributed to the relief shipments that the Japanese agreed to receive. But these were few in number, and the distribution of this limited aid was entirely in Japanese hands. Intelligence about prisoners of war, moreover, remained a kind of drip-feed throughout the war, so far as official Japanese sources were concerned. Direct communication with prisoners of war, by radio and mail, provided some additional information, but this source, too, was irregular. Moreover, given that messages to and from prisoners were transmitted through Japanese channels, these were viewed by Australian authorities as an unreliable source and potentially damaging to domestic morale. A final option of making contact with the prisoners by launching military operations to rescue them was considered once, in the case of Sandakan in north Borneo, but, for reasons which remain controversial, this plan was never translated into action.

The Pacific War ended, therefore, with little achieved in terms of relief for, or communication with, Australian prisoners of war. Their liberation in August 1945 confirmed the worst fears of their government and families. The scale of the deaths – some 35 per cent of the Australians captured[1] – and the visible ravages of disease on survivors' bodies meant that the impact of captivity was felt throughout Australian society. Although prisoners had to confront, both within themselves and official-dom, some ambiguity about their having surrendered, progressively they positioned their experience of captivity within the national narrative of war, the Anzac legend. In particular, when the late-20th-century memory 'boom' gave prominence to modes of remembering which privileged victimhood and trauma, prisoners of war assumed a central place in the national memory of the Second World War.

THE AUSTRALIAN EXPERIENCE OF CAPTIVITY

Captivity features so large in Australians' memories of the Second World War because of its scale. In the three months after Pearl Harbor some 22,000 Australians became prisoners of the Japanese: around 15,000 surrendered when Singapore fell in February 1942; 2736 were captured in Java; 1137 on Timor; 1075 on Ambon and 1049 on New Britain.[2] A further 38 Australian Army nurses were taken prisoner; six of them at Rabaul, New Britain; and 32 on Sumatra, after the ship on which they were being evacuated from Singapore was sunk.[3] This disaster eclipsed the number of Australians taken prisoner in North Africa and Europe. Some 8591 were captured in those theatres, most of them in the Greece and Crete campaigns of April–May 1941, but many were also shot down over Germany when serving with Bomber Command.[4] Moreover, whereas 2.4 per cent of Australians captured in Europe and the Mediterranean died, over a third of those held by the Japanese perished. The number of prisoners who died in the war against Japan almost matched those killed in combat in that theatre.[5]

Shocking through these statistics are, the experience of captivity in the Asia-Pacific region was not uniformly one of unremitting violence, malnutrition, starvation and death, as many publications today imply. Certainly, these were the experiences of many prisoners, but conditions varied significantly across the camps in which they were held from 1942 to 1945. Many variables shaped the experience of captivity, including the progress of the war, the geographical location of the camp, the working conditions within it, the particularities of the local Japanese command,[6] the rank a prisoner held in his own military unit,[7] and, though this is difficult to verify empirically, the emotional and psychological resources on which individuals and collectives could draw for resilience. Each of these variables is a topic in itself, well beyond the scope of this chapter, but for the prisoners themselves, and the Allied authorities who were trying to reach them, location was one of the most critical.

Many prisoners had multiple places of internment during the war. Recognising the value of the Allied prisoners as a labour force, the Japanese constantly relocated them to work sites around the region. Hence, many of the Australians captured on Singapore spent only weeks or months at the Selarang Barracks, Changi, in which they were interned initially. (Not until mid-1944 were prisoners housed in Changi Prison, the iconic site later conflated in popular memory with the barracks.)[8]

Figure 4.1: Prisoners of war laying railway track, Thai–Burma Railway, c. 1943. (Australian War Memorial P00406.027)

In May 1942, the first of many labour parties, A Force, left Changi for Burma (now Myanmar). Here it first constructed airfields in coastal towns; then, later in 1942, it began work as part of a multinational force on the Thai–Burma Railway, which the Japanese had decided to build to substitute for the increasingly vulnerable sea routes to Burma.[9] A further 1000 Australians from Java, including survivors from the HMAS *Perth* which had been sunk in the Sunda Strait off the Netherlands East Indies on 28 February 1942, joined the workforce in Burma in late 1942 and early 1943.

Since the Japanese decided to build the railway from both ends simultaneously, several more multinational forces were transported in crowded cattle railway trucks from Changi to Thailand in 1942–43. The first Australians to arrive, in January 1943, were a force of nearly 900 men, Dunlop Force, named after its commanding medical officer, Lieutenant-Colonel Edward (Weary) Dunlop. Captured on Java, these men had been interned on that island throughout 1942, until they were routed to Thailand through Changi. Three larger forces ranging from 3000 to 7000 Australian and British prisoners, D Force, F Force and H Force followed in March to May 1943. They were joined in June and August 1943 by around 200 British medical personnel, K and L Forces, who were sent to try and remedy the catastrophic health situation of the thousands of Asian labourers, or *rōmusha*, who had been induced or conscripted to work on the railway.

Over a similar period, July 1942 to March 1943, B and E Forces were sent to Borneo, where most of them were imprisoned in the north around Sandakan. Senior officers were interned in Kuching on the west coast. Japan was the destination for yet more prisoners. Three main forces (of mixed nationalities) were shipped from Changi: C Force in late November 1942; G Force in late April 1943; and J Force in mid-May 1943. These men were followed in June to July 1944 by Australians shipped from Java and Timor; a further group from Singapore; and in September 1944 by prisoners who had completed the building of the Thai–Burma Railway. Tragically, some of those who had survived this experience, including A Force's commanding officer Brigadier A. Varley, were killed when the ship on which they were travelling was sunk by US submarines.

In addition to these large movements of prisoners were a plethora of smaller ones. Senior officers above the rank of colonel, initially interned at Singapore, were transferred to Formosa (now Taiwan) in August 1942 and then, in October 1944, to Manchuria. The Australians captured on Dutch Timor were moved off the island, in July and September 1942, and ultimately scattered across locations ranging from Manchuria to Java. The force that was overwhelmed at Ambon in February 1942 was split in October that year, with one third of the Australians going to Hainan. Most of the military personnel, nurses and civilians captured on New Britain were moved to Japan, but more than 1000 of them died when the ship in which they were travelling, the *Montevideo Maru* was sunk by the USS *Sturgeon* off the Philippines in July 1942. Such disasters became increasing prevalent in the last 18 months of the war, as US submarines came to dominate the sea lanes to Japan. By one estimate, 19,215 prisoners and civilian workers of various nationalities perished at sea; around 87 per cent of them died in the last 20 months of the war.[10]

Of all the locations in which Australians were interned, those that were geographically remote seemed to have been the most perilous. On the Thai–Burma Railway, for instance, the men of F Force were forced to march 300 kilometres from the railhead at Ban Pong before they reached their primitive camps close to the border with Burma. The single road supplying the workforce broke down during the monsoon of mid-1943 and, with almost no access to outside supplies, 29 per cent of the Australians died of overwork, cholera and other illnesses of malnutrition.[11] Further down the line, working conditions were often as frightful (for example, at the notorious Hellfire Pass, or Konyu Cutting), but the death toll was kept at a lower rate. This was probably because the prisoners could supplement the starvation rations and meagre supplies of medicine provided by the Japanese by trading with the local population and members of the Thai resistance. Likewise, it would seem that on Ambon it was a combination of isolation and the malicious cruelty of the Japanese administration which resulted in the appalling death rate of 77 per cent: 40 per cent of these deaths occurred in May to July 1945 when the island was completely blockaded.[12] The catastrophe at Sandakan, where only six of around 2500 Australian and British prisoners survived many months of malnutrition and brutal forced marches in early 1945 to Ranau, again owed something to isolation. The Japanese were indisputably culpable, in that they must have known that few of their prisoners would survive the gruelling trek, but the shortage of food on Borneo was partly a function of the last year of the war: US bombing had forced the local populations to move inland, leaving their crops unharvested, and the Japanese garrison was cut off from external supplies. It too suffered severe privations and losses as it withdrew into the remote sections of the island to take up new defensive positions in early 1945 as the Allied invasion of Borneo loomed.[13]

In contrast, those camps which were close to human settlements had higher rates of survival. Changi may have become a byword for the horrors of captivity in the post-war years, but it was in fact 'almost a heaven on earth compared to some of the dreadful places to which [prisoners] were taken', as Stan Arneil put it later.[14] The camps in Japan, meanwhile, varied considerably, ranging from the extremes of Naoetsu, 'where sixty Australian prisoner of war died (a large proportion of the 190 Australian prisoners of war killed in Japan), to the less brutal camps of Zentsuji, Kawasaki, Nakama or Kobe, where although conditions were tough prisoners had a far better chance of survival'.[15] But in all instances the prisoners had the opportunity for contact with Japanese civilians.

Even more importantly, in most camps in Japan prisoners had access to the ICRC, whose delegates regularly forwarded reports about the prisoners' conditions to the relevant national governments. The principles of mutual benefit, reciprocity and fear of reprisal inform the 1929 Geneva Convention. As some Allied governments, including Australia, themselves held Japanese prisoners, the Japanese may have mitigated the treatment of prisoners in those camps which they knew were being monitored.

RELIEF FROM OUTSIDE

The vast majority of Australian prisoners, however, saw almost nothing of the ICRC, thanks to the Japanese refusal to give access to camps south of Hong Kong. Nor did most prisoners have much access to external relief in the form of food, medicines and other 'comforts' funded and packaged by national Red Cross societies and anxious families at home. In Europe, these parcels played a significant role in mitigating the hardships of captivity.[16] However, in the Asia-Pacific theatre the Japanese rarely cooperated with Allied efforts to ship relief supplies.

These efforts, which rarely feature in accounts of Allied captivity, began almost immediately after Pearl Harbor, when the American Red Cross sought Japanese government approval to send a ship carrying relief supplies. Similar requests followed from the British Red Cross, which spoke also on behalf of the various Dominion, Indian and colonial Red Cross societies.[17] It seems that the Australian government, with a young, small diplomatic service and a history of reliance on imperial advocacy, accepted that greater diplomatic traction could be gained with the Japanese government through agencies such as the Imperial Prisoners of War Committee in London, on which Australia was represented. Australia also agreed, in view of the chronic shortage of shipping, that it would be more effective to collaborate with other Red Cross societies, pooling Allied relief efforts. Supplies for prisoners in Japan, China, Hong Kong and (eventually) the Philippines would be sourced from the US and Canadian Red Cross societies; those for Singapore and the Netherlands East Indies, from the Australian Red Cross.[18]

In mid-1942, the Japanese agreed to cooperate by allowing Allied relief supplies to be loaded onto a Japanese vessel involved in a diplomatic exchange of Japanese and Allied personnel at Lourenço Marques in Portuguese Mozambique. These supplies, which the Japanese vessel carried on its return journey, were predominantly food and medicines, since reports emerging from Asia already indicated that these commodities, and heavy winter clothing for prisoners in Japan, were in greatest demand. Frustratingly, the Japanese vessel cut short its stay in Lourenço Marques, and considerable quantities of the Allied supplies were left in store. However, some 40,000 shipping tons were eventually offloaded for distribution at Singapore, Hong Kong and finally Yokohama.[19]

This practice of using vessels engaged in diplomatic exchange to carry relief supplies was repeated twice, but as a means of getting aid to prisoners it was unpredictable and limited in capacity.[20] The British and US governments and the ICRC therefore sought alternatives, including offering ships to the Japanese at various times in 1943 and 1944. None of these were accepted.[21] Finally, after prolonged negotiations including the United States, Japanese and Soviet governments, it was agreed that relief supplies could be sent to Vladivostok. The Soviet Union was not then at war with Japan, and the Japanese could collect the supplies and distribute them to the prisoners of war.[22] The supplies were sourced from a central pool, to which the Australian Red Cross contributed £100,000 (as well as paying 40 per cent of the shipping costs).[23]

The relief supplies reached Vladivostok in November 1943, but more than six months passed before the Japanese collected them from the Soviet port of Nakhodka (which was less militarily sensitive than Vladivostok). Only in November 1944 and early 1945 did the Japanese start distributing the supplies to prison camps in Japan, Manchuria, Korea, China and the southern occupied territories (Singapore, Indochina and the Netherlands East Indies).[24] The Allies guaranteed the Japanese vessels carrying relief supplies safe conduct. However, on 1 April 1945 one of the two vessels, the *Awa Maru*, was sunk by a US submarine as it returned from unloading supplies in South East Asia![25] The loss of life was heavy and the Japanese denounced the sinking as the 'most outrageous act of treachery unparalleled in the world history of war'.[26] The US government acknowledged responsibility and court martialled the submarine commander,[27] but refuted the Japanese claim that the sinking was deliberate and wilful. It denied also that there was any 'valid connexion [sic] between this disaster and matter [sic] of treatment to be accorded prisoners of war and civilian internees in Japanese custody'. However, such minimal trust as had been created in the previous relief negotiations seems to have been destroyed. With the war nearing an end, no other relief shipments were made, much to the frustration of the Australian Red Cross, which from April 1945 repeatedly urged the Australian government to hand over a vessel to the Japanese.[28]

With so few relief supplies being shipped to prisoners of war, the Allied governments considered other options, including air drops. Many of the camps in which Australian prisoners were interned were within reach of Allied air forces by 1944. Indeed, camps on Ambon and in Burma were bombed in 1943 with some loss of Australian life.[29] The Thai–Burma Railway also was constantly attacked after its completion in October 1943, and the steel railway bridge at Kanchanaburi, which was in the immediate vicinity of the British prisoner camp, Tamarkan, was severely damaged in late 1944 and early 1945 (in raids which again caused prisoner casualties).[30] However, it seems that relief air drops did not have a priority with the Allied military authorities. One proposal in late 1944 was rejected by South East Asia Command on 'security grounds' and the unlikelihood of the Japanese cooperating.[31]

Another, ultimately more effective, approach adopted by national Red Cross societies from 1943 onwards was to transfer cash (via the ICRC in Geneva) to nominated representatives in Thailand, Japan and Singapore. With this money, local purchases of food and comforts could be made on behalf of prisoners and internees, and cash (or 'pocket money') could be given directly to them to make local purchases themselves.[32] In Bangkok a remarkable circle of relief activity emerged, with a local 'agent' of the ICRC, W. Salzmann, working in collaboration with the Swiss Consul (the Protecting Power),[33] the Thai Red Cross Society and local businessmen who advanced loans when remittances from Geneva were delayed. Large quantities of food and medicines were purchased, of necessity on the black market, and between October 1943 and July 1945, nine relief shipments were handed over to the Japanese for distribution to prisoners and internees. However, Salzmann was denied direct access to the prisoner-of-war camps managed by the Japanese military along the Thai–Burma Railway. It was not until February 1945 that he was permitted to take five cargo boats carrying 43 tons of food, medicines, clothing, cigarettes and other commodities to Ban Pong.[34] As his group made their way along the waterways they saw prisoners of war 'working in shorts or just bathing slips, some with hats, and all with a reddish brown skin', but they could only wave to them. When the goods were handed over to the Japanese at Ban Pong, Salzmann was not allowed any contact with camp doctors or spokesmen.[35]

It is difficult to tell how much of this aid, delivered at such effort, reached Australian prisoners of war, given that the Japanese were always responsible for its distribution. Some of the goods delivered via the Vladivostok shipment were reported as reaching camps in Japan;[36] while further south, in Changi, Red Cross goods were distributed at various times from 1942 to 1944.[37] Dunlop, too, noted in his diary on four occasions in 1944 and 1945 that Red Cross supplies were received at the hospitals of Chungkai and Nakom Patom in Thailand.[38] Dunlop, incidentally, thought they were American supplies, a conclusion that would have agitated some Australian officials, who feared that the system of pooling Allied relief might render Australian aid invisible.[39]

Yet it is unclear what proportion of the total supplies provided by the Allies reached prisoners, and relief shipments seem never to have reached camps on the fringes of Japanese-occupied territory. It would seem also that some Red Cross goods were appropriated by the Japanese or hoarded, only to be released when the war ended.[40] One Australian prisoner in Japan recalled on 15 August 1945, 'All the time we'd been prisoners we'd seen Red Cross parcels on only two occasions and then it was one parcel to five men, but now they made a distribution of one parcel to two men. We knew that something was really cooking'.[41]

COMMUNICATING WITH PRISONERS

The attempts of the Australian government to communicate with prisoners also had only limited success. One of the key problems facing Australian authorities was that the Japanese never provided complete nominal rolls of the men they had captured. Nor, for obvious reasons, did they supply details of the thousands of deaths that were occurring in captivity. Rather, information about prisoners was released in a sporadic fashion that aggravated the anxiety and frustration of those waiting for news at home. By June 1943, about 6600 names of Australians had been provided through Geneva, and a further 1500 names were released officially a few weeks later. This made a total of 8100 names of 23,400 men thought to be missing![42] Other details of prisoners were released from late 1942 by Japanese shortwave radio broadcasts. Mail from prisoners of war, though infrequent and confined to relatively uninformative standard postcards, also added to the pool of intelligence.

For families, any information was welcome, no matter how slight or in what manner it had been gained, but the Australian authorities were sceptical about the value of the shortwave prisoner broadcasts. As they saw it, these were probably a propaganda exercise and 'conducive to a weakening of Australian morale'. Prime Minister John Curtin wrote on 5 December 1942:

> The general tone of the letters would indicate that they are carefully edited to combine the expression of longing for home with grateful appreciation of Japanese treatment, in order to induce a feeling of war weariness among listening relatives and to create among Australians an attitude of mind favourable to giving up fighting.[43]

There was even a suggestion from the Defence Committee in late 1942 that the broadcasts be jammed. The Cabinet sensibly decided against this, but families were warned 'against a too ready acceptance of [the letters from prisoners] as completely authentic'.[44] Then, when the Australian Broadcasting Commission began in 1943 to broadcast replies by families to the letters they had received, the government intervened to stop this practice. For the Prisoners of War Relatives' Association this was 'merely vexatious' and indicative of 'a deplorable lack of interest in POW in official circles'. But Curtin continued to argue that 'while prisoners of war [were] being used as propaganda bait, resumption of the broadcasting of messages would be playing into the hands of the enemy'.[45] A year later the government seems to have repented and in August 1944 introduced an Australian Radio Message Service, through which 300 messages (of no more than 25 words, excluding address) were broadcast each week.[46]

As it happened, this coincided with an offer from the Japanese, unprecedented to this time, to establish through the ICRC a regular telegram service between prisoners and internees and their families.[47] The Japanese motives were unclear, and they required the costs of the transmissions to be borne by the relatives sending the message. Fortunately, the Australian Red Cross, which was deeply frustrated by the ICRC's past lack of progress, was eager to expend some of the £4.36 million it had accumulated through fundraising.[48] It agreed to provide £100,000 to support the scheme: as the Australian Red Cross Society saw it, 'the people have given the money for these services ... if we cannot feed them we can feed their minds'.[49] The scheme, which limited outward communications to one telegram per year, was launched in January 1945 when some 25,788 message cards were issued to next of kin. Within three weeks, 18,339 messages had been lodged for transmission, climbing to 21,296 messages by early April 1945.[50]

By mid-March some 710 replies had been received from prisoners,[51] but neither this scheme, nor the earlier broadcasts and irregular mail, provided the comprehensive and authoritative information about the circumstances of prisoners that families and officials craved. Even in March 1945, the Australian Red Cross Society's list of prisoners, compiled from mail and broadcasts, included 8000 men who had not been confirmed by the Japanese as prisoners.[52] One of the 59 inbound messages received in April 1945 was from a prisoner of whom nothing had been heard previously![53] As the war came to an end, then, there were still thousands of Australians captured in 1942 of whom nothing was known.[54] For those on Hainan, for example, there was 'a lack of all information'.[55]

ATTEMPTS AT RESCUE

Despite this, the Australian government and public knew in a general sense that the conditions many Australians were experiencing in captivity were dire. From a variety of sources it was known by early 1944 that the Japanese were committing atrocities, and that prisoners in Java and Thailand were working on roads and railways without adequate food, clothing and medicine. On 28 January 1944, the British Foreign Secretary Anthony Eden made this knowledge public in a speech to the House of Commons that was widely reported in the Australian press. Additional intelligence about the suffering of prisoners was gained from men rescued when the ships in which they were being transported to Japan were sunk by US submarines in 1944 – sinkings which 'deeply shocked' the Australian public.[56] By April 1945, it was concluded in London that an 'appreciable proportion' of prisoners had died.[57]

Given this knowledge, it might be asked whether the Australian government could have attempted to rescue some of the prisoners of war. A bitter public debate on this issue erupted in late 1947 when the Australian Commander-in-Chief, Field Marshal Thomas Blamey, announced that plans to rescue prisoners of war on Sandakan were aborted when the Allied command failed to make available the necessary aircraft. There is, in fact, no evidence to support Blamey's claim, but the controversy as to whether the rescue operation was feasible has resonated down the decades. The more measured accounts of the subject suggest that it was not. There was not enough reliable intelligence about the precise location of the prisoners in early 1945 to rescue large numbers of them, and, had the rescue operation been launched to coincide with the Allied attacks on Borneo and Tarakan in May to July 1945, it would have been too late (most of the prisoners had died or left Sandakan for Ranau by this time). It is also possible – though this too is contestable – that the Japanese might have massacred the prisoners in response to any rescue operation. Yes, there *were* successful rescues of US prisoners in the Philippines in early 1945, but, in contrast to Sandakan, here the Americans already had troops and facilities nearby and could draw on the support of hundreds of pro-Allied guerrillas.[58]

Some of the arguments against the Sandakan rescue operation apply with equal force to other sites where Australians were being held captive in the last year of the war (the only time when the Allies were in the position to consider any liberation operations). It was not simply that there were other strategic priorities, and that Singapore, Ambon and Java were being bypassed in the Allied drive towards Japan. It was that no one knew with any certainty where many of the prisoners captured in 1942 were located by this stage of the war. Hence, the Australian government's position remained, as the External Affairs Minister Dr H. V. Evatt told the federal parliament in early 1944: 'Nothing less than the complete and final defeat of Japan will bring about the release of these captives'.[59] Only when that defeat was achieved was the Australian government galvanised into action, implementing, with the assistance of the ICRC and the Australian Red Cross Society, a very successful and rapid liberation and repatriation of those prisoners who had survived.

PRISONERS OF THE JAPANESE
IN AUSTRALIAN MEMORY

Given the high death toll suffered by Australian prisoners of the Japanese, it is not surprising that in time they came to hold a central place in the Australian national memory of the Second World War. This recognition, however, was not immediate. On their return to Australia, prisoners of the Japanese attracted considerable publicity and compassion, and popular interest in their stories was fuelled by the publication in the next decade of a stream of memoirs and fictional accounts of captivity. Many of these sold exceptionally well and remained in print for decades. Predictably, these early publications focused not on the impotence of Allied relief efforts but on the brutality of their captors as the root cause of the prisoners' suffering. Beyond that, some of these memoirists chose to position their experience of captivity within the language of the Anzac legend, which since the First World War had become the dominant mode of remembering Australians at war. In some ways this was incongruous, since the archetypal Anzac was supposedly a superlative fighter, not a soldier who had been defeated. But ex–prisoners of war stressed that even in surrender and the passivity of captivity they had manifested the mythic qualities of Anzacs, in particular resourcefulness, laconic humour, the capacity to survive against the odds, and a powerful mateship which enhanced their chances of survival.[60]

Yet, for all these attempts at a positive construction of captivity, prisoners of war found in the immediate post-war period that there was some ambivalence about their having surrendered, which manifested itself particularly in a reluctance on the part of Australian officials to treat their claims for compensation and post-war benefits generously.[61] It was only when the so-called memory boom of the late 20th century began to represent soldiers as victims of trauma that prisoners of war were able to take a central place in the rituals of national commemoration and remembrance.[62] Not only did this turn to the past generate another wave of memoirs from prisoners of war, who, in their later years of life, were motivated to confront, and find meaning, in their traumatic past. In the 1980s prisoners of war were also 'discovered' by popular historians and the academy. Engaging with history 'from below', scholars captured the memories of ageing ex-prisoners through oral histories, which, in turn, fuelled popular and family interest in the prisoner-of-war narrative.

Then, in the 1980s and 1990s, when the Labor governments of Bob Hawke and Paul Keating initiated the significant government investment in commemoration that continues to this day, prisoners of war were enshrined in officially sponsored rituals of commemoration. To name only some of a plethora of activities: an official 'pilgrimage' was taken to Singapore on the 50th anniversary of its fall in 1992; a memorial museum to Australian prisoners of war was constructed above Hellfire Pass in Thailand in 1998; and the year-long official memory fest 'Australia Remembers', which commemorated the 50th anniversary of the end of the Second World War in 1995, adopted an image of the homecoming of a prisoner of war as its leading logo. The depicted prisoner had admittedly been interned in Germany, but in the wider campaign the memory of prisoners of Japan featured prominently. Meanwhile, the prisoner-of-war doctor 'Weary' Dunlop was translated into one of the nation's most iconic figures of war, embodying the softer values of mateship, compassion and sacrifice that the Anzac legend was now coming to enshrine. His image was engraved on a 1995 coin, and his statue was installed in the vicinity of the Shrine of Remembrance, Melbourne, at his home town of Benalla, and, most significantly, outside the Australian War Memorial, Canberra. Here he now stands as a Second World War counterpart of Gallipoli's Simpson and the donkey. Dunlop's statues are, in fact, tributes to all Australian doctors and other medical staff who served Australian prisoners of war in the Asia-Pacific region, but only the most attentive visitor would notice this inscription at the statues' bases.

By 2013 it seemed that the positioning of the prisoner of the Japanese at the heart of the national memory of war was complete. As the minister of defence, Stephen Smith said at the Anzac Day Ceremony at the Commonwealth War Graves Commission Cemetery at Kanchanaburi (where the remains of many Australian prisoners who died in Thailand are buried),

> The Australian sacrifices that we honour today helped forge our national identity, helped forge our natural characteristics and helped set our national values and virtues. A nation egalitarian in spirit and independent by nature. A belief in a 'fair go' for all and in not leaving the weak or vulnerable behind. Optimism about what can be achieved by ingenuity and hard work. And the courage to work together to achieve in the face of adversity. The traditions forged at Gallipoli, and later by the POWs who suffered and sacrificed on the Thai-Burma Railway, have become an indelible part of our history.[63]

'Indelible' is an absolute word, its synonyms being 'permanent', 'ineradicable' and 'ineffaceable'. But although all collective memory is contingent and evolves with the changing values of successive generations, there seems no reason at the time of writing to challenge this judgement about the place of Australian prisoners of war in national memory.

FURTHER READING

Joan Beaumont, 'Hellfire Pass Memorial Museum, Thai–Burma Railway' in Martin Gegner and Bart Ziino (eds), *The Heritage of War*, Routledge, New York, 2012, pp. 19–40.

Joan Beaumont, Lachlan Grant and Aaron Pegram (eds), *Prisoners of War in the Twentieth Century*, Melbourne University Press, Melbourne, 2015.

Department of Veterans' Affairs, *Australian Prisoners of War*, Canberra, 2009.

Sue Ebery, *Weary: The Life of Sir Edward Weary Dunlop*, Viking, Melbourne, 1994.

Cameron Forbes, *Hellfire: The Story of Australia, Japan and the Prisoners of War*, Pan Macmillan, Sydney, 2005.

Gavan McCormack and Hank Nelson, *The Burma–Thailand Railway*, Allen & Unwin, Sydney, 1993.

Lynette Ramsay Silver, *Sandakan: A Conspiracy of Silence*, Sally Milner Publishing, Binda, New South Wales, 2011.

Notes

1 For statistics, see Joan Beaumont, Lachlan Grant and Aaron Pegram (eds), *Beyond Surrender: Australian Prisoners of War in the Twentieth Century*, Melbourne University Press, Melbourne, 2015, p. 276.

2 Australian War Memorial Encyclopedia, Australian Prisoners of War: Second World War Prisoners of the Japanese, Australian War Memorial, Canberra, www.awm.gov.au/encyclopedia/pow/ww2_japanese/?query=prisoners+of+Japanese, retrieved 9 January 2015.

3 Australian War Memorial Encyclopedia, Second World War Nurses, Australian War Memorial, Canberra, www.awm.gov.au/exhibitions/nurses/ww2/?query=nurses+new+britain; Australian War Memorial Encyclopedia, Nurse Survivors of the Vyner Brooke, Australian War Memorial, Canberra, www.awm.gov.au/encyclopedia/nurse_survivors/?query=nurses+prisoners, retrieved 9 January 2015. Twenty-one nurses were massacred when they landed on Banka Island off Sumatra.

4 Australian War Memorial Encyclopedia, Australian Prisoners of War: Second World War Prisoners in Europe, Australian War Memorial,

Canberra, www.awm.gov.au/encyclopedia/pow/ww2/?query=pris-
oners+of+war+europe, retrieved 9 January 2015.

5   The official historian Gavin Long (*The Final Campaigns, vol. VII,
    Australia in the War of 1939–1945*, Australian War Memorial,
    Canberra, 1963, p. 634) cites for deaths in the war against Japan:
    8274 killed and missing in action, 1196 died of wounds and 8031 died
    while prisoners of war.

6   F and H Forces on the Thai–Burma Railway, for example, seem to
    have been at a disadvantage because they were under the control of a
    distant Malay command rather than Japanese command in Thailand
    (A. J. Sweeting, 'Prisoners of the Japanese' in Lionel Wigmore, *The
    Japanese Thrust, vol. IV, Australia in the War of 1939–1945*,
    Australian War Memorial, Canberra, 1957, p. 581).

7   Joan Beaumont, 'Officers and Men: Rank and Survival on the Thai–
    Burma Railway' in Beaumont, Grant and Pegram (eds), *Beyond
    Surrender*, pp. 174–95.

8   Joan Beaumont, 'Contested Transnational Heritage: The Demolition
    of Changi Prison, Singapore', *International Journal of Heritage
    Studies*, vol. 15, no. 4, 2009, pp. 298–302.

9   For an introduction to the railway see Sweeting, 'Prisoners', pp. 541–
    92 (from which most statistics and details of movements used in this
    chapter are drawn).

10 See Lachlan Grant, 'Hellships, Prisoner Transport and Unrestricted
    Submarine Warfare in the Second World War' in Beaumont, Grant
    and Pegram (eds), *Beyond Surrender,* pp. 204–5.

11 Sweeting, 'Prisoners', p. 581.

12 Joan Beaumont, *Gull Force: Survival and Leadership in Captivity*,
    Allen & Unwin, Sydney, 1988, pp. 135, 209.

13 See Michele Cunningham's measured, *Hell on Earth: Sandakan,
    Australia's Greatest War Tragedy*, Hachette, Sydney, 2013,
    pp. 140–1.

14 *One Man's War*, Sydney, Alternative Publishing Cooperative, 1980,
    p. 3.

15 Lachlan Grant, 'Breaking Barriers: The Diversity of Prisoner-of-war
    Camps in Japan and Australian Contacts with Japanese Civilians' in
    Beaumont, Grant and Pegram (eds), *Beyond Surrender*, p. 235.

16 See Peter Monteath, 'Behind the Colditz Myth: Australian
    Experiences of German Captivity in World War II' in Beaumont,
    Grant and Pegram (eds), *Beyond Surrrender*, p. 119.

17 Report on the Directorate of Prisoners of War and Internees at Army
    Headquarters, Melbourne, 1939–1951, pp. 331, 325, A7711,
    National Archives of Australia (NAA).

18 Ibid., p. 327; Melanie Oppenheimer, *The Power of Humanity: 100 Years of Australian Red Cross, 1914–2014*, HarperCollins Australia, 2014, p. 110.

19 Report on the Directorate of POWs, pp. 327, 334.

20 Memo for Secretary Prime Minister's Department (PMD), Canberra, 23 July 1945, A1066 IC45 6/1/2, NAA.

21 The offers of ships were two from the US government (February 1943 and March 1944), one from the British government (May 1944) and one from the ICRC (1944): J. Newman Morris, Chairman Australian Red Cross Society to Prime Minister (PM), 17 April 1945, A1066 IC45 6/1/2, NAA. See also Report on the Directorate of POWs, pp. 329–3.

22 Australia House to Secretary, PMD, 19 June 1944, A1608 G20/1/1 pt 2, NAA.

23 ARCS Report on Conference relating to Prisoners of War and Internees in the Far East (Sydney), 28 November 1944, A989 1943/925/1/23, NAA.

24 Department of External Affairs to High Commissioner's Office, London, 19 February 1945, A1608 G20/1/1 pt 2, NAA.

25 High Commissioner's Office, London to External Affairs, no. 5069, 6 May 1945, A1066 IC45 6/1/2, NAA.

26 Washington Embassy to Foreign Office, tel. no. 3629, 24 May 1945; tel. no 3630, 25 May 1945, A1066 IC45 6/1/2, NAA.

27 Department of State press release, 13 July 1945, A1066 IC45 6/1/2, NAA.

28 Newman Morris to PM, 17 April 1945, Alfred Brown (ARCS) to External Affairs, 10, 11 August 1945, A1066 IC45 6/1/2, NAA.

29 Joan Beaumont, *Gull Force* pp. 102–08; Sweeting, 'Prisoners', p. 554.

30 The Thai–Burma Railway and Hellfire Pass [website], Remembering the Railway: The Bridge on the River Kwai, Department of Veterans' Affairs, Canberra, http://hellfire-pass.commemoration.gov.au/remembering-the-railway/bridge-on-the-river-kwai.php, retrieved 16 February 2015.

31 Report on the Directorate of POWs, p. 330; R. H. Wheeler, Australia House, London, to Secretary, PMD, 3 November 1944, A1608 G20/1/1/ pt 2, NAA.

32 ARCS Report on Conference, 28 November 1944, A989 1943/925/1/23, NAA.

33 A Protecting Power is a state which represents in another state the interests of the citizens of a third state.

34 W. Salzmann, Report on the Activity of the International Red Cross Delegation for Siam during the period 1/5/1943–15/8/1945, 16

February 1946, BG 017 07–141, International Committee of the Red Cross (ICRC) Archives, Geneva.

35   Dr K. Laupper, My First Journey with a Relief-Shipment for POW Camps in Thailand, 18 March 1945, BG 017 07–141, ICRC Archives.

36   Letter, J. M. Fraser to PM, 5 April 1945, MP 742/1 255/15/748, NAA; Rowley Richards, *A Doctor's War*, HarperCollins, Sydney, 2005, p. 257.

37   R.P.W. Havers, *Reassessing the Japanese Prisoner of War Experience: The Changi POW Camp, Singapore, 1942–5*, RoutledgeCurzon, London, 2003, pp. 46, 48, 88, 104, 157.

38   Diary entries, 16 May 1944, 22 May 1944, 15 November 1944, 13 August 1945, E. E. Dunlop, *The War Diaries of Weary Dunlop: Java and the Burma–Thailand Railway 1942–1945*, Nelson, Melbourne, 1986, pp. 351, 355, 366, 380.

39   Report of Standing Conference POW and CI (Far East), ARCS, 22 March 1945, A1066 IC45/48/9; Memo W. Howlett, to Secretary, PMD, 23 July 1945, A 1066 IC45 6/1/2, NAA.

40   Havers, *Reassessing*, p. 162; Richards, *A Doctor's War*, p. 272

41   Bill Haskell cited in Patsy Adam-Smith, *Prisoners of War: From Gallipoli to Korea*, Viking, Ringwood, Vic., 1992, p. 441.

42   Response to High Commissioner's Office, London, no. 23405, 4 June 1943; High Commissioner's Office, London to PMD, no. 5896, 19 June 1943, B3856 172/77/308, NAA.

43   War Cabinet Agendum, 'Japanese Propaganda: Prisoner of War Letters', 5 December 1942, A705 32/6/51 pt 1, NAA.

44   Ibid. For Curtin's public announcement and warning to families see, for example, Hobart *Mercury*, 9 December 1942.

45   Sydney Smith, Honorary Secretary, Australian Prisoners of War Relatives' Association, to Curtin, 31 May 1943; Curtin to Smith, 14 July 1943, A663 031/2/204, NAA.

46   Tel. 141 to High Commission, Delhi, 17 August 1944, A705 32/6/51 pt 1; ARCS Report on Conference 28 November 1944, A989 1943/ 925/1/23, NAA.

47   High Commissioner's Office London, no. 10013, 31 August 1944, B3856 144/2/5, NAA.

48   Oppenheimer, *Power of Humanity*, p. 127.

49   'Rush to Send POW Cables', 17 January 1945; Conference held . . . to discuss proposal for the exchange for exchange of telegrams, 24 November 1944, B3856 144/2/5, NAA.

50   Secretary, External Affairs, Secretary, Department of Army and Director-General, Posts & Telegraphs, 7 April 1945, B3856 144/2/ 5, NAA.

51 Australian Red Cross Society Standing Conference, 22 March 1945, A1066 IC45/48/9, NAA.
52 Cable ARCS Headquarters to London Committee of Australian Red Cross, 26 March 1945, B3856 144/2/5, NAA.
53 Ibid.
54 ARCS Standing Conference, 22 March 1945, A1066 IC45/48/9, NAA.
55 High Commissioner's Office, London to PM, no. 5383, 16 May 1945, A1066 IC45 6/1/2, NAA.
56 ARCS Report on Conference 28 November 1944, A989 1943/925/1/23, NAA.
57 N. Howlett, Australia House, London to Secretary, PMD, A1066 IC45 6/1/2, NAA.
58 I owe these arguments to Michele Cunningham. *Hell on Earth*, pp. 213–51.
59 *Commonwealth of Australia Parliamentary Debates, House of Representatives*, 9 February 1944, p. 16.
60 See Joan Beaumont, 'Prisoners of War in Australian National Memory, in Bob Moore and Barbara Hately-Broad, *Prisoners of War, Prisoners of Peace*, Berg, Oxford, 2005, pp. 185–94.
61 See Christina Twomey, 'Compensating Prisoners of War of Japan in Post-war Australia', in Beaumont, Grant and Pegram (eds), *Beyond Surrender*, pp. 259–66.
62 Christina Twomey, 'Trauma and the Reinvigoration of Anzac: An Argument', *History Australia*, vol. 10, no. 3, 2013, http://journals.publishing.monash.edu/ojs/index.php/ha/article/view/988, retrieved 20 October 2014.
63 Minister for Defence: Address at the Anzac Day Service, Kanchanaburi Thailand, Department of Defence Ministers, Canberra, www.minister.defence.gov.au/2013/04/25/minister-for-defence-address-at-the-anzac-day-service-kanchanaburi-thailand/, retrieved 26 September 2014.

CHAPTER 5

TOTAL WAR ON THE AUSTRALIAN HOME FRONT, 1943–45

Michael Molkentin

At a press conference on 17 February 1942, two days after the British surrender at Singapore, Prime Minister John Curtin announced that Cabinet had ordered 'a complete mobilisation of all Australia's resources, human and material', to meet the Japanese threat. As Curtin explained, the decision put 'every human being in this country, whether he likes it or not ... at the service of the Government to work in the defence of Australia'. Later that day, during a lunch time Liberty Loan drive in Martin Place, Sydney, Curtin spoke of the diversion of the nation's 'money, machinery, buildings [and] plant' to the war effort. 'Nothing you have', declared the Prime Minister, 'shall be withheld if the Government says that that is proper for fighting a maximum war'. From the outset, the press referred to this as 'the Government's plans for total war'.[1]

The legal basis for such an unprecedented extension of economic and social management by the state had been established in September 1939, with the parliament's passing of the *National Security Act*. This provided the governor-general with authority to issue regulations 'for securing the public safety and the defence of the Commonwealth', a power the government wielded with moderation between 1939–41, but used extensively following the Japanese attack on Pearl Harbor.[2] Indeed, between December 1941 and April 1943 the *Manual of National Security Regulations* index doubled in length, providing the Commonwealth with the means to direct people and their property in support of the war effort. By August 1944 the *Manual* comprised two volumes, spanning over 1500 pages. Its rules and regulations were administered by various government departments and covered activities as diverse as trading rabbit skins and storing wheat, to rationing, labour dilution, civil defence and measures to control the spread of venereal disease – but all had the purpose of maximising Australia's war effort.[3] Through regulations issued under the *National Security Act*'s authority the Commonwealth came to control where people worked, what they consumed, the information they received and a myriad of other things that Australians took for granted before the war. 'In effect', as David Lee puts it, 'the whole productive system of the nation was placed under government control and direction and many of the incentives for individuals operating in a market system were suspended'.[4] Never before or since has the Australian government had such control over the everyday movements and activities of white Australians.

The extent of Australia's involvement in the war hinged on the government's capacity to both increase the production of goods essential to the war's prosecution and to divert a finite supply of labour from 'non-essential' industries to those deemed most important to the war effort. From 1942 on this involved the maintenance of Australian forces in the field, the provision of food assistance to Britain, and the feeding and housing of US forces in the region, an obligation formalised when the Commonwealth signed a reciprocal lend-lease agreement with Washington in September 1942.[5] Besides increasing Australia's productivity, Australian policy makers had the difficult task of balancing industry and agriculture's need for labour with that of the armed services, and convincing the Australian public that shortages of consumer goods, degraded working conditions and intrusions on civil liberties were, in fact, necessary. This task became more difficult as the war went on, especially after mid-1943 when the apparent risk of a Japanese invasion of the Australian mainland receded.

Despite the attenuation of a direct Japanese threat, Australia would maintain a total war effort throughout the conflict. Perhaps contrary to popular imagination, which focuses on the dramatic days of 1942, Australia's economic and military contribution culminated in what proved to be the final year of the war. This resulted from the government's commitments to support US strategy in the Southwest Pacific Area (SWPA), to provide logistical support to a British Pacific fleet in late 1944, and to employ Australian forces in several separate campaigns in the Pacific during 1945. Indeed, although the strategic centrality of Australian operations declined in 1944–45, the size and intensity of operations did not.

Underlying Australia's obligations was an expectation that Japan would not surrender and that an invasion of the Japanese Home Islands would extend the war – and Australia's commitment to it – at least until 1946.[6]

This chapter outlines the manner in which Curtin's 'maximum war' transformed the Australian home front between 1943–45. It takes a thematic approach, identifying four areas in which government control redefined the lives and activities of Australian civilians, and dealing with each in turn: manpower controls, the regulation of consumption, censorship and attacks on Australian territory. The chapter concludes with a brief assessment of how the total war effort affected politics in Australia during the latter part of the war.

Manpower

During the war's first two years the Commonwealth applied National Security Regulations to restrict the enlistment of men employed in occupations considered essential to the war effort. Before Pearl Harbor it applied industrial reservation sparingly. The policy affected approximately one in four Australian workers and, as Lenore Layman demonstrates, it had loopholes that these employees in 'reserved' occupations could exploit to join the services.[7]

This changed with the Japanese thrust into the SWPA. In January 1942, the War Cabinet established a Directorate of Manpower to compile a national register of workers and manage labour deployment. The Curtin Government initially maintained the cautious approach of its predecessor, but in October 1942 it was compelled to extend the Manpower Directorate's powers when it became clear that war-related sectors faced acute labour shortages. The Directorate henceforth had authority to compulsorily call-up women into work, to transfer workers between industries without reference to their employers, and prosecute those who failed to comply.

Under these regulatory powers, which remained in place for the rest of the war, the Directorate acquired control of both labour engagement and direction, that being: the employment of workers and their placement in particular occupations. Direct government control over labour appointments commenced in March 1942 and, by August, as the Director General of Manpower explained, 'practically all labour movements were subject to official sanction'.[8] Regulatory statutes restricted both government and private employers from engaging workers directly; they could only advertise positions through a National Service Office. As the war went on, fewer sectors received exemptions to advertise and appoint workers independently. At the same time breaches concerning the engagement of labour by employers became one of the most typical infringements prosecuted under National Security regulations.

Once a worker was engaged, the Directorate had regulatory powers to appoint them to a particular position, hold them there, and move them elsewhere as it considered necessary. The reservation of essential occupations remained an important administrative instrument until mid-1943, but thereafter became superseded by other, more extensive regulatory powers. From March 1942 the Directorate acquired the authority to declare sectors of industry 'protected', thus freezing workers to their jobs and preventing them from leaving or being dismissed, for any reason – enlistment or otherwise. Initially applied to Commonwealth munitions plants, aircraft factories and shipyards (and the private contractors that supported them), protection came to affect parts of the mining, building, transport and public-service sectors. Between September 1942 and July 1944, the number of protected occupations in Australia more than doubled, increasing from 8585 to 19,654.[9] In January 1943 the Directorate of Manpower also acquired the authority to direct workers into particular occupations, including away from where they lived.[10] During the following 18 months nearly 10,000 individuals (a third of them female) received compulsory direction orders – though these only comprised 1 per cent of work placements administered by the Directorate.[11] The threat of being compelled into a job seems to have encouraged civilians to seek work in a war industry of their own choosing. As Niall Brennan, a wartime university graduate recalled, his most pressing concern was to get 'into a good position as quickly as possible', otherwise 'you had to go where you were sent' and remain there for the war's duration.[12]

With the majority of eligible male and female civilians engaged in war work by the middle of 1943, Manpower authorities turned to another potential source of labour: civilian foreign nationals ('aliens' in the bureaucracy's vernacular) and prisoners of war. The former, which included all civilian non-British subjects of 18 years of age and older, were obliged to register under the National Security (Aliens Control) Regulations and, from May 1943, could be drafted to serve in the Civil Aliens Corps. Cabinet approved this measure in an attempt to meet a shortage of manpower and granted the Minister of the Interior authority to conscript any male refugee or enemy alien between the ages of 18–60 into its service and to set the conditions of their employment. In the event, the Civil Aliens Corps call up only yielded 1671 of the 15,601 eligible aliens who registered between June 1942 and February 1945. Manpower authorities granted most exemptions as they were already employed in war industries.[13]

Italian prisoners of war, of which some 18,400 came to Australia during the war, had, in the words of the Director-General of Manpower, 'a significant effect in relieving the acute labour shortage which had developed in rural industries in 1943–44, when expanded food programs were required'.[14] In April 1943 Cabinet approved the private employment of prisoners of war on the land and the following month authorised the 'transfer of up to 10,000 Italian prisoners of war from India for employment in Australia'.[15] By January 1944, 7000 Italian prisoners were engaged in food production in Australia, and, that May, a review of the scheme for Cabinet noted an increase in rural production and minimal public opposition. It urged the program's further extension – though a shortage of shipping and Italy's capitulation in June 1944 would limit the number of Italian prisoners of war that reached Australia.

Aliens were not the only Australians the government monitored. A compulsory national civilian registration program provided the Directorate with the administrative machinery to comprehensively manage the deployment of labour and enforce its regulations. Registration of all civilians over 16 years of age commenced in March 1942 and was extended to 14 year olds a year later when the Directorate realised that some 216,000 civilians who had left school before turning 17 were unemployed – a move that prompted alarming rumours that schoolchildren were next to be 'manpowered'.[16] Registered civilians received an identity card, which they were required to carry at all times and present to obtain new rationing books.

The Manpower Directorate used the threat of prosecution to enforce compliance. Its statutory rules detailed a range of offenses including absenteeism, refusal to comply with direction orders and failure to register, and magistrates had the authority to apply heavy fines and prison sentences of up to six months. From April 1943 manpower officials raided hotels and other places of leisure to catch absent workers and unregistered civilians. As one young female worker recalled, 'they used to get around in a car like police officers and we were very afraid of them … people were really too scared to have time off work without just reason'.[17] Statistics for both New South Wales and Queensland indicate that while non-compliance remained relatively limited, it increased as the war progressed. In Queensland the number of prosecutions grew from 31 in 1943 to 567 in 1944. Authorities in New South Wales had collected £1270 in fines up to the beginning of 1944 and then twice that amount in the following 12 months.[18] Enforcement continued until the end of the war, a Perth café owner, for example, being fined £10 in August 1945 for hiring four employees outside official channels.[19]

In relative terms industrial disputes had a limited impact on the government's drive to maximise Australia's war effort. From the 3 billion days Australians worked during the war 5.8 million were lost to strikes.[20] This figure equates to 0.19 per cent of working days lost and puts the recent claims of conservative commentators that unions engaged in 'sabotage' and 'treasonous behaviour' into some perspective.[21] The incidence of strikes tended to reflect the strategic situation: industrial action declined sharply in 1942 but trended upward as the Japanese threat subsided in 1943–44. The number of industrial disputes 'soared' in the war's final months, although, as the government had improved its machinery for arbitration, the number of working days lost remained lower than at earlier stages of the war.[22]

Australia's wartime gross domestic product peaked, in real terms, in 1943 at 41 per cent above its immediate pre-war figure. Food production, by 1945, had become capable of feeding between 12–13 million people: approaching double Australia's population size.[23] For the most part these considerable economic achievements had not resulted from increased participation in the workforce by previously unemployed Australians: the number of women working in 1944 was, in real terms, only 5 per cent higher than it had been in 1939.[24] Rather, substantial increases in state investment, especially in defence infrastructure, and innovation in production methods – such as the importation of US farming machinery through lend-lease – fuelled the economic growth. Crucial, however, was the Directorate of Manpower's organisation of labour. The cost of maximising the war-related output of Australia's finite labour pool, however, was that the Directorate's activities became the greatest source of disruption and degradation of personal liberties that Australian civilians faced during the second half of the war. For the vast majority of Australian civilians 'the manpower' defined their wartime experiences and had life-changing effects that never became established in the collective memory of the Second World War.[25]

RATIONING

Before 1942, the Australian public faced shortages in a number of consumer goods and experienced some regulation in the supply of products such as tobacco, fuel and newsprint. The second half of the war would see the extension of rationing to address shortages caused by the redeployment of over a third of the nation's primary industry workers to other sectors and the Commonwealth government's commitment to supply both the British nation and US forces in the Pacific with food.

Based on the British coupon-book system and administered by a Rationing Commission established in May 1942, clothing became the first item to be rationed during the Pacific War. It was followed by tea in July, sugar in August, butter in June 1943 and, finally, meat in January 1944. Of all these items, restrictions on the supply of clothing had the most significant impact on the consumption habits of Australians during the second half of the war. Each adult had 112 coupons with which to meet their annual clothing needs, the Rationing Commission setting values for garments in order to cut male consumption by half, female by a third and that of children by a fifth. Restrictions increased in later stages of the war, with household drapery added to the list of rationed textiles in June 1943 and a substantial reduction in woollen garments occurring in the winter of 1945. Nonetheless, according to the memories of civilians, the significant restriction on clothing consumption seems to have forced improvisation and caused mild embarrassment more than real hardship. Florence Paterson, a Sydney department store clerk remembered it as a 'time of make-overs' in which women adapted men's clothes and turned to un-rationed fabrics such as calico. Another woman lamented the shortage of rubber to make corsets, which prompted the slogan 'bulge for Britain'. One young man recalled being told his suit was so shiny that he should be 'run in for shining a light in the blackout'.[26]

The rationing of tea and sugar caused even less hardship. Initially set at 2 ounces (57 grams) per adult every five weeks, the Commission more than doubled the tea allowance in October 1942 when it became apparent that supplies from Ceylon were not as badly affected by the war as forecast. Indeed, for much of the war Australia had an 'embarrassingly abundant' surplus of tea – though restrictions remained in place given predictions of a post-war shortage.[27] Likewise, Australian sugar production did not decline as predicted. Though less than its pre-war average, the Australian ration – 1 pound (453 grams) a week per adult – was above that consumed in most other Allied nations and was supplemented by generous allowances during 1944–45. Twice, in 1944, for example, the Rationing Commission permitted an additional 6 pounds to 'persons who wish to make jams and preserves at home'.[28] Altogether the Australian population consumed 8 per cent less of both tea and sugar in 1945 than they had immediately before the war.[29]

More significant reductions in consumption occurred as a result of meat and butter rationing. The shortage of rural labour directly affected the availability of these products, as did substantial demands for both products from British and US authorities. The rationing of butter to 8 ounces (227 grams) per adult each week in June 1943, and the reduction of this by a quarter a year later, succeeded in curtailing consumption in Australia from 96,000 tons in 1942–43 to 72,000 in 1944–45 – though even then Australia never succeeded in meeting the British Ministry of Food's requirements.[30] The meat allowance likewise diminished as the war progressed, a final 9 per cent cut to civilian buying power occurring in February 1945. Altogether, and despite difficulties regulating such products, by 1945 the rationing of meat and butter curtailed average Australian consumption of both these goods by 25 per cent of pre-war averages. Nevertheless Australian civilians continued to consume almost twice as much meat and butter as their US counterparts and more of both than Canadian and British residents.[31]

Besides the handful of officially rationed products, the 1943–45 period was also characterised by periodic shortages in various types of other consumer goods. Those wanting to write letters often found stationary in short supply; school students had few books. Other civilians recalled a want of elastic, clothes pegs, firewood, picture wire and beer at various stages of the war. While the shortage of these items caused inconvenience, a dearth of housing had more serious implications for the standard of living in wartime Australia. A legacy of the Depression-era slump in housing investment, Australia entered the Second World War short of 120,000 dwellings – a figure that had tripled by 1945, the result of requisitioning by the services, the concentration of workers in certain areas and the diversion of builders, building materials and capital to the war effort.[32] The national accommodation deficit forced civilians to live in cramped conditions and sub-standard dwellings – an ordeal that exacerbated the experience of degraded conditions at work. It also undermined morale, indicating that some parts of the community were making greater sacrifices than others for the war effort. In 1945 a Great War veteran from Newcastle wrote in disgust of spacious homes in his neighbourhood occupied by childless couples or sub-let at 'exorbitant black market' rates. His wife and five children shared 'two rooms and [a] kitchen, deplorably ventilated, and dark even in daytime'. When his three serving sons came home on leave they had to stay with friends. 'Our case is typical of very many', he claimed, 'far too many others'.[33]

Besides housing though, rationing and shortages changed people's habits of consumption but did not, generally speaking, cause privation. 'Really and truly, we didn't go without', explained Lorna Fitzgerald, a Melbourne woman, then in her mid-twenties.

> We weren't starving of food or we weren't threadbare or anything like that. Everyone could get by on what we had but you weren't allowed to be extravagant . . . it wasn't rationing like in London . . . You always had butter . . . [and] . . . beef every week and that sort of thing . . . [It was] restricted, but you were able to buy it.[34]

Indeed, in 1945 the Commonwealth Nutrition Committee concluded that Australians had eaten well during the war and in most respects fared better, both in terms of quantity and variety, than civilians in Britain.[35]

Rationing and shortages nevertheless presented a source of discomfort, one that became more difficult for civilians to reconcile as the war moved further from Australia's shores. As with strikes and prosecutions for man-power offenses, offences connected with black market trading increased in number as the war progressed, providing another indication of war weari-ness and the government's difficulty in justifying the continuation of a total war effort once the direct threat receded. Indeed, wartime prosecu-tions for rationing offences peaked in 1945 with 55 people imprisoned and 560 fined.[36] The number of fines continued to increase after the war; tea and butter remained rationed until 1950.

CENSORSHIP

Responsibility for press censorship in Australia, along with the production and dissemination of official, war-related information, lay with the Department of Information, a ministry established by the Menzies Government in September 1939. Its specific functions, as well as the manner in which it censored the press, changed as the war progressed. Broadly speak-ing, however, its focus during 1940–41 was on the publicity of Australian involvement in overseas operations, an emphasis that shifted to guarding home front morale and operational security in 1942–43, before returning to cultivating Australia's overseas image during the war's final two years.

The New South Wales censor's treatment of a radio play in 1943, based on the Australian guerrilla operations in Timor, provides a snapshot of these various censorship objectives at work, as they stood in the middle of the war. The censor instructed the authors to keep their 'fiction within limits of military security'; that is, not provide operational details beyond what had previously been published in the reports of war correspondents. The censor's internal correspondence describes these details as 'service concerns'; they typically covered tactical matters (such as Sparrow Force's patrolling techniques), force structure and disposition, and details regarding military technology. The censor was also concerned with how the radio play's fictional representation might undermine the public's faith in official reports: it excised the imagined sinking of an aircraft carrier that might encourage rumours and 'weaken public confidence in GHQ communiques'. Finally, the censor sought to protect Australia's relationship with her allies. To this end it requested an apparently traitorous character 'Van Reisling' be renamed to 'Schultze' so as not to offend Netherlands East Indies authorities.[37]

During 1942 Australia's journalists largely complied. The New South Wales censor applied 'severe censorship treatment' to only four in 100 outgoing messages from the press, while his counterpart in Melbourne prohibited 1.39 per cent and significantly edited 2.45 per cent; just over 82 per cent passed with amendment. During 1943, however, censorship provoked protests from the nation's predominant newspaper proprietors, including Keith Murdoch and Warwick Fairfax, who represented their industry on a Press Censorship Advisory Committee, chaired by the prime minister. In March 1943, Murdoch and his counterparts complained about the suppression of criticism of the high command in the press and claimed that General Headquarters' communiques were too brief, 'lacking in colour' and that their accuracy was dubious. Curtin sided with his censors, considering criticism of command decisions bad for morale and trusting the judgement of MacArthur and his staff when it came to official communiques.[38]

Tensions between the government and the press remained in check throughout 1943 but re-emerged after Labor's September 1943 election victory, when Curtin appointed Arthur Calwell as Minister for Information and Chairman of the Press Censorship Advisory Committee. The newly appointed cabinet's least experienced minister, Calwell had previously been a vocal critic of the Department of Information and had a bad relationship with Murdoch, whom he saw as an enemy of the working class and representative of the anti-labour press. Tensions increased in January 1944 when Calwell issued a vitriolic response to the Australian Newspaper Proprietors Association's criticism of censorship, in which he accused the anti-labour press of putting profits and political objectives ahead of national security.[39] Matters came to a head on 15–16 April 1944 when, during the press debate over the government's plans to release service personnel to work on the home front, Consolidated Press's Sydney newspapers published with blank spaces, implying where the censor had excised text. When rival Sydney newspapers joined the protest on Monday 17 April the censor ordered Commonwealth Peace Officers to shut down distribution. A temporary High Court injunction obtained by the newspapers that afternoon permitted publication to resume while the matter went before the court. The case concluded in May with out-of-court negotiation when it became clear to both sides that the government's censorship powers had strong legal precedent.

Traditionally regarded as a victory for press, John Hilvert describes the revised censorship rules that the Department of Information issued as a result of the settlement as 'more symbolic than substantive'. They clarified the legal process of press censorship but did not, in effect, reduce the censor's powers. In any case, the data on censorship suppression orders indicates that as the Allies' strategic situation improved in the Pacific the censors had less cause to exercise their authority. After peaking in 1942 at an estimated national average of 56 censorship instructions per month, they declined to 35 in 1943, 17 in 1944 and 5.5 in 1945 (newspaper censorship ceased on 31 August 1945, with radio and cable following a fortnight later).[40]

Even so, Department of Information expenditure doubled between 1942 and 1945, a reflection of the fact that its focus shifted from ensuring operational security and protecting home front morale to cultivating a favourable impression of Australia overseas.[41] In part this involved ensuring publicity of Australia's efforts in the campaigns against Japan, but it also had the goal of promoting Australia to potential post-war investors, trading partners, migrants and tourists. During 1944–45 the Department established Australian News and Information Bureaus in New York and London, appointed press attachés to Canada, France, India and Brazil, and established a publicity unit in New Guinea. Through these overseas agents the Department of Information distributed over a million copies of pamphlets on Australia's war effort, conducted lecture tours, distributed educational films and fed local news agencies with Australian content. When questioned in parliament, in March 1944, about overseas publicity of Australia's contribution to the Allied cause, Calwell could provide figures to demonstrate that the London Bureau had secured Australia several times more column space in British newspapers than the other dominions, while its New York counterpart had established an Australian presence on US radio, and in newspapers and cinemas.[42]

ATTACKS ON AUSTRALIA

After breaking off their bombing campaign against mainland Australian targets in November 1942, Imperial Japanese Navy squadrons based in the Netherlands East Indies resumed sorties over northern Australia in January 1943. These raids would continue until mid-November 1943, though they would be of a more sporadic nature than in 1942 and mainly concentrated against military targets in the vicinity of Darwin.

Whereas during 1942 the US Army Air Force shouldered the burden of northern Australia's aerial defences, the 1943 campaign was fought by No. 1 Fighter Wing, a formation of three Spitfire squadrons provided by the British government at the Commonwealth's request. Nos 452 and 457 Squadrons were RAAF 'Article XV' units formed in accordance with terms of the Empire Air Training Scheme. The other fighter squadron, No. 54, was an RAF unit seconded to the command of the RAAF's North Western Area. The Japanese bombing and reconnaissance sorties, which were intended to suppress Allied air activity over the Japanese Empire's southwestern flank, failed in their objective. Allied aircraft based in northern Australia remained active over the islands to Australia's northwest throughout 1943. The Japanese air campaign could not even be said to have tied the Spitfire wing to Darwin; the American Fifth Air Force's leadership did not want the Spitfires in New Guinea on account of their limited range capability.[43] Still, it was not the loss of 28 Japanese aircraft on sorties over northern Australia during 1943 that forced Japanese authorities to abandon the campaign.[44] Rather, far more substantial aviation losses over the Solomons and Rabaul, and Allied advances in the SWPA during 1943 compelled a redistribution of air assets.

Meanwhile, until June 1943, shipping continued to come under attack by Japanese submarines in Australian waters. For a year up to that point, at least a dozen different Japanese submarines operated off the coast, sinking 19 vessels and attacking 15 others. Australian naval authorities managed to mitigate losses by instituting a convoy system along Australia's east coast and extending it to New Guinea. To support the Allied offensives there in 1943, 4155 ships were concentrated into 748 convoys, and a larger number of RAAF units remained in Australia on coastal patrol duties than went north to fight in New Guinea. The convoy system ended in March 1944 when it became evident that the Imperial Japanese Navy had withdrawn its submarines to fight a defensive campaign in the Pacific. During the summer of 1944–45, the German admiralty assigned four U-Boats to Australasian waters to keep Allied anti-submarine resources out of the Atlantic. Three of these raiders sank before scoring any successes and one, *U-862*, sank two US merchant vessels in Australian waters – one off Bermagui in New South Wales in December 1944 and another off Western Australia in February 1945.

Along with measures to protect shipping, air raid precautions (ARP) remained in place in various parts of Australia well into 1944. They were only gradually relaxed, as public concern about road safety and 'immoral' activities on blacked-out streets supplanted fear of Japanese bombs. Adelaide's residents were still participating in elaborate air raid exercises in July 1943, but by November the local ARP wardens were devoting most of their time to making toys for the Red Cross. In March 1944, Adelaide councillors petitioned the state's premier to have the city's dilapidated public trenches filled in on account of 'at least four serious accidents' and the 'disgusting' behaviour that took place in them.[45] With the federal Department of Home Security's sanction, the South Australian government closed public shelters and put its 20,000 ARP volunteers on reserve in September 1944. Perth's Civil Defence Organisation went into abeyance in November, a year after the last bombs had fallen in the Northern Territory, and Victoria followed in December 1944.

There is a sense in the government's gradual repeal of ARP measures of its apprehension that the population would be less willing to accept the exigencies of total war if they did not feel directly threatened by the enemy. Indeed, in April 1944 when the Defence Committee recommended a relaxation of civil defence measures in southern Australia given the improved 'strategical situation', the War Cabinet moved cautiously, reasoning that 'any wholesale demolition of protective measures would affect the public morale and not be in the interests of the war effort . . . '.[46] The War Cabinet agreed, in June, to permit a circumspect reduction in civil defence infrastructure where it impeded war work or presented a public danger – but it deferred further attenuation of civil defence measures for six months.[47] It was January 1945 before federal authorities sanctioned a general removal of air raid shelters and protective works Australia-wide.[48] As it had earlier, even at this late stage of the war the government's provision remained subject to the requirements of the total war effort: civil defence works could only be demolished if the relevant government authorities released the manpower and material to do so. Manpower, an overarching and absolutely fundamental aspect of Australia's war effort, thus also influenced the timeline on which ARP receded from the day-to-day lives of Australians.

THE POLITICAL RAMIFICATIONS OF TOTAL WAR

The extension of the federal government's powers to mobilise the nation's people and resources behind the war effort required a concomitant expansion of the bureaucracy, both in size and the role it played in policy initiation. Regulation, the gearbox of the total war machine, permeated Australian society between 1942–45. Its administration saw the number of federal departments grow from 12 in 1938 to 25 in 1945, with a commensurate doubling of the size of the public service. Most of this growth comprised temporary appointments (largely women and boys) out of fairness to those in the armed services, though the newly enlarged federal bureaucracy would survive into the post-war era. The complexity of the style of regulatory government that total warfare produced in Australia saw federal ministers delegate authority to senior public servants to an unprecedented extent in a way that gave them a new and unfamiliar presence in the press and public consciousness. 'The anonymity that had formerly cloaked the public servant', observed Gavin Long, 'largely disappeared.'[49] The delegation of ministerial responsibilities onto the bureaucracy also increased the involvement of senior public servants in policy formulation, where before the war their role had typically been confined to managerial and administrative work. This, in turn, along with the increased size and complexity of departmental administration, required a new kind of Australian public servant – one far more likely than before the war to have a university education.[50]

That the mass mobilisation and economic management of the 1942–44 period suited the Labor Party's political philosophies and gave federal Labor a new, if temporary, legitimacy is evident in the results of the 1943 election campaign.[51] The government's campaign focused on its war record and criticised the United Australia Party's handling of the war effort while in power early in the war. The United Australia Party meanwhile attempted to present the government's wartime controls as too heavy handed and accused it of using 'the war emergency to introduce Labour's socialistic policy, quite irrespective of adverse effects upon the war effort'.[52] The government's victory, which increased its hold on the House of Representatives from 36 to 49 seats and secured a majority in the Senate for the first time since 1917, illustrates how, at the time, a majority of Australians considered what the United Australia Party had disparaged as 'regulation mania', necessary.[53]

The limits of Labor's newfound legitimacy and, indeed, the extent to which Australians were willing to endure government regulation are apparent in the results of the 1944 referendum. After unsuccessfully attempting to convince the states to relinquish a set of powers in 1943, the federal government held a referendum, seeking a mandate to transfer 14 powers from state to federal control for five years following the war – including among other things, laws regarding companies, prices, employment, health and Indigenous Australians. The campaign played out more or less on political lines. The affirmative campaign, supported most vocally by Labor and Communist Party elements, emphasised the threat of unemployment and housing shortages after the war and expressed concerns over how ex-servicemen would fare. The Country Party and United Australia Party opposed it, presenting the bill as an attempt by Labor to 'destroy individual enterprise and freedom of choice, and to perpetuate after the war the present bureaucratic control and regulation of the lives and actions of the people'.[54] This spectre of continued rationing and industrial conscription resonated with Australians, the majority of whom voted 'no' at the polls on 19 August 1944. Only two states (South Australia and Western Australia) returned a majority in the affirmative. Paul Hasluck considered the result symptomatic of the public's weariness of regulation: 'With the outcome of the war no longer in doubt the urgency which the government claimed was less credible'.[55]

At the same time, in the 1944 referendum we can detect the genesis of the post-war struggle between conservative and Labor conceptions of economic management and social policy. Two months after the vote, a Non-Labour Unity conference of 13 political organisations associated with the United Australia Party resulted in the establishment of a federal Liberal Party, under the leadership of Robert Menzies. In announcing its initial program of policies, Menzies presented them as an alternative to what he saw as Labor's socialist agenda for post-war reconstruction. The movement resonated with the 'middle class backlash', as Michael McKernan describes it, that emerged in 1944 to the government's wartime controls and, in particular, its legislative attempts, following the referendum, to increase federal authority in matters of post-war economic and social policy.[56] By November 1946 the Liberal Party comprised over 1000 branches nationally, with 124,000 members. Although the Labor Party comfortably retained government at that year's federal election the Liberal/Country Party coalition secured a swing of 4.1 per cent against it and increased its share of the vote by 12.6 per cent more than the United Australia Party had achieved in 1943.

Figure 5.1: Crowds of civilians gather in Sydney to celebrate VP Day, 15 August 1945. (Australian War Memorial P02018.409)

CONCLUSION

By 1945, the Australian public's willingness to submit to the requirements of total war had worn thin. With the threat of invasion and air raids in the past, and a perception that Australian forces were engaged in 'mopping up' operations of no strategic significance, the justification that had made wartime controls seem necessary – or at least bearable – in 1942–43 no longer existed. As a Wilcannia newspaper editor observed in January 1945, there was a need for a suppression of liberties in wartime but things had reached 'a disgraceful state of affairs' in which common sense had been supplanted 'by a ton of red tape'.[57] His perception reflected the reality that regulation had persisted and, in a number of respects, increased as the battlefront receded from Australia's shores. Less apparent to him, however, was that as the Japanese threat waned the Australian government's commitment to furnish its Allies with food and infrastructure expanded, as did the extent to which Australian forces were engaged in operations in the SWPA that were large, complex and geographically dispersed.

On 16 August 1945, the *Sydney Morning Herald* reported that after the Victory in the Pacific (VP) Day celebrations the streets of the city were left littered with 'man-power forms, permit forms, application forms for this and application forms for that, priority forms, and forms to ensure supplies of other forms ... Feet fell on them happily'.[58] For Australians the end of war celebrations marked not only victory over Japan but, as an Adelaide newspaper editor put it, also their release from the 'painstaking regimentation of all our affairs' and the 'invasion of our fundamental liberties'. He had titled his editorial 'Strangling the Country by Red Tape'.[59]

FURTHER READING

Joan Beaumont (ed.), *Australia's War 1939–45*, Allen & Unwin, Sydney, 1996.

S.J. Butlin and C.B. Schedvin, *War Economy 1942–45*, Australian War Memorial, Canberra, 1977.

Kate Darian-Smith, *On the Home Front: Melbourne in Wartime, 1939–1945*, Melbourne University Press, Melbourne, 1990.

Jenny Gregory, *On the Homefront: Western Australia and World War II*, University of Western Australia Press, Nedlands, 1996.

Paul Hasluck, *The Government and the People, 1942–45*, Australian War Memorial, Canberra, 1970.

John Hilvert, *Blue Pencil Warriors: Censorship and Propaganda in World War II*, University of Queensland Press, St Lucia, 1984.

Wallace C. Wurth, *Control of Manpower in Australia: A General Review of the Administration of the Manpower Directorate, February 1942 – September 1944*, Wallace C. Wurth, Sydney, 1944.

Notes

1   'Total Mobilisation Ordered', *Sydney Morning Herald*, 18 February 1942, p. 9.

2   'An Act to make provision for the Safety and Defence of the Commonwealth and its Territories during the present state of War, No. 15 of 1939': Australian Government ComLaw: National Security Act 1939, www.comlaw.gov.au/Details/C1939A00015, retrieved 9 October 2014.

3   'Manual of National Security Regulations (Fifth Edition) as in force on 1st August, 1944, Volume 2 Regulations 'R' to 'Z' – Orders rules and index', NAA AA1966/5 404.

4   David Lee, 'Politics and Government' in Joan Beaumont (ed.), *Australia's War 1939–45*, Allen & Unwin, Sydney, 1996, pp. 82–106.

5   Paul Hasluck, *The Government and the People: 1942–45*, Australian War Memorial, Canberra, 1970, pp. 239–40.

6   Karl James, *The Hard Slog: Australians in the Bougainville Campaign, 1944–45*, Cambridge University Press, Melbourne, 2012, pp. 9–28.

7   Lenore Layman, 'I Was Manpowered: The Personal Impact of Labour reservation in World War II', in Bobbie Oliver and Sue Summers (eds), *Lest We Forget? Marginalised Aspects of Australia at War and Peace*, Black Swan Press, Perth, 2014, pp. 58–63.

8   Wallace C. Wurth, *Control of Manpower in Australia: A General Review of the Administration of the Manpower Directorate, February 1942 – September 1944*, Government Publishing, Sydney, 1944, p. 86.

9   Wurth, *Control of Manpower in Australia*, pp. 70–85.

10   Statutory Rules 1943 No. 23- Amendments of the National Security (Man Power) Regulations, 20 January 1943, www.comlaw.gov.au/Details/C1943L00023, retrieved 15 July 2015.

11   Wurth, *Control of Manpower in Australia*, pp. 97–111.

12   Joanna Penglase and David Horner, *When the War Came to Australia: Memories of the Second World War*, Allen & Unwin, Sydney, 1992, p. 140.

13   Paul Hasluck, *The Government and the People 1939–1941*, Australian War Memorial, Canberra, 1952, pp. 596–97.

14   Wurth, *Control of Manpower in Australia*, p. 212.

15   War Cabinet meeting minutes, 14 May 1943, NAA A5954 809/1.

16   Wurth, *Control of Manpower in Australia*, pp. 125–27.

17   Penglase and Horner, *When the War Came to Australia*, pp. 139–40.

18   'Manpower Fines Total £209', *The Courier-Mail* (Brisbane), 1 January 1944, p. 3; '567 Fined Here on Manpower', *The Courier-Mail* (Brisbane), 12 December 1944, p. 2.

19   'Café Proprietor Fined £10', *The Daily News* (Perth), 14 August 1945, p. 7.

20   Paul Hasluck, *The Government and the People 1939–1941*, p. 603.

21   See, for example, Hal Colebatch, *Australia's Secret War: How Unionists Sabotaged Our Troops in World War II*, Quadrant Books, Sydney, 2013; Miranda Divine, 'Unions Exposed as War Saboteurs', *Daily Telegraph* (Sydney), 2 November 2013.

22   Hasluck, *The Government and the People 1939–1941*, pp. 603–7.

23   Michael Bosworth, 'Eating for the Nation: Food and Nutrition on the Homefront', in Jenny Gregory, *On the Homefront: Western Australia and World War II*, University of Western Australia Press, Nedlands, 1996, 226–38, p. 234.

24   Kate Darian-Smith, 'War and Australian society', in Joan Beaumont (ed.), *Australia's War 1939–45*, Allen & Unwin, Sydney, 1996, 54–81, p. 63.
25   Layman, 'I Was Manpowered', pp. 74–7.
26   Penglase and Horner, *When the War Came to Australia*, pp. 193–6.
27   S. J. Butlin and C. B. Schedvin, *War Economy 1942–45*, p. 302.
28   'Sugar Ration for Preserves', *Western Herald* (Burke), 8 December 1944, p. 4.
29   Ronald Wilson, *Official Year Book of the Commonwealth of Australia No. 36 1944 and 1945*, Commonwealth Printer, Canberra, 1947, p. 1090.
30   Butlin and Schedvin, *War Economy 1942–45*, pp. 304–5.
31   Wilson, *Official Year Book*, p. 1101.
32   Darian-Smith, 'War and Australian Society', pp. 71–2.
33   'Housing Shortage', *Newcastle Morning Herald and Miners' Advocate*, 9 August 1945, p. 6.
34   Lorna Fitzgerald, interview 28 January 2004, Australians at War Film Archive, www.australiansatwarfilmarchive.gov.au/aawfa/interviews/1795.aspx, retrieved 22 October 2014.
35   Bosworth, 'Eating for the Nation', p. 236.
36   Butlin and Schedvin, *War Economy 1942–45*, pp. 308–9.
37   NSW State Publicity Censor minute, SPC/1549, 27 March 1943, NAA A11663 PA33.
38   Minutes of Press Censorship Advisory Committee Meeting, Canberra, 12 March 1943, NAA SP 195/1 72/26/3 Part 4.
39   'Daily Press Out-Censors Censor', *Worker* (Brisbane), 3 January 1944, p. 3.
40   John Hilvert, *Blue Pencil Warriors: Censorship and Propaganda in World War II*, University of Queensland Press, St Lucia, 1984, pp. 188, 220–2.
41   Wilson, *Official Year Book*, p. 705.
42   Commonwealth Parliamentary Debates (House of Representatives), 15 March 1944, pp. 1321–24.
43   Peter Helson, 'The Forgotten Air Force: The Establishment and Employment of Australian Air Power in the North-Western area 1941–1945', MA thesis, University College of the University of New South Wales, 1997, p. 106.
44   Anthony Cooper, *Darwin Spitfires: The Real Battle for Australia*, NewSouth, Sydney, 2011, p. 477.
45   'Another Protest on ARP Trenches', *Advertiser* (Adelaide), 7 March 1944, p. 6.
46   Hasluck, *The Government and the People, 1942–1945*, p. 665.
47   Minutes of War Cabinet Meeting, 29 June 1944, NAA A5954 817/2.

48   Minutes of War Cabinet Meeting, 24 January 1945, NAA A5954 811/1.
49   Gavin Long, *The Six Years War: Australia in the 1939–45 War*, Australian War Memorial and AGPS, Canberra, 1973, pp. 394–95.
50   Craig Matheson, 'Staff Selection in the Australian Public Service: A History of Social Closure', *Australian Journal of Public Administration*, 2001, vol. 60 (1), pp. 47–8.
51   Lee, 'Politics and Government', p. 82.
52   'Ministry Unfitted to Govern', *Sydney Morning Herald*, 23 June 1943, p. 7.
53   'Regulation Mania!', *The Argus*, 5 July 1943, p. 4.
54   Country Party press release, 21 June 1944, NAA SP286/16 12.
55   Hasluck, *The Government and the People, 1942–1945*, pp. 539–40.
56   Michael McKernan, *All in! Australia during the Second World War*, Thomas Nelson, Edinburgh, 1983, p. 143.
57   'Red Tape', *Western Grazier* (Wilcannia), 26 January 1945, p. 2.
58   Layman, 'I Was Manpowered', p. 69.
59   'Strangling the Country by Red Tape', *Chronicle* (Adelaide), 23 August 1945, p. 29.

PART 3

GREEN ARMOUR AND SPECIAL OPERATIONS

LEARNING AND ADAPTING FOR JUNGLE WARFARE, 1942−45: THE AUSTRALIAN AND BRITISH INDIAN ARMIES

Daniel Marston

Defeats in the Malayan, Papuan and Burma campaigns of 1942 convinced the Australian and Indian armies[1] that new tactics and training were required for new and challenging environments. In particular, it became apparent that basic training had been woefully inadequate for the rapidly expanded armies,[2] many of whom lacked a clear understanding of basic tactics, techniques and procedures. There were various pre-war manuals available, including *Field Service Regulations*, as well as branch-specific manuals such as *Infantry Training: Training and War*; these were still relevant and, with updating during the war, served as foundational resources.

The key lessons from the defeats of 1942 were the need for proper basic training and specialised training in jungle warfare for all the new units and formations. The latter, however, could follow only after foundational or basic training had been reformed and jungle warfare doctrine had been formulated. As the Australian jungle warfare manual stated in 1943,

> [I]t will be clear to all commanders that the information contained in this pamphlet will prove of little value unless the principles set out are closely studied and thorough training conducted in units and sub-units.

Figure 6.1: Troops jumping off a 20-foot-high platform with full kit at the Jungle Warfare School, Canungra, Queensland, 25 November 1943. (Australian War Memorial 060635)

> It presupposes that special training in jungle warfare is necessary, and should follow the completion of normal basic training.[3]

The British Indian Army Manual[4] of 1943[5] stated similar sentiments:

> [I]n principle there is nothing new in jungle warfare, but the environment of the jungle is new to many of our troops. Special training is therefore necessary to accustom them to jungle conditions and to teach them jungle methods.[6]

Training in jungle warfare was not a 'black art', but it did require some specialised thinking and training to adapt to the unique environment, even for veteran formations such as the 9th Australian Division.

By the end of 1944, both the Australian and the British Indian armies had become fully capable not only of operating in the jungle environment, but also of conducting open terrain, amphibious and combined arms operations against the Imperial Japanese Army in the Southeast and Southwest Pacific Command regions. They had, as institutions, integrated the knowledge that ongoing learning and adaptation were integral to their achievements. This chapter will analyse how and why these reforms came about. It will assess each army's attempts at reform through identification and dissemination of lessons, and subsequent changes to doctrine and training, through the experience of two battalions – the British Indian Army's 4/12th Frontier Force Regiment (FFR) and the Australian Army's 2/28th Infantry Battalion (and their respective formations, the 17th Indian Division and the 9th Australian Division) – as microcosms of the armies' learning and adaptation processes and to provide tactical context for other chapters in this book. I will consider the Indian Army's experience and performance first, since the 4/12th FFR fought against the Japanese in Burma in 1942 and experienced defeat firsthand, whereas the 2/28th and 9th Australian Division, flush with success in the Western Desert, did not see action against the Japanese until late 1943. I am discussing and comparing experiences and resources from both armies to provide a broader perspective on learning and adaptation initiatives across British Empire forces, and to analyse the Australian Army's performance in a larger context.

17TH INDIAN DIVISION – 4/12TH FRONTIER FORCE REGIMENT, 1942–44

The British commanders involved in the First Burma Campaign set out almost immediately to assess and learn from their defeats.[7] Others in General Headquarters (GHQ) India also recognised the need for tactical reform, and various units throughout India Command began to explore new ways of operating in the jungle. For many units, the Army in India Training Memoranda (AITM) and Military Training Pamphlets (MTPs)[8] published by GHQ India were the starting points for this process.[9] Veterans from the Malaya and Burma campaigns were sent by GHQ India to different formations to lecture about their experiences.

The principal methods of disseminating the new tactics being developed were the AITM and the MTPs. The number actually published was not large,[10] because GHQ anticipated that the pamphlets would be sent to the divisional HQs, and from there distributed to the various brigade HQs and so on, down to battalion HQs. Upon receiving these, commanders from the divisional level down generally would read the material with other officers and draw up inter-unit orders covering the most important points raised. However, the lessons provided were not universally applied; as well as producing these pamphlets, GHQ India also set up training schools, but there was apparently no system in place to ensure that the new tactics were being implemented.

The AITM No. 14 of February 1942 was the first to present jungle warfare tactics, in the context of a lesson from the fighting in Malaya.[11] Field Marshal

Wavell published his notes on the Malaya Campaign, focusing principally on the problems that the British Indian troops encountered against the tactics employed by the Japanese. His main argument was that it was necessary for troops to move off the roads and travel overland. He also discussed the concept of resupplying ground troops from the air, an idea that later became a cornerstone of jungle tactics. Other points raised included the necessity for rigid fire discipline in order not just to ensure adequate levels of ammunition, but also to avoid giving away one's position to the enemy.[12]

The AITM No. 15 of March/April 1942 described in more detail the problems of the Malaya campaign, noting first that 'tactics of jungle warfare are specialised and to employ them well special training is needed'.[13] This pamphlet also raised two other points that became as important to tactical development as the previously noted air supply and fire discipline. First, no linear defence was to be employed; instead, all-round defence would be used, with a mobile reserve to attack any penetrations into the defended areas. Second, it was necessary for units of all areas and services of the army to learn infantry tactics and to be able to fight as infantry in the jungle.[14] The final AITM of 1942 provided additional information from Burma and then from the Assam region. The principal theme was that every soldier must be trained to take part in battle;[15] everyone had to be involved in the fighting, from commanders down to privates, in order to provide defensive positions with mutual fire support.[16]

Following the withdrawal of the 17th Indian Division (including the 4/12th FFR) from Burma in May 1942, the Divisional Commander, Major General D. T. Cowan, set out to draw what lessons he could from the First Burma Campaign.[17] Some of the ideas worked out during this period changed over the course of the next few years, but many formed the basis of the tactical doctrine eventually adopted by most units in the field.

The first indication of reforms under way in the division appears in the June 1942 war diary. Training Instruction No. 1 for the 17th Indian Division appears in the appendix, and it begins with two important sentences: 'The division has acquired considerable practical experience of fighting against the Jap [sic] and many lessons have been learned from their methods which can be adopted by us ... [N]ow is the time to train and practice these new methods and to drive in the good lessons before they are forgotten.'[18]

The 17th Division distributed Training Instruction No. 2 on 24 June 1942. This requested that all veteran officers and men, before going on leave, relay their experiences and observations of battle to new men coming into their units via lectures and written notes. The final orders for 24 June indicated that all officers were to read the Cameron Report, AITM and the Malaya Report.[19]

Seven training instructions were written for the 17th Indian Division between June and December 1942; these became the basis for various exercises in the field. The 17th had the added benefit of Japanese troops stationed in the area as a training tool. As units were sent out to encounter the nearby enemy troops, a constant assessment of tactics could be undertaken and sent back to the various HQs for further analysis and dissemination to other units.[20] This reform and assessment process continued throughout 1943.

A limited counteroffensive was ordered for late autumn 1942 to seize Akyab Island in the Arakan (1st Arakan Offensive), where there was a strategically important airfield. The original plan called for the 14th Indian Division, under the command of Major-General W. L. Lloyd, to advance down to the southern tip of the Mayu Peninsula and draw Japanese forces away from the area. The plan was too ambitious, and the 14th suffered a major defeat.

The Arakan defeat was a significant blow to morale for the Indian Army; they had failed once again to defeat the Japanese. Units had been sent into combat with minimal training once again, and while some may have received some jungle warfare training, it was inconsistent and insufficient. The rising numbers of killed and wounded brought half-trained reinforcements into action, perpetuating the vicious circle. The debacle in the Arakan demonstrated conclusively the necessity for establishing an integrated and centralised program of retraining and reorganisation for the Indian Army, and in June 1943 an Infantry Committee was formed to take the matter forward.

INFANTRY COMMITTEE AND THE TRAINING DIVISIONS

The Infantry Committee's report was divided into seven sections, and its guiding principle was the conclusion that 'fundamentally the fighting spirit, physique and morale of both Indian and British units [was] unsatisfactory'. Part I highlighted the reasons for failures in the infantry units. Since jungle warfare was mainly an infantry war, the training of the infantry was most important. Reasons given for failures in infantry performance included lack of adequate basic training and of experienced leadership in infantry units. The necessity for British and Indian troops to fight on multiple fronts created complications of organisation, constant chaos of establishments and training difficulties. Other reasons cited included absence of adequate collective training, failure to relieve engaged troops and the consequent effect on morale and absence of adequate machinery to provide trained reinforcements.[21]

Part II focused more closely on specific problem areas, commenting that the lack of basic training was not only a problem for the Indian Army;

British reinforcements were also arriving untrained. The Committee recommended that, following the long journey from the United Kingdom, British troops should be sent to a reinforcement centre for proper acclimatisation, toughening and refreshing of basic training under actual jungle conditions. The Committee also pointed out the need for a simple, consistent and recognised jungle warfare doctrine, which must include cut-and-dried battle drills for training recruits. The Committee commented that there were numerous doctrines in circulation at the moment, some of them fundamentally different from others, and stressed that GHQ India needed to oversee the pamphlets so that trained soldiers could follow one consistent method.[22] Part II also stressed that all units should be trained for jungle warfare. To resolve the problem of reinforcements arriving with minimal training, the Committee recommended increasing the time period for basic training from three months to at least eight, with two to three months' additional training in jungle conditions. It also stipulated that training divisions be established to provide for the jungle warfare element of training.[23]

The rest of the report considered other, more specific problems. One of these was that the war in Burma required younger and fitter commanding officers (COs) to command battalions. The Committee recommended, as a general rule, that COs should be replaced after two years' service, as remaining with any one battalion for too long made them stale. In reality, most COs did not spend this long with their units; they were either promoted or sent to other units, and probably did not have the opportunity to become stale.[24]

The Committee's report also made recommendations regarding the separation of training responsibilities, suggesting that basic training should take place at regimental centres, and should focus on weapons training, discipline, indoctrination in regimental traditions, use of company and platoon weapons, and section and platoon training, with minimal reference to jungle warfare. This should be supplemented by two to three months' training with a jungle warfare training division. Officers were advised to put in a few months at their regimental training centre following officer training school. Following this, they would be posted to the training divisions for two to three months' additional training before being posted on to a unit in the field.[25]

Within two days of the submission of the Infantry Committee report, the General Staff in New Delhi was drawing up plans for the formation of two training divisions, for which each regiment of the Indian Army was required to provide a battalion. The 14th Indian Division was the first formation selected as a training division, and was posted to Chindwara, where jungle warfare camps had already been set up. Saharanpur, near Dehra Dun, was selected as the training ground in mid-June.[26] A separate

British brigade, the 52nd, was earmarked to receive British reinforcements.[27] There was a strong desire to form the training divisions quickly so that the process could begin as soon as possible, and all preparations were reported complete by 17 November 1943.[28]

Initially, the recruits would spend a month[29] in a base camp, where they would begin individual jungle warfare training, such as weapon training, battle drill, ground and field craft, principles of movement in the jungle, and digging. The second month they would move into the jungle with their training company and participate in patrolling, swimming with full kit, shelter building, defensive procedures, hygiene, track discipline, concealment, movement, and so on. This period was gradually built up with longer periods of time on patrol, and the exercises of the second month often ended with a two- or three-day patrol, complete with 'enemy' troops in the training grounds. Officers were placed in the rifle sections as ordinary riflemen for two months, and in a holding company for practice commanding a platoon or company.[30]

The training program was continuously updated with new lessons identified from the fighting in 1944 and early 1945.[31] Throughout the training period, all the officers and men lived in either the stationary camps or in the jungle, under jungle conditions. The goal was to completely acclimatise them before they were posted to their respective units.[32]

9TH AUSTRALIAN DIVISION – 2/28TH BATTALION

The 9th Australian Division was a veteran formation, which had been successful at Tobruk and the final battles at El Alamein. As orders were received to return to Australia and prepare for the war against the Japanese, the various commanders within the division were well aware of the need for specialised training in jungle warfare, as well as amphibious operations.[33]

The officers, non-commissioned officers and men of the 9th Division were able to seek information from veterans of the difficult early campaigns in Malaya and New Guinea. As their Indian Army counterparts were doing, many units and formations learned from defeat. These lessons were sought after, and Australian veterans from the first campaigns were sent far and wide to lecture to various units and formations to share their experiences. There had been some successes, notably at Milne Bay and the Kokoda Trail, but many within the Australian Army recognised the need both for better basic training and for specialised jungle training.[34] As with the Indian Army, the Australian Army identified the necessity for veteran troops to complete both specialised training and re-training.

Figure 6.2: Bayonet training at the Jungle Warfare School, Canungra, Queensland, 25 November 1943. (Australian War Memorial 060651)

In reforming training, the 9th Division was able to rely upon the various systems that had been created in 1942 by Advanced Land Headquarters (LHQ).[35] Two LHQ Training Teams were set up in 1942 to run training programs and disseminate lessons from Malaya and New Guinea, and a jungle warfare training centre was created at Canungra. Its mission was to train replacements for the various militia and Australian Imperial Force units forces in the SWPA Command, train independent (Commando) companies, and run a junior officer tactical school. By the end of 1942, LHQ had created large divisional areas on the Atherton Highlands in Queensland to train units and formations for operations in the SWPA.[36] The Australian and Indian armies were following a similar pattern: creation of training teams, specialised training camps and divisional-level training centres.[37] Both armies had official and unofficial lines of communications regarding transmitting lessons. Formations in both armies were creating their own doctrines by late 1942; however, in 1943, both HQs set out to create all-encompassing doctrine for units and formations to follow.[38] By mid-1943, both armies had tried to consolidate the various initiatives and create centralised systems. This was an important development, one that both armies continued to build on by assessing battlefield lessons and refining tactics accordingly for the remainder of the war.

The 9th Division and the 2/28th Battalion arrived at the Atherton Highlands in the autumn of 1943. Training teams with experience from New Guinea (from the 6th and 7th Divisions) were attached to units in the 9th Division. The first divisional training instruction, published on 14 April 1943, specified that 'formations will be well fitted to undertake operations in any type of country. At the same time, all formations will be trained to fit themselves for jungle warfare.' The first instruction highlights other key themes as well – notably, awareness of the enemy, the use of combined arms in the jungle environment and the need to train junior leaders. Divisional HQ created a series of training instructions that highlighted lessons from New Guinea, especially training of reinforcements and the need for better combined arms training. They also emphasised the key role of patrolling and the importance of 'object and lessons'. The instructions also requested lessons from training for further dissemination. During this period, the division was also reorganised with regard to equipment and numbers of men for the New Guinea front.[39] All of this activity was mirrored by the developments and thinking within the Indian Army at the same time.

Learning and adaptation were highlighted throughout as important features of the training period. In late May 1943, the division noted: 'during the preliminary training period many successful experiments have been carried out. It is desirable that information gained should be known throughout the Div.'[40] Space does not allow for a detailed description of the training efforts at the brigade level; however, the 24th Infantry Brigade, in which the 2/28th served in, followed the division's lead and created brigade-level training instructions, emphasising individual and collective training. The second training instruction reinforced a key theme: 'in tropical theatres of war great variations in country must be expected, and although jungle warfare must be learned thoroughly, the standard of training for operations in more open types of country must be kept at a high level.'[41]

The 2/28th Battalion followed suit; as with the higher level instructions, the battalion emphasised physical, individual and collective as well as night training. The battalion also provided detailed instructions encompassed in training syllabi for the officers, non-commissioned officers and soldiers,[42] who were specifically enjoined to read *MTP (Aust) 23 Notes on Jungle Warfare*. As their counterparts in other Australian and Indian units were doing, the 2/28th Battalion emphasised the key role of patrolling. The battalion also carried out the instructions of higher command and 're-organised' their battalion for the jungle environment.[43] They spent the months of June and July in continuous training and learning.[44]

By late July, the various units and formations of the 9th Division had completed their jungle warfare training. After carrying out amphibious warfare training for three weeks, they moved to Milne Bay in August for more training and acclimatisation.[45] By this point they were a veteran force, fairly well trained for the jungle environment; however, for both the Australians and their Indian counterparts, the true training and experience would occur in the jungle against the Imperial Japanese Army.

JUNGLE TACTICS CODIFIED IN DOCTRINE (AUSTRALIAN AND BRITISH INDIAN)

The tactics described here are from the Indian Army *Jungle Book* and the Allied Land Forces in SWPA Operations, MTP (Australia) No. 23, XX Jungle Warfare (provisional).[46] These were the first significant attempts to create centralised doctrines based upon lessons identified from the battlefields in Burma, Malaya, New Guinea and the Solomons. MTP (Australia) No. 23, describes itself as 'this pamphlet [which] endeavours to collect all the available information which has been gained from ... fighting under jungle experience'.[47]

The *Jungle Book* discusses the prerequisites for successful operation in the jungle: silent movement, concealment, deception, good marksmanship and physical fitness. The environment demands that 'command must be decentralised so that junior leaders will be confronted with situations in which they must make decisions and act without delay on their own responsibility'. Finally, a comparison is drawn between the difficulties of jungle fighting and night fighting. Both present limited vision and command and control problems, and require similar capabilities. Night training is recommended as suitable substitute preparation for jungle warfare, in the event that no jungle terrain is readily available.[48]

MTP (Australia) No. 23 follows a similar model, presenting core points up front. The Australian manual presents the topic of command decentralisation later in the narrative, but comes to similar conclusions:

> All our experience shows that in the jungle or similar enclosed country, command in battle is decentralised so that junior leaders are often confronted with a situation in which they must make a decision and act without delay on their own responsibility ... Junior leaders in particular must be trained and capable of taking the place of their superiors in the event of casualties.[49]

Both armies agreed that the chief element of success in the jungle was continuous patrolling, in both offensive and defensive situations. MTP No. 23 specifically stated: 'patrolling is the most important operation in jungle warfare'.[50] When companies or battalions were sent forward to attack and destroy known Japanese positions, both reconnaissance and fighting patrols were sent out on the flanks. Patrols were classified as either reconnaissance or fighting (listed as 'tiger' patrols by some Indian Army units). Reconnaissance patrols generally consisted of two or three men under the command of an officer or non-commissioned officer. The information they gathered was passed back to the company and battalion HQs, and decisions whether to send out fighting patrols were based upon this. Fighting patrols usually consisted of not less than a platoon of men and could be as large as a full company, and were sent out to lay ambushes or destroy Japanese patrols in the area.[51] The main advance was made in columns, designed to outflank the enemy or prevent him from outflanking the Allied force.[52] The nature of the terrain meant that units in the field did not have clear lines of defence, and there were frequently large stretches of no man's land between the British–Indian–Australian, and Japanese forces. The general principle behind active patrols was 'to make no man's land your man's land'.[53]

Battalions were deployed with companies stationed forward of the HQ. Within companies, patrol bases were set up still further forward, to support a variety of patrols. The patrol base had to be kept in the same area for as long as possible in order to maximise its success in gathering information. It had to be structured to limit enemy access and had to be able to defend itself,[54] necessitating the establishment of an all-round defence.

The *Jungle Book* and MTP (Australia) No. 23 describe the differences between frontal and flank attacks in more detail, as well as what each should comprise. Frontal attacks were only to be used if there were no alternatives, usually due to the terrain or the enemy having overextended its strength. The outflanking attack was regarded as more difficult but usually more successful, and was divided into four phases. The first group took up positions opposite the enemy and pinned him down, while the second and third flanking groups moved out to cut the lines of communication and attack from the flank or rear. The final group acted as the reserve. The flanking units had to provide all-round defence for themselves, essentially by patrols to engage any enemy approaching.[55] Flank attacks generally had a better chance of success than frontal attacks, but even so some of the fighting in 1943/1944 would be marked by frontal attacks. These were usually carried out due to terrain or time constraints.

The British/Indian 14th Army expanded and developed the box formation[56] concept for units from platoon to divisional level, the size of the box depending upon the unit involved. The basic design was for an all-round defence, structured so that all sides received sufficient fire coverage to stop a Japanese attack. As smaller units moved into the field, the standard order given was that movement stopped and defensive positions were dug two hours before sunset. If time permitted, the unit was to study the position to see from where the Japanese might attack and modify the layout of the box accordingly. Slit trenches were dug for rifle and Bren gun positions, and field of fire lanes cut in front of the position. Wire and *panjiis* (sharpened bamboo sticks) were set up outside the position. In certain cases, depending on the terrain and size of the box, heavier weapons were sometimes separated and put in a dedicated box at a distance to offer supporting fire for all the boxes in a given area.[57] Although stationary, the box formation encompassed an active defence. Half of the troops were stationed along the perimeter of the box. Another quarter was assigned to attack any Japanese penetration of the perimeter defences, while the last quarter was earmarked to attack Japanese movements outside the perimeter. Patrols also needed to be very active to deny reconnaissance information to the Japanese.[58]

The two manuals included considerably more detail than is presented here, on such topics as supporting weapons and air support. Both manuals also covered Japanese tactics as well as organisation. The one area where the two manuals diverged was in terms of illustrations. The Australian manual had a small amount of illustrations, whereas the *Jungle Book* had quite a few, including colour to provide greater detail.[59] Overall, the two manuals are very similar in topics, tactics, procedures and themes. As MTP (Australia) No. 23 noted:

> it will be clear to all commanders that the information contained in this pamphlet will prove of little value unless the principles set out are closely studied and through training conducted in units and sub-units. It presupposes that special training in jungle warfare is necessary, and should follow the completion of normal basic training.[60]

The Japanese high command had little inkling that these tactics were being developed and implemented by both the Australian and British Indian forces, and Japanese troops continued to fight through 1943–44 as if they were facing the same enemy that they had defeated so handily in 1942. Lieutenant-Colonel Fujiwara, staff officer with the Japanese 15th Army in Burma, stated that the Japanese failures in the Arakan and at

Imphal of 1944 were due to 'failure of recognition of the superiority of the Allied equipment and training in jungle warfare'.[61] Discussion of box formations figures prominently in another report written by Lieutenant-Colonel Kawachi and Colonel Kobayashi, described as both the tortoise and a bees' hive. They stated that 'until this time (1944) our forces did not encounter this type of enemy tactics . . . and therefore were unprepared to deal with them'.[62] Australian and British Indian troops in the field were not successful in every one of their efforts, but they learned quickly and constantly assessed themselves.

MILITARY MISSION 220

Throughout 1942–44, the two armies shared and disseminated lessons through official channels such as doctrine, manuals, training teams and observers. One overarching resource compiled the various initiatives undertaken by all the militaries engaged in fighting the Japanese: the 220 Military Mission. The lessons identified and recommendations proposed by the Mission influenced the training and organisation of the Australian, American and British Indian militaries during the final years of the war. Major General J. S. Lethbridge was tasked to form and head a military mission from the War Office, London to the United States, Australia, New Guinea, the Solomon Islands, New Caledonia, Burma and India to liaise with and report on the jungle fighting practices of the Allies generally and British Indian forces in particular. His report was intended for development into a training program for British units sent to the Pacific theatre as the war in Europe ended.

The 220 Military Mission began in June 1943, comprising 27 officers from all services, ordered to visit training areas and operational units in the jungle to assess the organisational needs of future units. Its report, submitted in March 1944, documented the requirements for units to become jungle-oriented and sufficiently adaptable to contend with the Japanese military.[63] The report reiterated what now had become a familiar theme: 'in conclusion we wish to emphasise that to enable troops to fight successfully in the jungle they must be thoroughly trained in normal basic infantry training, be imbued with a very rigid discipline, and be thoroughly physically fit'.[64]

Some other findings of the Mission are useful to state here, as they highlight how far the Allies had come over the previous two years in the war against Japan and how much had been shared between the various militaries. One of the key findings reported:

The Mission have seen tactical training in America, New Guinea, Australia and India and have found an almost startling agreement regarding main principles. An Australian Brigadier of considerable experience was recently touring India on a liaison visit, [and] remarked to the head of the Mission that when he was at the Indian Tactical School he could close his eyes and imagine himself back at the Australian Tactical School as the teaching was identical.[65]

The Mission's report was accepted by all the units and formations they visited across the Pacific, Southwest, Southeast and South Asia. The Mission felt that officers and non-commissioned officers they visited were keen to pass along their knowledge as well as learn from the Mission about other methods and tactics, techniques and procedures from other militaries.[66]

The report also highlighted a key theme for all aspects of warfare, whether occurring in the desert, beaches, jungle or arctic: 'the solution of these problems lies in the closest cooperation of all arms. The assault must be deliberately planned—a most closely coordinated attack by infantry, tanks and artillery'.[67] This philosophy would be a major theme in training for the final campaigns against the Japanese in Burma, New Guinea and Borneo.

POST-BATTLEFIELD ASSESSMENT FROM THE FIGHTING IN 1943–44 – DOCTRINE AND TRAINING

The experience of battle for the 4/12th FFR[68] and 2/28th Battalion in 1943 and 1944, as well as for their respective formations, helped to hone their battlefield skills, while the findings of the 220 Military Mission highlighted the learning and adaptation that had already occurred. Battlefield success did not make either army complacent; they knew that learning and adaptation must continue and that the cycle of debates, lessons identified, updated doctrine and ongoing training must continue in preparation for the coming battlefields of Central Burma and Borneo. Both armies also recognised that the battles would not remain limited to the jungle or closed country, but would encompass open-style fighting and river crossings, and amphibious, airborne and air-landed operations. Both armies had become learning institutions, and the process was integrated into their functioning.

DOCTRINAL LEARNING AND ADAPTATION, 1944–45

Doctrinal thinking had undergone a similar process of incorporating learning and adaptation from battlefield experience. In 1944, the Australians published *Tropical Warfare*, Pamphlet No. 1. As their British and American counterparts had done, the Australian manual expanded its remit beyond jungle warfare and discussed all sorts of operations in a tropical environment, commenting that,

> the principles of war apply equally as in any other theatre of operations. A commander is faced with the same problems in reconciling the different principles; he is likely to suffer equally from flagrant violations. The conditions to tropical areas will only affect the methods he must use to apply these principles ... It is necessary, therefore, that the conditions peculiar to tropical areas be studied in detail, and the limitations imposed by them thoroughly understood.[69]

The manual covers all the normal jungle warfare issues – patrolling, all-round defence, flank attacks and supply – as well as Japanese tactics, and notes that its conclusions are based upon lessons from New Guinea as well as other areas. Strangely, although well written overall the manual is devoid of any illustrations or maps.[70]

The Indian Army's documentation of doctrinal reforms began with AITM No. 24, March 1944. This manual focuses closely on the actions of 1944 under the heading 'Words of Wisdom from the Front', and is sub-headed with topics such as siting posts, preparation of posts, camouflage and track discipline, digging, wiring, and so on. These points, originally Messervy's notes, were reproduced not only in AITM No. 24 but also in the *Jungle Omnibus*.[71] AITM No. 24 also includes lessons from fighting in the Arakan and Assam, and stressed that it was crucial for all units to 'PATROL, PATROL, PATROL'. The manual also reiterates the critical need for units to dig in immediately after seizing a position, since the likelihood of a Japanese counterattack or at least a mortar attack was assessed as high. It also covers combined arms lessons from the Australians in New Guinea.[72]

AITM No. 25 went into more detail about lessons identified from the fighting in both the Arakan and Assam. The text noted that 'operations in ASSAM and the ARAKAN have demonstrated that a formal frontal infantry attack supported by a barrage and made against organised Japanese positions is rarely effective and often costly'. It also made the contention that one reason for the defeats tended to be the loss of the element of surprise, with an artillery bombardment indicating the direction from which the attack would come. The manual recommended a two-phase approach and reiterated that all firm bases had to employ an all-round defence. It also noted that artillery and air support could be used to pound Japanese positions, to smoke the area for an attack or to lay down deception fire on a specific area to make the Japanese think an attack was imminent there.[73]

AITM No. 25 also commented on other issues, including the need for proper training in minor tactics. The war in most cases was a platoon commander's war, and this meant that minor tactics played a significant role. Junior leadership was very important, and all moves had to have a plan. Another issue raised was fire discipline, which continued to be a problem. Not only was the loss of ammunition in arbitrary firing wasteful, but more importantly it also gave away positions to the enemy. A further suggestion was for all administration units to be trained to fight as infantrymen, able to carry out patrols, dig slit trenches and undertake wiring. The new *Jungle Omnibus* and the remaining AITM continued the practice of covering lessons from the Australian and US forces in the SWPA regions;[74] it's also worth noting that all this compilation and assessment was accomplished without any of the computer or communications technology considered necessary in our era.

LESSONS FROM BATTLE – 9TH DIVISION AND THE 2/28TH INFANTRY

Units from the 9th Division returned to Australia between January and March 1944 after carrying out successful operations against the Japanese in New Guinea. The division, commended for its professionalism by both Australian and Allied commanders, remained in Australia until April 1945; during this period many men, non-commissioned officers and officers went on leave, were posted out to other formations, or were released due to illness. As a result, records indicated that an estimated 50 per cent of the divisional units had new recruits to fill the ranks. This turnover meant that training became a major aspect of life for 9th Division units from April 1944 until early 1945.[75]

One of the first training instructions for the 9th Division, dated 10 May 1944, highlights a potential issue regarding composition of units: 'the big majority of troops in this division, having either fought in the jungle or having been trained in the jungle, are familiar with jungle conditions'.[76] So much personnel turnover raises the question of how experienced the division was about jungle conditions. The division tried to deal with this issue later in the month, announcing that more reinforcements were coming who needed to be imbued with not only the 'principles of war' but also the recent experiences of fighting in New Guinea. Training Instruction No. 5, 20 May 1944, specifically lays out how best to conduct training for both jungle and open-style warfare, asserting that

> any training in the open or semi-open will be done with the object
> of training principles or of demonstrating phases of jungle
> fighting . . . [T]raining in any phase of platoon, company or battalion
> tactics likely to be met in the jungle will culminate in exercises in the
> jungle.[77]

Following the model established in 1943, the division specifically called for individual and collective training in the basics, followed by specialisation; it also emphasised the need for better combined arms training.[78]

The Training Instructions continued from June through December; all emphasised the many different kinds of training that were needed: open-style, closed country, combined arms and amphibious, as well as discussion of key lessons identified from the fighting in New Guinea.[79] The 24th Infantry Brigade and 2/28th Infantry Battalion followed the divisional instructions and specialised their training accordingly,[80] and exchange of lessons among the Allies continued. The September 1944 War Diary includes a 'Precis on Notes on Recent Operations in the Arakan by GOC 36th [probably 26th] Indian Division' as an appendix, which lists and describes key lessons from recent fighting in the mountainous Arakan region. It covers the usual key issues, and does not underestimate the enemy, asserting that 'the Jap is a courageous and most tenacious infantry-man'.[81] The campaigns of 1945 would validate the value of these months of training, as the 9th Division would demonstrate during operations at Tarakan and North Borneo.[82]

LESSONS FROM BATTLE: 17TH INDIAN DIVISION AND THE 4/12TH FRONTIER FORCE REGIMENT

The 4/12th FFR and the 17th Indian Division fought with professionalism on the Imphal Plain in 1944 and, alongside units from IV and XXXIII Corps, destroyed the Japanese invasion. Even with successes in both the Arakan and Assam, commanders in the 14th Army and India Command felt that room for improvement remained in both tactical training and organisation.

One of the first recommendations that was made as a result of the fighting in the Arakan and Assam and the findings of the 220 Military Mission was to regularise the organisation of the infantry divisions in SEAC to create the 'standard division'. There were five different divisions in SEAC in the summer of 1944. At a conference held 26–27 May 1944 at 14th Army HQ, senior officers from the HQs of India Command, 11th Army Group, 14th Army and IV, XV and XXXIII Corps[83] decided that an infantry division should be capable of normal jungle fighting, being transported by air and amphibious landings. These changes were to be implemented over time; as each division was pulled out of the fighting, it would re-fit according to the new organisational structures. Discussion at the meeting also highlighted the need for serious training involving both tanks and infantry units; the recent fighting had indicated a poor level of coordination among units in the field.[84]

Each battalion and regiment that was withdrawn from the line and sent into reserve took with it not only a wealth of knowledge based upon the personal experiences of the officers and men, but also records that documented and made accessible that knowledge. Each battalion and regiment carried out retraining during the autumn of 1944 and winter 1944–45 before returning into battle. The 4/12th FFR held conferences where lessons were conveyed to all officers within the battalion. As with all units, retraining began with individual training and led to more advanced collective training. The 4/12th FFR adopted the new war establishment for infantry battalions, and was attached to the 48th Indian Brigade. It continued training with other units of the 48th Indian Brigade until December 1944. The HQ then distributed all relevant information to company officers, in both verbal and written form.[85]

In mid-December 1944, the 17th Indian Division received orders to proceed to Imphal. When the division arrived in early January, it adopted a new divisional structure. On 22 January, all units that were to be motorised were given jeeps and trucks and instructed to give up all animal transport. The 48th and 63rd Indian Brigades were among those chosen for the motorised role, and 4/12th FFR was required to send men on driving courses and learn the specific aspects of loading and unloading materiel and men with motorised transport. Units were given just short of one month of training before being ordered forward into Burma, but both brigades managed time to carry out further tank–infantry cooperation training with the 255th Armoured Brigade.[86] Officers from the 4/12th FFR noted that even in training men for the motorised role, jungle tactics were still evident, especially the use of boxes, planning for air resupply and organising foot patrols. The divisional General Officer Commanding, Major-General Cowan, noted: 'all round defence is just as important out of the jungle as it is in it . . . [O]ur basic training [jungle warfare] has stood the test now we have to adapt it to the new situation'.[87]

The 4/12th FFR, as part of the 48th Indian Brigade, crossed the Irrawaddy River on 18 February. The 4/12th FFR was successful in operating as lorry-transported infantry in the approach to Meiktila. Units set up boxes each evening, with constant patrols sent out to locate and destroy any enemy troops in the area.[88] It had not been overrun or surprised during the advance. The 4/12th FFR moved into and successfully fought in a built-up area of Meiktila; they effectively established roadblocks and set up ambushes on foot in the southwestern region of Meiktila. They had learned the lessons of the 1942–44 campaign, and were part of the destruction of the Japanese Burma Area Army.

CONCLUSION

The campaigns of 1945 clearly demonstrated that the Australian and Indian armies were capable of adapting to the changing conditions of terrain and operating environments. When troops were pulled out of the line in the spring and autumn of 1944 and jungle tactics further evaluated, the senior commanders also recognised that future fighting would eventually involve a very different terrain, open style, tighter combined arms, with airborne and amphibious operations. They could easily have been caught on the back foot emerging from the jungles of the Indo-Burma region and New Guinea, but by foreseeing potential problems they were able to adapt quickly and successfully to the change in terrain. Both armies had achieved a new level of professionalism by the time of the Japanese surrender; they were properly trained, capable of dealing with almost any tactical situation with which they might be presented, and imbued with the culture of learning and adaptation.

FURTHER READING

Peter Dennis and Jeffrey Grey, *The Foundations of Victory*, Army History Unit, Canberra, 2004.
Daniel Marston, *Phoenix from the Ashes: The Indian Army in the Burma Campaign*, Praeger, London, 2003.

T.R. Moreman, 'Remembering the War in New Guinea Jungle, Japanese and the Australian Army: Learning the Lessons of New Guinea', Symposium paper, 2000.

T.R. Moreman, *The Jungle, the Japanese and the British Commonwealth Armies at War 1941–45*, Frank Cass, London, 2005.

Garth Pratten, *Australian Battalion Commanders in the Second World War*, Cambridge University Press, Melbourne, 2009.

Notes

1 An equally important and successful reform process occurred within the US Army and the US Marine Corps during the same period. See *Jungle Warfare*: FM 31–20 and *Jungle Warfare*: FM 72–20 (1944). Both of these manuals discussed the need for all round protection, while the 1944 edition noted that jungle warfare does not alter the basic principles of war.

2 The Indian Army serves as a good example. It stood at 200,000 in 1939 and by 1941 was 1.5 million in strength.

3 Allied Land Forces in South-West Pacific Area Operations, Military Training Pamphlet (MTP) (Australia) No. 23, XX Jungle Warfare (provisional), 31 March 1943, Melbourne, Australian War Memorial (AWM) pp. 29–30.

4 Previous versions of this doctrine appeared in 1940 and 1942, however, many units and formations either never saw the various versions of the manual, or were so inadequately trained as to make the manual practically useless.

5 *Jungle Book* (Military Pamphlet No. 9), September 1943.

6 Ibid.

7 British/Indian Army officers and men who had escaped from the Malaya Campaign were also actively sought for their experiences and ideas.

8 The various training pamphlets developed by the War Office in London were also used to teach basic tactics and training. The 'jungle' tactics were drawn from the AITM and MTPs developed by GHQ India. MTP (India) No. 9: *Forest Warfare*, published in 1940, was revised as a second edition in 1942 as *Jungle Warfare*, and finally in 1943 as the third version, the *Jungle Book*.

9 The 14th Indian Division created a jungle warfare school at Comilla in mid-1942.

10 The attempt was made to get at least one copy of the *Jungle Book*, MTP No. 9, (and later the *Jungle Omnibus*) to all the officers in the field.

11 A manual published in 1940, *Tactical Notes for Malaya*, was used by British, Indians and Australians.

12 AITM No. 14 February 1942, National Army Museum (NAM), UK, p. 13.

13 AITM No. 15 March/April 1942, NAM, p. 2.

14 AITM No. 15 March/April 1942, NAM, pp. 3–4.

15 AITM No. 16–17, July and September 1942, NAM.

16 The formal beginning of the 'box' defensive positions, a staple of all later fighting in the war.

17 Brigadier R. T. Cameron, commander of the 48th Indian Brigade, wrote a report on the failings of the First Burma Campaign and possible solutions. This formed the foundation for the training of the 17th Indian Division.

18 WO 172/475 4/6/1942 National Archives (NA), UK.

19 WO 172/475 24/6/1942 NA.

20 WO 172/475 June–December 1942 NA.

21 L/WS/1/1371 Report of the Infantry Committee, India, 1–14 June 1943, Oriental and India Office (OIOC), British Library (BL).

22 Before this movement for centralisation and streamlining began, there were multiple doctrines being developed by units in India Command.

23 L/WS/1/1371 Report of the Infantry Committee, India, 1–14 June 1943, OIOC, BL.

24 L/WS/1/1371 Report of the Infantry Committee, India, 1–14 June 1943, OIOC, BL; see Pratten's *Battalion Commanders* for the debates within the Australian forces.

25 L/WS/1/1371 Report of the Infantry Committee, India, 1–14 June 1943, OIOC, BL.

26 General Staff Branch 16/6/1943 L/WS/1/1364 OIOC, BL.

27 War Office to Commander-in-Chief 19/8/1943 L/WS/1/1364 OIOC, BL.

28 L/WS/1/1323 Operations in Burma OIOC, BL.

29 This was cut back to two weeks as recruits arrived later in 1944 with adequate basic training.

30 Major General Curtis Papers, Imperial War Museum (IWM) UK.

31 Letter from Lieut. Alan Burnett, formerly with the 15/10th Baluch Regiment, training battalion 14th Division.

32 Major General Curtis Papers, IWM.

33 John Coates, *Bravery above Blunder: The 9th Australian Division at Finschafen, Sattleberg, and Sio*, Oxford University Press, Oxford, 1999, pp. 44–5.

34 See Moreman, *Jungle, the Japanese*, pp. 76–9 for more details.

35 Much of the work had been implemented by the Deputy Chief of the General Staff, Major General Frank Berryman in 1942. For a wider description see Peter Dean, *The Architect of Victory: The Military Career of Lt-General Sir Frank Horton Berryman*, Cambridge University Press, Melbourne, 2011, in particular, pp. 175–205.

36 See Moreman, 'Remembering the War in New Guinea' for a more detailed discussion and Moreman, p. 81. The training areas were commended by the 220 Military Mission. See below for more information.

37 See Marston, *Phoenix*, for an in-depth description of the various Indian Army divisional level attempts at creating training centres, disseminating lessons, creating doctrine within the divisions.

38 See below for a description of the manuals and tactics that were taught in 1943.

39 9th Division GS Branch War Diary, AWM 52 1/5/20, 18, 30 April and 9 May 1943.

40 9th Division GS Branch War Diary, AWM 52 1/5/20, 23 May 1943.

41 24th Infantry Brigade, War Diary, AWM 52 8/2/24, 29 April 1943. See March–May for more details.

42 See 2/28th Infantry Battalion, AWM 52 8/3/28, 12 May 1943, for a detailed description of the syllabi.

43 2/28th Infantry Battalion, AWM 52 8/3/28, May 1943.

44 See 2/28th Infantry Battalion, AWM 52 8/3/28, June–July 1943.

45 Coates, *Bravery above Blunder*, pp. 54–7.

46 These were not the end but the starting point for commanders to work from as they gained experience on the battlefield.

47 Allied Land Forces in South-West Pacific Area Operations, MTP (Australia) No. 23, XX Jungle Warfare (provisional), AWM, p. 3.

48 *Jungle Book*, Preface, p. 2.

49 Allied Land Forces in South-West Pacific Area Operations, MTP (Australia) No. 23, XX Jungle Warfare (provisional), AWM, pp. 29–30.

50 Ibid., p. 20.

51 Messervy Papers, File 5/8, 3/1/1944, Liddell Hart Centre Military Archives, Kings College, London, LHCMA.

52 *Jungle Book*, pp. 9–11 and see MTP (Australia) No. 23, AWM, p. 8.

53 *Jungle Book*, p. 19.

54 Brigadier Mizen 71/63/1 (9/12th FFR 20th Indian Division), IWM.

55 *Jungle Book*, pp. 10–1 and MTP (Australia) No. 23, AWM, p. 8.

56 The idea of the box formation originated in the fighting in the Western Desert. Despite their lack of success in the desert, boxes were tried again in jungle conditions and were implemented with considerable success.

57 Messervy Papers, File 5/1, 22/9/1943, LHCMA. These notes formed the basis for the section in AITM No. 24 'Defence', pp. 1–5.
58 *Jungle Book*, pp. 14–5.
59 MTP (Australia) No. 23, AWM. Platoon and section commanders manual had more illustrations as well.
60 MTP (Australia) No. 23, AWM, pp. 29–30.
61 SEATIC Bulletin 9/7/1946 Observations of the War in Burma, by Lieutenant-Colonel Fujiwara, Staff Officer with 15th Japanese Army, Lieutenant-General Evans Papers, IWM.
62 Japanese Studies of WWII No. 89 Operations in Burma 43–44, Lieutenant-General Evans Papers, IWM.
63 Major General J. S. Lethbridge Papers, 220 Military Mission Report, 2 vols, LHCMA.
64 Ibid., point 9, 'Training', LHCMA.
65 Ibid.
66 Ibid., points 53 and 54.
67 Ibid., point 14.
68 See Marston, *Phoenix*, for a detailed description of the performance of the 4/12th FFR on the battlefield in 1943–44.
69 Australian Military Forces, *Tropical Warfare*, Pamphlet No. 1, 1944, AWM, p. 9.
70 Australian Military Forces, *Tropical Warfare*, Pamphlet No. 1, 1944, AWM. The 1945 edition (Pamphlet No. 2, 1945), created for platoon and section level commanders, includes numerous illustrations.
71 *Jungle Omnibus*, January 1945, pp. 11–9. This manual collated all the materials covering jungle warfare that had been published in the AITM since 1942. The manual was intended for all new British and Indian army units arriving to fight in Southeast Asia; it was distributed to veterans as well, who continued to use the *Jungle Book* as well as the various unit and formation battle drills and TTPs.
72 AITM No. 24, pp. 18–21.
73 AITM No. 25. (*Jungle Omnibus*, pp. 24–6.)
74 See AITM No. 26 for major lessons dealing with combined arms in New Guinea from the US and Australian perspectives.
75 See 9th Division GS Branch War Diary, AWM 52 1/5/20, April–May 1944.
76 9th Division GS Branch War Diary, AWM 52 1/5/20, 10 May 1944.
77 Ibid., 20 May 1944.
78 Ibid., AWM 52 1/5/20, April–May 1944. See especially the Mountain Warfare section included in the war diary as a further example of learning and adaptation.
79 Ibid., June–December 1944; by October there were 25 training instructions.

80 See the 24th Infantry Brigade, War Diary, AWM 52 8/2/24, April–December 1944, the 2/28th Infantry Battalion, AWM 52 8/3/28, April–December 1944, war diary for a detailed description of the instructions and syllabi for the individual, collective, closed country, open country, combined arms and amphibious training.

81 9th Division GS Branch War Diary, AWM 52 1/5/20, 5 September 1944.

82 See Garth Pratten's chapter for more details.

83 This was held during the Imphal battles in the spring and summer, 1944.

84 30/6/1944 Protection of tanks in Far East L/WS/1/650 OIOC, BL.

85 WO 172/4979 July–December 1944, NA.

86 WO 172/7736 January–February 1945 and WO 172/7729 January–February 1945, NA.

87 Training Instruction, 23/1/45.

88 Interviews with officers of the 4/12th FFR.

CHAPTER 7

Intelligence and Special Operations in the Southwest Pacific, 1942–45

John Blaxland

When Gavin Long published the seventh volume of the official history *Australia in the War of 1939–1945: The Final Campaigns* in 1963, he ventured where few had gone before publicly by including an appendix on the Allied Intelligence Bureau – a secretive body responsible for some spectacular intelligence and special operations.[1] Until then, few Australians knew much about the world of intelligence and special operations outside the closed circle of practitioners. But even then, while certain aspects of the special operations realm were revealed, significant elements of the Allied wartime intelligence apparatus remained largely unheralded. Sworn to secrecy, insiders understood that the secret of success lay in keeping successes secret. One of the ironies of this was that for decades afterwards historical accounts were incomplete and analysis of Allied victories deeply flawed. As a result, for generations few would really understand the wartime role played by the intelligence and special operations domains.

Ultra Top Secret Codebreaking

More than a decade after publication of *The Final Campaigns*, and almost 30 years after the war's end, a retired Royal Air Force officer, Group Captain Frederick Winterbotham, published *The Ultra Secret*. This was a stunning revelation of how the German Enigma cipher machine functioned, how its codes were broken and how telegraphic traffic of the highest sensitivity was reported. The information was considered so sensitive it was described as being higher than simply 'most secret'. It was 'Ultra Top Secret', or simply 'Ultra'.[2]

Possession of Ultra gave the English-speaking Allies an extraordinary insight into Axis planning and operations. Indeed, at the end of the war British Prime Minister Winston Churchill told King George VI at a meeting with Sir Stewart Menzies, who was head of MI6 (Britain's secret intelligence service), that 'it was thanks to Ultra that we won the war'. Churchill may have been exaggerating, but Ultra did stave off several defeats early on from 1940 to 1942 and made a major contribution to the shortening of the war thereafter.[3]

Ultra, in fact, was an 'invaluable accessory' in planning Allied strategic initiatives from 1942 to 1945. It is widely known now that Ultra was pivotal for the success of the Allied landings in Normandy in June 1944. Ultra was also crucial to Montgomery's successes against Rommel in North Africa in 1942. Additionally, Allied successes against the German U-boats in the north Atlantic and Mediterranean in late 1941 were 'achieved entirely on the basis of Ultra'.[4]

But, as this chapter attests, the Ultra signals intelligence (sigint) was equally important in the Pacific War, enabling major strategic victories in the battle of the Coral Sea in May 1942 and at Midway the following month. These were the principal turning points in the Pacific War. Eventually the Allies were also able to build up a detailed picture of the Japanese order of battle. In the areas closest to Australia, the Allied forces under MacArthur were thus able to strike where the Japanese were weakest. Without sigint, the Allied losses would have been significantly greater.[5] What is often underappreciated is Australia's role in this critically important story.

Beyond the now well-known intelligence successes at the Coral Sea and Midway the years from 1942 to 1945 saw a large number of further revelations, which highlighted the success of Allied code breaking endeavours in the Pacific and Southwest Pacific theatres. With the Japanese relying on German cryptographic technology the ramifications of the Ultra breakthrough would be felt in both the European and the Pacific theatres of operations. Indeed, 1942 witnessed a significant expansion in capability across the board as Australia dramatically increased its efforts in the war against Japan. But before venturing further it is worth reflecting on the state of Australian security and intelligence affairs in the lead up to this period.

Nascent Intelligence and Special Operations Arrangements, 1939–41

At the outset of the Second World War Australia's intelligence architecture was rudimentary, relying primarily on material provided from British sources. At this time the British passed on what they thought Australians needed to know, while few Australian military officers were interested in intelligence. Not surprisingly, therefore, the intelligence services were of low quality and did not attract high calibre officers.[6]

Sensing the need for proactive measures in the lead up to conflict, the Director of Naval Intelligence arranged for representatives of Military and Air Force intelligence to consider what action might be taken. After a number of meetings and recommendations on 5 June 1939 the War Cabinet agreed to set up a defence security organisation responsible to the three chiefs of staff. But with rivalries and competing priorities this effort gained little traction.[7]

Following the declaration of war in September, a considerable expansion and development of the military's field intelligence and security arrangements took place. The expansion of the armed forces' intelligence staff had been complicated by the formation of the 2nd Australian Imperial Force for service overseas in late 1939. At home, since it seemed unlikely the army[8] would have to fight within Australia, the military intelligence staff in Australia did not pay much attention to operational intelligence. That was handled by the intelligence staff of the 1st Australian Corps that, from mid-1940, was based in the Middle East. In view of the lack of regular army intelligence officers, the key intelligence appointments went to militia officers, the senior most being Major John Rogers, who would subsequently become the army's Director of Military Intelligence (DMI).[9]

The DMI under Rogers came to include intelligence staffs at each level of command, including the lines of communications area headquarters in each state. Each service also had its own counter-intelligence staffs responsible for internal security, although the army had wider responsibilities with postal and telegraphic censorship.[10]

The DMI also established the nucleus of a cryptanalytic organisation in January 1940, when a Sydney University professor of pure mathematics, Thomas Room, along with his colleague, Richard Lyons, began studying foreign codes. They would subsequently form the nucleus of D Special Section, which focused on breaking the Japanese diplomatic codes for the rest of the war.[11] By October 1941, the Cypher Breaking Group was producing 'exceedingly good results', succeeding in breaking the Japanese LA code, a low-grade code used for consular traffic.[12]

In the meantime, the 2nd AIF deployed to the Middle East with its own signals intelligence unit. This unit served on operations in the Middle East from 1940 onwards, undertaking 'special wireless' code breaking and interpreting in Greece, Crete, Syria and North Africa. On return to Australia in 1942 this special capability was redirected towards the war against Japan, with the army special wireless units (essential signals intercept stations) intimately linked in with a research and control centre, which would become known as the Central Bureau.[13]

The Royal Australian Navy (RAN) also saw a massive expansion of its intelligence capabilities. The Director of Naval Intelligence, Commander R.B.M. (Rupert) Long, assisted by Commander Eric Feldt, established the Coastwatchers organisation prior to outbreak of the war in the Pacific. This involved a wide network of posts around Australia and the islands to the northeast. The Coastwatchers network was to prove of significant value to Australian and US forces and figured prominently in Allied intelligence cooperation. Their reports on air and shipping movements contributed a great deal to the war effort.[14]

By late 1940, the Royal Australian Air Force (RAAF) likewise initiated recruitment of area intelligence reporting officers to relay information on the movement of any enemy aircraft, ships or personnel. Participants were selected according to their access to radios that could transmit over long distances. They were located throughout New Guinea and around Australia. The Coastwatchers provided an invaluable service. But as the Ultra historian Ed Drea observed, 'perhaps the Coastwatchers' finest service was to shield, albeit unknowingly, the Ultra secret in the Southwest Pacific Area'.[15]

Australia in the meantime had made little progress in raising an indigenous sigint organisation, and as late as 1939 there was no sigint or cryptanalytic capability in Australia.[16] At Singapore, however, the British had established the Far Eastern Combined Bureau, primarily for eavesdropping on Japanese communications. While the Bureau was 'singularly ineffectual in forecasting Japanese strengths and intentions' it did possess some high quality personnel. For instance, Commander Eric Nave, 'Australia's codebreaker extraordinary', spent some time as a Royal Navy officer at the Far Eastern Combined Bureau before transferring to Melbourne. Toward the end of 1940 Nave established Australia's first Special Intelligence Section in Melbourne and tasked it to obtain information by radio direction finding, traffic analysis and cryptanalysis.

Nave was given high praise, as he was the first to unravel Japanese naval telegraphy and to break Japanese Navy codes. Radio intercept stations were established in Darwin (HMAS *Coonawarra*), Melbourne and Canberra (HMAS *Harman*) and the section concentrated on Japanese traffic in the Mandated Islands north of New Guinea. By October 1940, *Harman* had four full-time and six part-time Y operators (that is, sigint collections operators) and *Coonawarra* had four part-time ones. Between 1940 and 1942, Nave's Signals Intelligence Bureau almost singlehandedly made Australia as aware of Japanese intentions as the governments in the United Kingdom and United States.[17] However, these initial, limited cryptographic capabilities meant that the Australian sigint organisation could do little more than supplement the work of the British Far Eastern Combined Bureau in Singapore, and the Government Code and Cypher School at Bletchley Park in Britain (later renamed the Government Communications Headquarters or GCHQ).

The Australians were, however, to make some significant break-throughs. This included breaking the code used by the Japanese mission in Australia, the details of which were quickly passed on to Bletchley Park and Washington; and in September 1941 they intercepted a message instructing the Japanese Consul-General to find another neutral country to look after Italian interests (Japan had been looking after Italian diplomatic interests since Italy joined Germany in the war), and on 4 December they detected the Japanese order to burn all their codes and ciphers. Thus, by the outbreak of the war in the Pacific in December 1941 the Australians had developed promising, albeit limited, expertise in 'special intelligence'.[18]

At the war's outset a Central War Room had been established at Victoria Barracks, Melbourne, to coordinate Australia's war effort. This was supplemented by a Combined Operations Intelligence Centre (COIC) in late 1940. The COIC was set up as a joint service organisation to distribute coordinated intelligence to Australian commanders.[19] The COIC staff analysed, 'all intelligence material and provided the appreciations on strategic and other important problems upon which the Chiefs of Staff based their war plans'.[20] A Weekly Diary of Operational Intelligence commenced in January 1941. Commander Long was the driving force behind the creation of the COIC and soon became its director. By April 1942, the COIC was absorbed into General MacArthur's headquarters.[21] But it was staffed by officers from the three Australia services and would partly duplicate the work of its US counterpart: military intelligence (G2) organisation.[22]

WAR IN THE PACIFIC

The Japanese bombing of Darwin on 14 February 1942 and the surrender of Singapore the next day brought home to Australians the Japanese threat. Information and intelligence on Japanese equipment, tactics and intentions was passed to Australia in a steady flow following the invasion of Malaya. Even with this information, Australia still did not have sufficient aircraft, personnel or equipment to stem the Japanese advance. The intelligence effort was still embryonic and coming to terms with the enormity of developing a sophisticated intelligence capability.

ALLIED INTELLIGENCE ORGANISATION IN SOUTHWEST PACIFIC AREA, MAY 1943

It's important to note that the Pacific was carved up between the Allies and the US services. Britain was responsible for South East Asia Command covering Burma and India. After the collapse of the short-lived American–British–Dutch–Australian Command in the Netherlands East Indies (now Indonesia), the Pacific was divided into the Southwest Pacific Area (SWPA), under General Douglas MacArthur, and the Pacific Ocean areas, under the US Navy.

With the arrival of MacArthur in Australia in mid-March 1942, intelligence was coordinated through General Headquarters (GHQ) SWPA. Major General Richard Sutherland was MacArthur's Chief of Staff and Brigadier General Charles Willoughby was his Chief of Staff for Intelligence (G2). With Prime Minister Curtin's acquiescence, GHQ SWPA directly supervised the Central Bureau, the Allied Translator and Interpreter Service and the Allied Intelligence Bureau.

Eventually, as the war progressed, MacArthur wanted to move his headquarters northwards. Consequently, GHQ and Advanced Land Headquarters (Adv LHQ) moved to Brisbane in late July and August 1942. DMI Rogers and his deputy, Colonel Keith Wills, flew between Melbourne and Brisbane but would end up spending most of their time in Brisbane or visiting the intelligence staffs at forward army and corps headquarters in New Guinea or the Atherton tablelands (west of Cairns).[23] With the nation facing an apparent existential crisis, there was much work to be done, and some innovative ideas and organisations emerged as a result.

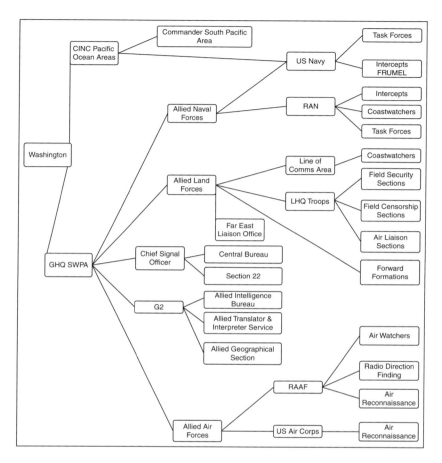

Figure 7.1: Allied Intelligence Organisation, Southwest Pacific Area, May 1943. (Letter Brig Rogers to DMI London, India, Middle East, Ottawa, Wellington, 10 May 1943, Adv. HQ AMF G Int. Sect. War Diary AWM 1/2/2 cited in Horner, *High Command*, p. 241.)

ALLIED INTELLIGENCE BUREAU AND SPECIAL OPERATIONS

In mid-1940, Australia had been encouraged to establish a special branch to organise fifth columnists to operate in territories likely to be occupied. Lieutenant Colonel J. C. Mawhood was sent to Australia by Britain's Special Operations Executive to assist in setting up an organisation to conduct irregular warfare. Mawhood got offside with his Australian interlocutors, however, and the plan for a centrally controlled irregular warfare force didn't materialise. But when the threat to Australia became clearer, the independent companies that emerged played a prominent role in the war thereafter in places like East Timor.[24]

The British saw special operations – that is sabotage and direct subversion – as a significant enabling capability in the European theatre. This was the case particularly during the early years of the war when there was little that direct, conventional military capabilities could do about Germany's iron grip on the continent. This faith in the utility of special operations was transported to Australia with a view to its application on operations throughout the occupied archipelago to Australia's north. As in Europe, however, special operations would have mixed results, with some successes and some tragic failures.

In May 1942, General Blamey advised MacArthur that secret intelligence and field intelligence behind enemy lines had to be carried out under separate organisations but with common direction. In July 1942, the Allied Intelligence Bureau (AIB) was set up and the Australian Colonel Caleb Roberts became its controller. He reported directly to MacArthur's Chief of Intelligence (G2), Brigadier-General (later Major-General) Charles A. Willoughby.[25] The AIB's mission was, 'to obtain and report information of the enemy in the SWPA, exclusive of the continent of Australia and Tasmania, and in addition, where practicable, to weaken the enemy by sabotage and destruction of morale'.[26]

The AIB was staffed by personnel from 10 armed services from Australia, Britain, the United States and the Netherlands East Indies. At its peak it controlled eight separate organisations, broken up into four sections. These sections were:

- Section A – Special Operations Australia with the cover name of Services Reconnaissance Department, including Z Special Force, focused largely on sabotage operations. This was formed with the assistance of the British Special Operations Executive;
- Section B – Secret Intelligence Service, which was an offshoot of the British Secret Intelligence Service (MI6);
- Section C – Combined Field Intelligence Service (incorporating Coastwatchers); and,
- Section D – Far Eastern Liaison Office, which was a pseudonym for the Military Propaganda Section, involved in a 'leaflet and radio war' of 'combat propaganda' and agent penetration of enemy-held territory across and beyond the Netherlands East Indies and New Guinea.[27]

The AIB included sections responsible for special operations in three sectors including the Philippines, the Netherlands East Indies and New

Figure 7.2: Lieutenant J. Sampson, Allied Intelligence Bureau, leading a patrol through the dense jungle behind the enemy lines, Tamkaidan, New Britain, Papua New Guinea, 15 January 1945. (Australian War Memorial 078363)

Guinea, along with nearby areas in the SWPA. It also included Secret (or Special) Intelligence Australia (ASIS), which was partly controlled by the British Secret Intelligence Service in London. Its task was to conduct special intelligence, or espionage, as distinct from the special operations carried out by the other sections of the AIB. By March 1945, 3046 people worked in the AIB of whom only 19 were American.[28]

Reflecting on the AIB's contribution to the war effort, historian Alan Powell observed that neither the achievements nor the costs were easy to measure. Over 100 decorations and awards were won; 264 party missions carried out, involving 164 operatives killed, 75 captured and 178 missing, against 7203 Japanese dead, 141 prisoners of war taken and 1054 Allied personnel rescued from enemy-held territory. This does not include the hundreds if not thousands of civilian lives lost as a direct result of these operations. There were undoubtedly some brilliant clandestine operations, not least of which were the daring raids on Japanese-held Singapore Harbour undertaken by Z Special Force.[29]

Operation Jaywick was perhaps the most renowned operation. This raid on shipping in Japanese-occupied Singapore Harbour occurred between

September and October 1943. The Z Special Force team included four British and 11 Australian service personnel disguised as Malay fishermen. The team travelled from Exmouth to an island close to Singapore in a captured boat, renamed the MV *Krait*. This was a 20-metre-long, slow-moving, wooden-hulled vessel with sporadic engine trouble. On reaching the designated island, the team launched their canoes, paddled into Singapore Harbour and proceeded to attach limpet mines to the ships in harbour. They then paddled another 80 kilometres to rendezvous with *Krait* six days later. When the mines exploded, seven ships were sank or badly damaged. The *Krait* recovered the team and returned to Exmouth a couple of weeks later.[30]

The success of Operation Jaywick prompted a follow-on and more ambitious Operation Rimau in September and October 1944, but the mission ended in tragedy when the vessel was approached and the team opened fire. With the element of surprise gone, the mission was abandoned. In seeking to escape back to the rendezvous point, all of the 23 members were tracked down and killed by the Japanese.[31]

The occasional dramatic success had come with other such notable disappointments. The initial progress against the Japanese in Portuguese Timor, for instance, was cause for encouragement. But as Japanese pressure mounted successive operations were compromised and defeated in detail, and it became clear that piecemeal special operations were unlikely to generate significant momentum for victory in Timor. The early successes also were seen by many to be largely negated by the eventual abandonment of efforts there and the retributions suffered by the Timorese at the hands of the Japanese.[32] Many of the submarine-supported clandestine insertions around the islands of the Netherlands East Indies also generated considerable backlash by Japanese forces against collaborators.[33] This was a high price to pay as there was little evidence of long-term strategic benefits to the Allied cause beyond tying down Japanese occupation forces.

In light of the variable successes and the unusual collection of international components within the AIB, it is not surprisingly therefore, that it was quickly disbanded once the war was over. Still, the experience of special operations and the perceived need to maintain such a capability for *in extremis* circumstances would resonate in Australian defence and security policymakers' minds for generations. In fact, after the war the special operations function would be performed by Commandos and by the Special Air Service once it was formed in 1957. Only a limited capability remained as part of the mandate of the Australian Secret Intelligence Service, but even that would be curtailed after the botched Sheraton Hotel raid in 1983.

CENTRAL BUREAU AND SIGNALS INTELLIGENCE

Without question, the AIB provided significant intelligence support to the Allied cause.[34] But the accomplishments of the Central Bureau were in a league of their own. The Central Bureau was a secretive signals intelligence codebreaking unit focused on sigint that was established in Melbourne in April 1942. Established by the Australian Signal Officer-in-Chief, Major General Colin Simpson, drawing on the Army Special Wireless Group, and by MacArthur's Chief Signal Officer, Brigadier-General (later Major-General) Spencer Akin. Unlike the AIB, which reported to the G2, Willoughby, the Central Bureau reported to headquarters through Akin. This separate reporting line led to considerable friction and hampered coordination and dissemination of all-source intelligence reports.[35]

By September 1942, the Central Bureau had moved to Brisbane. In terms of cryptanalysis, this was the SWPA equivalent of Britain's Bletchley Park. The bureau was widely regarded by those briefed to know as 'stunningly successful', and the intelligence it gathered played an important role in operations ranging from New Guinea up to the Philippines.[36] The Central Bureau had four tasks: providing radio intelligence derived from Japanese military signals, ensuring Allied communications security in the SWPA under MacArthur's command, collaboration with the US Navy's Signal Intelligence Service in Washington to solve Japanese Army codes; and the supply and exchange of intelligence with the US Navy.[37]

By 1943 over 1000 men and women worked as part of the Central Bureau, with more than 100 intercept stations and other supporting sigint facilities established in and around Australia. Organising this sigint network had been what Ball and Horner call an 'outstanding achievement' and one that would pay rich dividends on the battlefield.[38] By May 1945, when its advanced headquarters moved to Manila, there were over 4000 people involved. The number of staff assigned pointed to the confidence authorities placed in the reliability and utility of Central Bureau's reports. In fact, as Horner observed, the Allied successes against the Japanese fleet in the battle of the Coral Sea and Midway as well as the shooting down of Admiral Yamamoto and the enormous successes of Allied submarines 'can all be attributed to cryptanalysis'.[39] In essence, effective and precise targeting was facilitated by sigint, which identified enemy schedules and routes in advance.

There were numerous instances of sigint tip-offs making a real difference to the outcome of combat actions. For instance, in June 1944 the Central Bureau reported an imminent Japanese attack against an isolated Allied position at Aitape. The news was surprising but came in time for reinforcements to bolster the position and ensure the Japanese were soundly defeated. In the words of the official report, this was 'a brilliant example of the tactical application of this type of secret information'.[40] But there were occasions when intelligence assessments arrived too late or proved inaccurate.

MacArthur was always extremely sensitive to criticism of their intelligence estimates, so he sought to restrict the flow of intelligence to London and Washington. He was also anxious to avoid passing it to Australians who might inform London. MacArthur didn't want the Australians having a standalone intelligence assessments capability that he didn't control. So the Central Bureau was established with 50 per cent staffing by US Army and Air Force personnel and the other 50 per cent by Australian Army and Air Force personnel, but under US control. Recognising the significance of the sigint capability, Australia continued to try to provide around 50 per cent of the people to run the Central Bureau. This was at least in part an effort to ensure that if the Australian component was separated it could form a viable organisation.[41]

The Bureau's Australian Army component came mostly from the Australian Special Wireless Group, which had been established at Bonegilla in Victoria to recruit and train intercept operators in the field. Australian Army and RAAF personnel together with US Intelligence personnel who escaped from the Philippines and some British military personnel who had escaped from Singapore became part of what was to be the most important but most secret section of intelligence work. Their job was to research and decode army and air intercept traffic and work in close cooperation with sigint centres in the United Kingdom, United States and India.[42] Canada also contributed an army unit, supplying No. 1 Special Wireless Group, which operated in Darwin.[43]

Interestingly, though, MacArthur so valued the work of the Central Bureau that he ensured their participation in the Philippines Campaign from May 1945 onwards – at a time when no other Australian land force units were committed on operations in the Philippines.[44] Indeed, despite MacArthur's foibles, the utility of British–US sigint cooperation, and its extension to the three Commonwealth countries of Canada, Australia and New Zealand, would be an enduring legacy of the wartime international sigint cooperation.

SECTION 22

Yet another Allied intelligence group was Section 22, which was responsible for radar and radio countermeasures, at times operating behind enemy lines. In essence its functions revolved around technical and geolocation intelligence derived from non-communications electronic radiations. This would come to be known as electronics intelligence or ELINT. In essence Section 22 collected Japanese radar signatures, which, once ascertained, could help warn Allied units of approaching enemy aircraft and ships. Section 22 was responsible to GHQ and operated separately from Central Bureau, but like Central Bureau it reported through the Chief Signals Officer rather than the G2. It included at least two field units; Section 22 employed RAAF and Women's Australian Air Force personnel to collect information on Japanese radar and radio systems, analyse and disseminate the resulting intelligence and requisition and assign electronic countermeasures/reconnaissance personnel and equipment. By mid-1943, Section 22 was assembling a detailed picture of the Japanese radar network.[45]

Section 22 came to realise the effectiveness of electronic warfare (EW) collection operations using EW-dedicated US Army Air Force B-24 Ferret aircraft. This then forced the US Navy operating nearby in the Pacific theatre into a similar mode of operation. Section 22 also operated PBY-5A (Black Cat) Catalina seaplanes that were modified for electronic reconnaissance using ARC-1 receivers equipped with a direction-finding antenna system. The Black Cats operated in New Guinea, flying electronic reconnaissance missions from the seaplane bases at Port Moresby and the Samari Islands. The B-24D Ferret was also equipped with the SCR-587 receiver and a developmental version of a radar pulse analyser which became a vital tool to assist the airborne operators in identifying the type of enemy radar being intercepted.[46]

FLEET RADIO UNIT, MELBOURNE

Fleet Radio Unit, Melbourne (FRUMEL) was another critical intelligence unit, but it was separate and distinct from Central Bureau, drawing on British elements from Singapore, US elements from Corregidor in the Philippines and Australia's Eric Nave and his team from (and subsequently absorbing) the Special Intelligence Bureau. FRUMEL was a United States–Australian–British signals intelligence unit, based in Melbourne.[47] Much of the deciphering work was undertaken by members of the Women's Royal Australian Naval Service.[48]

At the height of the war FRUMEL maintained four intercept stations at Moorabin (near Brisbane), Cooktown (in north Queensland, covering Solomon and Gilbert Islands), at Exmouth Gulf (Western Australia) and Adelaide River (South of Darwin) with the latter two also used for high-frequency radio direction finding.[49] The station at Adelaide River, for instance, was established in 1943 and tasked to intercept radio communications from across the archipelago from Singapore to Makassar to Manila. By May 1945, the station employed 73 enlisted personnel and three officers. Sixty-eight were operations personnel, with 43 assigned to intercept, eight each to teletype and 'scrambler' operations, five to general service circuits and four supervisors. From March to August 1945 the stations reportedly intercepted an average of 760 messages per day.[50]

Unlike Central Bureau, FRUMEL was under US Navy control and appears to have had an acrimonious relationship with Central Bureau. It was one of two major Allied signals intelligence units, called Fleet Radio Units, in the Pacific theatre, the other unit being FRUPAC (also known as Station HYPO), in Hawaii. FRUMEL played a significant role in supporting the Battle of the Coral Sea, reporting on Japanese intentions and actions. But there were some difficulties with the arrangement. FRUMEL, as an inter-Navy organisation, was subordinate to the Commander of the US Seventh Fleet. Part of the difficulty arose because the reporting chain was to Hawaii and not to anyone in MacArthur's headquarters. In addition, the US Navy officer in charge, Lieutenant Commander Rudolph Fabian, was known to be ill-disposed to the British and to the Central Bureau's Commander Eric Nave. Some speculated the Americans wanted to dominate Japanese naval cryptography at the expense of the British. The confluence of factors led to FRUMEL gaining notoriety for its lack of cooperation or helpfulness to Central Bureau, despite its evident utility for naval operations in the Pacific theatre.[51]

ALLIED TRANSLATOR AND INTERPRETER SERVICE

In order to ensure a comprehensive intelligence capability in the SWPA, GHQ SWPA needed to be able to understand what was being collected in documents, interrogations and over the airwaves. For this, additional services like translators and interpreters were required. These functions were performed by the Allied Translator and Interpreter Service, a joint Australian–US Second World War intelligence agency which served as a centralised Allied intelligence unit for the translation of intercepted Japanese communications, interrogations and negotiations in the SWPA between September 1942 and December 1945. The service originally consisted of 25 officers and 10 enlisted men, and grew rapidly along with the scope of its operations, supported by a language school established at Point Cook, near Melbourne. At the height of operations in 1945 almost 4000 men and women were employed of whom most were second-generation Japanese Americans, known as Nisei.[52]

Several notable events occurred during its operation, including the translation and analysis of the captured Z-Plan[53] in 1944. This was an outline of Japan's defensive plans against Allied attacks on its Pacific territories, such as the Mariana Islands in the northwest Pacific. These translated documents proved of immense value. The Allied Translator and Interpreter Service also interpreted millions of captured documents, intercepted messages and interrogated thousands of Japanese prisoners of war during the Second World War.[54] During the last few months of operations and after the Japanese surrender the primary focus was on the investigation of Japanese war crimes, where the service played a pivotal role.

ALLIED GEOGRAPHICAL SECTION

The Allied Geographical Section was another important adjunct to the Allied intelligence capabilities. Established in July 1942, the section was tasked to undertake terrain studies to include maps and photographs of the areas to which Australian troops might be sent. The Allied Geographic Section was predominantly an Australian–US Army unit, with representatives from the other two services as well as the Dutch. The unit was devoted to the collection and collation of information of geographical significance. Its primary task was to provide basic geographical information and detailed terrain appreciations for the use of operational commands and combat forces. They prepared maps, guidebooks and terrain profiles were an integral part of the Allied intelligence set-up.[55] Starting in Melbourne, the unit subsequently moved to Brisbane. From 1943 onwards the RAAF also played an important role, supplying mainly photo-technicians, typists and draftsmen.[56] This was linked to the important work the RAAF undertook in the realm of air intelligence.

AIR INTELLIGENCE

RAAF wireless units were some of the most significant intelligence elements operated by the RAAF. They were tasked with the interception of enemy air communications which provided vital warning of Japanese aerial attacks on northern Australia. Later, these units followed General MacArthur's forces to the Philippines.[57] By the end of the war the RAAF had five wireless units operating in Darwin, Hollandia and the Philippines.[58] The army likewise had wireless units operating in Darwin and New Guinea.

The Air Industry Section was another group tasked with identifying enemy aircraft production volumes and sites through the decoding of aircraft name plates. This section deduced that aircraft engine production facilities were a critical vulnerability and subsequently made a priority bombing target.[59]

The Central Interpretation Unit was another significant air intelligence unit focused on photographic interpretation, three-dimensional terrain modelling and 'flak intelligence'. The unit housed photographic inter-preters, graphic artists, support personnel and a printing capability, including a mix of Australian service personnel as well as other nationalities. The unit's main location was in Brisbane, but later in the war it had teams in Morotai and Lae.[60] Flak intelligence included the creation of mosaics showing the disposition of enemy anti-aircraft positions to inform tactics.[61]

The Allied Technical Air Intelligence Unit was yet another wartime creation. This unit was tasked to investigate Japanese air technical cap-abilities and trends by obtaining crashed or abandoned Japanese aircraft and equipment from wherever they could be recovered in the SWPA. Teams would be sent to newly captured airfields to investigate Japanese aircraft before souvenir hunters could strip the aircraft of valuable com-ponents. Captured aircraft and wrecks were inspected, all name plates removed, airframes measured, engines disassembled for examination, changes in cockpit layout recorded and, in some cases, entire aircraft were sent back to Australia for more detailed analysis.[62]

By 1943, the RAAF had reconnaissance versions of the Lockheed P-38 Lightning, the F-4A, on strength for photo-reconnaissance missions in New Guinea. Air Force Intelligence Officers who had access to Ultra code-breaking considered photographic interpretation as 'probably the most valuable source of intelligence'.[63] Some claimed that '80 per cent of all intelligence in World War II came from aerial intelligence'.[64] This is a debateable figure, but even if it is discounted in part as an exaggeration expressed by practitioners, photo intelligence was still significant. Their efforts formed the foundation for post-war photo-reconnaissance capability fostered in the RAAF. While the RAAF developed such niche intelligence capabilities, the army was also required to perform a range of intelligence and security functions in support of dispersed land combat units.

ARMY INTELLIGENCE IN THE FIELD

Army intelligence cells were to be found at the various levels of head-quarters up and down the army's chain of command across all theatres of operations and all types of formations. This included intelligence staff at battalion headquarters, and at successive higher headquarters at brigade, division, corps and army levels. Battalion level staff, for instance, would draw on the patrol reports from their own companies and platoons to piece together a picture of what the enemy's capabilities, dispositions and intentions were. Captured enemy prisoners of war would face interrogation with the support of translators from the Allied Translator and Interpreter Service. These reports helped commanders to understand the enemy's capabilities and intentions. These were supplemented by reports passed from flanking units and higher headquarters. The reports emanating from the work undertaken by RAAF aerial photography and imagery analysts proved handy on numerous instances as well, particularly for the planning of operations. Higher-level headquarters intelligence staff would study trends in enemy actions and capabilities to discern changes in weapons and tactics that could then inform Australian and Allied tactics and techniques. They would then prepare intelligence bulletins for broad dissemination to help ensure units and formations stayed abreast with the latest developments.[65]

The intelligence picture was also supplemented by maps provided by the Allied Geographical Section and, at times, radio intercepts of Japanese actions and locations provided by units from the Army Special Wireless Group linked to the Central Bureau. Army's special wireless units sometimes delivered remarkable results, occasionally with the help of accidental discoveries. In January 1944, for instance, the 9th Australian Division captured the site of the 20th Japanese Division at Sio on the north coast of New Guinea. The Division's crypt library, with all the major codebooks of the high command system – minus their covers which had been returned for 'destruction' – had been abandoned in a deep water-filled pit. With the covers accounted for, the Japanese considered the material to have been destroyed and did not fear compromise. Consequently for two full months the Japanese messages could be read immediately on receipt. Although subsequent changes were introduced, they were frequently passed over the wireless, making it relatively easy to keep up with the code changes.[66] This provided the Allied land forces operating in the area a remarkable advantage.

'Field security', involved efforts by army intelligence corps personnel to ensure compliance with security regulations to protect operational security. This was intended to complement and not duplicate the internal security work of the Commonwealth Government's Security Service (the precursor to the present day Australian Security Intelligence Organisation

(ASIO).[67] In the line of communications and rear echelon areas around Australia, such concerns remained the priority for field security sections. Complementing their work, the Army Special Wireless Group Type C Sections monitored Allied communications for security purposes and Type D Sections developed counter measures against clandestine missions within Australia – although there was admittedly 'very little subversive broadcasting within Australia during the war'.[68] Still, security about sensitive intelligence sources was of the highest concern, notably around protecting Ultra and an even more secret discovery – Venona.

ULTRA LEAKS AND THE VENONA SECRET

The British and the Americans established Special Security Officers stationed at all headquarters for the safe transmission and handling of Ultra material. At Hollandia on 22 November 1944, the US Special Security Officer informed General Berryman that Ultra signals showed that by 11 November Tokyo knew the Allied estimates of Japanese forces in the Philippines. Furthermore, the figures related to those that had appeared in the *Australian Military Forces Weekly Review* No. 118.[69]

The leaks next appeared to have come from a Department of Information circular sourced to the Soviet Ambassador in Australia. The Soviets were not yet at war with Japan. Messages sent from Canberra or Sydney to the Soviet Consulate in Harbin, Manchuria, could easily have been acquired by the Japanese. The British Head of the Ultra Security Liaison Unit, Group Captain Frederick Winterbotham, arrived in Brisbane on a world tour to inspect the security of Ultra transmissions. He considered the leakages had global implications.[70]

The secrecy of Venona – the Allied cryptanalytic operation that exposed Soviet espionage activities during the war – was even greater than that accorded Ultra. During the war it had been necessary to distribute Ultra to dozens of US, British, Australian and other commands and agencies, on a worldwide scale and in an expeditious manner. The only people who needed to know about Venona, however, were the cryptanalysts and the sigint personnel who supported them in obtaining, decrypting and translating Soviet traffic, and those intelligence and counter-espionage personnel who were directly involved in exploitation of the Venona material.[71]

The Australian government was apprised of the information leaks in January 1945. Sigint activities, involving the interception and decryption of foreign signals, had definitely proved the leakages, but their method and origin remained to be ascertained. Within four years, however, US and

British cryptanalysts had decrypted substantial portions of the KGB cable traffic between Moscow and Canberra from 1943 to 1948. These decrypts provided an extraordinary picture of Soviet espionage activities in Australia, including the identities of the Australian agents and contacts involved.[72]

In their book, *Breaking the Codes*, published in 1998, Desmond Ball and David Horner made clear, using documentary archival material, that allegations of security breaches were not trumped up, that there was a real espionage ring and that ASIO would be subsequently established specifically to deal with it.[73] This was elaborated upon in Horner's *The Spy Catchers*, the first volume in a three-volume official history of ASIO.[74]

CONCLUSION

This chapter has argued that good intelligence proved to be one of the most important elements of wartime decision-making. During the Second World War, Australia advanced from a position of being almost totally dependent upon British intelligence to a point where it had relatively large and effective intelligence organisations integrated with counterpart Allied organisations. This was a substantial achievement that was to have important repercussions for the future.[75]

Australia's experience with special operations left a mixed legacy. Special operations had generated spectacular and morale-boosting successes. But operations often unravelled and led to many otherwise-avoidable deaths with little direct strategic effect on the course of the war. When created in the early 1950s, ASIS would be tasked with maintaining a residual special operations authority for wartime. Over time and following the establishment of a counter-terrorism capability within the Army's special forces, that function would be transferred away from ASIS.

It is noteworthy that the Allied Intelligence Bureau, the Allied Geographical Section, the Allied Translator and Interpreter Service and the Central Bureau were all built upon Australian foundations and most would have organisations with functions that echoed theirs a generation later in what was to emerge as the Australian Intelligence Community. Although MacArthur's headquarters had the responsibility for their overall control, Australia provided the majority of personnel, and catered for most of their needs. The increasingly accurate and voluminous intelligence enabled confident and precise decision-making on the employment of military forces. If the major decisions of 1941 and 1942 were based on inexact knowledge, by mid-1943 and into 1944 and 1945 the government could be sure that not only was Australia secure, but that victory was assured.[76]

Of enduring significance was that virtually all of the major national intelligence and security agencies had their antecedents in this period. This included ASIO, ASIS, the Defence Intelligence Organisation, the Australian Signals Directorate and even the Australian Geo-spatial Intelligence Organisation (echoing the work of the Allied geographical section and air intelligence). In addition, all were intimately linked with their Allied counterparts and were to be quite dependent on them for the provision of much of the raw data but also for a considerable portion of its assessment. In 1947 much of this relationship was codified in the then highly secret UK–USA Agreement, to which Australia, Canada and New Zealand were included.[77] Having developed unprecedented specialist intelligence capabilities throughout the war, the services intelligence components also retained residual elements of most of these capabilities. In the years that followed, as Australia grappled towards a more self-reliant security posture, many of these capabilities would be called upon again, repeatedly. While decades would pass before the achievements recounted here could be publicly revealed, Australia emerged from the war with a relatively advanced national intelligence architecture – one which would play an important but discreet role in support of Australia's efforts to engage with what was called the 'Far East' – but which for Australia was the near north.

FURTHER READING

Desmond Ball and Keiko Tamura, *Breaking Japanese Diplomatic Codes: David Sissons and D Special Section during the Second World War*, Asian Studies Series Monograph 4, ANU Press, Canberra, 2013.

Desmond Ball and David Horner, *Breaking the Codes: Australia's KGB Network*, Allen & Unwin, Sydney, 1998.

Geoffrey Ballard, *On Ultra Active Service: The Story of Australia's Signals Intelligence Operations During World War II*, Spectrum, Melbourne, 1991.

Jean Bou, *MacArthur's Secret Bureau: The Story of the Central Bureau General MacArthur's Signals Intelligence Organisation*, Australian Military History Publications, Loftus, 2012.

Reuben R.E. Bowd, *A Basis for Victory: The Allied Geographical Section, 1942–1946*, Canberra papers on Strategy and Defence No. 157, Strategic and Defence Studies Centre, ANU Press, Canberra, 2005.

David Horner, *The Spy Catchers: The Official History of ASIO, 1949–1963*, Allen & Unwin, Sydney, 2014.

Ian Pfennigwerth, *A Man of Intelligence: The Life of Captain Eric Nave Australian Codebreaker Extraordinary*, Rosenberg, Dural, 2006.

Alan Powell, *War by Stealth: Australians and the Allied Intelligence Bureau 1942–1945*, Melbourne University Press, Melbourne, 1996.

Judy Thomson, *Winning with Intelligence: A Biography of Brigadier John David Rogers, CBE, MC, 1895–1978*, Australian Military History Publications, Loftus, 2000.

F.W. Winterbotham, *The Ultra Secret*, Weidenfeld and Nicholson, London, 1974.

Notes

1 Gavin Long, *Australia in the War of 1939–1945: The Final Campaigns*, Australian War Memorial, Canberra, 1963.

2 F.W. Winterbotham, *The Ultra Secret*, Weidenfeld and Nicholson, London, 1974.

3 Desmond Ball & David Horner, *Breaking the Codes*, Allen & Unwin, Sydney, 1998, p. 3.

4 Ibid.; and F.H. Hinsley and Alan Stripp, *Code Breakers: The Inside Story of Bletchley Park*, Oxford University Press, Oxford, 1993.

5 Ball and Horner, *Breaking the Codes*, p. 3. For details of the critical operational value of Ultra see Geoffrey Ballard, *On Ultra Active Service: The Story of Australia's Signals Intelligence Operations During World War II*, Spectrum Publications, Melbourne, 1991, pp. 253–61.

6 David. Horner, *High Command: Australia and Allied Strategy, 1939–1945*, Allen & Unwin, Sydney, 1982, p. 225.

7 Ball and Horner, *Breaking the Codes*, p. 19.

8 The Australian Military Forces were not formally called 'The Australian Army' until after the Second World War. Hence the 'Australian army' is referred to here informally in lower case as short hand for the Australian Commonwealth Military Forces.

9 Ibid., p. 20.

10 Ibid., p. 38. See Judy Thomson, *Winning with Intelligence*, AMHP, Canberra, 2000.

11 See Desmond Ball and Keiko Tamura (eds), *Breaking Japanese Diplomatic Codes: David Sissons and D Special Section during the Second World War*, Asian Studies Series monograph 4, ANU E Press, Canberra, 2013, pp. 15–51.

12 David Horner, 'Special Intelligence in the South-West Pacific Area in World War II', *Australian Outlook*, vol.32, no.3, 1978, p. 310; and Ball and Horner, *Breaking the Codes*, p. 52.

13 See Ballard, *On Ultra Active Service*.

14 Horner, *High Command,* p. 226; and Thomson, *Winning with Intelligence*, p. 138.

15 Edward J. Drea, *MacArthur's ULTRA: Codebreaking and the War against Japan 1942–1945*, p. 54, cited in Alan Powell, *War by Stealth: Australians and the Allied Intelligence Bureau 1942–1945*, Melbourne University Press, Melbourne, 1996, p. 48.

16 Ball and Horner, *Breaking the Codes,* p. 49.

17 For a biography of the life of Captain Eric Nave see Ian Pfennigwerth, *A Man of Intelligence*, Rosenberg, Dural, 2006.

18 Pfennigwerth, *A Man of Intelligence*, pp. 153–77.

19 Horner, *High Command*, p. 237.

20 Douglas Gillison, *Royal Australian Air Force 1939–1942*, Australian War Memorial, Canberra, 1962, p. 93.

21 Thomson, *Winning with Intelligence*, p. 138.

22 Ball and Horner, *Breaking the Codes*, p. 38.

23 Ibid., p. 39.

24 Horner, *High Command*, p. 225; and Thomson, *Winning with Intelligence*, p. 138.

25 Ball and Horner, *Breaking the Codes,* p. 37.

26 Powell, *War By Stealth*, p. 24.

27 Ibid., p. 25; Peter Dunn, Australian's at War www.ozatwar.com/sigint/aib.htm, retrieved 14 November 2014; and 'Special Operator', RAN, 'The Story of FELO', *As You Were, 1949*, pp. 68–72.

28 Powell, *War by Stealth*, p. 358.

29 Ibid.

30 Operation Jaywick, 'The Raid on Singapore Harbour', Australian War Memorial, www.awm.gov.au/encyclopedia/operation_jaywick/, retrieved 15 November 2014.

31 Powell, *War by Stealth*, pp. 124–31.

32 Ibid., pp. 132–50.

33 Ibid., pp. 151–81.

34 Horner, *High Command*, p. 237; and Ball and Horner, *Breaking the Codes*, p. 37.

35 Horner, *High Command*, p. 227.

36 See Jean Bou, *MacArthur's Secret Bureau*, AMHP, Loftus, 2012. Central Bureau files are at NAA B5436, MP 508/1, A6923, A816 and A649.

37 Ball and Horner, *Breaking the Codes*, p. 64.

38 Ibid., p. 66.

39 Horner, 'Special Intelligence in the South-West Pacific Area in World War II', p. 315.

40 Special Intelligence Bulletin no. 417, 27/28 June 1944 cited in Horner, 'Special Intelligence in the South-West Pacific Area in World War II', *Australian Outlook*, p. 322.
41 Horner, *High Command*, pp. 242–3.
42 Thomson, *Winning with Intelligence*, p. 141.
43 Horner, *High Command*, p. 243.
44 Horner, 'Special Intelligence in the South-West Pacific Area in World War II', p. 324.
45 See Kevin Davies, 'Field Unit 12 Takes New Technology to War in the Southwest Pacific', *Studies in Intelligence*, vol. 58, no. 3, September 2014, pp. 11–20; and Horner, *High Command*, p. 237.
46 See 'Section 22' at www.ozatwar.com/sigint/section22.htm, retrieved on 14 November 2014; and 'RAAF Command – Establishment – Section 22', NAA A11093/320/3J5.
47 Bou, *MacArthur's Secret Bureau*, pp. 7–8.
48 FRUMEL Records NAA B555; and World War Two – FRUMEL, Women's Royal Australian Naval Service Officers, NAA A10909/3.
49 Desmond Ball, 'Fleet Radio Unit Melbourne (FRUMEL) 28 June 1943 – 2 September 1945', unpublished manuscript.
50 Report, 'SRH-316 US Navy Supplementary Radio Station Adelaide River Northern Territory Australia 23 March 1943 – 21 September 1945', NARA (copy held by author).
51 Bou, *MacArthur's Secret Bureau*, pp. 7–8 and 43–44; and Pfennigwerth, *A Man of Intelligence*, pp. 169 and 186–9.
52 See Allison B. Gilmore, 'The Allied Translator and Interpreter Section: The Critical Role of Allied Linguists in the Process of Propaganda Creation, 1943–1944', in Peter Dennis & Jeffrey Grey (eds.), *The Foundations of Victory: The Pacific War 1943–1944*, Army History Unit, Canberra, 2004, pp. 149–67; and Kieran Laurence Miles, 'A History of the Allied Translator and Interpreter Section Southwest Pacific Area WW II', Postgraduate Dip Arts thesis, University of Queensland, 1993.
53 Greg Bradsher, 'The "Z Plan" Story Japan's 1944 Naval Battle Strategy Drifts into US Hands', *Prologue Magazine Fall 2005*, vol. 37, no 3. www.archives.gov/publications/prologue/2005/fall/z-plan-1.html, retrieved 15 November 2014.
54 Gilmore, 'The Allied Translator and Interpreter Section'.
55 Reuben Bowd, *A Basis for Victory: The Allied Geographical Section 1942–1946*, ANU, SDSC, Canberra, 2005.
56 Ibid., pp. 11–17, 34.
57 Jack Bleakley, *The Eavesdroppers*, Australian Government Publishing Service, Canberra, 1992; and Jack Brown, 'Katakana

Man', 2006, http://airpower.airforce.gov.au/Publications/Details/246/Katakana-Man.aspx, retrieved 17 November 2014.

58 Ball and Horner, *Breaking the Codes*, p. 64.

59 See N. B. Tindale, 'History of Air Industry Section', AWM 173, 9/25.

60 'Intelligence Reports, Headquarters Allied Air Forces SWPA Directorate of Intelligence Central Interpretation Unit, AWM 54, 423/6/20.

61 Report, 'History of Flakintel – Section RAAF 1944', AWM 54, 32/9/5 and 32/9/7.

62 Report, 'Allied Technical Air Intelligence Unit – A General History', NAA A9696/603.

63 John F. Kreis (ed.) *Piercing the Fog*, Air Force History and Museums Program, Bolling, DC, 1996, p. 80 (http://www.afhso.af.mil/shared/media/document/AFD-101203–023.pdf, retrieved 14 November 2014).

64 Roy M. Stanley II, *World War II Photo Intelligence*, Scribner, New York, 1981, p. 3.

65 See the AWM54 record series.

66 Ballard, *On Ultra Active Service*, p. 194.

67 LHQ Intelligence Instructions no. 31, *Field Security Wing – Australian Intelligence Corps, August 1944*, Museum of Australian Military Intelligence (MAMI), Canungra.

68 Ballard, *On Ultra Active Service*, p. 233.

69 Berryman Diary, 22 November 1944, AWM PR84/370, Item 4, cited in Thomson, *Winning with Intelligence*, p. 186.

70 Thomson, *Winning with Intelligence*, p. 187.

71 Ball and Horner, *Breaking the Codes, p. 5*.

72 Ibid., p. xiv.

73 Ibid., p. xvii.

74 David Horner, *The Spy Catchers: The Official History of ASIO from 1949 to 1963*, Allen & Unwin, Sydney, 2014.

75 Horner, *High Command*, p. 246.

76 Ibid.

77 Desmond, J. Ball, 'Allied Intelligence Cooperation Involving Australia during World War II', *Australian Outlook*, vol. 32, no. 3, 1978, p. 299.

PART 4

THE NAVAL AND AIR WAR

CHAPTER 8

THE RAN AT WAR, 1944−45

Ian Pfennigwerth

The dawn of 1944 revealed a Royal Australian Navy (RAN) still spread across several theatres of operations. While the last Australian ships had been withdrawn from the Mediterranean after the invasion of Sicily in 1943, a number of RAN officers and men remained serving with British and Canadian forces in the Atlantic and Mediterranean. Many were to be decorated for their gallantry in the series of amphibious landings, commencing at Anzio in January 1944, Normandy in June 1944, the South of France in August 1944 and in several smaller operations along the eastern coast of Italy as the allies pushed to reduce the defensive lines fiercely contested by the Germans. Several Australian naval personnel were, unfortunately, to lose their lives in these operations, while others fought on and under the sea to defeat the Germans. A few examples will illustrate the contribution made by the RAN in bringing the European war to its conclusion.

In a British midget submarine Lieutenant Hudspeth RANVR (RAN Volunteer Reserve) took reconnaissance parties onto Normandy D-Day beaches and then on D-Day endured the uncomfortable experience of acting as a beacon to guide the landing forces onto the beaches while under fire from both friend and foe. Lieutenant Thomas Foggitt, RANVR, a veteran of the Dieppe raid in 1943, won a Distinguished Service Cross for his gallantry in taking command of his landing craft when the commanding officer was hit and, although wounded himself, pressing on with the task of landing Royal Marines against ferocious German opposition at Walcheren Island near Antwerp in 1944. RANVR Lieutenant

Commander Stanley Darling and two bars set an unequalled record by sinking three German submarines in the space of six months in the Atlantic in his Royal Navy frigate, while the men of the Render Mine Safe force continued to win awards for bravery both in the United Kingdom and, as the Allied forces advanced into Europe, in the ports which were liberated from the Germans. A George Cross was awarded to Lieutenant George Gosse RANVR for his gallantry and technical skill on the day following the German surrender, when he successfully defused one of the deadly German 'Oyster' pressure-activated mines in Bremen Harbour. Several of these officers returned to Australia in 1944–45 and were involved in the countermeasure operations against ordnance and booby traps left by the Japanese in New Guinea and the Philippines.[1]

At home and abroad, the RAN continued to grow. With more than 35,000 men and women in naval uniform, it was manning 324 vessels and 10,000 shore positions and had over 3000 officers and men serving with other navies. In the pipeline were another destroyer, more corvettes, a new class of 22 frigates and 17 minor war vessels. The Navy wanted more: discussions on the transfer of an aircraft carrier and a modern cruiser from the Royal Navy were underway, and six more destroyers had also been offered. These would require an increase in RAN strength of about 5000, but the Australian government had serious concerns over manpower. The RAN was told 'steady as she goes', while efforts were made to build up the Royal Australian Air Force (RAAF) to 53 squadrons and the Army began to demobilise from January 1944 to meet civilian demands for workers. These decisions – setting an upper limit of six divisions for the Army – were reinforced following meetings in London in May 1944, even though the War Cabinet had agreed to construct an additional cruiser for the RAN. A modest increase in the RAN by 350 per month to December 1944 was all that the Chief of Naval Staff could extract from the politicians. The British offer of additional ships was held over for 12 months, and was finally declined in July 1945.

THE INDIAN OCEAN 1944

With the Army and Air Force largely committed to operations in the Southwest Pacific Area (SWPA), the importance of the Indian Ocean theatre in the conduct of the war can often be – and is – forgotten by Australians. The surrender of Italy in September 1943 opened the Mediterranean as a transit corridor for Allied shipping. This not only shortened the voyages to the Middle East, India and Southeast Asia, which had previously had to sail via the Cape of Good Hope, but it also proved a safer route across the Indian Ocean to Australia. In 1943 the Germans had dispatched a squadron of submarines – the Monsoon Group of 11 boats – to join their Japanese counterparts based on Penang in what is now Malaysia, whence the five survivors of the voyage were able to conduct a successful campaign against Allied shipping transiting the Indian Ocean. In mid to late 1943, losses in the Indian Ocean were the most severe of any theatre. The magnitude of the shipping using the area, including supplies being transferred to the USSR through Iran, is frequently underestimated; by December 1943 shipping sailed in convoy through the Straits of Hormuz topped 10,000,000 tons. The scale of the losses to German and Japanese attacks were a function of there being insufficient escorts for convoys and the complete absence of the kind of air support which was now routine for Atlantic shipping. Priority demands for escorts for the major amphibious operations planned and executed in the Atlantic and the Mediterranean soaked up the available resources. Not until these operations had been completed could ships be released to join the hard pressed British Eastern Fleet in tackling the submarine menace.

A similar observation applied to the Eastern Fleet itself, whose main strength of slow, over-age battleships had been carefully preserved out of harm's way in a defensive deployment against any possible descent by the Japanese upon the Bay of Bengal. The fleet counted in its strength six RAN destroyers and 13 Bathurst Class corvettes which, together with the few British destroyers that could be spared from other theatres and the ships of the Royal Indian Navy, attempted to meet the heavy demands placed upon them. There were occasional successes but, until a major expansion of the surface forces assigned to the Eastern Fleet in April 1944, convoying was a difficult and demanding task conducted in monsoonal conditions or in the restricted visibility in the vicinity of the Red Sea.

The Indian Ocean also featured in discussions on Allied combined strategy. The United States wanted to bring pressure upon the Japanese by supporting Chinese armies in central China through Burma. This theme in US planning since 1942 naturally appealed to the Chinese as well. However, to achieve this would have required the British to recapture Japanese-held territory. A British attempt to implement a modified advance into Burma from the sea was defeated in May 1943, after which the recapture of Burma in 1943–44 was not considered feasible. Nevertheless, efforts to improve upon the situation were underway, and in November 1943 Lord Louis Mountbatten assumed duty as Supreme Allied Commander Southeast Asia with his headquarters in New Delhi.

In a series of three conferences between Allied leaders in Cairo and then Teheran in November 1943 and again in Cairo in December between the British and Americans, the future course of the war in the Indian Ocean was debated. The outcomes of these summits were to influence the Australian Navy's contribution to the war. Mountbatten was not backward in putting forward plans for an amphibious assault on the Andaman Islands at the entrance to the Malacca Strait, a good jumping off point for an assault on Rangoon, at the Cairo conference in December that year, but this was deemed not possible because of the need to preserve landing craft for the European theatre. Thus the proposed Andaman operation was abandoned because of the lack of resources to carry it out, and this was only the first disagreement between the Allies on priorities for naval operations east of Suez. The most serious bone of contention was an American wish to confine the Royal Navy to operations in the Indian Ocean, a concept initially favoured by Prime Minister Churchill but not by his Chiefs of Staff. They believed that the Royal Navy should be involved in the assault against the Japanese Home Islands, which had to be weighed against the British desire to reclaim captured territories in Southeast Asia, but there was not sufficient force to do both. For the Americans, especially the Chief of Naval Operations, Admiral Ernest King, taking on the Japanese was a task for the United States alone. While these discussions were continuing, the Eastern Fleet began to receive substantial reinforcements.

This followed a disastrous first two months of 1944, when the Indian Ocean again earned the unhealthy distinction as the main theatre of Allied shipping losses. While these were not large in number, their cargoes were sorely missed in Southeast Asia Command as the Eastern Fleet planned a move forward from its African bases to Sri Lanka and a troop build-up for operations in Burma continued. At that point there were several successes against Japanese boats and the Germans began to make plans to withdraw their submarines in the role of blockade runners. The British advance was cautious: while the aim was to make its Sri Lankan base at Trincomalee secure, intelligence demonstrated that the Japanese still retained in Singapore a powerful force capable of overwhelming the Eastern Fleet. It was not obvious that the Japanese Navy's attention was firmly held by events in the central Pacific, and a raid by three Japanese cruisers in March through Sunda Strait, which resulted in the sinking of only one merchant ship, and the subsequent massacre of most of its passengers,[2] appeared to demonstrate determination to resist the British advance.[3] However, by the end of March the Royal Navy had reoccupied Trincomalee, where it was joined by US ships, including an aircraft carrier. On 23 April, the Eastern Fleet attacked Sabang at the tip of Sumatra in a diversionary attack to coincide with MacArthur's assault on Hollandia. Damage was done to Japanese ships and defences but there was no counterstroke. The Indian Ocean had slipped out of Japanese strategic calculations. A second diversionary attack made by the Eastern Fleet with US Navy reinforcement on Surabaya on 17 May as MacArthur's troops landed in Wakde was also successful, but the Australian Chief of Naval Staff judged it as of questionable military value. It also failed to divert Japanese attention from their main target – the US Pacific Fleet.

In June, a new squadron of seven German submarines was sent to the Indian Ocean. The promised British escorts did nothing immediately to solve this renewed problem being faced by Admiral Somerville. However, the submarine threat was about to collapse, with the Japanese pulling all but three of their boats out of Penang to go to the Pacific in accordance with their fleet doctrine of 'decisive battle'. Three German submarines were accounted for by the Eastern Fleet, and an aerial mine-laying campaign targeting Penang forced the remaining U-boats to withdraw to Jakarta in October. A final effort to transport strategic materials back to Germany by U-boat failed utterly, with all boats sunk on passage. The final successful attack of the war by an enemy submarine in the Indian Ocean was carried out by *U-862* on 5 February 1945.

At the request of Admiral King, with the aim of sowing confusion in Japanese minds, on 17 October the Eastern Fleet carried out a diversionary raid on Japanese bases in the Nicobar Islands as if in preparation for an amphibious assault, with air strikes and bombardments by cruisers and destroyers. Three RAN destroyers participated but the effort was only modestly successful and could not divert the Japanese attention from Leyte. What remained of the Combined Fleet was already steaming to meet its destiny in the Philippines Sea. Meanwhile, the land advance by the British Fourteenth Army into Burma necessitated the establishment of a maritime base to support its operations from the sea. Akyab was chosen because of its airfields and the British advanced by land with gunfire support from RAN destroyers *Napier* and *Nizam* from 17 December. On 3 January 1945, the two destroyers with other vessels carried an assault force to Akyab, with *Napier* having the honour of being the first British ship to enter the port since May 1942. During January and February, the Australian ships also participated in the occupation of Ramree and Cheduba Islands, which marked the end of the Burma campaign, but they then were detached to join the British Pacific Fleet.

The British Pacific Fleet

As the war continued, so did discussion on what the role of the Royal Navy should be in bringing the war with Japan to a close. Various strategies were proposed, including one for a British Empire assault to parallel that of MacArthur. It seems to have been an Australian suggestion that General MacArthur's lack of organic sea power could be filled by the British Fleet, which tilted the arguments towards a Pacific strategy in conjunction with the Americans. At the Octagon conference in Quebec in September 1944, Churchill made this offer to President Roosevelt. The President's reply – 'No sooner offered than accepted' – put an end to Admiral King's objections. It was now time for the British to make good on the offer.

The British desire to participate in naval operations in the Pacific had faced other problems besides Admiral King's active discouragement. The first was that the Fleet would need a base to provide it with major personnel, logistics and engineering support, airfields and aircraft maintenance facilities and ammunition depots; the only possible site for this would be Australia, with advanced bases further towards the Japanese islands. Thus, from April 1944 the British began a series of meetings in Australia to develop this concept. The second operational problem for the Royal Navy was that of the need for the fleet at sea to be supported by stores ships, tankers, ammunition ships, repair vessels, hospital ships and so forth, known by the general title of a 'fleet train'. Working out of bases in the British Isles, even on trans-Atlantic operations, British naval forces need not be accompanied by these vessels as the warships could be refuelled, rearmed and replenished on either side of that ocean. This was not possible in the Pacific. To bridge the gap between its bases in Australia and its area of operations close to Japan there would need to be considerable investment in ships to support the British fleet at sea, an issue of some magnitude.[4]

By August, the planned size of the British force was made clear – four modern battleships, six fleet carriers, 19 smaller carriers, 20 cruisers, up to 50 destroyers and around 100 escorts, plus the fleet train. Not all of these would be British; Australia would be asked to contribute destroyers and two flotillas of minesweeping corvettes as well as support ships. The British contingent would number 120,000 personnel of whom nearly 30,000 – virtually as large as the entire RAN – would be shore-based. This mass of men and machinery would begin to arrive in Australia in December 1944. A committee set up to examine the proposal and its ramifications recommended in November that the assistance that should be offered by Australia amounted to £21 million worth of goods and services and that around 4500 men and women would be required to deliver it.[5]

On 22 November 1944, the Eastern Fleet was disbanded and its assets transferred to the British Pacific Fleet under the command of Admiral Sir Bruce Fraser. The advance guard arrived in Fremantle on 10 December, with the remainder of the Fleet joining on 4 February 1945.

THE PACIFIC OCEAN 1944

In 1944, the two great Allied – essentially US – thrusts against the Japanese Empire in the Pacific were able to combine for the first time. The Quadrant conference in Québec in August 1943 had decided that the Japanese fortress of Rabaul should be isolated and bypassed. The landings at Cape Gloucester and Arawe at the western extremity of New Britain in December 1943, consolidated by early February 1944, had established the means to cut off Japanese forces there from support from the New Guinea mainland. The link-up of Australian and US forces at Saidor at the same time secured the western side of the vital Vitiaz Strait separating New Britain from New Guinea. The only source of support to the Japanese in Rabaul now available was from Truk, but on 17 February 1944 Admiral Nimitz ordered a massive air attack on this outpost by his Central Pacific carrier force. The success of this removed the possibility of reinforcement for Rabaul and its fighter protection was withdrawn to Truk two days later. Until the landing of the Australian 5th Division at Jacquinot Bay in November 1944, the Japanese forward positions were harried and over-run by a Melanesian guerrilla force led by RAN Coastwatchers, driving the enemy back behind fixed defences erected around the Gazelle Peninsula. With Rabaul neutralised, the Japanese submarine threat was also diminished; convoying south of Townsville was discontinued in February 1944.

The identification of bases to support naval assaults on Japanese-held territories was not only a matter for the British. Similar facilities had to be established to support the US-led advance across Central Pacific to the Philippines and from the Southwest Pacific to the same destination. For the Central Pacific forces, the island of Kwajalein in the Marshall Islands would be captured. The assault by a force of over 290 ships and 54,000 marines and soldiers on 31 January took a week to subdue the defenders with moderate losses to the attackers. Although the next attack, on Eniwetok, was not scheduled until March, Admiral Spruance committed his reserve from Kwajalein and assaulted the island on 17 February, the same date of the aerial attack on Truk. The assault was also successful, so by March the Marshall archipelago, which had been expected to present a major obstacle to the advance through the Central Pacific, had come under US control.

In SWPA it was agreed that Manus Island in the Admiralty Group would provide a secure fleet anchorage, the capacity to hold a large number of major ships and the land on which to construct the necessary support facilities, workshops, stores, ammunition dumps and airfields. MacArthur's Fifth Air Force had been conducting bombing operations against the Admiralty Islands from late January and reported no resistance and few signs of Japanese occupation. MacArthur thus committed the American 1st Cavalry Division to land in a 'reconnaissance in strength' on the 29 February. The naval supporting force assigned was Task Force 74, comprising Australian and US cruisers and destroyers, commanded by Royal Navy Rear Admiral Crutchley. In the attack its destroyers would provide naval gunfire support to suppress Japanese defences while the troops would land from US Navy destroyer transports of Admiral Barbey's VII Amphibious Force, MacArthur's means of delivering amphibious assaults. The initial lodgement was successful, but the Japanese put up an unexpectedly stout resistance. Reinforcements and more destroyers under the command of RAN Captain Emil Dechaineux attempted to force the passage into the magnificent Seadler Harbour by destroying Japanese defences, but the Japanese played 'possum' and resumed their fire on the US troops once the destroyers had been withdrawn. The matter was resolved after three reinforcement echelons of troops had been landed and Crutchley's cruisers were assigned to the task, which secured the entrance to the harbour and allowed the minesweeping force to conduct its operations in preparation for the arrival of major naval forces. In commenting on the support his troops had received, the divisional commander made the laconic remark that 'The Navy didn't support us, they saved our necks!'

Manus was secured by 3 April at a cost of over 1200 US casualties, and within a few weeks it was on track to become a major naval base. By September, anchorages for 44 capital ships, 104 cruisers and 114 destroyers had been established and there were 37,000 personnel in the area manning hospitals, stores, repair facilities, messing and recreation facilities and staffs. There was even a floating dock capable of taking 100,000-ton ships.

For Task Force 74, the Admiralties operations brought to a close a period of leave and refitting in Sydney in preparation for the amphibious assaults to come. The destroyers had been deployed in the attack on Saidor in January with the cruisers reserved for bombardments in support of Army operations in February, but by the end of the month the task force was back up to strength with three cruisers and five destroyers under Crutchley's command. Coincidentally, while fighting raged around Manus, a decision of great significance for the RAN had been taken in Canberra. The government advised that all future senior naval appointments should be held by Australian officers as soon as possible, and there was some posting activity in preparation for the next step in June 1944 when RAN Commodore John Collins took command of the Australian Squadron on the completion of Admiral Crutchley's term of loan service.

In mid-March, Task Force 74's destroyers carried out a shipping strike bombardment on Wewak, a major Japanese base. This was also the target for successive attacks by MacArthur's air force, as it was the headquarters of the Japanese XVIII Army of three divisions, spread out over a distance of more than 900 miles. This activity was aimed at weakening Japanese capabilities in Eastern New Guinea while disguising the fact that MacArthur's next target for assault was Hollandia in Dutch New Guinea. At the end of March Admiral Spruance's US Fifth Fleet made major attacks on Palau, inflicting heavy losses of aircraft on the Japanese and convincing Admiral Koga, commander of the Combined Fleet, to evacuate his headquarters to Davao in the southern Philippines. In the process he was killed in an air accident. Meanwhile, preparations continued for the assault on Hollandia in which MacArthur was counting on the growing power of his air forces to neutralise Japanese attempts to reinforce and protect the base, bolstered by aircraft carriers from Nimitz's forces cooperating with MacArthur for the first time. Hollandia's airfields were expected to provide bases from which his heavy bombers could strike targets in the eastern Indonesian archipelago.

For the Japanese, the loss of the Admiralty Islands and Palau and increasingly effective US air and submarine interdiction of the means of resupplying their forward bases meant a complete reconsideration of their strategic plan. The initiative at sea had shifted decisively to the Allies who were able to operate and to strike virtually at will against Japanese targets, leaving garrisons and outposts not essential to Allied planning to wither on the vine. Before his death, Admiral Koga had formulated the 'Z–Plan' and received approval to implement it by concentrating his forces to attack the Pacific Fleet when the Americans entered the Philippine Sea – the long sought 'decisive battle'. This fixed Japanese eyes firmly on the Pacific and negated diversionary operations in the Indian Ocean.

The attack on Hollandia, with a concurrent assault on Aitape to capture the nearby airfield from which to support the operation, went in on 22 April and was a complete success. The Australian warships were engaged in supporting the landings at Tanahmerah Bay, west of the town in which the RAN landing ships delivered their US troops onto the beaches. Resistance was slight, and the two Allied forces linked up four days later. The airfield at Aitape was also captured, although the area was not yet totally in Allied hands. Japanese forces along the north coast of the island of New Guinea were now isolated from each other. The Allied pressure was relentless, and in a series of assaults MacArthur's forces took the islands of Sarmi and Wakde, 193 kilometres west of Hollandia, and then on 27 May assaulted Biak, a further 290 kilometres westward. The ships of TF 74 supported all three landings and *Manoora* landed US troops at Wakde on 16 May. US bombers from Wakde flew over Mindanao in the Philippines for the first time in two years on 27 May.

The Allied assault on Biak now triggered partial execution of the Japanese 'Z-Plan'. The strength of the Japanese Navy had been concentrated in the southern Philippines close to oil supplies from fields in Borneo. The fleet, including the two super-battleships *Yamato* and *Mushashi*, was now ordered into action against the Allied forces off Biak while a hurriedly assembled troop reinforcement was despatched to the beleaguered island. Fortunately for Seventh Fleet, the Biak assault had been scheduled to coincide with an assault by Nimitz against Guam, Tinian and Saipan in the Marianas. This seemed, at last, to present the Japanese with their decisive battle opportunity, and the battle force was recalled to the Philippines Sea. In the meantime, Kinkaid's cruisers and destroyers under Crutchley's command intercepted and drove off the Japanese reinforcement force.

The Battle of the Philippines Sea between the Japanese fleet under Admiral Ozawa and the US Fifth Fleet under Spruance was fought on 18–19 June. Essentially a battle between aircraft carriers, assisted by submarines on the US Navy side, it was a total defeat for Ozawa who retreated to Okinawa, having lost three of his nine carriers and all but 100 of his aircraft. American casualties were negligible in comparison. The battle signalled the end of the Combined Fleet as a serious threat to Allied dominance of the seas in the Pacific.

Behind the Allied front advancing towards the Philippines, fighting to dislodge and destroy the Japanese forces in New Guinea and New Britain continued. The major fighting in South Pacific Command concluded with the occupation of Emirau off New Ireland in March. It now became a rear base area headquartered in Noumea, and Admiral Halsey joined Nimitz as the commander of the US Third Fleet – which was the same as the Fifth Fleet, but changed its designation as Halsey and Spruance rotated through command. The Japanese remained in Rabaul and in possession of the northern areas of Bougainville. The isolated garrisons in the Madang area were mopped up by the Australian Army in April–May with the support of RAN destroyers and corvettes. Wewak remained a major base, and in July the XVIII Army was advancing thence westward to recapture Aitape. After supporting a further landing at Noemfoor west of Biak on 2 July, on 10 July Commodore Collins was ordered to supress Japanese barge traffic supporting the advance and was then directed to Aitape where the Japanese had breached the US defensive perimeter. Attacks by US Navy Patrol Torpedo boats and bombardments by TF 74 stopped the Japanese and forced their withdrawal, having lost half their strength. Japanese garrisons now marooned on scattered offshore islands were harassed, and their lines of communication were disrupted by the motor launches of the RAN as Wewak was left to wither for the moment. Greater plans were in progress.

In the Marianas, Guam had fallen to the United States a month earlier. The Japanese defensive island barrier around the empire had also been seized and crumbled. What would be the next target? Differences between MacArthur and Nimitz on this were resolved in August by President Roosevelt with a decision that was to shape the remainder of the war. The Philippines were to be recaptured first, after which the Japanese Home Islands were to become the focus of Allied power, determinations endorsed at the Octagon conference in Quebec in September. The Philippines assault would be a joint venture between forces from SWPA and the Pacific Command and, for political reasons, the troops landed were to be American. For MacArthur, this meant his landing force had to be assembled from a number of scattered locations in Bougainville and New Guinea and that they needed to be replaced first by the Australian Army. The navies were thus kept busy ferrying troops thither and yon.

As directed, MacArthur paused only to seize the island of Morotai in the Halmaheras to act as a jumping-off point for aircraft destined for Leyte before embarking on his assault on the Philippines. Despite the existence of very large Japanese garrisons on islands south of Morotai, so complete was Allied control of the air and sea that no attempt was made to disrupt the operation on 16 September, in which TF 74 provided its valuable

Figure 8.1: The landing ship HMAS *Kanimbla*, 1945. (Australian War Memorial 300850)

bombardment services against minimal opposition while *Manoora* and *Kanimbla* landed troops. MacArthur then confirmed the date of 20 October for the assault at Leyte Gulf. The Central Philippines Attack Force under the command of Vice Admiral Kinkaid comprised 550 ships made up of the Seventh Fleet, including 37 Australian cruisers, destroyers and survey vessels, escorts, minesweepers, landing ships and logistics ships, augmented by major vessels from the Pacific Fleet, including carriers and battleships. The assault by 14 divisions was launched on eight beaches along Leyte Gulf, with close support by battleships, cruisers and destroyers, and by the aircraft of 18 escort carriers. The support force under Admiral Halsey comprised six battleships and 17 carriers plus 73 cruisers and destroyers.[6] The task of assembling this huge force and organising its transit to the operations area was successfully completed and the attacks went in on 20 October as planned. Japanese resistance, at first, was light and that afternoon MacArthur waded ashore to fulfil his promise, made in 1942 in Australia, that he would return.

The Japanese response was threefold. Troops from other parts of the Philippines were rushed to strengthen the battlefront and contain the Americans, enormous numbers of land-based aircraft were directed at stopping the Americans and driving off the invaders and the Imperial Japanese

Navy planned a final attempt at battle, albeit directed against the landing force rather than Halsey's battleships and carriers. They would be lured out of the way by a feint by the remaining Japanese carriers and their few serviceable aircraft to the north of the Philippines on the assumption that no US admiral worth his salt would pass up the opportunity to destroy these. Spruance might have, but Halsey rose to the bait: at the critical moment when Japanese forces succeeded in entering Leyte Gulf he was hundreds of miles away.

However, returning to the Japanese riposte at Leyte, dawn on 21 October brought the first concerted air attacks, and at 0605 *Australia* had the dubious distinction of being the first ship struck by a suicide aircraft. This was the forerunner of a concerted campaign of this type delivered by the *Kamikaze* – 'divine wind' organisation.[7] The plane hit the cruiser's foremast and crashed through the air defence positions onto the bridge, killing 30 men, including the captain, and wounding 64, including Commodore Collins. Unable to continue the fight *Australia* was withdrawn and sailed to Espiritu Santo for repairs. She was only the first of many ships damaged or sunk in this way during the remainder of the Pacific War.

The Japanese had split their surface force into two pincers, one to enter the Philippines Sea from the south of Leyte though Surigao Strait, and the other to track north and enter through San Bernardino Strait. The forces diverged on 22 October and from 24 October were under concerted US air and submarine attack. The carrier diversion plan was activated the same afternoon, causing Halsey to leave the seaward entrance to San Bernardino Strait, but the southern exit into the Philippines Sea was securely blocked with a force of battleships, cruisers and destroyers, including *Shropshire* and *Arunta*. In the early hours of 25 October battle was joined – the last battleship action in history. *Arunta* led an attack on the Japanese with torpedoes and *Shropshire* took the battleship *Yamashiro* under fire with her guns. US battleships finished off the Japanese force: only four ships survived.

Meanwhile, the Japanese northern pincer had emerged into the Philippines Sea without encountering the expected US surface force. Leyte Gulf and its collection of irreplaceable amphibious assets was open to Japanese attack despite a heroic attempt to stop them by jeep carriers under Rear Admiral Sprague. However, on the brink of a stunning victory, the Japanese Admiral decided that it was too risky to fulfil his orders to destroy the Allied ships and retired. The land battle for Leyte continued and Australian ships contributed with survey, convoy and air defence missions until TF 74 was withdrawn to Manus to prepare for the next operation – the invasion of Luzon through Lingayen Gulf. Japanese resistance on Leyte ceased on 20 December after a landing on the western shore of the island by US forces on 9 December. RAN ships also supported a US landing on Mindoro on 13 December where the force was strongly attacked by *Kamikaze* aircraft, fortunately with no losses to the Australians.

While the fighting continued in the Philippines, the RAN was kept busy in supporting operations closer to home. On 4 November the Australian 5th Division was landed in Jacquinot Bay on the south coast of the Gazelle Peninsula of New Britain following a survey of the proposed landing site by HMAS *Kiama* in September in conjunction with the Coastwatchers. *Swan* conducted a bombardment of Japanese positions during the landing.

PACIFIC 1945

After Leyte, the combined Allied force was again divided, with Nimitz's forces continuing their island-hopping progress towards Japan while MacArthur was to capture Luzon. To move his force from the Leyte area to Lingayen would require MacArthur's ships to transit the western coasts of the Philippines still in Japanese hands, exposing them to potential attack by the remnants of the Imperial Japanese Navy still in Southeast Asian waters and running the gauntlet of more than 70 Japanese air bases. Despite misgivings, the operation went ahead with landings planned for 6 January 1945. TF 74, rejoined by *Australia*, and with Commodore Harold Farncomb now in command of the Squadron,[8] would participate along with the survey force, including two of the new frigates, and all three landing ships. All now bristled with additional anti-aircraft armament.[9] The 650 ships of the assaulting forces sailed from Hollandia and Manus in late December and were joined by the support force from Leyte. Enemy reaction began as soon as the ships entered the Sulu Sea, with bombing, *Kamikaze* attacks and a threatened surface attack which failed to materialise.

Arunta was hit by a *Kamikaze* on 5 January but emergency repairs enabled her to continue to Lingayen Gulf where on the following day the action became heated. Several ships of the bombardment force were hit, including *Australia*, and *Warramunga* towed a burning US destroyer clear of the action and rescued her survivors. No ship was safe from the new weapon, and over the five days of the assault the force had to deal with almost 400 attacks. Of the support force only two cruisers, one of them *Shropshire*, and half the destroyers remained undamaged. *Westralia* was also damaged but continued her role of landing troops as the assault went in on 9 January, the beaches and approach channels having been surveyed by *Warrego* and *Gascoyne*. The hardest hit was *Australia*, with four more strikes by *Kamikazes*, one of them blowing a hole in her side. The casualties among her upper deck guns crews were severe – 48 dead or missing and many others wounded – but she continued her mission of bombardments and was withdrawn only when this was completed. It was the end of her part in the war for this stout ship and her gallant company.

Surveying the battered force, the US Admiral in command singled out the Australian ships for praise, noting *Warramunga*'s role in saving the US destroyer, *Arunta*'s performance off the beaches and *Shropshire*'s '. . . excellent air search radar equipment and her accurate and complete reports on air contacts', as well as her bombardment performance. *Australia* was farewelled with affection and gratitude: Farncomb was congratulated on the performance of the Squadron in its most challenging battle yet.

Shropshire, *Warramunga* and the two survey frigates remained in Philippines waters, participating in operations to re-take Subic Bay and the attack on the fortress of Corregidor at the entrance to Manila Bay, as well as joining the covering force formed to protect the Philippines in the event of an enemy surface attack. The fighting ships returned to Manus on 1 March, where *Hobart* rejoined the Squadron after her repairs following the torpedo attack in 1942. *Warrego* conducted the survey of the beaches for the American assault on Zamboanga in the southern Philippines where the Japanese attacked her survey launches, fortunately without loss, and for the landings at Ilo on Panay Island. By the time she left in May she had also conducted check sweeps of Manila Bay, re-established the navigation lighting in Surigao Strait and checked a passage from Morotai to Brunei in preparation for landings there. *Hobart* rejoined the war with bombardments during the assault on Cebu on 26 March.

Meanwhile, the campaign to reclaim Australian territory in New Guinea continued, on a smaller scale but with no less determination. The 6th Division, fighting its way eastwards from Aitape, received the assistance of *Swan*, fresh from a harassment and interdiction mission with other RAN ships in the Halmaheras, with bombardments on 24 February and interdiction of Japanese barge traffic with the assistance on the motor launch force. She was switched to New Britain for the latter half of March to work with the 5th Division and returned to the 6th Division in April, where plans for an amphibious assault on Wewak were being developed. Joined by corvettes and motor launches, and renamed 'Wewak Force', this small flotilla supported the landings on 9 May with the help of *Hobart*, *Arunta*, *Warramunga* and the Royal Navy cruiser *Newfoundland*, which were transiting to Borneo. The 6th Division had vanquished the Japanese defenders by the end of May.

On the wider Pacific canvas, Halsey's force conducted raids on Japanese-held territories in reach of his carriers throughout January before retiring to Ulithi to hand over command for the next assault, Iwo Jima, which was attacked on 17 February. This was a bloody affair, with the island – to be used as a landing strip for B-29 bombers – not taken until 16 March. Meanwhile, the fleet, now joined by the British Pacific Fleet as Task Force 57, began the pre-assault attacks on Okinawa. In the British escort force were *Quickmatch* and *Quiberon*. Troops were landed on 1 April, meeting no resistance, but retaliatory air attacks commenced the following day. Damage was restricted to two ships, although the Australians recognised that the British were not armed sufficiently against the *Kamikaze*.[10] On 18 April, the 7th Destroyer Squadron joined TF 57, bringing the total of RAN ships engaged to six, not counting the support ships and corvettes guarding the logistics force.

While ships in the Okinawa operation battled air attacks, the Squadron had become part of the support force for the first of three amphibious operations conducted against Japanese positions in Borneo. The enemy threat was non-existent, although the Japanese garrisons put up their usual stout defence when troops were landed. Pre-assault surveys were again carried out by the RAN survey frigates at Tarakan (1 May), Labuan Bay (10 June) and Balikpapan (1 July), and the landing ships delivered their Australian clients from the 9th Division onto the designated beaches, controlled in this campaign by the RAN Beach Commandos. The biggest threat to the landing forces were mines laid by the Allies and the Japanese in the approaches to these anchorages. All three objectives were taken with light losses.

The sea war against Japan now moved to direct attacks on the Japanese Home Islands. Third Fleet began its attacks on 10 July with strikes by aircraft from its 16 carriers in the Tokyo area. On 16 July it was joined by the British – now TF 37 – with *Quiberon* and *Quickmatch* the RAN representatives. The RAN destroyers of the 7th Squadron were assigned as escorts to the logistics force. Besides air sorties, the British component also carried out bombardments of the Japanese coast north of Tokyo with its battleships, with *Quiberon* keeping company. Meanwhile, plans for a landing on Kyushu in November – Operation OLYMPIC – were being developed with the commitment of the RAN Squadron and discussion over a possible role for the Australian Army and RAAF. Before these could be concluded, the Japanese accepted the Allied surrender terms and hostilities ceased on 15 August.

The shooting had stopped but not the work of the RAN. Its ships were deployed widely, taking the surrender of Japanese garrisons and supervising their disarmament, recovering prisoners and internees, arresting suspected war criminals and transporting troops and refugees back to where they had come from. This took up to three years in some cases, and during this time the RAN also provided warships for the British Commonwealth Occupation Force in Japan as well.

The war itself had seen RAN ships and men fight on all the oceans of the world against all the King's enemies. Wherever they operated they acquitted themselves well on, under or over the sea. The Navy had expanded fivefold to man at its zenith 337 ships with just short of 40,000 personnel. These had received almost 1200 decorations and awards for gallantry or service, including 67 from foreign governments. The cost of the war to the RAN was 1947 dead and 11 ships lost to the enemy, but it emerged as a stronger and more confident service with a tradition of excellence which would stand it in good stead as the painful process of post-war political and strategic adjustment now began.

FURTHER READING

John Alliston, *Destroyer Man*, Greenhouse Publications, Melbourne, 1985.

Daniel E. Barbey, *MacArthur's Amphibious Navy: Seventh Amphibious Force Operations, 1943–1945*, United States Naval Institute, Annapolis, Maryland, 1969.

Hugh Campbell, *Notable Service to the Empire: Australian Corvettes and the British Pacific Fleet 1944–45*, Naval Historical Society of Australia, Sydney, 2000.

Eric Feldt, *The Coast Watchers*, Penguin Books, Melbourne, 1991.

Marsden Hordern, *A Merciful Journey: Recollections of a World War II Patrol Boat Man*, Miegunyah Press, Melbourne, 2005.

Shirley F. Huie, *Ship's Belles: The Story of the Women's Royal Australians Naval Service in War and Peace, 1941–1985*, Watermark Press, Sydney, 2000.

Stan Nicholls, *HMAS Shropshire*, Naval Historical Society of Australia, Sydney, 1989.

Alan Payne, *HMAS Australia: The Story of the 8-inch Cruiser*, Naval Historical Society of Australia, Sydney, 1988.

Ian Pfennigwerth, *The Royal Australian Navy and MacArthur*, Rosenberg Publishing, Sydney, 2009.

David Stevens (ed.), *The Royal Australian Navy in World War II*, Allen & Unwin, Sydney, 2005.

Frank B. Walker, *Corvettes-Little Ships for Big Men*, Budgewoi, Kingfisher Press, New South Wales, 1995.

Notes

1 Details of these and other RAN activities during the Second World War are to be found in G. Hermon Gill's two-volume official history *Royal Australian Navy, 1939–42* and *Royal Australian Navy, 1942–1945*, Canberra: Australian War Memorial 1968. A more recent and shorter history of the RAN in the war in the Southwest Pacific Area is Ian Pfennigwerth's. *The Royal Australian Navy and MacArthur*, Sydney: Rosenberg Publishing, 2009.

2 A total of 89 men, women and children were killed in one of the cruisers after they had been recovered from the sinking ship. This act of barbarity earned the Admiral in charge seven years imprisonment before the War Crimes Tribunal in Tokyo after the Japanese surrender. It was also a practice of Japanese submarine commanders to machine-gun their enemies' survivors, a fact that caused great concern among crews of merchant ships sailing independently of naval escorts.

3 Interestingly, the advance of these ships into the Indian Ocean caused the withdrawal of US tenders supporting the US submarine force in Fremantle to Albany in Western Australia as a safety measure and preparations for an air strike on the ships should they approach the West Australian coast.

4 When it commenced operations in February 1945 the British Fleet train comprised 44 ships. When hostilities ceased in August it had grown to over twice that size and incorporated several RAN and Australian commercial vessels.

5 This was an underestimate. In January 1945, the War Cabinet authorised an additional £5 million and the manpower to construct works required by the Royal Navy.

6 These were not the only Australians present. General Headquarters so respected the work of the codebreakers in the Central Bureau Brisbane that a special RAAF field unit was formed to accompany the staff to Leyte to warn of Japanese aircraft activity. Other RAN personnel went ashore with US Navy Render Mines Safe units to clear obstacles, unexploded ordnance and booby traps.

7 While accounts vary, it is generally agreed that the crash was a deliberate act. The *Kamikaze* weapon was first employed four days later against US aircraft carriers off Leyte.

8 Farncomb had been sent to command a British aircraft carrier as part of the RAN senior officer succession plan. He served with distinction in the Mediterranean before being recalled because of Collins's incapacity after Leyte.

9 Experience demonstrated that if a *Kamikaze* pilot evaded the fighter screen and focused on a target ship the only way to defeat the attack

was to interrupt the trajectory of flight. In practical terms this meant knocking the aircraft to pieces. The weapon of choice was the Swedish-designed Bofors 40mm gun firing 120 rounds per minute and great ingenuity was applied to getting as many of these mountings into ships as was possible, with or without official sanction.

10 The Japanese had recognised the power of the *Kamikaze* as a weapon and had regrouped their air assets into squadrons to conduct mass suicide attacks on Allied ships, under the code name *Kikusai*. The first of 10 *Kikusai* operations against the Allies of Okinawa on 6 April comprised 355 *kamikaze* and 341 bombers, which resulted in the sinking of three US destroyers, two auxiliaries and damage to another 10 ships, all destroyers. By the time of the final attack on 21/22 June the Japanese has lost almost 1500 aircraft in exchange for sinking 30 naval ships and damaging 368, and killing almost 5000 Allied men. The Americans were avenged by the sinking of the super-battleship *Yamato*, herself on a suicide mission to attack the fleet off Okinawa, on 7 April.

CHAPTER 9

'ON THE SCRAP HEAP OF THE YANKS': THE RAAF IN THE SOUTHWEST PACIFIC AREA, 1944-45

Mark Johnston

Early in 1944, the Royal Australian Air Force (RAAF) was able to send out unprecedentedly large forces to bomb Japanese targets. This spoke well of the force's organisation and skill. Its aircrew and ground personnel were more experienced and able than ever before. The Allies' strength made eventual victory certain, and Australia contributed to that victory. Yet the years 1944 and 1945 were in many respects deeply unsatisfying for the RAAF. A critical factor was Australia's relationship to the United States. The US Army Air Force (USAAF) had been growing much faster than the RAAF in the Southwest Pacific Area (SWPA): whereas in March 1943 the two forces had rough parity in squadrons, one year later the Americans had 82 squadrons to the RAAF's 45. The US squadrons boasted advanced types like the P-38 Lightning, while the Australian squadrons included obsolete types like the Vultee Vengeance dive-bomber, three squadrons of which the Americans banished from New Guinea in March 1944. This move and the sending of three Kittyhawk squadrons from New Guinea to New Britain represented the sidelining of No. 10 Operational Group, an Australian force established in September 1943 at the request of the Commander of Allied Air Forces, General Kenney, for operations in the forward areas of SWPA alongside the Fifth Air Force USAAF. No. 10 Operational Group was efficient and hard working. For example in

February 1944, 78th Squadron racked up 1007 operational hours, as opposed to the 600 that was typical of RAAF fighter squadrons. That 600-hour figure was based on RAF standards, whereas General Whitehead demanded up to 1500 hours per month for his Fifth Air Force squadrons.[1] Whitehead required the RAAF squadrons to increase their flying hours too, if they wanted a share of the confined airfield space in New Guinea. Group Captain Fred Scherger, the able and amenable commander of No. 10 Group, obliged. His force had been created to advance alongside the Americans. From March 1944 that was clearly most unlikely.

The Americans pointed to a silver lining on these dark clouds. The Vengeance crews were to be retrained to fly modern B-24 Liberator bombers, thus fulfilling a long-cherished Australian government and RAAF desire for four-engine heavy bomber squadrons of their own.[2] The Australian government hoped that this indicated that Australian forces would be participating in the drive on Tokyo, but they were to be disappointed. Kenney intended to base the retrained squadrons in Darwin, so he could release the US bombers based there for more important work.

The decline of Japanese air power exacerbated the Australians' loss of self-respect. After February 1944, there were no Japanese aircraft defending Rabaul, which had been the focus of much Australian and US air action for the previous two years. In February 1944, MacArthur completed the isolation of Rabaul by occupying Los Negros in the Admiralty Islands. No Japanese aircraft arrived to support their ground forces, while Australian Kittyhawks gave useful ground support to the Americans in the fierce and successful fighting. Five RAAF radar stations were sent to the Admiralty Islands.

From mid-March 1944, No. 78 Wing's Kittyhawks, with No. 10 Operational Group at Cape Gloucester, were also providing air support for appreciative Americans, this time Marine Corps troops fighting on New Britain. In April, the hard-working wing was ordered to move again to support the important US amphibious invasion at Hollandia, on the north coast of Dutch New Guinea. They hoped for air combat.

HOLLANDIA AND AITAPE

With the threat from Rabaul removed, MacArthur had more freedom of movement, and the success of his bold operations in the Admiralties encouraged him to make daring leaps to fulfil his promised return to the Philippines. That return was part of plans developed by the Allied Combined Chiefs of Staff in December 1943 to launch two great simultaneous drives against Japan: one across the Central Pacific, the other via New Guinea and the Philippines. MacArthur was ordered to invade Hollandia in April 1944, and then the Philippines in November. By monitoring Hollandia's wireless traffic, the Darwin-based No. 3 Wireless Unit RAAF gathered valuable intelligence. The Japanese had three airfields on this distant target with aircraft capable of intercepting bombers, but Kenney's P-38 Lightnings could fly to Hollandia and stay overhead for an hour before returning to Nadzab. These P-38s escorted more than 60 Liberators to Hollandia on 30 and 31 March. Among the Liberator crews were Australian airmen learning to fly B-24s in preparation for the creation of RAAF Liberator squadrons. Flying them was physically hard, and they were not particularly robust. But as anticipated they came across virgin territory, to which just days previously the Japanese Fourth Air Army had withdrawn from its pulverised Wewak base. The poorly dispersed aircraft at Hollandia were smashed: 340 aircraft wrecks were later counted on its three airstrips.[3]

On 22 April, US forces landed at Hollandia and, 160 kilometres east, at Aitape. The RAAF contributed substantially to the success of the Aitape landings. These bases were so far from the nearest Allied airfields that it was imperative to make Aitape's strip, at Tadji, operational quickly. RAAF Wing Commander Bill Dale, an exceptionally able and experienced leader, was given command of 2500 Australian and US engineers to make the airfield ready for fighter aircraft the day after the landing. Outstanding work, especially by the veteran RAAF construction squadrons Nos. 5 and 6, ensured that 50 hours after Dale came ashore, Allied fighters were flying from the 1188-metre long steel matting on Tadji airfield to support US ground forces on Hollandia.[4] No. 11 Repair and Salvage Unit RAAF did a remarkable job in ensuring that the Kittyhawks of No. 78 Wing were fit to operate at Tadji just weeks after being warned of the move from Cape Gloucester and Nadzab. This effort, involving two daily shifts of 12 hours, exemplified the unsung but essential work of RAAF salvage and repair units in the SWPA. Australia's repair system was more efficient than Japan's. Tadji was crowded and a hive of disease, but from it Australian aircraft provided valuable ground support to the advancing Americans and escorted air transports to Hollandia. A further 13 Allied squadrons based in the Northern Territory bombed, mined and strafed Japanese forces in support of the Hollandia-Aitape operation.

In addition to supporting MacArthur's thrust along the north coast of New Guinea, RAAF Catalina squadrons Nos. 22, 20, 42 and 43 undertook minelaying in the Netherlands East Indies. The effectiveness of these operations worried the Japanese to the extent that they allotted 30 ships and some 1500 men to mining countermeasures there. By September 1944, 25 ships were credited as sunk or damaged in the Netherlands East Indies, for the loss of just six Catalinas and four crews: one 'Cat' per 95 sorties.

When Cliff Hull was forced to ditch his Catalina in the open sea after losing an engine to flak at Macassar in October 1944, a 42 Squadron Catalina under Armand Etienne rescued this crew in waters perilously close to four Japanese airfields. This has been described as the longest air–sea rescue of the Pacific War. In 1945, dangerous minelaying missions would be flown from Morotai and the Philippines to Surabaya in Java, Formosa, Hong Kong and the China coast. An operation to Wenchow, at 28 degrees north of the equator on the Chinese coast, in May represented the RAAF's most northerly operation in the Pacific War. After the war, the US Joint Army–Navy Assessment Committee concluded that mines laid by RAAF Catalinas sank nine ships totalling 21,033 tons. The RAAF claimed 23 sunk and 27 damaged.[5] The US figures probably underestimated the Australian contribution, but even had the Australian estimate been correct, that total was small relative to the 266 Japanese vessels lost to mines during the war. Yet tonnage sunk is not the only measure of the effectiveness of RAAF mining. Also significant was time lost to ships trapped in harbours or forced to take roundabout routes. Keeping ships out of harbours made them vulnerable to US submarines, the success of which was a key factor in Allied victory over Japan.

STIFF UPPER LIP AT AITAPE

In May 1944, the Beauforts of Nos. 8 and 100 Squadrons contributed to the bombing of Wewak from their base at Nadzab. In June, they moved again to Aitape, as did 30 Squadron's Beaufighters. The latter destroyed 18 barges in three weeks, but this was not simply a period of 'happy hunting'. Raynor Barber, a 30 Squadron pilot, talked later of immense stresses on men expected to display a stiff upper lip under all circumstances. In his case the stress derived from the expectation that the flak would eventually bring him down, the loss of a string of tent-mates, the fear of Japanese soldiers raiding the base, but also from a series of incidents which scarred him mentally: being menaced by scores of sharks as he waited to be rescued after ditching in the sea; trying fruitlessly to rescue a fellow pilot trapped in a burning Beaufighter; telling a widow of the death of a fellow pilot and mate he permitted to go on 'one last flight' before returning home. After returning from missions and reporting, Barber would lie down for an hour 'to alleviate the shaking'.[6] Some members in the squadron even tried intentionally to avoid missions: one deliberately spent hours staring at blindingly white coral, until his self-induced eyesight problems had him sent home.

When Japanese troops launched an offensive to recapture Aitape in July 1944, Beauforts and Beaufighters flying from Tadji helped to halt them. Beaufort crews were each flying a very demanding four sorties a day. Thick jungle made it hard to determine the effectiveness of their raids, but a captured soldier reported that a July raid by 100 Squadron killed 70 Japanese.[7] On 7 August, No. 8 Squadron flew a record 64 sorties in one day and dropped nearly 400 bombs. One diarist claimed that the two squadrons had killed 2000 Japanese 'observed'.[8] The Beaufighters poured more pressure on the enemy by seeking enemy barges at night. It was dangerous but often fruitful work: three Beaufighters were lost on 13 July 1944.

LOW PRIORITY, HARD DOGFIGHTS

MacArthur now implemented his 'island hopping' or 'leap frogging' strategy, bypassing rather than destroying isolated Japanese garrisons and attacking only those locations he wanted as bases to facilitate his drive on the Philippines. The strategy was valid, but not only left the Japanese behind but also the RAAF. As advances outran supply the RAAF became an even lower priority. Operational bases such as Port Moresby, Dobodura, Milne Bay, Kiriwina, Woodlark and Goodenough – all vital at some point – became superfluous. More forward airfields were seized at Wakde, Biak, Noemfoor and Sansapor (on the Vogelkop Peninsula). Nos 75, 78 and 80 Squadrons supported all these moves, still averaging 1400 hours monthly.

On 4 March 1944, when 14 Kittyhawks of 75 Squadron fought off Oscar fighters attempting to intercept USAAF Liberators near Wewak, it was the squadron's last aerial combat of the war: an extraordinary fact given that 75 Squadron was the RAAF's most successful squadron in the Pacific and that the war still had 17 months to run. Another rare but dramatic RAAF flying battle occurred on 3 June 1944, over Biak. Sixteen Kittyhawks of 78 Squadron under Flight Lieutenant

Robert Osment surprised a group of enemy aircraft. For the loss of one P-40 and its pilot, whose parachute failed to open, the Australians shot down seven Oscar fighters and two Kate torpedo bombers in about 45 minutes. It was the squadron's first aerial battle and the RAAF's last major flying battle in the Pacific. With all Japanese naval aircraft withdrawn to defend the Marianas, only a few Japanese Army Air Force aircraft remained in New Guinea. The last RAAF aerial victory over New Guinea occurred on 10 June 1944, when 78 Squadron Kittyhawks downed a lone Tony fighter.

NEW GUINEA, NOEMFOOR, NORTHWESTERN AREA

There was no question, however, of the operational Kittyhawk squadrons becoming idle: in May–June 1944, 78 Wing's three squadrons (75, 78, 80) averaged 1406 flying hours per month, which was more than similar US squadrons. A US commander said of an Australian squadron's support of one US attack: 'Close support mission early this date tremendous success. Air strike broke up Jap counterattack on our bridgehead.'[9] The RAAF fighter squadrons worked mainly on ground attack, with P-40s now often carrying three 500-pound bombs. Two squadrons were disbanded to sustain this rate of effort. From early 1944 the P-40N, the final operational variant, equipped virtually all Kittyhawk squadrons.

No. 10 Group moved to Noemfoor Island in July 1944. Allied air domination was so complete that the previous day aircraft could fly over the invasion area to spray DDT. Dale's Australian works squadrons lengthened the airfield from 100 to 1830 metres in just a week. RAAF bomb disposal squads cleared enemy mines and defused many unexploded US bombs. Air Commodore Harry Cobby, Second World War air ace, took command of 10 Group in August. The group, based in western New Guinea, remained under Fifth Air Force Command. While many Fifth Air Force airmen were granted leave in Australia, No. 78 Wing was undertaking daily patrols. No. 77 Wing, including squadrons 22 and 30 with their Bostons and Beaufighters, also arrived at Noemfoor. Beaufighters, Bostons and Kittyhawks attacked Japanese airfields in the Netherlands East Indies, even though these were generally unused. More than 700 sorties from Northwestern Area, based on Darwin and Western Australia, supported the Noemfoor landing. Beaufighters of 31 Squadron brought down a Nick over Flores Island, while Spitfires downed a Dinah reconnaissance aircraft at Darwin in July: thereafter not even Dinahs came to the area.

NEW AUSTRALIAN AIRCRAFT

RAAF Liberators first went into action in August 1944. Drawing on seemingly limitless US production, Kenney planned to equip seven RAAF squadrons with Liberators and use them to relieve his No. 380 Bombardment Group in the Northern Territory. Australia's first heavy bomber squadrons in the Pacific War were costly to administer, requiring more fuel, vehicles and personnel than the typical squadron. Whether their strategic value to Australia repaid the cost and risk involved is debatable, but their crews loved them. Another addition to the RAAF arsenal were rockets, fitted to Beaufighters and destined to make the 'Beau' an even more effective ground attack aircraft. By late 1944, Beaufighters were Australian rather than British-built.

INVASION OF THE PHILIPPINES

October 1944 brought the long awaited invasion of the Philippines. RAAF aerial support of the invasion at Leyte was indirect, through bombing and patrolling in rear areas. It was still intense work. In October 1944, No. 77 Wing Bostons and Beaufighters sank 24 vessels. As the Japanese drew aircraft from surrounding areas like the Netherlands East Indies to send to the Philippines, up to 400 Allied aircraft could range from New Guinea to Java with no aerial opposition. The only major Australian unit to participate in the ground invasion was No. 3 Airfield Construction Squadron RAAF, part of the first wave of invaders on Mindoro Island in the Philippines. It established an airstrip by 19 December, ahead of schedule.

FIRST TAF CREATED, RAAF RELEGATED

In October No. 10 Group was renamed First Tactical Air Force (TAF, or, in rhyming slang, 'TAF-RAAF'). It was a sizeable force, comprising two fighter wings, an attack wing and two airfield construction wings. However the US command was not dissuaded from its intention to leave First TAF in New Guinea to support Australian Army operations. The Australian government also naturally wanted the RAAF to prioritise supporting Australian ground forces wherever they fought, but in addition wanted Australian forces to accompany the main US advance towards Japan. Neither MacArthur nor Kenney shared that desire.

In June 1944, the US Fifth and Thirteenth Air Forces were combined in the Far East Air Force, under General Kenney. He also commanded the

Australian and Dutch air forces, some US Marine and naval air units and Royal New Zealand Air Force units. Henceforth the 'Allied Air Forces' would comprise only RAAF, Royal New Zealand Air Force and Netherlands East Indies units, with any US forces Kenney chose to attach. Operational control of the First TAF was transferred from the Fifth Air Force to the Thirteenth. The Fifth Air Force was designated the vanguard in the drive on Japan, with the smaller Thirteenth – and by implication First TAF – playing a supporting role. These measures marked the definitive relegation of the RAAF to Second XI status. As late as March 1945, the War Cabinet believed that the expected arrival of 100 Lincoln bombers would, together with the Liberator squadrons, allow Australia 'to offer a substantial force in the final bombing of Japan'.[10] Yet with the European war winding down, so much material was available to the Pacific that giving meaningful work to all available forces became impossible. Consequently the RAAF became an even lower priority to the US.

To Morotai

In September, MacArthur ordered Australian troops to replace US forces fighting bypassed Japanese garrisons in New Guinea, New Britain and Bougainville. To support them 31, 452 and 457 Squadrons would leave Northwestern Area and join First TAF by February 1945. From November 1944, First TAF moved to Morotai Island. From there it attacked enemy airfields and other targets in the Celebes, Vogelkop Peninsula, Ambon-Ceram, Halmahera, Mindanao and Borneo. Results were rarely fruitful, and 'Saw nothing, sore behind', was a common summary of many sorties.[11] The Japanese Army Air Force could only reply with small-scale night raids. On 22 November, eight Bostons made the first Australian strike on the Philippines, followed by eight Beaufighters. These were tiny numbers compared to the 517 USAAF aircraft over the Philippines that day.

The following night, nine Japanese bombers made an unusually destructive raid on Morotai's congested airstrips. Nine of the 15 aircraft they destroyed were Bostons of 22 Squadron RAAF, which for lack of replacements had to retrain and rearm with Beaufighters. The Australians on Morotai got some revenge on 24 December, when in view of thousands of applauding Australians and Americans a newly arrived 452 Squadron Spitfire brought down a nocturnal raider. The raids diminished thereafter.

BOUGAINVILLE, NEW BRITAIN, AITAPE-WEWAK

Though undermanned and underequipped, No. 84 Wing backed Australian troops effectively on Bougainville from November 1944. While Royal New Zealand Air Force Corsairs provided the cutting edge, RAAF Boomerangs and Wirraways assisted them, and the Australian ground forces, by finding and marking enemy targets. These 'eyes of the Army' also called in mortar shoots, strafed and dropped supplies. Auster light observation aircraft did valuable reconnaissance and liaison work, while RAAF Beauforts and Dakotas dropped supplies and performed anti-malarial spraying. Beauforts and Boomerangs supported ground operations on New Britain, while Beauforts continued attacks on Rabaul.

Air supply was essential to the 6th Australian Division advance towards Wewak from late 1944, especially on its inland axis. Between November 1944 and January 1945, RAAF Beauforts flew some 500 ground-support sorties per month. Attacking Wewak was perilous, especially as its anti-aircraft defence was notoriously accurate. Though low on personnel, fuel and bombs, the Beauforts and Boomerangs made a substantial contribution to a crucial battle at Nambut Hill in February 1945, dropping 500-pound bombs onto mortar smoke markers just 150 metres in front of Australian infantry. This helped pave the way for a rapid coastal advance and set a precedent of very close cooperation and fellow-feeling between Army and RAAF in this campaign. The main objective of the inland advance was Maprik airfield and Beauforts offered excellent support though at the cost of heavy casualties, especially though accidents. Though the RAAF dropped more than 1000 tons of bombs supporting the 6th Division in May, they were so short of bombs they were resorting to unreliable Japanese ones. In the 12 months that the Beauforts were in the Aitape-Wewak area, they reportedly accounted for half the bombs dropped by the RAAF in the SWPA in that period.

'MUDDY BLOODY MOROTAI'

Life for the 3000 TAF personnel on Morotai by January 1945 was unpleasant. Ground and air transport and rations were meagre, unlike the mud. While US forces conquered the Philippines, First TAF was well behind the advance, attacking or watching bypassed targets. Australian casualties continued to rise and included three airmen captured and bayoneted after their Kittyhawks got lost on the way to Morotai. The slow attrition and lack of significant targets affected morale within First TAF. The maximising of sorties and flying hours that the USAAF demanded of the Australians in early 1944 was continuing at the end of that year, even though the RAAF was far behind the main game. Their targets were often airstrips, usually defended by flak. Veteran Jock Scott remarked pointedly '. . . All we did was to make the Japs use up their endless supply of anti-aircraft ammo and improve their shooting. They were isolated, unsupplied, ineffectual and without an effective role to play in the war – except to shoot at stupid buggers in Kittyhawks'.[12]

When Group Captain 'Woof' Arthur arrived at Noemfoor in December 1944 to take command of No. 81 Wing, the waste and unnecessary danger in the campaign soon unsettled the air ace. He drew up an 'operational balance sheet' and concluded that in October–November, the wing had lost 11 pilots and 15 aircraft, while destroying just 12 barges and six vehicles.[13] In turn Cobby drew up his own statistics that showed the numbers of aircraft destroyed by flak were only one in 862 sorties in November 1944, two in 2249 in December, and five in 2037 sorties in January. Yet Arthur's point was that the losses were not balanced by substantial gains. Caldwell of 80 Wing and Cresswell of 81 Wing felt the same. Others complained about insufficient flying hours and their disjointed and disorganised lifestyle, especially on Morotai.

The Japanese were of course far worse off. By March 1945, Japanese air strength in the SWPA was estimated at 161 aircraft, far fewer than the 663 RAAF aircraft. In February 1945, about 60 Kittyhawks and 28 Beaufighters hit Tondano in the Celebes in one of the largest RAAF attacks of the war. It was the first time the three Beaufighter squadrons, including the refitted 22 Squadron, had worked together.

The combat fliers knew that if they crashed or had to ditch over enemy territory or in the great stretches of open water, there was a rescue organisation with aircraft manned by crews prepared to risk everything to save them. RAAF Catalina crews did most of this work, as well as transporting personnel and supplies and laying mines. Catalina crews, many of which logged over 2000 hours, rescued some 540 Allied pilots.

The petty struggles between Air Vice-Marshals Jones and Bostock at the top of the RAAF dragged on. Australian and US leaders were unable and unwilling to resolve the issue, which 'had an unsettling effect on the force', although many of the rank and file knew nothing about it.[14]

As the number of RAAF personnel on Morotai grew, so did their frustration. At various times hundreds of men were sleeping in the open due to a lack of tents. Australian and US aircraft kept the four crowded airstrips in constant use: from Wama alone, Australian flying control personnel handled as many as 400 aircraft daily. Rations were monotonous, especially after Australian Army rations replaced US ones in April. Many airmen on Morotai had completed 20 months without returning to Australia after the regulation 15-month tour of duty, primarily because of a lack of transport. Life on this isolated island, almost on the Equator, was monotonous. Alcohol was available in small amounts on Morotai and Noemfoor: beer for the men, beer and spirits for the officers. Business-minded Australian airmen, including officers, swapped or sold their beer to Americans. Flying in beer supplies had always been a tempting challenge for squadrons and Cobby tried unsuccessfully to stop the illicit trade in alcohol.

It was Cobby's failure to end the RAAF's wasteful policy towards its flying squadrons that prompted 'Woof' Arthur to take decisive action. In March 1945, he went to Morotai and found that other senior veterans felt as he did. They included Group Captain Caldwell (No. 80 Wing), Wing Commander 'Bobby' Gibbes (an air ace in the Middle East, now No. 80 Wing), Squadron Leader John Waddy (80 Squadron, one of Australia's top aces in the Middle East) and Squadron Leader Doug Vanderfield (110 Mobile Fighter Control Unit). The group were on the point of taking action when two of them, Caldwell and Gibbes, were accused of trading alcohol.

This accusation had not been resolved when on 19 April eight senior First TAF officers tried to resign their commissions over the wastefulness of operations. Their resignations said simply: 'I hereby respectfully make application that I be permitted to resign my commission as an officer in the Royal Australian Air Force, forthwith.'[15] Cobby was unable to persuade them to explain further. At Morotai Bostock interviewed the eight officers, whom he found 'respectful but bitter and unrelenting'. They would not withdraw their resignations, but agreed to change 'forthwith' to 'at the end of current operations'. Bostock found the morale of First TAF at a 'dangerously low level'.[16] Cobby disagreed.

After speaking to the eight, Kenney felt that they were sincere and their complaints understandable. He warned Jones not to punish them. Bostock's solution was to ask RAAF Headquarters to relieve of command three other senior officers, including Cobby. For once, Jones agreed. The Australian government sent Mr Justice Barry to investigate this 'Morotai Mutiny', though they and Jones emphasised the alleged illegal trading in liquor rather than First TAF's operations and why morale on Morotai was so low. Barry found that discontent stemmed largely from disquiet about those operations and about the three sacked senior officers. Like Arthur and a contemporaneous RAAF Operational Research section report, Barry found that expenditure on operations far outweighed the return. Concern with this imbalance, rather than the trying living conditions or the command scandal was the key reason for the mutiny. Ineffective leadership was another. The mutiny itself affected the atmosphere in First TAF, focusing attention on the negatives. But at least one group of airmen arriving at Morotai in May were eager to be there. 'The war at last!' wrote the 23 Squadron diarist when, from their US Liberty ship, the squadron saw Morotai on the horizon.[17]

TARAKAN, NORTH BORNEO AND BALIKPAPAN

Some 20 squadrons of First TAF supported the Australian landings at Tarakan, North Borneo and Balikpapan. So did squadrons based at Darwin and Western Australia. RAAF planning was essentially independent, as from early 1945 RAAF Command was responsible for all operations south of the Philippines. Tarakan Island was the first objective, primarily because of its airfield (the RAAF's contribution to that campaign is explained above). In planning the operation Bostock had at his disposal the resources of the First TAF, as well as the Thirteenth and Fifth Air Forces and RAAF heavy bomber squadrons based in the Northern Territory and Western Australia. Cobby and 'Woof' Arthur, now commanding 78 Wing, would oversee air operations at Tarakan, though as Cobby discovered just the day before the landing he was about to be sacked on Bostock's recommendation. Bostock himself had a moment of deep embarrassment when during the preliminary bombardment on the day of the landing only US Air Force bombers flew overhead as MacArthur and other senior officers looked on. During the radio silence enforced while the fleet was sailing, Jones had grounded the RAAF squadrons as they had completed their allotted monthly hours. When Bostock explained, Kenney offered his sympathy. A leading RAAF historian calls this incident 'the most shameful example of the depths to which the [Bostock/Jones] feud sank'.[18] The succeeding operations also reflected poorly on RAAF planning, intelligence and cooperation with the Australian Imperial Force (AIF). Another postscript to the sordid command scandal was Jones' report on 23 May that 'RAAF fighter aircraft were now operating from Tarakan'.[19] It would be another month before this was true. Yet while Tarakan reflected poorly on the RAAF, its support of the later Borneo operations was well planned and executed.

For the second Borneo operation, the seizure of Brunei Bay in North Borneo, First TAF allotted three Kittyhawk squadrons, one Spitfire squadron, an army-cooperation wing, an attack wing of Beaufighters and Mosquitos, and newly arrived No. 13 Squadron's Venturas. In the five days preceding the landings, more than 3000 sorties were flown, but of these the RAAF flew only a small proportion.

RAAF Liberators did constitute about one-quarter of the bombers that hit the enemy beaches on 10 June, the day of the landing which was unopposed. Among the invasion force were 6000 RAAF personnel from a broad range of support units and squadrons. The following day saw four supporting RAAF aircraft and seven aircrew lost in accidents. By 17 June, Labuan Island was available as an airstrip, while Tarakan, which had been seized to provide an airbase to support the other landings, was still unusable. Within three days, Australian Kittyhawks and Spitfires destroyed three enemy aircraft. There were ground targets too: 77 Squadron's pilots claimed they killed 100 Japanese on the ground and 30 swimming on 5 July. Between 4–6 July RAAF Kittyhawks, Spitfires, Wirraways and Austers supported ground operations with 230 sorties. No. 86 Wing's Mosquitos (No. 1 Squadron) and Beaufighters (93 Squadron) arrived in late July, and shared three operations between them.

For Balikpapan, the final Oboe target, Kenney delegated the detailed planning to Bostock, but offered him any Far East Air Force resources he wanted. Bostock would use Liberators operating from Australia, but his plan to employ RAAF Beaufighters and Kittyhawks foundered on delays at Tarakan. Instead he depended on land-based and carrier-based US fighters. Some 40 squadrons with 300 aircraft were at his disposal, whereas Japanese strength was estimated at just 17 fighters, 17 bombers and a few float-planes. Air operations at Balikpapan were primarily American: for example, only six of the 123 Liberators that bombed Balikpapan on 27 June were Australian. However, the RAAF did provide nearly one quarter of the 82 Liberators that participated on the day of the landing, 1 July.

The combined aerial and naval bombardment of the beach defences ensured that the 17 assault waves of infantry suffered no casualties in the landing. Once ashore, RAAF air liaison and support parties accompanied the troops and relayed many calls for air support to headquarters ships. US Liberators provided most of that support. On the first day, the Australian Infantry Commander Major-General Milford insisted against Bostock's advice that US Navy dive-bombers provide a supporting air strike. The naval aircraft missed their target, killing or wounding 17 Australians instead. Three RAAF Liberators on observation missions were also shot down in quick succession. By mid-July Kittyhawks and Spitfires had free rein at Balikpapan. 'Army elated with support given', wrote an airman at 78 Wing Headquarters.[20] The Japanese launched their biggest raid of the Borneo campaign on Balikpapan on 24 July, dropping 25 bombs. A 452 Squadron Spitfire shot down one of the aircraft. Five RAAF Liberators were destroyed in July along with the lives of 48 RAAF personnel, and several AIF and American men who flew with them. One of them, under Flight Lieutenant Kenneth Hanson of 21 Squadron, crashed over the Celebes, where several of its crew were captured and executed. Two, Arnold Lockyer and George Lindley, were tortured, then chloroformed and buried alive on 21 August 1945, after the war had ended.

On the eve of victory, Australia lost pilots such as Barney Newman of 79 Squadron on 2 August. Just weeks before, his Commanding Officer Ken James had described Newman as 'a definite asset to any squadron'.[21] Eldred Quinn of 80 Squadron was the last RAAF airman to die over Borneo, killed trying to crash land his P-40 after it was hit by ground fire on 9 August. His and Newman's many fine qualities were lost to Australia on the eve of victory.

THE WAR ENDS

In July, First TAF launched an impressive 877 sorties, but this effort was dwarfed by the more than 10,000 US sorties against Japan in just one week of July. The Japanese managed just 235 sorties. US airpower had already destroyed 80 per cent of Japan's cities by the time the war's ultimate aerial weapon, the atomic bombs, finally brought the conflict to an end. By then, on 15 August, the RAAF was flying support missions for Australian ground forces in Borneo, New Britain, Bougainville and the Aitape-Wewak area. Just before the word came to cancel missions, 30 RAAF Beauforts carried out what may have been the war's last bombing raid. By then, 137,208 members of the RAAF were serving in the Pacific theatre. The force's 54 operational squadrons and 3187 aircraft stood in stark contrast to the 12 incomplete squadrons and 250 obsolescent aircraft of the 1939 RAAF. Moreover, by 1945 its frontline airmen and commanders were combat veterans backed by an efficient infrastructure.

The RAAF took a leading role in aiding and repatriating thousands of Allied prisoners. It also repatriated Australian airmen in the SWPA, but it was a process lasting into early 1946, to the chagrin of many RAAF personnel. More than 2000 members of the RAAF would never return from the war against Japan.

The RAAF had fought from the first to the last day of the Pacific War. It had done so with inferior tools. One pilot who was still flying 'clapped out' P-40s in 1945 asserted that 'The RAAF went through the war on the scrap heap of the Yanks'.[22] A RAAF photographer reported Americans telling him throughout the war: 'You Aussies, you can fly alright, if you only had some ships to fly.'[23] For most of its aircraft the RAAF was dependent on its allies, just as after 1942 it depended on US commanders to allocate it roles that they deemed suitable. In 1944–45, these roles were secondary ones to those given to the larger, more concentrated and more up-to-date US forces. By July 1945, US Fifth Air Force squadrons were in Okinawa, part of Japan, while the leading Australian squadrons were closer to Australia than to Japan. Apart from the blemish of Tarakan, the RAAF performed their assigned tasks with commendable efficiency. Nevertheless, RAAF members saw themselves as a Second XI or what 'Woof' Arthur called 'a toothless poodle'.[24] By 1944, such a self-image was affecting the RAAF's morale. Attacking its isolated opponents in New Guinea, Bougainville, New Britain and Borneo brought Japan no closer to defeat, but was risky to the attackers. Indeed had these Japanese not been attacked they could have made no contribution to the war effort, while the Australians committed there might have made a more useful contribution elsewhere. It was an illogical policy and arguably an immoral one.

In 1944–45, Japan's air forces were unable to fight back effectively. Their aircraft were outdated, their pilots no longer the elite who had begun the war, and their support services such as rescue and transport inadequate. The few resources they did have were directed against Americans, not Australians, on key fronts such as the Philippines. In the seven months to 1 July 1945, there were only nine recorded Japanese air attacks in the entire SWPA, made by only 17 aircraft. In the war's last nine months the First TAF had just five contacts with airborne enemy aircraft. Some of the top RAAF aces had returned to Australia from the European theatre since 1942 but they had no chance to demonstrate their skill. The RAAF seems to have brought down just 20 Japanese aircraft between 1 January 1944 and the end of the war: an average of one per month for what by war's end was the world's fourth largest air force. Nine of these fell in the one air battle, over Biak in June 1944.

The RAAF's lack of enemies to fight, its dependence on its allies and its inadequate aircraft hampered its performance in 1944–45. So did continuing conflict at the top of the command structure, which affected the

Figure 9.1: This Liberator B-24 bomber aircraft of 24 Squadron, RAAF, was set on fire by Japanese fighter aircraft and subsequently crashed into the sea near Sumba, Netherlands East Indies, in April 1945. (Australian War Memorial AC0075)

organisation's efficiency. In late 1944, the Secretary of Defence, Sir Frederick Shedden, prophesied that one day there would be 'an outcry about the relatively poor RAAF effort in the Southwest Pacific Area'.[25] He blamed the organisational set-up, and not those he called the 'magnificent' men of the squadrons. This adjective was not misplaced, for it described men whose attributes were at least the equal of the army's soldiers, who achieved more in these two years. Indeed aircrew had to meet much higher standards to be accepted in their force. The reason the army achieved more was primarily a matter of opportunity. These 'magnificent' men were also part of an organisation that was not without some laudable qualities. It was a fully integrated force, with its own senior commanders, unlike the RAAF squadrons in Europe, and despite the distracting bickering of Jones and Bostock, both deserve some credit for organising a powerful Australian Air Force. Further credit goes to many superb leaders at lower levels, such as 'Woof' Arthur and Dick Cresswell. These daring men drew a great deal from their machines, inferior as these often were, and from their squadrons, who before and after the 'Morotai Mutiny' fulfilled their thankless tasks to the end as if they were fighting over Tokyo rather than over surrounded and forsaken enemy forces well behind the main front.

FURTHER READING

Eric M. Bergerud, *Fire in the Sky: The Air War in the South Pacific*, Boulder, Colorado, 2001.

Mark Johnston, *Whispering Death: Australian Airmen in the Pacific War*, Allen & Unwin, Sydney, 2011.

Sir George Jones, *From Private to Air Marshal: The Autobiography of Air Marshal Sir George Jones*, Greenhouse Publications, Melbourne, 1988.

Colin M. King, *Song of the Beauforts: No. 100 Squadron RAAF and the Beaufort Bomber Operations*, Air Power Development Centre, Canberra, 2007.

Lisa Mariah, *Touched By War: Memoirs of a Beaufighter Pilot*, Australian Military History Publications, Sydney, 2006.

Michael V. Nelmes, *Tocumwal to Tarakan: Australians and the Consolidated B-24 Liberator*, Banner Books, Canberra, 1994.

George Odgers, *Air War Against Japan, 1943–45*, Australian War Memorial, Canberra, 1957.

N.M. Parnell, *Beaufighters in the Pacific: A History of the RAAF's Beaufighter Squadrons in the South-West Pacific Area*, N. M. Parnell, Sydney, 2005.

Alan Stephens, *Power Plus Attitude: Ideas, Strategy and Doctrine in the Royal Australian Air Force, 1921–1991*, AGPS Press, Canberra, 1992.

——*The Royal Australian Air Force*, Oxford University Press, Melbourne, 2001.

Notes

1 Odgers, *Air War Against Japan*, p. 193.
2 Stephens, *Power Plus Attitude*, p. 80.
3 John O'Keeffe, 'Reminiscences of Second World War', p. 32, AWM PR01563; Odgers, *Air War Against Japan*, p. 212.
4 Odgers, *Air War*, pp. 205, 210; Stephens, *The Royal Australian Air Force*, p. 157.
5 Odgers, *Air War*, p. 373.
6 Mariah, *Touched By War: Memoirs of a Beaufighter Pilot*, Australian Military History Publications, Sydney, 2006, p. 54.
7 Odgers, *Air War against Japan*, p. 254.
8 LAC E. Hubbard, 8 Sqn, diary 7 August 1944, AWM PR00239.
9 Odgers, *Air War against Japan*, p. 223.
10 Stephens, *Power Plus Attitude: Ideas, Strategy and Doctrine in the Royal Australian Air Force, 1921–1991*, AGPS Press, Canberra, 1992, p. 82.

11 J. Scott, 'World War Two, as Seen by One Participant', memoir, pp. 18, 24 AWM MSS1510.
12 Ibid., p. 17.
13 Odgers, *Air War against Japan*, p. 388.
14 Ibid., p. 439.
15 ibid. p. 444.
16 ibid., p. 445.
17 Nelmes, *Tocumwal to Tarakan*, p. 110.
18 Stephens, *The Royal Australian Air Force*, p. 120.
19 Peter Stanley, *Tarakan: An Australian Tragedy*, Allen & Unwin, St Leonards, 1997, p. 133.
20 WO K. Ellis, 78 Fighter Wing, diary 24 July 1945, AWM PR87/150.
21 Service record for 'Newman, Benjamin Bernard', p. 30, NAA 9300.
22 H. James-Martin, memoir, p. 27, AWM MSS1514.
23 John Harrison interview 1991, Tape 2 Side A, AWM Murdoch Sound Archive, S01504.
24 Wilfred Arthur interview, Tape 3 Side B, AWM Murdoch Sound Archive, S00731.
25 Quoted in Stephens, *The Royal Australian Air Force*, p. 109.

PART 5

THE NEW GUINEA
CAMPAIGN

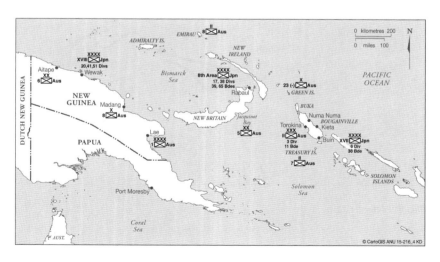

Map 6: Papua New Guinea

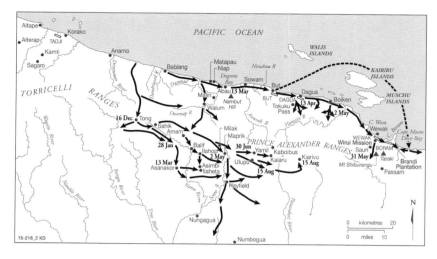

Map 7: Wewak

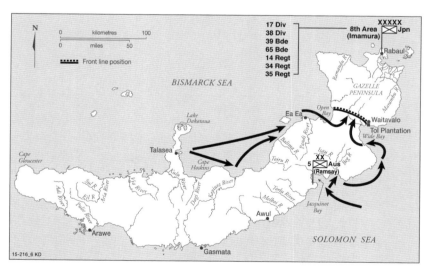

Map 8: New Britain

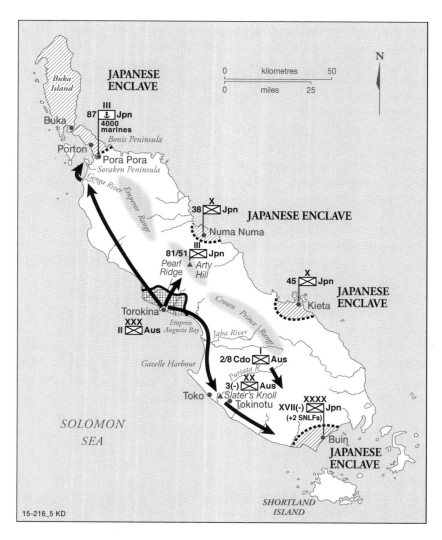

Map 9: Bougainville at the end of the war, 20 April 1945

CHAPTER | 10

'GIVEN A SECOND RATE JOB': CAMPAIGNS IN AITAPE-WEWAK AND NEW BRITAIN, 1944–45

Lachlan Grant

Like the other Australian operations in the south Pacific in 1944–45, the campaigns in Aitape-Wewak and New Britain during those years have been tarred with the label of 'unnecessary'.[1] Certainly, there were soldiers fighting in these campaigns who were frustrated by their circumstances. Some Australian 6th Division veterans felt that they were 'first rate troops given a second rate job'.[2] Conversely many historians have argued that it is inaccurate and misleading to regard these campaigns as unnecessary (see chapter 1),[3] but leaving aside the debates surrounding 'mopping up' at Aitape-Wewak, this campaign was one of the longest fought by Australian troops during the war, in some of the toughest and most unpleasant conditions.

THE AMERICANS AT AITAPE

The northern coast of New Guinea between Aitape and Wewak is characterised by low-lying swamps, thick vegetation and numerous streams prone to flooding. The coastal plain is hemmed in by the Torricelli Mountains, whose grassy foothills steadily rise, forming steep gullies and ridges above the coastal plain. On 22 April 1944, the US 163rd Regimental Combat Team of the 41st Division landed at Aitape. Their job was to capture and defend the nearby Tadji Airfield and to help block the Japanese Eighteenth Army, based around Wewak, from interfering with operations further westward at Hollandia. The Eighteenth Army, commanded by Lieutenant General Hatazō Adachi, had been in a continuous westward retreat along the coast since the Allied advances along the Huon Peninsula and Finisterre Range the previous year. On 3 May, the 163rd Regimental Combat Team was replaced by the US 32nd Infantry Division and the 112th Cavalry Regiment, and they were later joined by the 124th Regimental Combat Team of the 31st Infantry Division, as well as the 43rd Infantry Division. The task of the Americans was to protect the airfield, and they stayed mostly within their small perimeter. Between 10 July and 25 August, a major battle took place at the Driniumor River, 32 kilometres east of Aitape. On the night of 10–11 July, some 10,000 Japanese attacked the US positions across the Driniumor River. The attackers suffered appalling losses from machine-gun and artillery fire, and over the following weeks fell back to the Wewak area. During the initial attack, one Japanese battalion was hit by an artillery barrage and was reduced from 400 men to 30 within minutes.[4] In one of the costliest battles in New Guinea for the entire war (exceeded only by the beachhead battles of Buna, Gona and Sananada between November 1942 and January 1943), over 8000 Japanese were killed. Losses for the Americans were 440 killed and 2560 wounded.[5]

In July 1944, MacArthur informed Blamey that Australian units were required to relieve the six American divisions then in the New Guinea area. Disagreements over the size of the replacing force (see chapters 1 and 2) eventually led Blamey to remove the 6th Division from the I Australian Corps and allocate it to New Guinea in order to meet MacArthur's demands. The 6th Division was chosen simply because it was the only Australian Imperial Force division that was ready for operations at this point, and was therefore tabled to replace the US forces at Aitape.[6]

ARRIVAL OF THE 6TH DIVISION

Following the battle of the Driniumor River, the Americans were happy to hold their positions, and there were no more major actions before the arrival of the 6th Division in mid-October. Due to the shortage of shipping (with priority given to expediting the extraction of the American divisions destined for the Philippines) the various elements of the 6th Division arrived in a trickle. The vanguard was provided by the 2/6th Cavalry (Commando) Regiment (2/7th, 2/9th and 2/10th Commando Squadrons); they were followed by the 19th Brigade (2/4th,

2/8th and 2/9th Battalions) by 19 November, the 17th Brigade (2/5th, 2/6th and 2/7th Battalions) by 7 December, and the 16th Brigade (2/1st, 2/2nd and 2/3rd Battalions) by the end of December. Although the 6th Division was the senior Australian Imperial Force formation, the 19th Brigade had spent the majority of 1943–44 garrisoning northern Australia and thus had not been in action since May 1941, when they had fought the Germans on Crete. However, the division's other two brigades had previously served in the Southwest Pacific with distinction; the 16th in Papua during 1942 and the 17th at Wau-Salamaua in 1943. Throughout the division a majority of the officers were veterans of the earlier campaigns, and had served with the division since 1939. However, among the rank and file veterans numbered only a small percentage.[7]

When the 6th Division arrived at Aitape it was believed the Japanese Eighteenth Army numbered approximately 30,000, although the actual number was closer to 35,000.[8] The three Japanese divisions within the Eighteenth Army – the 51st, 41st and 20th Divisions – had each suffered appalling hardships and casualties in the previous New Guinea campaigns. Each had been in constant retreat along the coast since facing the brunt of the Australian advances in Lae-Salamaua, the Ramu Valley and Huon Peninsula in 1943. As Lieutenant General Yoshihara recalled:

> There were no clothes, no shoes, no blankets, no mosquito nets, no tools, no ammunition, no medicine, and there was, of course, a shortage of food but bravely and tenaciously our troops continued their garrison efforts, with no sleep and no rest.[9]

Disease was rife, and there was no air or naval support. Following the battle for Driniumor River, the Japanese had avoided contact with the Americans, and had mostly withdrawn to areas in which they could grow and cultivate their own food in gardens, but ammunition was so low that troops were eventually prohibited from shooting wild game. Although the Japanese had become relatively self-supporting, grim conditions prevailed. Hungry, weak from malnutrition, and often sick with disease, many were in bad shape. In one instance, the Australians found stolen Australian clothes in the possession of a Japanese soldier killed while infiltrating a night-time position; the clothes he'd taken had been hung out to dry the night before in the encampment.[10] In fact the circumstances were so desperate that Japanese troops resorted to eating grass, leaves and bark to stave off their hunger and in more extreme cases there were incidents of cannibalism.[11] Similarly, just as Australian troops felt frustrated that they had been sidelined from the main battles elsewhere, the Japanese also felt that the war had passed them by, with the real action taking place in the Philippines. They too felt that their presence in New Guinea served political, rather than military or strategic concerns, but they realised that they could still help their homeland if they were able to tie down large numbers of Allied troops in New Guinea.[12]

Australian policy in taking over from the Americans was that the garrison would defend the airfield and radar installations in the Aitape-Tadji area, contain the Japanese forces based at Wewak, and seize any opportunity to destroy this force. They would also give maximum assistance to the Allied Intelligence Bureau and Australian New Guinea Administrative Unit patrolling the area.[13] Since the Americans had had little contact with the enemy since July and August, the General Officer commanding 6th Division, Major-General Jack Stevens, had little information when he arrived regarding the enemy forces that might be opposed to his division. He therefore instructed his forward units of the 2/6th Cavalry (Commando) Regiment to conduct vigorous patrols beyond where the Americans had established their perimeter.[14] In November, Stevens' orders from Lieutenant General Vernon Sturdee at First Australian Army headquarters were for the 6th Division to undertake small raids and patrols 'within the resources available' to gain information and maintain an 'offensive spirit in the troops'. Within these limitations, Stevens' course of action was to launch a two-pronged advance. Along the coast, the 19th Brigade would move eastward to make contact with the enemy, while inland in the Torricelli Mountains the 17th Brigade, when ready, would advance eastward along the range parallel to the coast, thus blocking any Japanese forces intent on coming down from their gardens. The 16th Brigade would remain in reserve on garrison duty around Aitape and the Tadji Airstrip, and be ready to rotate through the front.

When the brigades moved forward to replace the commando squadrons, they had already penetrated inland 32 kilometres into the Torricellis and 64 kilometres along the coast from Aitape to the Danmap River.[15] At first, the going was slow. The numerous rivers, streams and swamps to be crossed along the coastal sector proved difficult, as did the thick jungle and mountainous terrain inland. Making matters worse was the northwest monsoon, which ran from November until April. Monsoonal rains caused havoc at river crossings. These crossing were named after places through which the division had previously journeyed – such as Bardia, Tobruk, Derna, Benghazi, Athens, Olympus, Corinth, Suda Bay, Heraklion, Damascus, Ceylon, Kokoda, Buna, Gona, Wau, Mubo; these names reminded the men of previous battles and campaigns, and of the long journey taken by the formation since 1939.[16]

The terrain and weather were not the only problems that the division faced. A lack of suitable port facilities at Aitape made it difficult to maintain a force of divisional strength. There were no piers at Aitape, and the anchorage offered very little protection from the strong monsoonal winds. The heavy swell and crashing surf on the beach also meant that small landing craft – designed to carry 14 tons of stores – could only carry and unload 2½ tons at a time on the back of a 2½ ton truck. Compounding this difficulty were the limited number of supply ships and landing craft available, as the priority for shipping had been given to the US offensives in the Philippines. This situation prevented the 6th Division from mounting any major offensive operations, and by the beginning of February 1945 it also meant that there were only seven days' rations at Aitape, though this situation was significantly improved by April.[17]

From December 1944 to early January 1945, the 19th Brigade had made a steady advance along the coastal stretch, crossing the Danmap River to Matapau and beyond. There had been a number of small, sometimes sharp, clashes with the enemy during the period, but on 2 January the forward patrols began to encounter well-defended pockets offering stiff resistance. This began several days of close-quarters fighting, with the infantry calling on the support of the Royal Australian Air Force and artillery as well as calling up two tanks and a bulldozer to help dislodge the Japanese at Niap. By 20 January, the advance had reached Abau, while in the foothills and mountains steady progress was also being made, with several contacts occurring with small groups of enemy soldiers. On this date, Stevens ordered the 16th Brigade forward to relieve 19th Brigade.[18]

From 21 January, torrential rain caused severe flooding of the Danmap River. The flood destroyed a bridge that was being constructed by the 2/2nd Field Company, sweeping three men out to sea, who were later rescued. On 26 January, a machine-gun platoon of 2/3rd Battalion found itself on a newly formed island amid the raging torrents. That evening the island became submerged and as the water climbed six metres over its banks the noise was so loud that shouted communications became inaudible. Those who had clambered to safety high in the treetops watched as whole trees, said to be up to 18 metres long and over one metre in diameter, swept passed at 50 kilometres per hour.[19] Lieutenant G. H. Fearnside, a veteran of Tobruk and El Alamein, found this night the most terrifying experience of his life.[20] He later wrote that 'some were killed outright in that mad onslaught of frenzied water and green timber; others were swirled beneath the press of timber and drowned; others were knocked unconscious and their bodies snatched and sent racing downstream, turning over and over, like otters'.[21] The next day, survivors who had been washed away – or floated away on logs – and made it safely to the banks, began arriving at the battalion area. However, seven men of the company had drowned as had four more men of the 2/9th Commando Squadron, while seven bridges that had been supporting the advance had been washed away.[22]

In the mountains with the supply situation steadily improving, Stevens told the 17th Brigade to continue to maintain the pressure on the enemy. Leading the line at this point was the 2/5th Battalion, and by the end of January they had carried out 77 patrols, making regular contact with enemy parties, and had 'expedited the enemy's withdrawal' from a mountainous area measuring about 19 by 13 kilometres.[23]

While the supply situation had been improving, it was still insufficient to support a major offensive; maintenance and communication were also major problems. There were many river crossings requiring bridges (including those damaged in floods). In total, throughout the campaign 118 bridges, with spans totalling 2.7 kilometres, were constructed between Aitape and Wewak. In one case, the 2/8th Field Company took 10 days to construct a 72-metre bridge, with 42 piles, across the Driniumor River.[24] The effort required to maintain these river crossings and roads was compounded by the unavailability or shortage of bulldozers, tip-trucks or graders (of which there was only one). In addition, there were few small landing craft available at this point to help with the coastal advance.

The foundation of Stevens' plan was the parallel advance along the coast and the Torricellis. While the 6th Division was undertaking these operations (within the limitations presented by the lack of shipping and transport, and an inability to stockpile supplies) at no point was consideration given to cancelling either the push. To have done so would have enabled the Japanese to withdraw from the coast to the areas in the mountains where they had cultivated their gardens, or even further into the Sepik Valley. In fact, Stevens had hoped to drop a parachute battalion south of the Torricellis to block the Japanese withdrawal further inland in the face of the Australian advance. To do this, however, would require 50 C-47 Dakotas and a fighter squadron for support. As it was, at this point he had only one C-47 at his disposal to supply the troops slogging it out in the hills. It was therefore an unlikely scenario – soon confirmed – that more transportation aircraft would be made available. Despite these difficulties, on 10 February Sturdee ordered the 6th Division to carry on with its coastal advance towards Wewak 'within the limit of its own resources and without becoming involved in a major engagement'. The operations would, according to Stevens, be conducted under 'greater handicaps than those just completed'.[25]

With the 16th Brigade now having replaced the 19th Brigade on the coastal sector, supply problems (that had been made even more acute by the floods) were relieved by the capture of Dogreto Bay. This was the first beach along the coast from Aitape suitable for landing craft. Between 15 and 20 January the 6th Division generally had four Landing Craft Tanks and 15 to 20 Landing Craft Mechanized at its disposal. The advance was moving at such speed now that on 31 January, when a patrol of the 2/3rd Battalion camp came across a large encampment of Japanese on a spur near Mima Creek, the Japanese were unaware of the presence of the Australian forces. The Japanese were going about their daily business, working around the camp, and some of the prepared machine-gun pits were unmanned. Remaining concealed within metres of enemy, the 2/3rd patrol led by Lieutenant Gilbert Cory – after whom the spur would be named – launched a surprise attack, killing 33 of the 62-strong Japanese.[26] On 15 February, Stevens issued orders to his brigades, outlining his intention to continue the eastward advance and capture Wewak on the coast, and the colonial administrative centre of Maprik in the mountains.[27]

By 18 February, Nambut Hill, an important feature overlooking Dogreto Bay, was in the hands of the 2/1st Battalion after severe close-quarters fighting dislodged the enemy from their strong position. A month later on 17 March, the 2/2nd Battalion had captured But, a missionary outpost which was important due to its jetty, sheltered harbour and air-field. With such facilities now at hand, But became the site of a forward base to supply 6th Division's approach to Wewak, and on 25 March a second airstrip was captured further along the coast at Dagua.[28]

In the face of this rapid advance along the coastline, the Japanese were in disarray, but at Tokuku Pass in the heights overlooking Dagua they anchored their defence, providing stubborn resistance. The subsequent battle to seize control of Tokuku Pass – essential to protect the right flank of the coastal advance – saw the most severe fighting up to that point in the campaign. It was during this battle, on 25 March, that Lieutenant Albert Chowne of the 2/2nd Battalion was killed leading his platoon in a bayonet charge against a Japanese strongpoint, an action for which he was posthumously awarded the Victoria Cross.[29] Four days of heavy fighting followed, after which Tokuku Pass had been seized and the nearby Wonginara Mission occupied. Another notable action occurred on 2 April near Wonginara, when two companies of the 2/3rd Battalion were directed by local guides to Lieutenant-General Masutaro Nakai's 20th Division headquarters, and in a surprise attack killed 28 of 40 Japanese (including five staff officers, but not the general).[30] Among the Australians killed in this action was Lieutenant Robert Varley, the son of Brigadier Arthur Varley, who had been captured at the fall of Singapore. Varley senior had commanded the 22nd Brigade in Malaya, and as a prisoner of war commanded A Force on the Thai–Burma Railway. Unbeknownst to his son or family at the time, Varley senior had also been killed, having perished at sea following the sinking of the *Rakuyō Maru* on 12 September 1944.[31]

The battle of Tokuku Pass also saw the first use of flame-throwers by the Australians in the war. Although the 6th Division had requested the weapon in December 1944, competing priorities meant that it was only issued in March 1945.[32] Troops were instructed that the flame-thrower had a 'powerful psychological effect'. Not only did the flames and smoke 'have considerable blinding effects', the resulting gases were toxic and caused 'immediate disablement when breathed by direct scorching of the lungs, whilst the poisonous effects of carbon monoxide and the lowered oxygen content can also cause casualties'. The jet of flame did not, therefore, have to make direct contact with an enemy to be deadly. Not only could a jet of flame follow the contours of a dugout or bunker, but its radiant heat and toxic gases could also kill.[33] A horrific weapon, flame-throwers were highly valued in the Pacific during the later stages of the war, and reports stated that it boosted morale among 6th Division troops during the Aitape-Wewak campaign. Effective in destroying prepared Japanese defences, flame-throwers were claimed to have saved the 6th Division many more casualties than would have occurred in clearing such pillboxes in a more conventional manner, using squads of men armed with small arms and grenades.[34] During the operations at Wewak, it was reported 'in all cases where possible the Japanese vacated his position screaming before the flame throwers were in range'.[35] Similarly, near Maprik on 8 May, the enemy abandoned 30 weapon-pits, fleeing in the face of a 2/7th Battalion soldier armed with the weapon.[36]

Meanwhile in the Torricellis, the advance toward Maprik continued. When a landing strip was completed at Balif on 20 February, it provided great relief to wounded requiring evacuation, since the journey by stretcher back down the mountains was a six-day affair.[37] As with earlier campaigns in Papua and New Guinea, the advance in the Torricellis was dependent upon the lines of local carriers.[38] Employed by Australian New Guinea Administrative Unit, not all carriers were volunteers, and many were in fact conscripted against their will. As one Australian New Guinea Administrative Unit officer concerned by the treatment of New

Guineans during the Aitape-Wewak campaign cynically wrote in a letter home, '[I] am engaged in some slave trading this trip'.[39]

By the first week of March, operations in the area had slowed considerably, but the availability of a second C-47 Dakota markedly improved the supply situation. However, the sluggish progress to this date had allowed the Japanese to reorganise their forces in well-defended localities, and they grew more aggressive as the Australian forward patrols edged closer to Maprik.[40] On 13 March, a troop of the 2/10th Commando Squadron became surrounded by a much larger Japanese force. Besieged, the Australians thwarted persistent attacks over five days and four nights before they reopened their line of communications. Nearby, other troops of the 2/10th Commando Squadron were also attacked or ambushed. By late March it was becoming clear that a commando squadron was not sufficient to provide the vanguard for the advance on Maprik, and with the supply situation improving by the day, the worn-out commandos, whose morale was deteriorating, were relieved by the 2/6th Battalion.[41] In April, the 2/7th Battalion and 2/6th Battalion continued the slog towards Maprik. In the face of fierce resistance, Maprik was occupied on 22 April and repairs were undertaken immediately on its airstrip.[42] Nearby, a second strip was also constructed and within weeks was able to accommodate C-47 Dakotas. Notably, it was during the fighting for Maprik that the newly commissioned Lieutenant Reginald Saunders, the first Indigenous Australian to obtain the rank of officer in the Australian Army, led his platoon into battle for the first time.

Enduring the tough monsoonal conditions throughout February, March and April, troops of the 6th Division became ever more convinced that the campaign in which they were engrossed was not worth the cost. Casualties had been slowly building; by the end of April, the 6th Division had lost 196 killed and 457 wounded.[43] The close-quarters fighting in the jungle, swamps and ridges meant that often the best and most experienced men – forward scouts, platoon and section leaders, often popular and much admired veterans of earlier campaigns in the Mediterranean and Papua – were the ones being killed and wounded. Concerns were further reinforced by the fact that the division had not been allocated adequate shipping, transport aircraft, and heavy engineering equipment.[44] Use of the term 'mopping up' by politicians and the press caused great resentment. One soldier wrote in a letter home – intercepted by the censors – that the term made the men 'feel like a lot of bludgers. It's not much compensation for the hardships and hard fighting we are enduring'.[45] They had the sympathy of a war correspondent, writing to a friend, whose mail was also intercepted by the censors. 'Everyone insists on calling this "mopping up" and that annoys me', he wrote. 'These boys are mopping up tens upon tens of thousands of Japs, and getting neither praise nor any publicity for it.' It was not spectacular, 'but it is the filthiest, most tedious and sustained heroism that any war can produce anywhere'.[46]

Compounding the problems of morale was the malaria epidemic that struck the 6th Division in the early months of 1945. At the end of January, Stevens had ordered that Atebrin doses be doubled, and a daily Atebrin drill undertaken at which an officer administered the dose, placing the tablets in each soldier's mouth. The soldier then had to show he had swallowed the dose and would then have his name marked off a roll. These parades were deemed to be degrading and insulting, and malaria cases in fact continued to rise. However, it was not a lack of discipline that led to an increase in malarial cases, as it was later discovered that a particularly virulent strain of malaria, resistant to Atebrin, was widespread in the area.[47]

Battle for Wewak

On 27 April, Stevens issued the orders for the 19th Brigade to capture Wewak. The coastal area of Wewak featured three small peninsulas: from east to west, Cape Wom, Wewak Point and Cape Moem. Along the coast, the 2/4th Battalion and 2/7th Commando Squadron advanced to capture Cape Wom (which was achieved on 4 May), while the 2/8th Battalion advanced inland to capture Yarabos (captured on 7 May). On this day a squadron of American P-38 Lightnings, on a sortie to soften up the defences on Wewak Point, inadvertently attacked the Australian position at Cape Wom, killing 11 and wounding 21.[48] On 10 May, the strongly defended position of Wewak Point was seized by the 2/4th Battalion, though one pocket of Japanese held out until the morning of 11 May. Supported by a heavy artillery and air bombardment, the troops approached the peninsula across a 30-yard sand spit covered on either side by swamp and sea. Fighting continued throughout the day as the Japanese resisted strongly from their concrete bunkers, dugouts, and caves connected by tunnels up to 90 metres long within a steep 30-metre escarpment that formed the peninsula.[49] Supporting the infantry were Matilda tanks, artillery and flame-throwers. When the Japanese would not surrender, cave entrances were piqueted until engineers came forward to blow up the entrance, sealing in the occupants. Possibly 200 Japanese were killed at Wewak Point. The 2/4th Battalion had lost just two killed and 17 wounded.[50]

Slightly inland, the 2/11th Battalion, after wading waist-deep through swamp and thick jungle, attacked the Wirui Mission, the key point of defence on a steep 90-metre hill overlooking Wewak. This point fell on 14 May after it was partially surrounded by the 2/4th Battalion, with tanks in support approaching from the opposite direction.[51] It was for his exploits in silencing a series of enemy bunkers during this action that Private Edward Kenna was awarded the Victoria Cross.[52] On 11 May, an amphibious landing, Operation Deluge, took place at Dove Bay, just a few kilometres east of Wewak. The purpose of the landing was to seize the coastal roadway and therefore cut the Japanese retreat from Wewak. With strong air and naval support from the cruisers HMAS *Hobart* and HMS *Newfoundland*, destroyers HMAS *Arunta* and *Warramunga*, the sloop HMAS *Swan*, and the corvettes HMAS *Dubbo* and *Colac*, the 2/6th Cavalry (Commando) Regiment with supporting elements was successfully landed. The beachhead was quickly secured and a perimeter established, blocking the Wewak road.[53] By 22 May, the 2/8th Battalion had occupied Boram Airfield and the heavily booby-trapped Cape Moem; by the end of the month the area around Wewak had become stabilised. For the 6th Division, in the heaviest fighting of the campaign, the capture of Wewak came at the cost of 81 killed and 208 wounded, while Japanese losses were 1355 killed and 69 taken prisoner.[54]

The 6th Division had now driven the remnants of the Japanese Eighteenth Army out of Wewak, forcing them southward into the mountains. During pursuit of the enemy, heavy fighting continued throughout June as the battalions of the 19th Brigade fought for three heavily defended positions at Mt Kawakubo, Mt Tazaki and Mt Shiburangu. The approach to each mountain was a slow process, and the Japanese provided strong resistance from well-prepared and sited positions on the sharp, steep spurs, ridgelines and knolls that characterise the range. After days of heavy fighting, on 14 June Mt Kawakubo fell to the 2/4th Battalion; Mt Tazaki fell to the 2/4th on 22 June, and the 2/8th Battalion occupied Mount Shiburangu on 27 June. By 5 July, the enemy had been cleared from the ridgelines connecting each of these features.[55]

Throughout the period that the fighting had raged around Wewak, the 17th Brigade had continued its steady advance in the mountains, meaning that Adachi's force was now partially surrounded. Through July and into August, aggressive patrolling continued. When the war came to an end, the 6th Division had advanced during its 10-month campaign 112 kilometres along the coast from the Driniumor River to Wewak, and then 16 kilometres inland, while in the Torrecellis the advance had covered 72

Figure 10.1: Private Arthur Willett, 2/8th Battalion, using a flame-thrower in an attack on a Japanese position, Wewak, 10 May 1945. (Australian War Memorial 091749)

Figure 10.2: Evacuating wounded during the fighting at Wewak Point, 10 May 1945. (Australian War Memorial 091729)

kilometres. The total area cleared of the Japanese was in the region of 7770 square kilometres. The 6th Division had inflicted heavy casualties on the Japanese, killing approximately 7200 and capturing 269 prisoners of war. Japanese estimates were 6400 killed in battle with an additional 14,600 dying of illness or malnutrition. Therefore, of the 35,000 Japanese in the Wewak area when the 6th Division arrived in October 1944, only 14,000 were still alive at war's end. Australian casualties were 587 killed (442 killed in action) and 1141 wounded. During the 10-month campaign, tropical diseases caused the greatest number of casualties, with the number of 6th Division troops admitted to medical units for malaria totalling more than 6200, and for other diseases 11,300.[56]

THE RETURN TO NEW BRITAIN

The situation facing the Australian 5th Division (Militia) on New Britain was cause for a different approach. The island fell to Japan in January 1942, and Allied forces returned during Operation Cartwheel in 1943. In December of that year, the US 112th Cavalry Division landed at Arawe on the southwest coast and the US 1st Marine Division landed on Cape Gloucester, on the western tip of New Britain. Both were relieved in April 1944 by the US 40th Division. The Americans mostly stayed garrisoning air bases around Arawe and Cape Gloucester, the Japanese having withdrawn into the hinterland, or they stayed around their main base in the Southwest Pacific (and head-quarters for the Eighth Area Army at Rabaul) on the northeastern tip of New Britain, known as the Gazelle Peninsula. The US and Japanese forces thus sat at opposite ends of the island. In between, patrols, mostly Australian-led, of the Allied Intelligence Bureau waged a small guerrilla war against enemy patrols and outposts. When the 5th Division arrived in October 1944 to replace the US 40th division (which was bound for Luzon in the Philippines), the Allies believed that the Japanese forces on the island numbered about 38,000. At the end of the war it was learnt that the number of Japanese was actually around 93,000.[57]

Rather than stay on the western tip as the Americans had done, Blamey had decided to establish the Australian base at Jacquinot Bay on the southeast coast, with a smaller base established at Cape Hoskins on the northern coast. The commander of the 5th Division, Major-General Alan Ramsay, ordered that the role of the division was to relieve the US forces and protect the western part of New Britain. The division's main task, therefore, was to contain the Japanese on the Gazelle Peninsula and continue to collect intelligence for future operations.[58]

Using barges, the Australians launched a series of two-pronged advances along the north and south coast, toward the neck of the Gazelle Peninsula. Most of the contact with the enemy during this period was limited to small skirmishes; however, in order to secure the Waitavalo-Tol area and enable the division's forces to establish a perimeter across the neck of the Gazelle Peninsula, a series of actions lasting six weeks began in March 1945 to dislodge the Japanese from a succession of fortified positions on Mount Sugi. The offensive involved two river crossings (though torrential rain the night after the Wulwut River was bridged washed the bridge and a ferry out to sea), and a beach landing. It led to the eventual capture of an elaborate system of Japanese defences along a series of ridgelines approximately 2.3 kilometres in length, and rising steeply above the Wulwut River and Henry Reid Bay to a height of approximately 180 metres.[59] The rain had turned these steep slopes into a slippery mess up which the Australians troops had to advance, an approach made more treacherous by mortar fire and machine-gun fire from well-concealed pillboxes.[60] The most notable action in this campaign was the seizure on 18 March of the final defensive point, a feature known as Bacon Hill. After securing Mount Sugi, troops in April began the gruesome discovery in the Tol Plantation of skeletons and remnants of Australian equipment. These were the remains from the massacre of captured members of Lark Force that had taken place there in 1942.[61]

The capture of the Japanese strong points in the Waitavalo-Tol area was the final major engagement of the New Britain campaign, and with the division now having fulfilled its task of establishing a line across the neck of the Gazelle Peninsula, the final four months until the end of the war consisted of maintaining the line and forward patrolling. Many troops complained of boredom, and as in Aitape-Wewak there were frustrations over the lack of recognition given to New Britain in the press. 'Some of those chaps have spent over three years in the islands and aren't given any recognition', a veteran of the desert war now serving with the 29th/48th Battalion wrote. 'It's really not fair for most of them are only kids.'[62] The Japanese, having long expected a major Allied attack on Rabaul, had kept their forces within a strong defensive perimeter around the former administrative centre. Regardless of the lack of Japanese aggressive spirit on New Britain, the raw troops of the 5th Division, with relatively few casualties, had achieved their task of keeping a large Japanese force in check. In 10 months, between October 1944 and August 1945, 53 Australians were killed in combat on New Britain (and a further 21 died from other causes), with 140 wounded. Most importantly, the liberation of Rabaul on 6 September 1945 brought freedom to 5589 Indian prisoners of war, 1397 Chinese, 688 Malayans, 607 Indonesians and 28 Europeans held as internees.[63]

CONCLUSION

The final campaigns in New Guinea and New Britain in 1944–45 have remained controversial. While the veteran 6th Division was fighting a limited offensive at Aitape-Wewak aimed at destroying Japanese forces in New Guinea, in New Britain the relatively inexperienced 5th Division was also fighting a long campaign. However, unlike at Aitape-Wewak, the 5th Division pursued a policy of containing – rather than destroying – the Japanese forces that remained on New Britain. While the policy of containment employed has been seen as the correct approach, exemplified by the relatively low rate of casualties sustained by the 5th Division, the conduct of the Aitape-Wewak campaign is still a cause of debate.[64] Could the same containment policy carried out on New Britain have been applicable at Wewak? Certainly, the geography of New Britain, being an island with the Japanese fortifying their defences around Rabaul, made it a more suitable ploy to bottle up the Japanese forces. Such an approach on the north coast and mountains of New Guinea would have been less practical, and throughout the early months of the campaign it was planned that the 6th Division would later be deployed elsewhere, either for campaigns on Java or for the final assault on Japan itself. To free the division for future operations – and only with hindsight do we know that the war would suddenly end in August 1945 – required the destruction of the large Japanese forces that remained in the Australian mandated territory of New Guinea.[65]

The final campaigns in New Guinea and New Britain were some of the longest fought by Australia during the Second World War, and in the case of Aitape-Wewak, troops of the 6th Division were in almost constant contact with the enemy.

Perhaps the last word should be left to Major General Jack Stevens, who later pondered:

> Why was it fought? What did it achieve? No one in the 6th Division was happy being involved in it [more] than was absolutely necessary. We were all dismayed at being sent to Aitape and our one hope – in fact, our prayer – was to get out of it and to participate in something which, in our view, would contribute to the ending of the struggle ... Whatever the reason, it was a heartbreaking campaign. The objective was not clear; its value uncertain; it was a horrible area in which to fight ... we

lost good men whose lives, it seemed, might have been profitably employed in operations aimed at Japan's main forces. However a fine fighting Division was committed to it and my task as commander was to accomplish the task with the minimum number of casualties.[66]

FURTHER READING

Phillip Bradley, *Hell's Battlefield: The Australians in New Guinea*, Allen & Unwin, Sydney 2012.

Peter Charlton, *The Unnecessary War: Island campaigns of the South-West Pacific, 1944–45*, Macmillan, Melbourne, 1983.

Peter Dean, *The Architect of Victory: The Military Career of Lieutenant-General Sir Frank Horton Berryman*, Cambridge University Press, Melbourne, 2011.

Karl James, 'The Unnecessary Waste: Australians in the Late Pacific Campaigns', in Craig Stockings (ed.), *Anzac's Dirty Dozen: 12 Myths of Australian Military History*, NewSouth Publishing, Sydney, 2012, pp. 138–63.

Mark Johnston, *Fighting the Enemy: Australian Soldiers and their Adversaries*, Cambridge University Press, Melbourne, 2000.

Mark Johnston, *The Proud 6th: An Illustrated History of the 6th Australian Division 1939–45*, Cambridge University Press, Melbourne, 2008.

Gavin Long, *The Final Campaigns*, Australian War Memorial, Canberra, 1963.

Notes

1 Peter Charlton, *The Unnecessary War: Island Campaigns of the South-West Pacific 1944–45*, Macmillan, Melbourne, 1983.

2 Margaret Barter, *Far Above Battle: The Experiences and Memory of Australian Soldiers In War*, Allen & Unwin, Sydney, 1994, p. 235.

3 Karl James, 'The Unnecessary Waste: Australians in the Late Pacific Campaigns', in Craig Stockings (ed.), *Anzac's Dirty Dozen: 12 Myths of Australian Military History*, NewSouth, Sydney, 2012, pp. 138–63; Peter Dean, *The Architect of Victory: The Military Career of Lieutenant-General Sir Frank Horton Berryman*, Cambridge University Press, Melbourne, 2011, p. 295–7.

4 Report on American operations, New Guinea and Dutch New Guinea, 1944. Aitape – the battle of Driniumor, Japanese 18th Army, July 1944, p. 2, AWM 54 603/8/1.

5 Robert Ross Smith, *The Approach to the Philippines*, US Army Center for Military History, Washington DC, 1953, p. 204.

6 David Horner, *High Command: Australia and Allied Strategy 1939–1945*, Allen & Unwin, Sydney, 1982, pp. 335–8.

7 Gavin Long, *The Final Campaigns*, Australian War Memorial, Canberra, 1963, p. 273–4.

8 Long, *The Final Campaigns* p. 272.

9 Yoshihara Kane, *Southern Cross*, http://ajrp.awm.gov.au/, retrieved 20 November 2014.

10 A. G. Leverett, papers, AWM PR85/236.

11 Yoshihara, *Southern Cross*; Mark Johnston, *The Proud 6th: An Illustrated History of the 6th Australian Division, 1939–45*, Cambridge University Press, Melbourne, 2008, pp. 197–8.

12 Aitape-Wewak Campaign – Reports: History of Japanese Operations in New Guinea, p. 13, AWM54 603/7/3.

13 6th Division War Diary, '6 Aust. Div. Operational Order 1', 27 November 1944, AWM52 1/5/12.

14 6th Australian Division Report on Operations Aitape-Wewak campaign 10 October 1944 – 13 September 1945, p. 3, AWM54 603/6/5.

15 Long, *The Final Campaigns*, pp. 279–80.

16 6th Division War Diary, 'Making of Bridges East of the Nigia River', 11 December 1944.

17 Long, *The Final Campaigns*, p. 281.

18 Long, *The Final Campaigns*, p. 286.

19 2/3rd Battalion War Diary, 27–28 January 1945, AWM52 8/3/3.

20 Johnston, *The Proud 6th*, p. 200.

21 Geoffrey H. Fearnside, *Half To Remember: The Reminiscences of an Australian Infantry Soldier In World War II*, Haldane Publishing, Sydney, 1975, pp. 184–5.

22 Long, *The Final Campaigns*, pp. 288–9.

23 2/5th Battalion War Diary, 31 January 1945, AWM52 8/3/5.

24 6th Australian Division Report on Operations Aitape-Wewak, Engineers Appendices, AWM54 603/6/5.

25 6th Australian Division Report on Operations Aitape-Wewak, p. 8.

26 2/3rd Battalion War Diary, 31 January – 4 February 1945, AWM52 8/3/3.

27 6th Division War Diary, '6 Aust/ Division Operation Order Number 7', 15 February 1945.

28 6th Australian Division Report on Operations Aitape-Wewak, pp. 9–11.

29 Lionel Wigmore, *They Dared Mightily*, Australian War Memorial, Canberra, 1963, pp. 258–9.

30 Long, *The Final Campaigns*, p. 325.

31 Lachlan Grant, 'They Called Them "Hellships"', *Wartime*, no. 63, July 2013, p. 33.
32 6th Australian Division Report on Operations Aitape-Wewak, p. 11.
33 6th Division War Diary, December 1944, Part 2, appendices, 'Notes on flamethrowers', p. 1.
34 6th Australian Division Report on Operations Aitape-Wewak, p. 11 and weapons and equipment appendices.
35 Copy of report on 'Deluge' Operations, p. 2, AWM54 603/7/28.
36 2/7th Battalion War Diary, 8 May 1945, AWM 52 8/3/7.
37 Long, *The Final Campaigns*, p. 304.
38 Ibid., pp. 325–6.
39 Australian Field Censorship Coy report dealing with comments and complaints by troops – 1944–1945, 29 March 1945, AWM54 417/1/4.
40 6th Australian Division Report on Operations Aitape-Wewak, p. 10.
41 Long, *The Final Campaigns*, pp. 307–8.
42 6th Australian Division Report on Operations Aitape-Wewak, p. 13.
43 6th Australian Division Report on Operations Aitape-Wewak, p. 13.
44 Long, *The Final Campaigns*, p. 327.
45 Australian Field Censorship Coy Report, 27 April 1945.
46 Ibid.
47 Johnston, *The Proud 6th*, pp. 201–2.
48 19 Brigade War Diary, 7 May 1944, AWM52 8/2/19.
49 6th Australian Division Report on Operations Aitape-Wewak, p. 17.
50 2/4 Battalion War Diary, 8–10 May 1945, AWM 52 8/3/4; Long, *The Final Campaigns*, p. 347.
51 6th Australian Division Report on Operations Aitape-Wewak, p. 17.
52 Wigmore, *They Dared Mightily*, pp. 263–4.
53 Copy of report on 'Deluge' Operations, p. 1.
54 6th Australian Division Report on Operations Aitape-Wewak, pp. 17–18.
55 Ibid., p. 20.
56 Long, *The Final Campaigns*, p. 385; 6th Australian Division Report on Operations Aitape-Wewak, p. 20 and medical appendices; Aitape-Wewak Campaign – Reports: History of Japanese Operations in New Guinea, appendix A.
57 Long, *The Final Campaigns*, p. 241.
58 5th Division War Diary, Operational Instruction 19, 7 October 1944, AWM52 1/5/10.
59 Long, *The Final Campaigns*, pp. 256–9.
60 *Stand Easy*, Canberra, Australian War Memorial, 1945, p. 139; 5 Division War Diary, 16–18 March 1945, AWM52 1/5/10.

61 Ron Blair, *A Young Man's War: A History of the 37th/52nd Australian Infantry Battalion In World War Two*, 37nd/52nd Battalion Association, Melbourne, 1992. p. 278.
62 Australian Field Censorship Coy report, 28 July 1945.
63 Long, *The Final Campaigns*, pp. 269, 557.
64 James, 'The Unnecessary Waste', p. 162.
65 Dean, *The Architect of Victory*, pp. 295–7.
66 Jack Stevens, Papers, p. 93, AWM 3DRL/3561.

CHAPTER 11

MORE THAN MOPPING UP: BOUGAINVILLE

Karl James

Bougainville was one of the largest campaigns fought by Australians during the Second World War. More than 30,000 Australians served on the island, over 500 were killed and two Victoria Crosses were awarded. By 1945, Australia had been marginalised from the key battles that would defeat Japan, relegated instead to bypassed areas in Australia's Mandated Territory of New Guinea and Bougainville, and on Borneo. The necessity of these campaigns was debated in parliament while the press echoed such criticisms. Soldiers too had their own opinions. Brigadier Heathcoat 'Tack' Hammer, who commanded an infantry battalion at El Alamein and an infantry brigade on Bougainville, later commented: 'everyman knew, as well as I knew, that the Operations were mopping up and that they were <u>not</u> vital to the winning of the war'.[1] As this author has argued elsewhere, Bougainville was a necessary campaign. It fulfilled the Australian government's long-stated policies of maintaining an active military effort and employing Australian forces in Australian territory, and was conceived when the war was expected to continue until at least 1946.

Commanded by Lieutenant General Stanley Savige, the Australian operations on Bougainville were initiated in order to shorten the campaign in the Mandated Territories, with the ultimate goal of freeing up manpower. The alternative was to statically garrison the island indefinitely. Crucially, the campaign was initiated when the Australians mistakenly believed they outnumbered the Japanese.[2] A Great War veteran, Savige had commanded a brigade in North Africa in 1941 and a division in New Guinea in 1943. A strong supporter of General Sir Thomas Blamey, Savige was no stranger to controversy.

Savige tightly controlled the campaign. He divided the island into three areas: the Central, Northern and Southern Sectors. In the Central Sector, the Australians crossed the Numa Numa trail over the island's mountainous spine. This was the 'nursery sector' where units gained combat experience before being deployed to more active areas. In the Northern Sector, the Australians followed the northwest coast towards Buka. The advance went well until a small force made a disastrous landing at Porton Plantation in June 1945. It was the only Australian defeat of the campaign. The main fight, however, was in the Southern Sector where the Australians advanced towards Buin, the major Japanese base on the island. The war the infantry knew was one of patrolling along stinking, humid jungle tracks and putrid swamps; the strain eroded some men's morale. In April 1945, the Japanese launched a major counterattack but were defeated with heavy losses at the battle of Slater's Knoll. The Australians continued the advance against over-whelming stubborn and skilful Japanese resistance until virtually the end of the war.

THE NEUTRALISATION OF THE JAPANESE

On 2 August 1944, MacArthur directed that the minimal forces to be employed in relieving the American garrisons in the islands, including the use of four Australian brigades on Bougainville. Another brigade was distributed among Emirau, Green, Treasury and New Georgia Islands – collectively referred to as the 'Outer Islands'. Consequently Lieutenant General Vernon Sturdee's First Australian Army headquarters moved from Queensland to Lae, in New Guinea, where it replaced New Guinea Force headquarters, which in turn formed the headquarters for Savige's II Corps. Savige's corps consisted of Major General William Bridgeford's 3rd Division (7th, 15th and 29th Brigades) along with Brigadier John Stevenson's 11th Brigade and Brigadier Arnold Potts' 23rd Brigade. The 3rd Division and 11th Brigade were sent to Bougainville, while the 23rd Brigade was distributed among Green and the Outer Islands.

The forces Blamey had to commit were considerably larger than he thought necessary for garrison duties. The Australians were fresh, well supplied and, in New Guinea and Bougainville at least, were thought to outnumber the isolated Japanese, estimated at only 13,400 on Bougainville, while they actually numbered around 40,000.[3] On

18 October, Blamey issued Sturdee with the order for 'offensive action
to destroy enemy resistance as opportunity offers without committing
major forces'.[4] Not surprising, Sturdee queried this vague and contra-
dictory order. On 7 November, Blamey replied that 'action must be of a
gradual nature' to 'locate the enemy and continually harass him, and
ultimately, prepare plans to destroy him'.[5] Blamey was ordering a limited offensive. What was of overriding importance, though, was keeping
Australian casualties to a minimum.

The largest island in the Solomon Islands chain, Bougainville had been a
German territory but was mandated to Australia by the League of Nations
following the First World War. The Japanese invaded Bougainville on
30 March 1942, landing at Kieta, on the island's east coast, followed up by
landings at Buka, in north Bougainville, on 1 April, and at Buin, in south
Bougainville, a week later. After their defeat at Guadalcanal in early 1943,
most of Lieutenant General Hyakutake Harukichi's Seventeenth Army
were evacuated to Shortland and Fauro Islands with the army's headquarters established around Buin. Bougainville was also reinforced from
Rabaul with troops, weapons and equipment, although there were only
enough food reserves for four months.

On 1 November, the US 3rd Marine Division landed at Cape Torokina,
in Empress Augusta Bay, on the island's west coast. A fortnight later they
were replaced by the US Army's XIV Corps consisting of some 62,000 men
from the 37th Infantry and the American Divisions. The Americans
established a large base at Torokina with airstrips and a fortified perimeter. In March 1944, Hyakutake attacked Torokina in a major
offensive, but the Japanese were beaten back with heavy casualties, losing
an estimated 3500 men killed and 5500 wounded.

The main focus of the Japanese subsequently became horticulture,
growing fruit and vegetables. By their own calculations, 30 per cent of
their overall strength on Bougainville during 1944 were sick. Of the
remainder, 35 per cent were working in gardens while 15 per cent were
on transport duties. Only 20 per cent of Japanese forces were deployed in
frontline areas.[6] In May and June 1944, approximately 4000 Japanese
died from disease and malnutrition. Once their gardens began yielding
produce in late 1944 mortality rates began to drop to 850 a month.[7]

TOROKINA AND THE OUTER ISLANDS

Brigadier Arnold Potts' 23rd Brigade (7th, 8th and 27th Battalions) began
to relieve the small US garrisons in the Outer Islands in early October.

Potts placed his brigade headquarters along with the 27th Battalion in Green Island group, a coral atoll lying 60 kilometres northwest of Buka. The group consisted of Green Island, also known as Nissan Island, and two smaller islands. The 8th Battalion was sent further afield to Emirau Island, 400 kilometres northwest of Rabaul. The 7th Battalion, meanwhile, went to the Treasury Islands group, and a company was sent to Munda, New Georgia. The Treasuries were 45 kilometres south of Bougainville and consisted of Mono and the smaller Stirling Islands.

A Great War veteran, Potts commanded the Australian forces during their withdrawal along the Kokoda Trial where he was controversially relieved of his command. Now, Potts was to cause his corps commander many headaches with what Savige thought were 'hare brained adventures' for plans to attack the Japanese on nearby islands.[8] Eventually, at the end of December, Savige recommended the island garrisons be reduced and the main body of the brigade brought to Torokina. MacArthur's headquarters approved this request in January 1945.

The first Australians to arrive at Torokina disembarked on 8 September 1944. Torokina was a semi-circle with nearly 10 kilometres of beach frontage, a perimeter that extended for 22 kilometres and was 6 kilometres across at its broadest point. The perimeter was a continuous line of pillboxes and machine-gun positions, connected by wire and minefields. Torokina was hardly comfortless. There were tennis courts and baseball fields, even plants for making ice cream and soft drinks. Sport and inter-unit sports competitions were routine, and swimming carnivals were also held. The Americans and Japanese largely observed an unofficial 'live and let live' policy. The Americans had not kept an accurate list of Japanese units and estimated that there were only 2000 combat troops out of the estimated 11,000 Japanese thought to be on the island.[9]

As with the army, the US Army Air Force and US Marine air squadrons in the northern Solomons were relieved by those from the Royal New Zealand Air Force. Initially two New Zealand fighter squadrons, flying Corsairs, were based at Torokina, but from April 1945 this was increased to four squadrons. The Royal Australian Air Force provided an army cooperation wing comprising No. 5 Tactical Reconnaissance Squadron, flying Wirraways and Boomerangs, along with smaller units flying twin-engine Beauforts for aerial dropping of supplies and equipment, and Auster light aircraft used as 'spotters' for the army.

A problem of the Australian build-up was the difficulty in recruiting enough Bougainvilleans to work as carriers. They were vital for the conduct of the campaign, but at the time of the Australian takeover there were only 300 male Bougainvilleans fit enough to work as carriers. To make up for the initial labour shortage, the Australian New Guinea Administrative Unit, whose role was to recruit and provide native labour, brought over 2000 carriers from New Guinea and recruited – conscripted – the remaining labour from surrounding villages. Bougainvilleans were paid between 5 and 15 shillings a month as well as food, depending on the work. In normal country, the carriers' load was about 18 kilograms, or 15 kilograms in rough country. The Bougainvilleans also worked in plantations, built huts and crewed small watercraft. The Australian New Guinea Administrative Unit also became responsible for administering the refugee compounds in liberated territory where the Bougainvilleans received rations and medical treatment.[10] Many villages conducted their own guerrilla war against the Japanese, killing straggling individual Japanese soldiers or operating under the control of Australian officers as part of the Allied Intelligence Bureau.

SAVIGE TAKES COMMAND

At one minute past midnight on 22 November 1944, Savige and II Corps assumed command of operations in the North Solomons. He had issued his first orders one day earlier. General Bridgeford's 3rd Division and Brigadier Stevenson's 11th Brigade were to relieve the Americans along the Torokina perimeter. Savige wanted a battalion from the 7th Brigade in the mountains, along the Numa Numa Trail, blocking the overland approach to Torokina. The bulk of Japanese were deployed in southern Bougainville and on the island's east coast. Savige wanted to build up detailed information about the Japanese and the terrain before formulating plans for future operations.[11]

Savige knew that he did not have the means to conduct a major offensive, so he tightly controlled the deployment and use of his troops. 'Time and again', he later wrote, 'I was forced not only to improvise but to shape the garment according to the cloth available.' His solution, 'was based on economy of force, and building up a firm base on attaining an objective from which to launch the next attack'.[12]

THE CENTRAL SECTOR

Some of the first troops to move beyond Torokina's perimeter were from the 7th Brigade (9th, 25th and 61st Battalions) with the 9th Battalion relieving the Americans on the feature named 'George Hill' along the

Numa Numa Trial. With rainforest-covered hills, sheer slopes and numerous streams, the country was difficult to supply. Only one battalion could be forward, with each of its companies deployed in a line along the narrow razorback. From George Hill the Australians could look down on the Japanese outpost on Little George Hill just 45 metres away, and beyond that 'Artillery Hill'.[13]

On 29 November, the 9th Battalion heralded the opening of the Australian campaign with an attack on Little George Hill. Advancing under a bombardment of artillery, mortar and machine-gun fire, the infantrymen captured and cleared the feature in 50 minutes, killing 20. Twenty-eight-year-old Spanish-born Private Edwin Barges, a stretcher-bearer, was killed in action and another private died of wounds. Six other Australians were wounded. The battalion went on to capture Artillery Hill on 17 December before being relieved by the 25th Battalion a few days later.

Pearl Ridge, the dominated high ground across the Empire Range, was set as the next objective. Its capture would block the Japanese's eastern approach to Torokina from Numa Numa and Kieta, and harass the Japanese lines of communication along the east coast, preventing any large movement of Japanese troops between the north and south of the island.

The offensive began on 30 December. In what become the usual pattern of attack, Australian Boomerang pilots directed mortar fire to mark targets on the ridge before leading in New Zealand Corsairs for their bombing runs. As the aircraft circled overhead, infantry from the 25th Battalion began moving along Artillery Hill pushing up onto the ridge, but the Japanese resisted skilfully and fighting continued into the next day. The Japanese abandoned the ridge on New Year's Day.

In early January 1945, the 11th Brigade (26th, 31st/51st and the 55th/53rd Battalions) assumed responsibility for the Central Sector. Brigadier John Stevenson had a busy time during the first months of 1945, with his battalions divided between Torokina, and the Northern and Central Sectors. Having commanded a battalion in Syria and on the Kokoda Trail, Stevenson realised the importance of improving the lines of communications in the Central Sector. A jeep track from Barges' Hill to Pearl Ridge was developed as well as an air-dropping ground. A light-rail link was even built up the face of Barges' Hill. During their 14 weeks in the sector, the 11th Brigade patrolled continuously. Patrols penetrated deep into Japanese territory, with one patrol even reaching Numa Numa plantation on the island's east coast. They had accounted for 236 Japanese killed, 15 possible 'kills' and four prisoners, for the loss of four Australians and 19 wounded.[14]

On 18 April, Potts' 23rd Brigade, recently arrived from the Outer Islands, became responsible for the Central Sector. The 27th Battalion began patrolling on 21 April, ambushing, snipping, raiding and generally harassing the enemy. The battalion's war diarist commented:

> After three and a half years of hard training … the unit has at last been committed to an operational role, and is fighting live enemy … The troops are in high spirits and the great majority are very keen to get at grips with the Jap.[15]

By early June 1945, the campaign on the island was going well for the Australians. As well as virtually controlling the Numa Numa Trail, the 11th Brigade in the north had pushed the Japanese back to the Bonis Peninsula while in the south the 3rd Division was threatening the main Japanese garden areas and was only 45 kilometres from Buin. With the 23rd Brigade's arrival on Bougainville, Savige's force, as of 9 June, numbered about 32,000 troops. The best estimates of the Japanese strength were considerably lower. In April, the total number of Japanese army personnel thought to be on Bougainville was 11,000. By June this figure had risen to an estimated 14,500. It was thought that there were 1780 soldiers in the north; 1630 around Numa Numa; 1130 in Kieta; 7850 in Buin, and an estimated 1310 soldiers on Shortland, Fauro and other nearby islands. It was also estimated that 1400 Japanese civilian labourers plus up to 3000 naval personnel where spread across the island. The total estimated Japanese strength was between 19,000 and 20,000. (The estimate for the army's strength was almost accurate, but once naval and civilians were included, whose numbers were double what was estimated, the actual Japanese strength was about 24,000.)[16] Savige's ultimate goal was the 'annihilation of the Japanese'. To do this he had to concentrate his forces in the south for the final advance on Buin, while still keeping enough forces in the other sectors to keep pressure on the Japanese. Savige decided the 23rd Brigade would become responsible for both the Northern and Central sectors. This would give the 11th Brigade a brief respite in Torokina before joining the 3rd Division in the Southern Sector.[17]

Savige now eased his earlier restrictions in the Central Sector and Lieutenant Colonel Harry Dunkley's 7th Battalion unleashed a new offensive. Savige told Dunkley the battalion was expected to 'inflict casualties of at least four to our one'.[18] Dunkley exceeded Savige's expectations. Between 7 June and 15 August, the 7th Battalion captured 25 Japanese positions and claimed 181 Japanese killed for the loss of 25 Australians and 54 wounded.[19]

On 10 August, First Australian Army warned II Corps that Japan's surrender was imminent. This message was immediately passed to all forward units. The next day, General Sturdee signalled Savige that, in view of the probability of cessation of hostilities, all operations were restricted, patrols were to be recalled, and that every effort must be made to avoid further Australian casualties. They could defend themselves if attacked, but hostilities were otherwise suspended.[20] During the morning of 13 August, the Japanese opened fire on an Australian platoon, killing Private Eric Bahr and wounding three others. A shearer from northwest Victoria, 26-year-old Bahr was the last Australian killed in action in the campaign. His death came just as Dunkley was informing his company commanders of his instructions for the Japanese surrender.[21]

THE NORTHERN SECTOR

As the Australians wore down the Japanese in the Central Sector, the campaign in the north also gathered momentum. With the cutting of Japanese communications between the north and south by controlling the Numa Numa Trail, Savige wanted the Japanese in the north contained to Buka Island and the narrow Bonis Peninsula on Bougainville's northern tip. The Americans had patrolled along the northwest coast to Cape Moltke and Kuraio Mission, about 30 kilometres from Torokina, once a week by landing craft. Prior to the 11th Brigade's takeover of the sector, Savige stressed to Stevenson, who passed it on to his battalion commanders, that there was no need for haste; they were to 'proceed cautiously' and 'avoid costly frontal attacks'.[22]

Moving from Torokina by foot and by landing craft along the coast, the Australians progressed steadily, and by mid-January 1945 the 31st/51st Battalion had reached Tsimba Ridge, a strongly fortified Japanese position honeycombed with elaborate trench systems and gun emplacements, and supported by artillery, including 75-millimetre mountain guns.[23] The battalion unsuccessfully attacked the ridge on 21 January and also tried to outflank the feature. Tsimba Ridge and the nearby area were finally captured on 9 February. The Australians acknowledged the skill and formidability of their foe. An after-action report stated Tsimba Ridge's defences were 'characterised' by 'stubborn and determined resolve' to hold this stronghold 'at all costs'. Japanese camouflage was 'excellent' and accurate Japanese snipers caused many casualties.[24]

The 31st/51st Battalion was relieved by the 26th Battalion in late February. The incoming battalion conducted a complicated series of manoeuvres, cutting the Japanese lines of communications, outflanking and forcing them to abandon one position after another. By employing a series of amphibious landings on Saposa and Taiof Islands, and Soraken Peninsula, the battalion cleared the peninsula by the end of March. The 26th Battalion remained at Soraken while the 55th/53rd Battalion took over in April, pushing north, through mangrove swamps on the coast and rugged foothills. Australian patrols met little resistance, but the difficult country slowed their progress and they were shelled continually. By mid-May, the Australians had established a line across the neck of the Bonis Peninsula, a front about 8 kilometres long.[25] The Japanese, however, were increasingly aggressive. Patrol clashes occurred daily: there were regular attacks on the 55th/53rd Battalion's thinly deployed companies, and more than 700 shells fell in the battalion's area.[26] The 26th Battalion relieved the fatigued 55th/53rd Battalion in mid-May, although the former was not much better off. Stevenson even described the 26th Battalion as being 'a little sore' at being sent back into action without a rest in Torokina.[27]

The Bonis Peninsula was laced with Japanese pillboxes and bunkers, and in order to overcome these defences an ambitious plan was devised where a small force would land by barge at Porton Plantation and push inland to link up the with main Australian force moving north. Early on 8 June, a force based around the 31st/51st Battalion's A Company, commanded by Captain Clyde Downs, landed at Porton. They established a small u-shaped perimeter, but from the outset the tactical plan went wrong. The barge carrying the force's heavy weapons became grounded on a reef offshore, and within 50 minutes of the first troops coming ashore they were under machine-gun fire. By dawn it was clear that the perimeter was ringed by pillboxes and the Japanese were reinforcing the area. The situation deteriorated throughout the day. It was only the accurate artillery support, firing from Soraken and called down skilfully by Lieutenant David 'Pete' Spark, which prevented the Japanese from overrunning the beachhead. Attempts to reinforce Downs during the night had to be abandoned when the Australian landing craft came under intense fire. Stevenson consequently decided to evacuate Downs' force.[28] An officer later described the conditions in the perimeter:

> Our sector was subject to rifle fire from hidden snipers making it impossible to raise one's head ... Eating, drinking and movement were impossible, personnel were cramped from lack of movement and the

continued immersion in swamp water, and sun heated our rifles until they were almost too hot to handle.[29]

The rescuing landing craft broke through to evacuate Downs' men late in the afternoon. Overloaded, three craft became ground. One floated off, but the other two remained stuck fast. Low flying Boomerangs and Corsairs, as well as ongoing artillery fire, tried to protect the trapped men, but they still came under fire from the Japanese on the shore, and from soldiers who tried to swim out to the vessels. One of the two stranded craft drifted off during the night, but the other remained stuck. A soldier afterwards described the desperate conditions in the remaining landing craft:

> The intense heat of the day, fatigue and exposure, plus the fact that we had not slept for three days and nights was beginning to take effect. Men often collapsed due to their exhaustion. A few were delirious. Men were half deaf from the continual explosion of bombs, shelling, and machine-gun fire.[30]

Finally, in the early hours of 11 June, the survivors were rescued. Of the 190 members of Downs' company group, 22 were killed or missing, including Downs, and 62 were wounded. More were hospitalised. Five more men were killed from the landing craft company, and seven were wounded.[31]

Brigadier Potts' 23rd Brigade began taking over the Northern Sector on 20 June. Potts was enthusiastic, but Savige was not interested in the brigadier's plans for an offensive push into the Bonis Peninsula. Having only just avoided a total disaster at Porton, Savige was not prepared to risk another major operation in an area that had 'no great bearing on the general campaign'.[32] While his caution is understandable, Savige's restrictions on Potts surrendered the initiative to the Japanese and put the Australians well and truly on the defensive.

By late June, the 23rd Brigade's 27th and 8th Battalions were experiencing the same setbacks as the 11th Brigade. To counter the Japanese tactics, the Australians placed standing patrols to guard the main roads. These patrols stayed in position from dusk until late morning, while ambush positions were manned 24 hours a day. Patrols hunted for ambush parties and searched the roads and tracks for mines.[33] Such efforts met with only limited success. It tied down and fatigued soldiers, and limited the number available for offensive patrolling. The Japanese simply carried on using other numerous small paths off the main tracks. In early

July, a troop of four Matilda tanks from the 2/4th Armoured Regiment were allocated to the Northern Sector. The swampy terrain and heavy rains limited their usefulness. The Matildas were more symbolic than practical; there was no better way to boost the infantry's morale. Savige and Potts decided to abandon the Ruri Bay position and concentrate both the 27th and 8th Battalions around the Ratsua–Buoi Plantation area. This was a shorter front, at less than 3 kilometres.[34]

On the 24th, the 8th Battalion attacked a series of Japanese bunkers named 'Base 5'. Despite already being wounded twice in the left arm and once in the thigh, Private Frank Partridge rushed forward under heavy fire, retrieved a Bren light machine gun from the dead gunner and fired into the Japanese bunker. Handing the Bren to another man; Partridge threw a smoke grenade into the bunker. The grenade exploded and Partridge dived in, killing the surviving occupant with a knife. He then went on to clear another bunker before blood loss finally forced him to stop. Others rushed forward and held the ground long enough to collect the dead and wounded. For this action Partridge was awarded the Victoria Cross.

The Australians attacked Base 5, now renamed 'Part Ridge', again on 5 August and captured the position. The Australians were slowly regaining control of the sector, but by now it was too late. The campaign in the Northern Sector ended in a stalemate.

THE SOUTHERN SECTOR

About 70 per cent of the Japanese on Bougainville were around Buin, although at least half were in no condition to fight a strenuous campaign. As their rations dropped, the numbers of Japanese suffering dysentery, malaria and malnutrition rose.[35] Savige outlined his plans to General Bridgeford for the sector on 23 December. The 3rd Division's ultimate role was to 'destroy [the] Japanese forces in Southern Bougainville'. Its immediate task was to clear the area south of the Jaba and move forward to the Puriata River. Once there, patrols were to push southward in preparation for the next advance. Keeping with Savige's policy governing the campaign, however, nothing larger than a battalion would be committed to an attack without his prior approval.[36] He also insisted Bridgeford rotate each of his three brigades through the area, shifting in turn from the front to the reserve, then the rear. Savige did not loosen his grip with time. When the Southern Sector was later divided between the south axis, along the Buin Road, and north axis, along a second track named the Commando Road, Savige insisted that a battalion advance along each axis with the third battalion in reserve. Savige directed: 'Not a single man more than was absolutely essential would be employed in the area' and 'Not a single ration would be consumed in these areas by any man whose presence was not absolutely essential to the conduct of the operation.'[37]

By the end of January 1945, the 29th Brigade (15th, 42nd and 47th Battalions) were across the Jaba River and reached Mawaraka by the middle of the month. It was relieved by the 7th Brigade soon afterwards. The 7th Brigade would advance to the Puriata River in three axes. The 9th and 61st Battalions would each head inland to Mosiegetta along different routes while the 25th Battalion would follow the coast around Motupena Point to Toko. The 61st Battalion's Sergeant John Ewen recorded in his journal the fatigue experienced by frontline soldiers. On 17 February, he commented they were 'just about had':

> Living on your nerves in mud, rain, sleeping in holes in the ground soon wears a fellow down. I have watched the boys faces get drawn and haggard, and their movements slow and listless. I suppose I must look the same.[38]

Throughout February and into March, Ewen's journal is full of descriptions of patrols, ambushes and attacks. These contacts were small but frequent, and each night the men expected an attack. Stress was constant.[39] The 9th Battalion was also tiring. By the end of January there were several instances of company commanders reporting their men being 'too frightened' to leave their positions and refusing to go on patrol. One company commander 'cracked up'.[40] The 9th and 61st Battalions reached Mosiegetta in mid-February. The 61st Battalion's own regimental medical officer noted a marked decline in each of the four rifle companies from the second and third weeks in March. Soldiers, non-commissioned officers and even a few subalterns were anxious and nervy, and several platoon commanders stated that their men refused to go on patrols.[41] On 19 March, the battalion's commander, Lieutenant Colonel Walter Dexter, wrote to his brigadier commander asking for his battalion to be relieved. Although he considered his men had so far 'done a magnificent job', Dexter conceded his battalion had 'reached such a state of mental and physical strain that it can no longer be regarded as an efficient striking force'.[42]

Following the battle of Slater's Knoll, both the 9th and the 61st Battalions remained in action into April. On the 17th Lieutenant Colonel Geoff Matthews, commanding the 9th Battalion, recorded a platoon had 'the jitters' and were about to have a 'sit down strike'. He cheered them up a little, and the patrol set off. The rest of the company were also a 'bit nervous', so Matthews told them he would relieve them from patrolling for as long as he could. 'The word got around quickly and spirits went up.'[43] A forceful commander, Matthews was able to use persuasion and patience to coax his 9th Battalion through its problems.

The situation in the 61st Battalion was bleaker. 'Bn is in a bad way as the men are all cracking up', Sergeant Ewen wrote on 9 April, with the soldiers refusing to go on patrol: 'Nearly all the boys have a vacant look in their eyes and look dazed.'[44] On 7 April, shortly after the battle of Slater's Knoll, Dexter was evacuated suffering from neuritis. He never returned. Having enlisted in the 1939 as a private, Dexter's own physical and emotional decline left him unable to encourage or manage his men's exhaustion and frayed nerves. The 'jack ups' or 'strikes' that occurred in the 9th and 61st Battalions are examples of what can happen when front-line soldiers were pushed beyond their limits of endurance.

The 25th Battalion's experience in the Southern Sector, however, was the exact opposite. At the start of January, the 25th Battalion's operations were focused on securing the coastline from Gazelle Harbour to the mouth of the Puriata River.[45] This was done in a series of small amphibious landings that cleared Motupena Point and moved on to Toko in early February. Toko subsequently became a major base for the Australians. In March the battalion crossed the Puriata River and advanced down the Buin Road with orders to clear the enemy to the Hongorai and then the Hari Rivers. In one action, on 22 March, after two men were hit, Corporal Reginald Rattey ran forward, firing his Bren from the hip. Reaching a Japanese weapon pit, he flung in a grenade, and called his section forward. He then cleared another pit using the same tactics. Still under heavy fire, he returned to his section, collected two more grenades, and went on to kill the Japanese in a third pit and captured a machine-gun post as his company moved up and consolidated the position. Rattey was awarded the Victoria Cross.

In response to the strong Australian push along the Buin Road, Lieutenant General Kanda Masatane, who replaced Hyakutake after he had a stroke, ordered the Japanese 6th Division to launch a full-scale attack on the Australians if they crossed the Puriata River. This counterattack was to inflict as many casualties as possible and delay the Australian advance, so as to allow Kanda time to prepare for Buin's defence. The focus of the attack would be against a feature called *Goshu-dai* (Australian Heights) – Slater's Knoll.[46]

The Japanese offensive began with an artillery barrage on 26 March followed by assaults on the 25th Battalion's most forward companies along the Buin Road the next day. By 31 March, the Australian companies where besieged. If it had not been for the relief column lead by Matilda tanks from the 2/4th Armoured Regiment, the Australians would have been overrun. Emerging from the jungle, the Matilda tanks opened fire and 'blasted and machine-gunned the Japs out of their pits' who 'fled in disorder'.[47] Thereafter a slight lull followed. Before the 25th Battalion's headquarters company, along with the battered survivors of B Company, who were dug-in on Slater's Knoll were hit by the Japanese just before dawn on 5 April. The attackers rushed headlong into barbed wire and ferocious machine-gun and rifle fire. Bodies were scattered over an area less than 170 square metres.[48] A Japanese officer afterwards likened it to being 'caught in a rain of bullets'. Men were tangled on the wire and killed. Those following behind used their bodies to climb the wire.[49] Fighting continued throughout the morning. At 12.50 p.m., two Matildas reached Slater's Knoll from the battalion's rear echelon, escorted by men from the 61st Battalion. Again the Matildas' firepower proved decisive. Individually and in small groups, the Japanese broke. They were shot down as they ran. Some Australians even stood up in their weapon pits to get a better shot.[50] Mopping up continued for about an hour, but the battle of Slater's Knoll was over.

The fighting left the survivors with powerful memories. An Australian sergeant remembered the Japanese screaming as they attacked: 'They came at us over and over again.' Some Japanese came within metres of the Australians' weapon pits and 'were shot at point-blank range or hit with a bayonet but a lot more collided with the barbed wire and were picked off in mid-stride'.[51] A Japanese lieutenant likened the battle to a scene from hell. The wire was tangled with the heaped bodies of the dead and the groans and cries of the dying. He saw one Japanese soldier, with an arm missing and covered in blood, crawling on his knees trying to get away. Elsewhere, wounded cried out for water while others begged to be killed.[52]

All told, between 28 March and 5 April, 620 Japanese dead were counted. As a point of comparison between January and April, the 25th Battalion lost 36 officers and men killed and 154 wounded. The 7th Brigade's total losses during this time were 70 dead and 260 wounded.[53] Slater's Knoll brought the 7th Brigade's campaign to a close.

Brigadier Hammer's 15th Brigade (24th, 57th/60th and 58th/59th Battalions) now advanced on a two-battalion front: one battalion along the Commando Road and another on the Buin Road. The two roads were connected by lateral tracks, which had been improved to allow Matilda tanks to move from one road to the other.[54] By comparison to earlier phases of the campaign, the 15th Brigade enjoyed an almost luxurious amount of

Figure 11.1: Brigadier Heathcote Hammer points out a map feature to Lieutenant General Vernon Sturdee (left), watched by Major General William Bridgeford and Lieutenant General Stanley Savige, Bougainville, 12 May 1945. (Australian War Memorial 091857)

air, artillery and armour support. Hammer's tactic was to drive the Japanese back into confined areas, with patrols harassing their flanks, and then employing the Australians' superior firepower to destroy them. When a 'worthy' target was found, he reported, 'we hit hard and often'. His approach was to use firepower as much as possible to save manpower and casualties. Approximately 68,000 artillery shells, 38,000 mortars and 768 tonnes of bombs were fired and dropped in support of his brigade.[55] By the end of the first week of May, the 24th Battalion's lead company reached the Hongorai River. It took 31 days to advance 6.5 kilometres.[56] Further inland, the 57th/60th Battalion on the Commando Road reached the Hongorai River in mid-May. The brigade continued on to the Hari and the Mivo Rivers in June.

Savige considered the 15th Brigade his 'most efficient and best fighting brigade', but he was mindful of it becoming too exhausted.[57] He consequently ordered General Bridgeford to relieve it with the 29th Brigade. As mentioned earlier, in June Savige reviewed the overall situation on Bougainville, with the object of 'completing the annihilation' of the remaining Japanese. Savige felt that he was in a good position to take a more aggressive approach. Using Brigadier Stevenson's 11th Brigade and the 3rd Division, Savige would build up a concentrated force in the Southern Sector large enough to destroy the Japanese in Buin. After this was done, he felt that the 'elimination' of the Japanese in the other sectors would be a relatively 'simple task'.[58]

The 29th Brigade began relieving the 15th Brigade around the Mivo River in early July. Torrential rain and floods hit the Southern Sector in the middle of the month. The Mivo River rose 2 metres; bridges were destroyed; the corduroy surfaces of roads and tracks floated away; and the Buin Road was reduced to a sea of mud. Water dripped from the men; clothes, boots and socks were sodden. Eating was an ordeal; sleeping was worse. Equipment and ammunition deteriorated quickly if not stored undercover and properly maintained. Stores became mouldy. Throughout it all, the Japanese continued to probe, setting mines and booby traps.

The 15th Battalion, around Siskatekori, where the Buin Road crossed the Mivo, was subjected to intense action. Patrols reported large clashes with the enemy. A series of minor attacks against the battalion culminated in a major assault on D Company on 9 July. Fighting continued for much of the morning. More than 30 Japanese bodies were counted afterwards. The 15th Battalion was pounded by Japanese artillery, sometimes being hit by more than 200 shells a day. By August, over 3000 rounds had landed in the battalion's area.[59]

At 10 a.m. on 15 August, Australian Prime Minister Chifley announced in a radio broadcast that the war was over. After the Japanese began shelling Soraken at 7 p.m., a soldier in the 8th Battalion wrote in his diary: 'Who said the war was over?'[60] The mood was very different in Torokina where celebrations erupted like 'wildfire'.[61] II Corps was not going to take any chances. Forty-five minutes after Chifley's broadcast, four specially prepared Beauforts took off from Torokina on a leaflet-dropping mission, dropping more than 230,000 leaflets over the main Japanese areas on Bougainville. Each Beaufort also had 'Japan surrenders' painted in large Japanese characters on the underside of the wings. A few weeks later, in a highly choreographed and formal ceremony in Torokina on 8 September, General Kanda and Vice-Admiral Baron Samejime signed the instrument of surrender in Savige's headquarters. All Japanese forces on Bougainville and the adjacent islands surrendered.

CONCLUSION

Bougainville did not change the outcome of the war nor contribute to its end. But it *was* a justifiable campaign, one conducted by Australian forces with brutal skill and efficiency. From the very outset, the ultimate

Australian objective was the 'destruction' of the Japanese. When the war came to an end, II Corps controlled about two thirds of Bougainville: in the Central Sector, the Japanese were harassed and contained around Numa Numa; in the Northern Sector, although still aggressive, the Japanese were contained in the northernmost tip of the island; and in the Southern Sector preparations were underway for the final advance on Buin. This advance came at a price. Between October 1944 and August 1945, 516 Australians died on Bougainville and another 1572 were wounded. The infantry suffered most of these casualties.

The Japanese fared far worse. When the Americans landed at Torokina in November 1943, about 65,000 Japanese occupied the island. When the Japanese surrendered nearly two years later there were just over 23,800. The US Marines and the US Army's XIV Corps estimated they had killed 9890 Japanese between November 1943 and November 1944. From November 1944 until August 1945, II Corps claimed 8789 Japanese killed; this figure included those killed by the Bougainvilleans. This meant that 17 Japanese soldiers died for every Australian killed, while another 138 Japanese were taken prisoner. The exact number of Japanese deaths, however, will never be known. Some 30,000 died from sickness and disease.[62] Any assessment of the campaign should also consider the people of Bougainville. Their support and assistance was vital to the Australians. From Bougainville's pre-war population of 52,000 people it is thought up to a quarter died either during or as a result of the war.[63]

Bougainville will always be a controversial campaign. Torokina, Pearl Ridge, Porton and Slater's Knoll will never become household names. But the campaign should never be dismissed. 'As somebody who was there throughout the campaign', a soldier later wrote, 'it certainly was not just "mopping up".'[64]

FURTHER READING

Audrey Davidson, *Porton A Deadly Trap: The Battle that Vanished*, Boolarong Press, Brisbane, 2005.

Harry A. Gailey, *Bougainville: The Forgotten Campaign, 1943–1945*, University of Kentucky, Lexington, Kentucky, 1991.

Karl James, *The Hard Slog: Australians in the Bougainville Campaign, 1944–45*, Cambridge University Press, Melbourne, 2012.

Gavin Keating, *A Tale of Three Battalions: Combat Morale and Battle Fatigue in the 7th Australian Infantry Brigade, Bougainville, 1944–45*, Land Warfare Studies Centre, Canberra, 2007.

Gavin Long, *Australia in the War of 1939–1945, series 1, vol. VII, The Final Campaigns*, Australian War Memorial, Canberra, 1963.

Peter Medcalf, *War in the Shadows*, Queensland University Press, Brisbane, 1986.

Tod Schacht, *My War on Bougainville*, Australian Military History Publications, Sydney, 1999.

Notes

1 Hand written notes on Bougainville by Major General H. H. Hammer, p. 5, AWM93, 50/2/23/440. [Unless otherwise stated all archival material is from the AWM.]

2 See Karl James 'The Unnecessary Waste: Australians in the Late Pacific Campaigns' in Craig Stockings, (ed.), *Anzac's Dirty Dozen: 12 Myths of Australian Military History*, NewSouth Publishing, Sydney, 2012, pp. 138–64; Karl James, *The Hard Slog: Australians in the Bougainville Campaign, 1944–45*, Cambridge University Press, Port Melbourne, 2012, pp. 9–28.

3 Gavin Long, *The Final Campaigns*, Australian War Memorial, Canberra, 1963, pp. 22–3.

4 Sturdee to Blamey, letter, 31 October 1944, 3DRL 6643, 2/35 (2 of 3).

5 Blamey to Sturdee, letter, 7 November 1944, 3DRL 6643, 2/35 (2 of 3).

6 History of the Japanese Occupation of Bougainville, p. 13, AWM54, 492/4/4 part 1.

7 Information on Japanese operations in Solomons, p. 5, AWM54, 423/6/15; Bōeichō Bōei Kenshūjo Senshishitsu (ed.), *Senshi sōho: Minami Taieiyō Rikugun sakusen <5> Aitape, Puriaka and Rabaul* [War History Series: South Pacific Army Operations (vol. 5), *Aitape, Puriaka, and Rabaul*], Asagumo Shinbunsha, Tokyo, 1975, p. 227.

8 Savige to Sturdee, letter, 3 December 1944, 3DRL 2529, 84.

9 Report on visit to HQ XIV Corps, 3DRL 2529, 68.

10 James, *The Hard Slog*, pp. 53–5.

11 II Corps Operation Instruction No. 1, AWM54, 613/4/15.

12 Savige, notes on 'To Slater's Knoll and Soraken', p. 1, 3RDL 2529, 128.

13 Long, *The Final Campaigns*, p. 108.

14 Report on Operations 11th Brigade, p. 29, 3DRL 2529, 73.

15 27th Battalion war diary, 17 April 1945, AWM52, 8/3/65.

16 Long, *The Final Campaigns*, p. 217.

17 Report on Operational and Administrative Activities, pp. 18–21, 3RDL 2529, 73.

18 Biographical additions, chapter 9, 'The Floods and the Cease Fire', AWM67, 3/113.

19 Report on Operations of 23rd Brigade, p. 21, AWM54, 613/6/37.

20 II Corps war diary, 10–11 August 1945, AWM52, 1/4/8.
21 James, *The Hard Slog*, p. 112.
22 Savige to Sturdee, letter, 18 February 1945, 3DRL 2529, 84.
23 11th Brigade Report on Operations, p. 2, 3DRL 2529, 72.
24 Report on operations, Tsimba–Genga River, pp. 4–5, AWM54, 613/
    4/46A; 2 Aust. Corps (AIF) in the North Solomons, p. 83, 3DRL
    2529, 72.
25 2 Aust. Corps (AIF) in the North Solomons, p. 9, 3DRL 2529, 72;
    11th Brigade Report on Operations, pp. 11–14, 3DRL 2529, 73.
26 Long, *The Final Campaigns*, p. 208.
27 Notes on the Official History, chapter 8, p. 7, AWM67, 3/382.
28 11th Brigade war diary, 'AQ' war diary notes for 8 June 45, Appendix
    28, AWM52 8/2/11.
29 Audrey Davidson, *Porton a Deadly Trap: The Battle that Vanished*,
    Boolarong Press, Brisbane, 2005, p. 78.
30 Report on events subsequent to boarding stranded ALCA on
    Porton beach until rescued by Private W. J. Crawford, p. 6,
    AWM54, 613/7/7.
31 Davidson, *Porton*, pp. 168–72. The casualty figures in the official
    history are slightly lower, giving 23 killed and 106 wounded. Long,
    The Final Campaigns, p. 215.
32 Savige to Sturdee, letter, 15 July 1945, 3DRL 2529, 84.
33 James, *The Hard Slog*, p. 148.
34 Report on Operations of 23 Brigade, p. 40, AWM54, 613/6/37.
35 History of the Japanese Occupation of Bougainville, pp. 18–19,
    AWM54, 492/4/4 part 1.
36 II Corps Operation Instruction No. 3, 23 December 1944, AWM54,
    613/4/15.
37 2 Aust Corps (AIF) in the North Solomons, p. 15, 3DRL 2529, 72.
38 Ewen, book 1, 17 February 1945, PR89/190.
39 See, for example, ibid., 23–28 February 1945.
40 See, for example, Matthews, diary 13, 29–31 January & 1 February
    1945, PR89/079, 5.
41 Medical report on battalion, 3DRL 6937, 32.
42 James, *The Hard Slog*, p. 179.
43 Matthews, diary 13, 15 & 17 April 1945, PR89/079, 5.
44 Ewen, book 2, 9 April 1945, PR89/190.
45 7th Brigade Report on Operations, p. 17, 3DRL 2529, 71.
46 James, *The Hard Slog*, p. 191.
47 Report on Operations in South Bougainville, p. 23, AWM54, 613/
    7/68.
48 Long, *The Final Campaigns*, p. 163.
49 Diary of Tsutsutani Toshiyasu, n.p., author's copy.

50 Halstead Press, *Tank Tracks: The War History of the 2/4 Australian Armoured Regimental Group*, Halstead Press, Sydney, 1953, pp. 43–4.

51 Patricia Shaw, *Brother Digger: The Sullivans, 2nd AIF*, Greenhouse Publications, Melbourne, 1984, pp. 138–9.

52 Bōeichō Bōei Kenshūjo Senshishitsu, *Aitape, Puriaka, and Rabaul*, p. 253.

53 Long, *The Final Campaigns*, p. 164; 7th Brigade war diary, April 1945, AWM52, 8/2/7.

54 15th Brigade Report on Operations, pp. 1–2, 3DRL 2529, 74.

55 Notes on Bougainville – by Hammer, pp. 10–11, AWM93, 50/2/23/440.

56 15th Brigade Report on Operations, p. 9, 3DRL 2529, 74.

57 Savige to Sturdee, letter, 1 July 1945, 3DRL 2529, 84.

58 II Aust. Corps (AIF) in the North Solomons, p. 19, 3DRL 2529, 72.

59 29th Brigade Report on Operations, p. 7, AWM54, 613/6/1, part 1.

60 Gunner P. Gilders, diary, 15 August 1945, 3DRL 3383.

61 Captain S. A. Sly, interview, S00510.

62 James, *The Hard Slog*, pp. 266–7.

63 Hank Nelson, 'Bougainville in World War II', in Regan, A.J. and Griffin, H.M. (eds), *Bougainville before the Conflict*, Pandanus Books, Canberra, 2005, pp. 194–5.

64 R. G. Sainsbery, letter to author, 26 August 2012.

PART | 6

THE BORNEO
CAMPAIGN

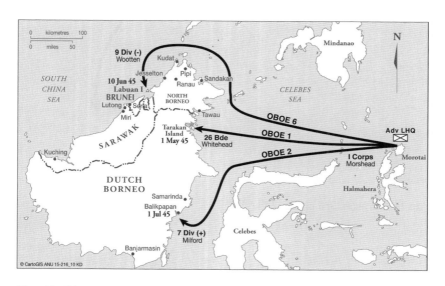

Map 10: Oboe overview

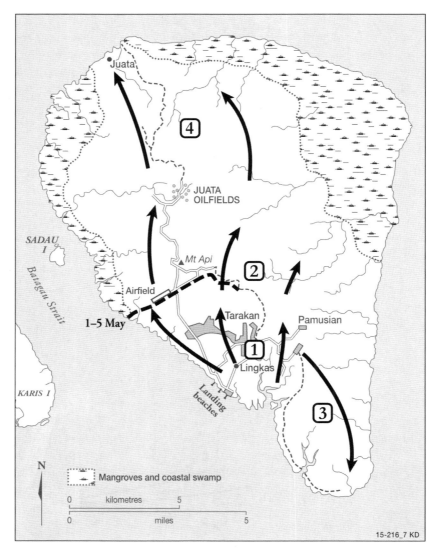

Map 11: Tarakan, 3rd phase, 2 May

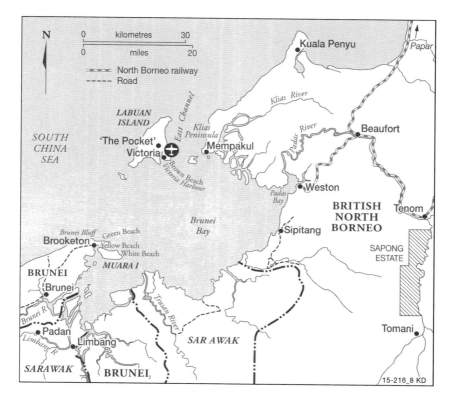

Map 12: Labuan Island, 19 April

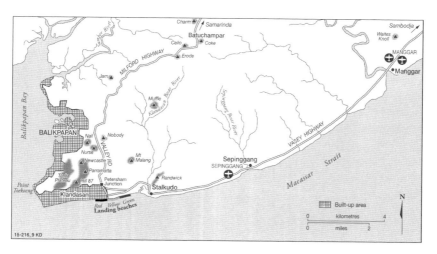

Map 13: Balikpapan, 2 May

AMPHIBIOUS WARFARE: TRAINING AND LOGISTICS, 1942–45

Rhys Crawley and Peter J. Dean

To Major-General George Vasey the situation on 13 January 1943 was one of despair. His division, the 7th Australian, had been fighting the Japanese in Papua since October 1942, had driven them out of Kokoda and the mountains, had crushed Major-General Horii's South Seas Force at the battle of Oivi-Gorari in early November, and had then pursued the Japanese to the coast. But with months to prepare their defences and with their backs to the Bismarck Sea, the final Japanese defences at the beachheads were proving formidable. Heavily dug in and reinforced, they had inflicted serious casualties on the Australians and Americans at Gona and Buna. Disease in the low-lying marshland on the north coast of Papua had taken an even bigger toll on the Allies. After months of grinding attrition, Gona and Buna had fallen; now only the last Japanese bastion, Sanananda, remained. The day before, 12 January, one of Vasey's infantry brigades, supported by tank and heavy artillery fire, had again assaulted the Japanese at Sanananda. Once more, they made no progress. Vasey and his troops, who could no longer call on armoured support, were exhausted and despondent.

With all this on his mind his corps commander, the American Lieutenant General Robert Eichelberger, and the corps Chief of Staff, the Australian Major-General Frank Berryman, now joined Vasey. They arrived at Vasey's headquarters (HQ) tent to discuss future operations, but the 7th Division's commander was out of troops and short of ideas. He argued to his visitors that to continue the attack against deeply entrenched Japanese positions using only infantry was inviting a repetition of the 'costly mistakes of 1915–1917' and those attacks were 'unlikely to succeed'. Outside intervention was needed, he argued, and an amphibious force should be landed by sea to outflank the Japanese and hit them from the rear.[1]

Berryman, however, did not think such an operation was viable. His reasoning, above all else, was that there was not enough shipping available. Eichelberger agreed, adding that the limited number of landing spots in the difficult terrain would mean that any force landed by sea could not be supplied properly due to the tidal flats in the area.[2] But, most significantly, 10 days earlier Berryman had presented to Blamey, Herring and Advanced New Guinea Force HQ a long and wide-ranging appreciation on the operations at Sanananda in which he had ruled out a seaborne assault due to the absence of suitable numbers of landing craft and a lack of troops who were trained in amphibious operations.[3] Instead of a landing from the sea, the three men decided upon a blockade of the Japanese and their attrition through artillery fire and air attacks.

THE ABSENCE OF A CAPABILITY IN 1942

The inability to land a force on the shores of northern Papua in 1943 was a reflection of a range of issues including: the time it took to develop an amphibious capability from scratch, the allocation of finite resources in the theatre, and the low priority accorded to the Southwest Pacific Area (SWPA) by the Allied Combined Chiefs of Staff, who were more concerned with supporting the war in Europe, and the US Joint Chiefs of Staff, who held command authority over the Pacific War.

Despite the defensive posture of the Allies throughout most of the Pacific War's first year, both the Australian and US high commands had been cognisant of the need to develop amphibious warfare skills and capabilities for offensive operations against the Japanese. In early March 1942, Deputy Chief of the General Staff in Australia, Major-General Sydney Rowell, had recommended the acquisition of specialist equipment and the establishment of a school of combined (joint) operations.[4] The Australians were also mindful of the need to undertake combined amphibious operations with their new US coalition partner.

A few months later, in June 1942, General Douglas MacArthur issued an instruction for the establishment of a Joint Overseas Operational Training School (JOOTS). This school was designed as a joint US-Australian, Army–Navy–Air Force endeavour. Its mission was the:

> Training of Land Forces in overseas operations in conjunction and cooperation with Naval Forces and Air Forces, both land and carrier

Figure 12.1: A landing exercise at JOOTS, Nelson's Bay, New South Wales, December 1942. (Australian War Memorial P02216.002)

based ... The task will involve the combat loading of ships, the disembarkation of troops and supplies in small boats in the face of an enemy, the landing on hostile shores, a rapid and strong thrust inland, and the occupation of hostile coast lines with continued operations into the interior, all tasks in coordination with Naval and Air support.[5]

At this stage, however, there were major restrictions on the development of an amphibious warfare capability in the SWPA. This mainly centred on a lack of trained and qualified instructors, a lack of equipment and an almost complete absence of landing craft and ships. While rudimentary training was undertaken at JOOTS at Nelson's Bay on the New South Wales mid–north coast and at the First Australian Army Combined Training School at Bribie Island near Brisbane in Queensland, from August 1942 the very troops that had received this preliminary training, the US 32nd and 41st Divisions, had their training cut short so as to be sent to the battlefields of Papua.[6] Thus, while there had been some solid progress made by the end of 1942, by the time of Vasey's request for an amphibious landing at Sanananda the partially trained troops were exhausted and their numbers depleted from months on the frontline. Moreover, the deficiencies in shipping, landing craft and equipment had still not been overcome. In reality, there was no amphibious capability. This meant that the beachhead battles were a slogging match, as both sides fought a land campaign in a maritime environment without sea control or the ability to undertake manoeuvre from the sea. In the end the Allied victory at Sanananda a few weeks later came only after the Japanese had decided to concede defeat and withdraw their remaining troops.

THE LACK OF AN AMPHIBIOUS TRADITION

One of the major factors for the lack of an amphibious warfare capability in early 1943 was the lack of attention that this type of warfare had received in Australia in the lead up to war. Australia's involvement in the First World War had started off with a focus on amphibious warfare. Both the Australian Naval and Military Expeditionary Force's landing near Rabaul, the capital of German New Guinea, on 11 September 1914 and the Australian and New Zealand Army Corps landing at Gallipoli on 25 April 1915 were joint amphibious operations. Yet, the amphibious character of these operations never embedded itself as part of the Australian military tradition. The Australian Imperial Force (AIF) was a land army, not a marine corps, and there were no Australian amphibious assaults to be found on either the Western Front or in the Middle East between 1916–18.

Amphibious warfare was also not a feature of Australia's inter-war defence planning, which centred on the Singapore naval strategy and the possibility of forming a second AIF for service outside of Australia. The result was that there was only one amphibious training exercise in the inter-war period, and this exercise, in 1935, was remarkable only 'for [its] air of unreality'.[7]

This meant that the raising of an amphibious warfare capability in Australia in 1942 to service the needs of both the US and Australian militaries in the SWPA had to occur from scratch. Both JOOTS, which initially focused on the staff training of junior and senior officers in amphibious warfare, and the school at Bribie Island, which focused on unit-level training, had to be built from the ground up. The Royal Australian Navy (RAN) also faced the same problems. It had to create an amphibious warfare training school, HMAS *Assault*, which it wisely co-located with JOOTS. These three organisations had to make do throughout 1942 with largely inadequate equipment while new landing craft were being built or imported from the United States. In addition, the RAN had no amphibious shipping and the armed merchant cruisers HMAS *Manoora, Westralia* and *Kanimbla* had only started the process of conversion into Landing Ships Infantry in late 1942 and early 1943. These ships would not be available for the Australian amphibious assault at Lae in 1943, and the requirement to produce crews for these ships hampered HMAS *Assault*'s ability to support the Army's training at JOOTS and at Bribie Island.[8]

While HMAS *Assault* was a navy facility, JOOTS and the School at Bribie Island both fell under General MacArthur's General HQ and General Blamey's HQ Allied Land Forces. This split in responsibility between Army and Navy only helped to exacerbate inter-service rivalry and competition for resources. The Australians' lack of experience in amphibious warfare meant that they were reliant in 1942–43 on a number of British officers as instructors or on Australians who had trained at the British Combined Training Centre in Kabrit, Egypt.[9] This fitted well, as the Australian services used the British doctrine, however, it soon led to a confrontation over amphibious techniques with the US commanding officer (CO) at JOOTS. The situation got so bad in August 1942, just a few months after the school was established, that JOOTS' CO Colonel B. Q. Jones (US Army) was sacked and the senior British officer at the school, Lieutenant-Colonel M. Hope (Royal Artillery)[10] was transferred to Bribie Island.

THE 7TH AMPHIBIOUS FORCE

Amphibious warfare training was only put on an even keel in the SWPA with the arrival of Rear Admiral Daniel E. Barbey (US Navy) and the establishment of the 7th Amphibious Force (7th AF) in the SWPA in December 1942. Barbey was given control over all amphibious warfare training in the SWPA from 8 February 1943, and he appointed Commander J. W. 'Red' Jamison (US Navy), who had served as a beach master in the North African landings,[11] to be the CO of the new 7th AF Amphibious Training Command (ATC) which absorbed JOOTS, the school at Bribie Island and HMAS *Assault*.[12] The ATC ran a joint and combined staff with officers from all three services of both countries as well as some officers from the US Marine Corps. The ATC standardised the training of units and formations. The courses previously set up under JOOTS, which included staff and command courses at the division, regiment and battalion levels, as well as specialist officer's courses on intelligence, logistics, engineering and medical issues, continued. Once these programs were completed, the units from which the officers had come then arrived at the ATC for unit training.[13] Jamison's team at the ATC was also given responsibility for developing doctrine and operational techniques in amphibious warfare for the SWPA.[14]

One of the most pressing problems for the ATC in 1943–44 was the dispersal of the different schools and their geographic distance from the troops in northern Australia and New Guinea. This had been an ongoing problem since the establishment of the schools in mid-1942 and General HQ undertook a review of possible suitable training grounds later in the same year, but it struggled to find any appropriate areas in northern Queensland.[15] Eventually, a decision was made to establish an ATC in Cairns, and this centre started operations on 25 June 1943 under Captain P. A. Stevens (US Navy). This was the location of the training ground for the US Army's 2nd Engineering Special (Amphibious) Brigade (2ESB), which was also incorporated into the 7th AF in mid-1943.[16] The Cairns ATC was to become the major training ground for Australian formations in amphibious warfare from mid-1943 until the end of the war, while JOOTS and the school at Bribie Island were eventually closed down. An ATC was set up at Milne Bay in late 1943 and in the Philippines in 1945. The ATC also overcame the distance issue by developing a number of Mobile Training Teams made up of Army and Navy personnel from both the US and Australia that moved around the SWPA training units and formations on location.[17]

AMPHIBIOUS TRAINING FOR OPERATION POSTERN

At the end of the Papua campaign, the majority of the troops returned to Australia for rest and retraining. I Australian Corps, stationed on the Atherton Tableland in northern Queensland, was reconstituted to include 7th Division and 9th Division, which had recently returned from the Middle East. Both of these divisions were assigned to the assault force for Operation Postern, the major Australian attack on Lae in New Guinea, earmarked for September 1943. The 9th Division, selected to undertake the amphibious landing (7th Division would be inserted by air and advance over land), began its planning with the US Army's 2ESB in May.[18] Each of the 9th Division's brigades was to undertake a two-to-three-week training program in amphibious operations with the small landing craft from the 2ESB starting on 16 June.[19] In order to facilitate training, Lieutenant-Colonel T. K. Walker Royal Marines was transferred from the staff at the old JOOTS to be the senior staff officer of the new Combined (Joint) Operations cell established at I Australian Corps HQ.

Unfortunately, the still evolving amphibious warfare training and operational requirements had a major impact on the 9th Division's training. Only the 24th Brigade went through a full training cycle. Wear and tear on the landing craft and strain on their crews meant that the 20th Brigade joined the 2ESB next, but its training was only half the length of the 24th Brigade, while 26th Brigade only received seven days training.

This training, which was intended to replicate the conditions in New Guinea, focused on preparing the division for jungle warfare. There was some limited practice in loading and unloading men and supplies from amphibious craft, and in caring for equipment in tropical conditions,[20] but in reality nothing was 'learned of the supply and maintenance problems' of amphibious operations.[21] The failure to prepare, both operationally and logistically, ignored a number of lessons that had been learned previously. In May, before training commenced, all senior commanders in the Australian forces had received a pamphlet outlining 10 general lessons for amphibious operations from US experience in North Africa and Guadalcanal, and British operations at Dieppe and Madagascar. Readers were told that 'adequate training and rehearsals are pre requisite to any operation', and that 'adequate personnel and material must be available for clearing the beach and dock areas of supplies'. The experiences of North Africa, in particular, emphasised the need for an organised beachhead, with men and vehicles to move stores to dumps rather than leaving them mixed on the beach.[22] Hindsight would prove just how apt these lessons were.

While the training was underway, a staff exercise, made up of divisional and corps HQ personnel and officers from the 2ESB, for the proposed landing revealed that the size of the Lae operations was beyond the capabilities of the 2ESB. Complicating matters further, 2ESB came under Barbey's 7th AF HQ at this time, changing the command structure and planning processes. 7th AF HQ also analysed the plan, agreeing with the Australian staff study, and proposed that the 9th Division be moved by the 7th AF's large ships and heavy landing craft and that the 2ESB be used for logistical maintenance of the division once ashore.[23] This decision meant that the 9th Division had little time to train and rehearse with the 7th AF before the assault.[24]

The landing, which took place outside Lae in September 1943, was the first time that the Australians had undertaken a major amphibious operation since Gallipoli in 1915.[25] The landing went well, and the 9th Division's troops performed admirably, but once ashore the limitations of their preparations and training became evident. The 2ESB did not have the capability to maintain the whole division ashore and the division also found out that it had completely miscalculated their logistical requirements in the beachhead.[26] Troops from a pioneer battalion and two infantry battalions had to be diverted from operations to help with the unloading of ships, the beachhead became congested, and supplies of food, ammunition and fuel remained intermixed and stacked closed to shore. Japanese aircraft destroyed fuel and ammunition dumps, and a determined Japanese bombing raid on the beachhead supply dumps could easily have terminated the entire division's advance from the coast to Lae. 9th Division's miscalculation had been so great that they had even rejected an offer for the 2/1st Ordnance Beach Detachment to be allocated to the division.[27]

While Lae was quickly captured, the 9th Division soon found itself preparing for a second major amphibious assault on Finschhafen only a few weeks later. Many of the same issues hindered this new assault, including the continued debate between the Army, Navy and Air Force over timings for the landing, air cover, reinforcement and resupply issues.[28] In addition, many of the landing craft veered off course for the assault and a lack of beach reconnaissance meant that a sand bar that ran across the main landing beach was not revealed until landing craft got stuck on it during the run into the beach. Captain Maxwell Worthley of the HQ staff 20th Brigade, who made the initial assault, called the landing 'a most ungodly balls up'.[29] Like Lae, however, Finschhafen was a success.

Logistic Lessons from Lae-Finschhafen

Of the 35 lessons identified by the 9th Division as stemming from the Lae and Finschhafen operations, nearly half dealt with logistics during the planning, training and assault phases. These reaffirmed many of the lessons that US and British forces had experienced in other theatres, and of which the Australians were already aware.

Logistic planning prior to the Australian landings was affected by late changes to the operational plans. The allocation of troops and stores to landing craft were continually altered because the Navy could not confirm how many craft would be available until a fortnight before the landings. Moreover, anticipating the potential destruction caused by Japanese aircraft, the Navy reduced the amount of time that amphibious craft could remain at the beaches, thereby allowing only three hours to offload the initial supplies. The division's post-mortem also recognised the need for a joint amphibious staff with the Army, Navy, and Air Force staffs co-located during the planning process, to work out these issues and alter plans accordingly. It believed that in future the division should be consulted prior to equipment tables being settled, thereby removing cases of unnecessary stores being loaded and transported to the beaches, as had occurred at Lae.[30]

The performance in both operations highlighted the results of deficient training and the importance of rectifying this in the future. Specifically, the supply and transport elements should undertake specialised training in loading and unloading supplies in the same type of craft to be used in an operation, and they should practise establishing stockpiles and constructing roads from the beaches into the jungle. Both operations reiterated that success relied on familiarisation, and that this would only come through training and experience.[31]

The main logistic lessons were to be found on the beachheads. Beach organisation, congestion, and forward supply could all be improved by better preparation and the formation of specialised units for work on the beaches. There was also an obvious need for additional labour, vehicles and small craft, in order to free up troops for operations and the army service corps for resupply purposes (as opposed to work on the beaches).[32] Specifically, a self-contained beach landing group, with its own staff and attached to the division, was 'a necessity' for work on the beaches.[33] This would eliminate the situation, as experienced at Lae, where the 9th Division had to provide 'practically the entire beach staff from within its own resources' to work the Beach Maintenance Area. It would also free up personnel for the quick preparation of beach exits and the formation of supply dumps, both essential elements in reducing congestion and clearing stores from the beach, where they were more vulnerable to air attack. The final, and most crucial, lesson was the requirement for better cooperation between the Army and Navy. The absence of a US Navy representative attached to the division was 'keenly felt' in both operations, and meant that there was no naval officer on the spot with the authority to call in naval craft and direct them where to land their men and supplies.[34]

LEARNING AND ADAPTATION

Notwithstanding the inexperience of the 9th Division's troops and the 7th AF in amphibious operations, the assaults at Lae and Finschhafen had been major factors in the success of the Australian liberation of north-eastern New Guinea. But they had also revealed a number of shortcomings in training, doctrine, planning and equipment. Work therefore began on learning from both of these operations as well as US amphibious landings in the SWPA and Central Pacific Area.

In December 1943, I Australian Corps issued a training instruction detailing the beach organisation and maintenance during combined amphibious operations. Importantly, it defined the service responsibilities and delineated the roles of various officers. Based on British doctrine and the methods then being employed in the Middle East, the instructions were not unlike those issued in the *Manual of Combined Naval and Military Operations* (1913), which guided amphibious operations during the First World War. The major difference was the creation of a beach group (and a naval beach commando) for landing supplies and organising the Beach Maintenance Area. It was clear that I Corps, in a doctrinal sense at least, now understood many of the problems associated with establishing a force ashore and then sustaining it during operations. Fundamental to this was 'the early establishment and smooth running of an efficient beach organisation'. The key message, reflecting 9th Division's lessons, was the need for cooperation between the services, and the flexibility to revise doctrine and adapt training following more experience in the SWPA.[35]

When I Australian Corps was pulled out of the line in New Guinea in early 1944 its future was unknown, but there were two things that remained certain. Both amphibious assaults and jungle warfare would figure prominently in any future operations. This realisation had resulted in some important developments in the organisation of the Australian Army. The most significant of these, reflecting the lessons of Lae and Finschhafen, was the formation of the 1st Australian Beach Group (ABG) in November 1943, and the 2nd ABG in May 1944. Based upon their British Army equivalents, but tailored for operations in the SWPA, each of these units was commanded by a Colonel, the Beach Group Commander, who was responsible to the divisional commander.[36] With 1800 personnel, each AGB consisted of army troops, a RAN Beach Commando, and a large collection of logistic units including engineers, signallers, medical staff, army service corps personnel, and ordnance and provost units. The role of the ABG was to facilitate the landing by unloading the landing craft, clearing the beach, liaising with the fighting forces and administering the beachhead.[37] In this respect, it was not dissimilar to the work carried out by the shore battalions in a US ESB.[38] Longer-term logistic support beyond the initial landing, when a base was up and running, became the responsibility of Base Sub Areas, another new organisation formed in 1944.[39]

The other major organisational moves were the establishment of a Military Landing Group (MLG), the Australian Combined Operations Section (COS) in I Corps HQ and the establishment of a number of specialist combined operations staff appointments to Advanced Land HQ. MLGs were created to provide divisional and brigade staff with specially trained officers to advise and assist in the requirements of amphibious warfare, including shipping, landing craft and the tactical embarkation of a force. They were made available for both training and well as operational support.

The COS consisted of seven officers specially trained in amphibious warfare for attachment to corps HQ. This included two senior Army staff officers, one each for operations and logistics, signals and engineering officers and a naval and Air Force officer. In addition, the COS provided a senior logistics staff officer to each of the divisional HQ. The role of the COS was wide ranging and included providing the training section in corps HQ, producing doctrine for the Beach Groups and Beach Commandos, supervising the MLG officers, operational planning, collating, preparing and disseminating reports on amphibious operations from across the Pacific and producing reports on Australian operations. The final support for amphibious operations came in the form of four specially trained lieutenant colonels attached to the operations section and two majors attached to the logistics section of the Army's senior operational HQ units, Advanced Land HQ and its Forward Echelon.[40]

The critical role of identifying and disseminating lessons in amphibious warfare from across the Pacific was undertaken by the COS and various other Australian HQ units and training schools. The Army also sent an officer to be attached to the British Combined Operations HQ in London. In addition, the Australians had a number of officers on the planning staff of the 7th AF including a senior operations planning officer, Brigadier Ronald Hopkins. Hopkins sent back regular reports on the operations he was involved in, as did other liaison officers.[41] In one of his reports, circulated to major Australian commands in July 1944, Hopkins explained that the only way to improve, particularly with regards to logistics on the beaches, was to test units in exercises and again in rehearsals before an operation.[42] His message was noted and repeated in the Australian Military Force's provisional guide for the training, planning, and conduct of future amphibious operations by Australian formations in the SWPA, issued in December 1944.[43]

DIVISIONAL TRAINING

In early 1944, the 6th Division, which had not participated in the New Guinea campaign, was at a more advanced state for amphibious operations than any other Australian formation. It had undergone amphibious training since August 1943, while the rest of the corps was still on the frontline. Although this training was somewhat disjointed, by mid-1944 the division was regarded as one of the best trained in Australia. Much of this training included logistic work with the newly formed 1st ABG. Training was as realistic as possible. Exercise Mittens in late December 1943, for instance, included loading assault craft, landing the force, developing a beachhead and delivering 500 tons of stores ashore, and was described as 'probably the best exercise the Beach Group ever did'.[44] Although this experience was invaluable for the 1st ABG, 6th Division was never able to put its skills to the test in a major landing. In late 1944, it was removed from I Corps and transferred to First Australian Army for operations in New Guinea around Wewak, where it remained until the end of the war.

For the rest of I Corps, staff training and combined operations courses were run from mid-1944, followed by brigade training with divisional attachments.[45] 9th Division was trained at Trinity Beach in Cairns at the end of 1944. The divisions worked on providing experience in amphibious operations to their reinforcements and refresher training to their old hands. In addition, like 6th Division, exercises were carried out with the new ABGs and with new equipment, including a small number of the new tracked landing craft or LVTs, and adapting to new procedures.[46] HQ staff also undertook a number of major planning exercises, up to corps strength using both divisions. Exercise Seagull, a corps level landing formed the last of the planning exercises at the end of January and represented the conclusion of the amphibious training cycle for the corps, which had started some six months earlier.[47] Both divisions were prepared, operationally and logistically, for their next big test: a series of amphibious assaults to liberate Borneo.

LOGISTIC PREPARATIONS FOR THE OBOE OPERATIONS

Although the idea had existed since 1944, detailed planning for the assaults on Borneo, codenamed Operation Oboe, began after MacArthur's GHQ issued orders in March 1945.[48] After a series of postponements, most of which were due to a shortage of shipping to move units from Australia to the staging base at Morotai, GHQ settled on three operations in three stages: Oboe 1, a landing by the 26th Infantry Brigade Group (9th Division) at Tarakan Island on 1 May; Oboe 6, by the remainder of the 9th Division at Labuan Island and Brunei Bay on 10 June; and Oboe 2, by the 7th Division at Balikpapan on 1 July. Each operation had a similar objective: to seize and destroy all enemy forces in the area, thus allowing the area to be used as a naval and air base for future operations, and, when possible, re-establish civil government.[49]

Logistics underpinned the entire planning and preparation process for these operations. After consulting with the relevant division, I Australian Corps issued a maintenance project for each operation.[50] The maintenance project was the force commander's administrative order, and defined the logistic considerations for the operation.[51] Crucially, it established the key dates and clarified who – including which service – was responsible for each component of supply, resupply and the ongoing maintenance of the force. In each of the Oboe operations, the Commander, Allied Land Forces, was responsible for providing the necessary supplies and equipment from Australia; the divisional commander, assisted by I Australian Corps and the US 93rd Division, was responsible for loading the assault convoy at Morotai; Commander, Allied Naval Forces, was then responsible for transporting the assault forces and their initial supplies from the staging base to the objective area; Commander, US Army Services of Supply (USASOS) was to provide bulk storage for ammunition and petroleum, including a floating reserve of each, and all transport for the resupply of the force.[52]

Troop movements from Cairns, Townsville and Brisbane to Morotai began on 12 March and continued at 6000–7000 troops, plus vehicles, equipment and stores, per week.[53] By the end of April, I Australian Corps HQ, with elements of 9th Division including the 26th Brigade Group – then preparing for Oboe 1 – was situated at Morotai. The remainder of the division was still on its way from Australia. 7th Division, which would form the nucleus of the Balikpapan force, was preparing to move from the Atherton Tablelands.[54] Almost all troop and cargo ships used for the concentration of troops, equipment, and supplies at Morotai, were provided by the USASOS.[55] Despite the problems of movement, by the time that the 7th and 9th Divisions departed Australia, I Australian Corps 'had been equipped to a level never previously achieved by an Australian Formation during this War'.[56]

Morotai, the staging base for all three Oboe operations, was a hive of activity and hard work in preparation for the embarkation of the assault convoys. These ships, mostly provided by the US Navy (although with RAN ships involved), would either run ashore or, in the case of Tarakan, offload using naval pontoons and amphibious craft at the objective area. They therefore had to be tactically loaded, so as to enable fast disembarkation by the Beach Groups and for their quick return to Morotai for resupply purposes.[57] In accordance with General HQ instructions, the loading of the

Figure 12.2: LVT-4 Alligator amphibious personnel carriers approach the beach at Balikpapan, July 1945. (Australian War Memorial 018812)

assault convoy was performed by Australian docks, labour and base personnel, supported by all Australian load-carrying vehicles and troops from the US 93rd Division.[58] The assault convoys, which left Morotai up to a week before the commencement of operations, carried with them minimal although sufficient supplies to establish the force ashore. In the case of Tarakan, this amounted to 18 days' supplies and 20 days' ammunition. If required, each force could call upon the USASOS floating reserve or, in an emergency, rations and ammunition could be delivered from Morotai by air.[59] The initial resupply, to boost the stocks carried in the assault waves, was also delivered from Morotai. After that, the maintenance of the forces – with the exception of Tarakan – shifted from Morotai to Australia, with shipping arriving at the sub bases on an as-required basis.[60]

Described by historian Ross Mallett as 'the high water of Australian Army logistics', the Oboe operations showed the Allied forces – air, sea, and land – at their most logistically proficient.[61] Where obstacles were faced, such as the difficulty of getting supplies ashore over Navy Lighterage Pontoons onto unsuitable beaches at Tarakan, the temporary breakdown of inter-service communication at Brunei Bay, or congestion on the beaches at Balikpapan caused by the destruction of piers, the ABGs, working with the fighting force, overcame them through familiarisation, improvisation, cooperation and hard work. Overall, and despite many small problems, the Oboe operations were a logistic success.[62] The forces achieved their objectives, and there were – with few exceptions – no real complaints about a lack of stores or supplies either in the initial stages or while following up the Japanese forces as they retreated inland. Indeed, the material discharged throughout the first three weeks of each operation amounted to an astonishing 177,953 tons (see Table 12.1). Between them, the 1st and 2nd ABGs, operating for the first time, handled, from ships to dumps, an average of 1500 tons daily.[63]

The reasons for this logistic success were many. As discussed earlier, I Australian Corps and Australian amphibious doctrine in general came to understand the importance of logistics and recognised that logistic proficiency came through proper planning, preparation and training. Increased amphibious lift capabilities, enabled by unprecedented US shipping support, meant that more troops and more supplies could be conveyed both to the staging base and the beaches than had hitherto been the case. Moreover, having learned the lessons of Lae, Finschhafen and a host of other amphibious operations in the European and Pacific theatres, the Oboe operations saw the Australian beach groups employed for the first time. The results, although not perfect, confirmed how important it was to have a properly functioning beach maintenance area and adequate cooperation between the forces, and the necessary labour and transport to perform the tasks and achieve the objectives as defined by General HQ.

CONCLUSION

The type and style of amphibious operations in the SWPA evolved radically between the Australian landings in New Guinea in 1943 and operations in Borneo in 1945. During this time, the Australian Army and RAN, supported by their US ally, had evolved from a force with no amphibious tradition, and thus no capability, to a proficient and well-trained amphibious force. Logistic deficiencies that had overshadowed the Lae and Finschhafen successes had been overcome. Shipping was available in large numbers to move Australian formations from Australia to Morotai, and thence to Borneo for the largest amphibious operations in Australian military history. Ashore, thanks largely to the establishment of the Australian beach groups and continued joint training and amphibious exercises, the Oboe operations were supported by a functioning logistic

Table 12.1: Discharge figures, Oboe operations, up to day 22.[64]

| | OBOE 1 | | | OBOE 6 | | | OBOE 2 | |
	No. of vehicles	Bulk stores DW tons	Total DW tons	No. of vehicles	Bulk stores DW tons	Total DW tons	No. of vehicles	Bulk stores DW tons	Total DW tons
Total	2477	13,615	33,431	4802	31,141	69,549	5562	30,477	74,973

Total deadweight (DW) tons = bulk stores DW + vehicles (average of 6 tons per vehicle, plus 2 tons per vehicle pre-loaded with stores).

system. While the 1943 landings were very similar to British doctrine, that being to land away from the enemy and manoeuvre to the objective, by 1945 the overwhelming logistical superiority of the Allies and the lavish amphibious assets available for operations, doctrinal development and specialised training, as well as air and naval supremacy, meant that the Australian landings in Borneo were reminiscent of the storm-landing techniques used by the US Marine Corps in the Central Pacific.

FURTHER READING

Daniel E. Barbey, *MacArthur's Amphibious Navy: Seventh Amphibious Force Operations, 1943–1945*, United States Naval Institute, Annapolis, 1969.

Hugh J. Casey, *Amphibian Engineer Operations*, Office of the Chief Engineer, United States Army Forces in the Pacific, Office of the Chief Engineer, US Government Printing Officer, 1959.

Peter J. Dean, 'Divergence and Convergence: Army vs Navy: Allied Conduct of the Pacific War', in Peter Dennis (ed.), *Armies and Maritime Strategy*, 2013 Chief of Army History Conference, Big Sky Publishing, Canberra, 2014.

Mervyn Eather and Bill Galmés, *Taken by Storm: The True Story of HMAS Manoora's Experiences in the South West Pacific Theatre of War*, HMAS *Manoora* Association, Melbourne, 1996.

Ross Mallett, 'Australian Army Logistics 1943–1945', PhD thesis, University of New South Wales, Australian Defence Force Academy, Canberra, 2007.

Seventh Amphibious Force Command History, 10 January 1943 – 23 December 1945, United States Navy, 1945.

W. N. Swan, *Spearheads of Invasion: An Account of Seven Major Invasions Carried Out by the Allies in the South-west Pacific Area during the Second World War, as Seen by a Royal Australian Naval Landing Ship Infantry*, Angus and Robertson, Sydney, 1954.

Notes

1 'Notes on Situation – Sanananda Area 13 Jan 43', War Diary, Adv NGF HQ, AWM52 1/5/51.

2 Summary of Events and Information, War Diary, 7th Australian Division, 13 January 1943, AWM52 1/5/14.

3 'Appreciation for GOC NGF by DCGS at Adv NGF', 1 January 1943, War Diary, Adv NGF HQ, AWM52 1/5/51.

4 'Long Range Planning for offensive Action – Landing operations', 13 March 1942, NAA, B6121 289. In the British, and thus Australian military, amphibious landings using more than one Service, were referred to as 'combined' operations. In this chapter the US terminology of 'joint' operations will be used for clarity, as this is now the universally recognised term.

5 Memo 'Combined Training for Offensive Operations', MacArthur to Blamey, 4 June 1942, NARA, RG 496, Box 667.

6 Combined Training School, Toorbul Point: Origin of the School, AWM54 422/7/8; A Summary of Combined operations Training in Australia (Amphibious) 1942–1945, AWM54 943/16/1. The First Australian Army School at Bribie Island had been established as a part of an Australian directed effort to develop amphibious warfare skills. This was undertaken before the decision was made by MacArthur's HQ to establishe JOOTS.

7 *Report on Combined Operations in Hobart to the Secretary of the Naval Board* (26 April 1935), as quoted in Parkin, 'A Capability of First Resort', p. 14.

8 A Summary of Combined Operations Training in Australia (Amphibious) 1942–1945, AWM54 943/16/1; AWM PR 00631, Papers of HMAS *Assault*.

9 'A Summary of Combined operations Training in Australia (Amphibious) 1942–1945', AWM54 943/16/1, p. 1.

10 Directive – Joint Overseas Operational Training School, 9 August 1942, GHQ SWPA, NARA, RG 496 Records of GHQ, G-3 General Correspondence, Box 667.

11 *Seventh Amphibious Force Command History*, USN, 1945, pp. II–11

12 Combined Operations—RAN Beach Commandos, NAA, B6121, 194B, p. 2.

13 *Command History of the 7th Amphibious Force*, p. II–13.

14 Barbey, *MacArthur's Amphibious Navy*, pp. 48–9. Doctrine in the SWPA in 1942–44 was different from that practised by the US Navy in the Central Pacific see Peter Dean, 'Divergence and Convergence: Army vs Navy: Allied Conduct of the Pacific War', in Peter Dennis, (ed), *Armies and Maritime Strategy*, Big Sky Publishing, Canberra, 2014, pp. 167–201.

15 See Selection of Alternative Site for Joint Overseas Operations Training School, 24 October 1942, NARA RG 496, Box 667 and Captain M. R. Kelly (US Navy) to MacArthur, RE: Selection of Alternative Site for Joint Overseas Operations Training School, 4 November 1942, NARA RG 496, Box 667.

16 *Command History of the 7th Amphibious Force*, pp. ii, 13–14.

17 See correspondence on the formation of the Mobile Training Teams, 25 December 1942–15 January 1943, GHQ SWPA, NARA, RG 496, Box 667.

18 This was confirmed in an order from GHQ to Commander Allied Land Forces, 15 May 1943. Operation Cartwheel – Correspondence – Messages and Plans, AWM54 389/3/10.

19 Berryman to Kruger, 6 May 1943, Correspondence, Memos and operation instructions for operation 'Cartwheel', April–December 1943, AWM54 589/3/11, Part 1.

20 '9 Aust. Div. Report on Operations and Capture of Lae and Finschhafen', n.d., AWM54 589/7/26 Part 3.

21 A Summary of Combined Operations Training in Australia (Amphibious) 1942–1945, AWM54 943/16/1.

22 Circular memo, 'Notes of Amphibious Warfare', 31 May 1943, AWM54 519/7/12.

23 Amphibious Operation Postern: Outline Plan, 14 July 1943, and Amphibious Force Seventh Fleet; Amphibious Operations for Operation II, Memos and Orders – Cartwheel – April–September 1943, AWM54 589/3/11.

24 Barbey, *MacArthur's Amphibious Navy*, p. 74.

25 The first Australian amphibious operations in the SWPA had occurred in October 1942 when a battalion was landed on Goodenough Island to destroy a Japanese force marooned there after their defeat at Milne Bay.

26 Mallett, 'Together again for the first time', p, 77.

27 Mallett, 'Logistics in the South West-Pacific 1943–1944', p. 113.

28 See Operation Diminish. 9 Aust. Div. Operational Order No. 15, 20 September. 1943, p. 3, HQ 9 Div. (G Br) WD, AWM52 1/5/20/37.

29 Worthly as quoted in Pratten, chapter 10, *Australia 1943: The Liberation of New Guinea*, p. 262.

30 '9 Aust. Div. Report on Operations and Capture of Lae and Finschhafen', n.d., AWM54 589/7/26 Part 3.

31 'Notes of S & T Services in Amphibious Operations – Based on experience of Lae-Finschhafen campaigns, Sept 1943 – Jan 1944', Lt-Col L. A. Withers, CASC 9th Aust. Div., n.d., AWM54 943/16/21.

32 'Extracts from report on operations in New Guinea by HQ 2 Aust. Corps 8 Oct '43 to 1 Mar '44', attached to minute, G1 (Op Reports) to Planning Section, 17 May 1944, AWM54 519/7/16.

33 '9 Aust. Div. Report on Operations and Capture of Lae and Finschhafen', n.d., AWM54 589/7/26 Part 3.

34 Ibid.

35 1st Australian Corps Training Instruction No. 2, 'Combined Operations: Beach Organisation and Maintenance', December 1943, AWM54 943/16/20.

36 'Report on Beach Group Organisation OBOE 1', CO 2 Aust. Beach Group, 15 May 1945, AWM54 617/7/5.

37 Karl James, '"Hell was let loose": Making Order from Confusion. The RAN Beach Commandos at Balikpapan, July 1945', *International Journal of Naval History*, vol. 8, no. 2, August 2009.

38 'Amphibious Warfare for Australian Forces in the South-West Pacific Area', December 1944, AWM54 945/7/3 Part 1.

39 Ross A. Mallett, 'Australian Army Logistics 1943–1945', PhD thesis, Australian Defence Force Academy, University of New South Wales, 2007, p. 329.

40 A Summary of Combined Operations Training in Australia (Amphibious) 1942–1945, AWM54 943/16/1 pp. 21–2, 25.

41 For instance see: General Notes on Woodlark Island, Lae and Finschhafen Landings, by Australian Liaison Officer, Seventh Amphibious Force, AWM54 591/7/7 and Operations against Morotai Island: A Report by British Combined Operations Observers, October 1944, AWM ORMF 80 527–30.

42 'General review of amphibious operations in the South West Pacific Area, December 1943 – May 1944', 13 July 1944, AWM54 945/7/7.

43 'Amphibious Warfare for Australian Forces in the South-West Pacific Area', December 1944, AWM54 945/7/3 Part 1.

44 A Summary of Combined Operations Training in Australia (Amphibious) 1942–1945, AWM54 943/16/1.

45 Amphibious Training: 1st Aust Corps, Command and Staff course 1944, AWM54 943/16/2.

46 Amphibious Training 1944, 1st Aust Corps training Instruction No. 6, AWM54 943/16/25.

47 A Summary of Combined Operations Training in Australia (Amphibious) 1942–1945, AWM54 943/16/1 pp. 19–20.

48 'Report on operations 1 Aust. Corps Borneo Campaign', Lt-Gen L. J. Morshead, GOC 1 Aust. Corps, 15 September 1945, AWM54 619/7/78 Part 1, pp. 7–9.

49 1 Aust. Corps Operation Instruction No. 1: OBOE ONE, 29 March 1945, AWM54 619/7/78 Part 1; Logistic Instructions No. 102/SOS, USASOS, 2 May 1945, AWM54 917/6/13.

50 'Report covering Q Branch and Services activities associated with the planning for operations OBOE ONE, OBOE SIX and OBOE TWO', DA&QMG, I Australian Corps, n.d., AWM54 617/3/11.

51 1st Australian Corps Training Instruction No. 2, 'Combined Operations: Beach Organisation and Maintenance', December 1943, AWM54 943/16/20.

52 Logistic Instructions No. 102/SOS, USASOS, 2 May 1945, AWM54 917/6/13.
53 'Report on operations 1 Aust. Corps Borneo Campaign', Lt-Gen L. J. Morshead, GOC 1 Aust. Corps, 15 September 1945, AWM54 619/7/78 Part 1, p. 13.
54 Ibid, p. 3.
55 Logistic Instructions No. 102/SOS, USASOS, 2 May 1945, AWM54 917/6/13.
56 'Ordnance Service – Report on Operations', n.d., AWM54 617/3/11.
57 'Report on operations 1 Aust. Corps Borneo Campaign', Lt-Gen L. J. Morshead, GOC 1 Aust Corps, 15 September 1945, AWM54 619/7/78 Part 1, pp. 11–13.
58 'Report covering Q Branch and Services activities associated with the planning for operations OBOE ONE, OBOE SIX and OBOE TWO', DA&QMG, I Australian Corps, n.d., AWM54 617/3/11.
59 Mallett, 'Australian Army Logistics 1943–1945', p. 341.
60 'Report on operations 1 Aust. Corps Borneo Campaign', Lt-Gen L. J. Morshead, GOC 1 Aust. Corps, 15 September 1945, AWM54 619/7/78 Part 1, pp. 18–19.
61 Mallett, 'Australian Army Logistics 1943–1945', p. 375.
62 For a detailed account of the Australian Army's logistic efforts during the three Oboe operations see: Mallett, 'Australian Army Logistics 1943–1945', pp. 340–75.
63 A Summary of Combined Operations Training in Australia (Amphibious) 1942–1945, AWM54 943/16/1.
64 'Consolidated report on the beach organisation in operations OBOE ONE, TWO and SIX', AWM54 619/7/62.

CHAPTER | 13

'To Capture Tarakan': Was Operation Oboe 1 Unnecessary?

Tony Hastings and Peter Stanley

Oboe 1 – the Allied campaign for the island of Tarakan off the northeast coast of Borneo – was the first of three major landings in Borneo by I Australian Corps. On 21 March 1945, MacArthur instructed the commander of I Corps, Lieutenant General Sir Leslie Morshead, to seize Tarakan and destroy the Japanese forces there. The Netherlands East Indies government was to be re-established and the oil installations conserved. As soon as the island's airfield was repaired, the Royal Australian Air Force (RAAF) planned to move in several squadrons to support the next two landings at Brunei Bay and Balikpapan.[1] Morshead allocated the 26th Brigade Group of the 9th Australian Division to assault Tarakan. The date of the landing was fixed at 1 May 1945. In contrast to earlier Australian campaigns, the Oboe operations would receive lavish support from Allied air and naval forces. But, despite this, Oboe 1 would prove to be far more difficult – and controversial – than expected.[2]

An 'Unnecessary War' in Borneo?

Tarakan has always been regarded as part of what journalist Peter Charlton called 'the unnecessary war': one of the 1945 campaigns that cost Australian lives in Borneo and the islands to no purpose.[3] More specifically, Oboe 1 was criticised in the Australian official histories as a costly failure because of the severe problems and long delay in establishing an air base on the island to support the later Borneo landings, and the heavy casualties suffered by the

Australian assault force.[4] The campaign last received an in-depth examination in 1997 in *Tarakan: An Australian Tragedy* by Peter Stanley (co-author of this chapter). While this work qualified Charlton's interpretation by stressing that US evidence made the genesis and justification for the operation more plausible, it accepted the conventional view that ultimately the operation was not worth the cost: hence the 'tragedy' in the title.[5]

Tarakan's enduring reputation as a futile campaign or wasted effort deserves to be examined afresh. By altering the thrust of historical enquiry, from the question 'why did Oboe 1 happen?' to 'what good did it do?' – and by re-examining the available literature and evidence – a new view of Tarakan emerges. The result of this approach has been both a reaffirmation of the essential narrative of the ground operations, but also a substantially new interpretation of the consequences of and justification for the campaign. The study demonstrates – if it needed to be demonstrated – the value of never accepting that subjects can be regarded as settled. Fresh evidence, new questions or novel perspectives can be productive.

GENESIS OF THE CAMPAIGN

The origins of what became Operation Oboe 1 went back to late 1944, when General Douglas MacArthur's General Headquarters' (GHQ) staff began looking beyond the campaigns in New Guinea and Luzon. GHQ outlined, under the 'Princeton' and 'Montclair' plans, a series of possible operations – Cringle, Victor, Oboe and Peter – that could take the Allied forces into the southwestern Philippines, into British and Dutch Borneo and ultimately into Java. As had become the pattern in the Southwest Pacific Area (SWPA), the lack of naval air cover committed the advance to landings to acquire airstrips to support future offensive moves: hence the need to seize Tarakan. However, MacArthur operated without reference to his nominal superiors, the Joint Chiefs of Staff in Washington, and never provided any clear rationale for the operation. His motives remained at the time opaque, but it became clear that obtaining Borneo's oil remained only a pretext. (Tarakan was one of three oil-producing areas in Borneo, and its high-quality output had been used by the Imperial Japanese Navy until mid-1944, once the oil wells had been repaired in 1942.) MacArthur seemed genuine in his desire to liberate 'a Dutch town of some importance', as he put it to George Kenney, the commander of the US Far Eastern Air Forces.[6] The argument that MacArthur devised the Oboe operations merely to make use of Australian troops he barred from the Philippines operations has no basis, given that the Borneo operations were planned (for US troops) late in 1944.

PLANNING OBOE 1

The Oboe operations (reduced in scale from six to three) began with the Tarakan landings. Troops of Brigadier David Whitehead's 26th Australian Brigade Group went ashore on 1 May 1945. Subsidiary operations had begun on the previous day with the destruction of the beach defences and the placement of an artillery battery on nearby Sadau Island. On the morning of 1 May 1945, Whitehead's battalions landed near Lingkas, the island's port, under the protection of a short but intensive naval and air bombardment. The fighting core of Whitehead's augmented 'Brigade Group' was the 3000 infantrymen of the 2/23rd, 2/24th, 2/48th Infantry Battalions, the 2/3rd Pioneer Battalion and the 2/4th Commando Squadron, supported by the tanks of the 2/9th Armoured Regiment and gunners of the 2/7th Field Regiment and the 53rd Composite Anti-Aircraft Regiment. Almost 6000 other troops arrived early in May, mainly members of 2nd Beach Group, divisional and base units, 4000 men of the RAAF and some 250 Dutch and 700 US troops. The RAAF contribution to the operation was to be the most controversial, and will be discussed in due course.

Tarakan's defenders comprised some 2400 troops, almost 900 army troops under Major Tadai Tokoi (who directed the defence) and 900 sailors, including the 2nd Naval Garrison Force under Commander Kaoru Kaharu. The remainder comprised Japanese officials, 350 civilian oil technicians, 280 Korean or Formosan naval pioneers and about 50 *Heihos* (Indonesian collaborators). Their heaviest weapons comprised heavy machine guns and four mountain artillery guns. They were opposed by an Allied force numbering over 15,000 men, supported by naval gunfire and heavy bombers, operated by a force enjoying total air superiority over Borneo.

As the first opposed landing made by Australian combat troops since the New Guinea campaign of 1943, the operation was able to draw on lessons learned by Australian, US and even British experience (the planners eagerly gleaned details of the Normandy landings of a year before). Though employing a large and seemingly generous US naval support and seven Royal Australian Navy vessels (and indeed, demonstrating notably positive relationship between Australian and US staffs and units at all levels), the operation did not proceed smoothly.

THE LANDING

The problems that were to bedevil the operation started in the weeks before it began, with the special forces parties sent to Borneo to gather intelligence.

The reconnaissance operation mounted by the Services Reconnaissance Department, codenamed 'Squirrel', ended farcically when radio failure prevented it reporting intelligence of minor importance only two days after the landing. Tarakan's beaches were atrocious – black mud and mangroves, protected by beach obstacles and pillboxes. Seven US Landing Ships, Tank were grounded on tidal mudflats, and the Air Force detachments' landing was haphazard and chaotic. A shortage of naval escorts had obliged the entire force to arrive together and land the embarked troops, regardless of when its components were needed, resulting in undue congestion on the beach and in what became the invasion force's rear area. Tanks struggled to get onto firm ground and most of the field guns were unable to open fire until the afternoon (though ample naval gunfire support was available, which meant that in fact the artillery was not need). Most distressingly for the liberators, they were unable to warn Tarakan's population before the landings, and at least 100, and probably more, Indonesian civilians were killed or wounded in villages hit by the supporting air and naval bombardment. Nevertheless, the lodgement proceeded with delay but

Figure 13.1: Machine-gunners of the 2/23rd Infantry Battalion give supporting fire to D Company patrols near Tarakan Hill, Tarakan Island, Borneo, 2 May 1945. (Australian War Memorial 089405)

without disruption, and all but one minor initial objective was captured by the end of 1 May at a cost to the invaders of 11 killed and 35 wounded.

The plan to seize the island's airstrip, 5 kilometres northwest of the landing beaches, however, almost immediately fell behind schedule. Tarakan's airstrip was supposed to be operational within six days of the landing. It fell after heavy fighting late on 5 May, and thereafter the RAAF airfield construction engineers arrived to survey the strip and plan its repair. What they saw was a mine-infested bog of overlapping bomb craters, and the struggle to get it operational lasted as long as the fighting on the island. As possession of the strip was the entire point of Oboe 1, its fate, and the consequences of what became a frustrating and embarrassing saga, is a vital part of the analysis of the operation's success.

Relations between the Australian Imperial Force (AIF) and RAAF on Tarakan remained poor throughout the operation. The tension of the landing, especially when overloaded RAAF lorries bogged in the beach exits, were exacerbated when Air Commodore Arthur Cobby, the RAAF Commander, declined to collocate his headquarters with David Whitehead, but instead placed it a kilometre away. Army provosts reported looting and three rapes committed by airmen, who were mostly idle until the airstrip could be secured. Unemployed airmen were put to work unloading stores, but worked only six hours at a time, compared to the 12-hour shifts worked by soldiers of the Beach Group.[7]

Oboe 1 manifested several differences to other operations, even other amphibious landings in Borneo. Japanese troops did not oppose the landings, but after losing the airstrip withdrew to an area of bunkers holding fortified hills behind Tarakan township. Over the following six weeks, Whitehead's four battalions pushed into the tangled jungle to overcome them one by one. For a further month, the three infantry battalions and the 2/3rd Pioneers attacked a series of Japanese positions. While able to call in armoured support (in the areas closer to Tarakan town), machine-gun and field-gun support throughout and backed by (mainly) US heavy bombers operating from the Philippines, the advance essentially saw sections of infantrymen moving through thick jungle against strong and often virtually invisible positions. Every patrol and attack saw casualties, but the AIF's dedication and professionalism did not falter, even in seemingly insignificant actions against an enemy unable to affect the course of the campaign, still less the war.

FUKUKAKU

If the planning and coordination of Oboe 1 exposed weaknesses and friction, the conduct of the gradual elimination of the island's Japanese defenders by

Whitehead's battalions demonstrated the expertise in close combat in the jungle that the Australian Army's units had attained by the war's final year. Though the seizure of the strip meant that the campaign's essential objectives had been taken, fighting continued against the island's defenders.

For the 26th Australian Brigade Group, the core of the fight for Tarakan involved a series of hard-fought actions in the dense jungle north of Snag's Track (the island's main lateral road), locating, reducing and eliminating Japanese resistance in the area that Kaharu had chosen to hold as the defenders' last-ditch positions. This entailed patrolling to find and plot the network of bunkers, most on hills codenamed after girls' names. Summarising from west to east, the 2/24th pushed eastwards from the airstrip, up Crazy Ridge and towards Sandy, Joyce and Clarice. The 2/23rd moved from the airstrip through Tiger to Margy and Janet. The 2/48th advanced from Sykes and Ostrich toward Agnes and Freda, and northward to Nelly, Linda and Faith. The 2/4th Commando Squadron supported the advance toward Agnes while the 2/3rd Pioneers advanced westward toward Helen, along John's Track. Each step involved careful and often costly probing into thick, jungle-clad hills against concealed machine-gun positions, which fell after prolonged air and artillery bombardment and then infantry assaults. The pioneers' week-long assaults on Helen, for example, assisted by 7000 rounds of 25-pounder shells and US medium and later heavy bombers dropping napalm, cost 20 killed and 60 wounded before the surviving defenders withdrew.

The defenders gradually retreated to the final Japanese position, named Fukukaku, located between Joyce, Clarice, Freda and Margy. The gradual closing in on Fukukaku took six weeks, in its final stages assisted by Matilda tanks, 25-pounder field guns and even 3.7-inch anti-aircraft guns brought over steep jungle tracks to fire directly at Japanese bunkers. Through June, the infantry completed the slogging fight to break into Fukukaku, and on 22 June Whitehead signalled that 'all organised resistance ceased'. A month after the landing, Australian staff officers estimated that about 875 Japanese had died, while over 600 remained: only 25 had been captured to date. While Japanese doctrine and Australian experience in New Guinea led both to expect that the defenders would fight to the last, in fact on Tarakan they did not. By the end of June, the defenders' morale collapsed, and while many insisted on dying, an unusually high percentage – about 15 per cent – decided to surrender. During the campaign's final 'pursuit' phase Whitehead's troops combed the island in what they called 'emu patrols'. Over 100 Japanese, many starving, lost and diseased, were rounded up on the island and more than 50 by 'barge patrols' in the sea and coastal swamps surrounding it. While 80 per cent of the Japanese defenders died in the fighting, the tally of prisoners was greater proportionally than in any comparable operation of the Pacific War.

By the war's end, Tarakan had cost the Oboe 1 Force 225 dead, 629 wounded and over 1400 evacuated because of illness (though including US, Dutch and other Australian personnel the deaths total approximately 250).[8] While its operations – the landing, lodgement, consolidation and liberation of Tarakan from Japanese occupation – unquestionably represented 'a justifiable use of an Australian national force acting as part of an international wartime alliance',[9] the operation's legitimacy and apparent success is, however, only part of the story. One of the other major and legitimate questions is, did Oboe 1 also make an effective contribution to Allied operations in the SWPA? That judgement essentially depends upon the extent to which Allied air forces were able to exploit the capture of Tarakan's airstrip. Therefore, the RAAF's part in the operation needs more detailed analysis.

Tarakan and the RAAF

In both the Army and Air volumes of the Australian official history, the Tarakan operation was described as an unambiguous failure. In *The Final Campaigns*, Gavin Long concluded that the 'airfield proved so difficult to repair that it was not ready in time for the opening of the operation against either Brunei Bay or Balikpapan'.[10] In *Air War Against Japan 1943–1945*, George Odgers claimed, 'Since the operation was undertaken primarily for the purpose of establishing an airfield for use against other points in the Netherlands East Indies, Tarakan must be regarded as a failure.'[11] Twenty-two pages later, however, Odgers somewhat contradicted himself, and Long, by stating that on 30 June 1945, the RAAF 'now began flying from Tarakan in support of the Balikpapan operation', that is, a day before Australian troops began landing there on 1 July.[12] He then went on to describe some of the RAAF operations from Tarakan.

Repairing the Tarakan airfield undoubtedly became the overriding problem for the RAAF. In the lead-up to the landing, Allied bombing badly cratered the already flooded strip, unintentionally turning it into a morass. Despite the efforts of the RAAF's airfield construction engineers, the strip opened too late to support the Brunei Bay landings, and it remained too rough to accommodate the full air garrison envisaged in the Tarakan invasion plan. Nevertheless, the RAAF force that eventually flew from the island made a measurable contribution to the Balikpapan landing and to operations further afield while operating from a barely adequate strip.

COMMAND ARRANGEMENTS AND FORCES

In order to understand Tarakan's relationship to the broader strategic thrust, it is necessary to see it in the context of Allied command arrangements. In the lead-up to the Borneo campaign, in a letter dated 27 February 1945, Curtin pressed MacArthur to ensure that the RAAF would take 'its rightful place in operations in the South West Pacific Area'.[13] Unfortunately, this goal was undermined by the corrosive internal power struggle between the RAAF's administrative and operational commanders, Air Vice-Marshals George Jones and William Bostock (see Chapter 9). As the RAAF's senior operational officer in SWPA, Bostock commanded RAAF Command Allied Air Forces. Up to this point, RAAF Command had been responsible for Allied air operations from the Australian mainland, including the air campaign over the northwest and the Netherlands East Indies. Following Curtin's letter, MacArthur agreed that Bostock would establish a headquarters in the forward area and take command of the RAAF outside the mainland as well.[14]

The RAAF's striking force in the forward area was the First Tactical Air Force (First TAF), commanded by Air Commodore Harry Cobby. He had assumed command in August 1944 after his predecessor, Air Commodore Frederick Scherger, had been injured in a jeep accident. First TAF, and its earlier incarnation, 10 (Operational) Group, had been under US control since 1943, but on 4 April 1945 it was transferred to Bostock's RAAF Command.[15] For the first time, all the RAAF's combat forces in SWPA came under the operational control of an Australian officer.

The American commander of Allied Air Forces in SWPA, Lieutenant-General George Kenney, delegated the planning and coordination of air support for the Borneo invasion to Bostock. In addition to First TAF, Bostock commanded the RAAF's heavy bombers in the Northern Territory and Western Australia. He could also call on the resources of the US Fifth Air Force on Luzon and the US Thirteenth Air Force in the Southern Philippines. The island of Morotai, which the Americans captured in September 1944, became the forward base for the Borneo landings. Bostock opened his Advanced Headquarters RAAF Command on Morotai on 15 March. By contrast, MacArthur decided that Blamey would not exercise operational control over the I Australian Corps, even though his Adv LHQ was also located on Morotai.

To ensure that the RAAF took its 'rightful place' in SWPA, Bostock decided that he would reinforce First TAF, which was building-up on Morotai, and reduce his forces in Australia and New Guinea. By April 1945, First TAF had grown into a powerful force with the following units in the field or slated to join: nine fighter squadrons, six attack squadrons, an Army cooperation wing and nine airfield construction squadrons, as well as numerous radar, technical, logistic and medical units.[16] Bostock also earmarked half a dozen medium and heavy bomber squadrons in Australia to move forward as the Oboe landings rolled out and more airfields were captured. By the end of April, First TAF had a strength of 16,894 men. By the end of June it had 20,646 men.[17]

But before the invasion of Borneo could get underway, First TAF was rocked by the 'Morotai Mutiny' (see Chapter 9 for a detailed account). On 19 April, eight senior RAAF combat officers submitted their resignations because they believed that Cobby's decision to order regular strikes against bypassed Japanese forces on neighbouring islands had resulted in unjustifiable losses. Bostock responded quickly, and on 22 April he recommended that Cobby should be relieved of his command. By this stage, Scherger had recovered from his injuries, so Bostock selected him to return to his former command. However, Scherger did not arrive to replace Cobby until 10 May. So during the eight days immediately before the Tarakan landing, and for 10 days after, First TAF was commanded by an officer that Bostock wanted sacked. The RAAF's Borneo campaign was off to a bad start, and the problems would continue.

TARAKAN AS AN AIR FORCE OBJECTIVE

MacArthur decided that the final sequence of the Borneo landings would be: Tarakan (Oboe 1), 1 May; Brunei Bay (Oboe 6), 10 June; and Balikpapan (Oboe 2), 1 July. While the strategic value of the Borneo campaign has been doubted, this sequence of landings made operational sense in terms of air power. Seizing Tarakan first meant that both Brunei Bay and Balikpapan could be brought simultaneously within the range of RAAF fighters and attack aircraft – assuming Tarakan airfield could be made operational. In particular, it would have allowed maximum air power to be deployed against the heavy Japanese fortifications of Balikpapan for the longest possible period.

In his report on Tarakan, Bostock noted that RAAF Command had three main tasks: to neutralise any enemy forces that could interfere with the operation, support the 26th Brigade and establish air forces at Tarakan to support the following Borneo landings.[18] According to intelligence estimates, the Japanese had only 48 fighters and 21 bombers in the whole of the Netherlands East Indies, so Bostock could be assured of overwhelming superiority.[19] However, the experience of the Philippines had shown that Japanese suicide planes could inflict severe damage on Allied ships, even if only a handful could sneak through a convoy's air cover.

Early in the planning phase, MacArthur's headquarters decided that the air garrison of Tarakan would include a fighter wing and an attack wing.[20] Cobby allocated 78 (Fighter) Wing with three Kittyhawk and one Spitfire squadrons and 77 (Attack) Wing with three squadrons of twin-engine Beaufighters, together with other specialist units.[21] The Oboe 1 plan anticipated that the Tarakan airfield would be ready to receive its first aircraft from 7 May.[22] To achieve this, two RAAF airfield construction squadrons of 61 Airfield Construction Wing would land immediately after the 26th Brigade and start work on the strip as soon as it was captured. The wing included 1 and 8 Airfield Construction Squadrons, which were specialist engineer units with heavy construction equipment. Airfield construction squadrons could also defend airstrips as they built them. To coordinate these forces Cobby and his Advanced Headquarters of First TAF would sail with the assault convoy.

During April, as planning proceeded for the establishment of a RAAF force on Tarakan, Bostock coordinated a series of preliminary air operations. US bombers from the Philippines and a detachment of RAAF Liberator heavy bombers from Morotai carried out the pre-invasion bombardment of Tarakan. In addition to bombing Japanese emplacements and troop concentrations, the airfield was bombed repeatedly – and excessively – to keep it out of action. Meanwhile, for 20 days before the landing RAAF Liberators from the Northern Territory and Western Australia struck at targets elsewhere in the East Indies as part of the wider effort to isolate Borneo.

During the opening phase of the operation, the RAAF experienced several problems. As the assault convoy sailed from Morotai to Tarakan, First TAF struggled to provide continuous air cover. According to Odgers, it was 'evident that the Australian pilots engaged in convoy escort had been given insufficient briefing'.[23] Fortunately, the Japanese air forces did not put in an appearance, and when the Thirteenth Air Force took over as planned, the provision of air cover went smoothly as the convoy approached Tarakan. On the day of the assault, 1 May, and the following few days, there were still more glitches. Bostock reported that the unloading of RAAF stores was difficult because the 'tactical loading of ships, though well planned, was badly executed. Beach control at the far shore was inadequately organised. Some communications equipment was unequal to the tasks required of it and breaches of close air support procedures occurred.'[24] Gary Waters noted in his study of Oboe air operations that 'there was almost a casualness to RAAF planning for Oboe One'.[25] Perhaps this was another reason why Bostock wanted to get rid of Cobby. Certainly, Morshead agreed that Cobby should be removed.[26]

But the problems did not end there. On 1 May, as MacArthur, Bostock and other senior officers watched the landing from a warship, only US aircraft could be seen pounding the island, even though RAAF squadrons were slated to be included. As Mark Johnston explains, 'Bostock was intensely embarrassed, and soon learned the reason: while the fleet was sailing, and radio silence was in force, his nemesis Jones had sent a message to RAAF squadrons telling them they were grounded as they had completed their allotted monthly flying hours!'[27] This fiasco was probably the worst example of the poisonous Jones–Bostock feud directly affecting operations.

TARAKAN AIRSTRIP

The repair of Tarakan's airstrip occupied the two RAAF airfield construction squadrons for seven weeks before it became operational in a limited way, and demanded continual repair for as long as it remained an Allied base. The strip had been bombed heavily and was severely cratered – more than it needed to be – by the preparatory air bombardment. (Not attacking it at all would have disclosed the objective, though it should have been obvious that a landing could only mean possession of the strip.)

RAAF reports of the strip's repair alternate between despondent chronicle and optimistic prediction negated day after day by the appalling challenge the engineers faced. Before the heavy construction equipment could move in, mines and booby traps had to be cleared. In two days an RAAF bomb disposal unit found and defused 114 mines.[28] An army sapper, glad he did not have to do the job, claimed that increasingly desperate RAAF construction men had filled craters with timber, pipes, concrete, steel mesh and boiler plate, all of which gradually settled into the ooze. Craters and boggy patches needed hundreds of 44-gallon drums packed with mud, while engineers laid miles of perforated steel Marsden matting. Pilots later claimed that the fill included a bulldozer that could not be extricated. The RAAF explained the delays by referring to abnormally heavy rain, infiltrators and air raids, but played down its own cratering of the strip. Successive deadlines were set and passed. George Jones repeatedly misinformed the Advisory War Council, claiming that the strip was usable while simultaneously describing it as 'little better than a mud patch'.[29]

In addition to the massive repair task, the rehabilitation of the strip was held up by bad weather. The history of RAAF airfield construction squadrons noted that at Tarakan there was 'perpetual competition between water and men. Bomb craters once pumped out, refilled with overnight rain and ground seepage', with one airman noting in his diary that 'machines were bogged everywhere'.[30] Local Indonesian labourers were put to work on the strip. The Netherlands East Indies Civil Affairs Unit provided 200 on 11 May, 240 on 15 May and 400 on 19 May.[31] To the chagrin of the RAAF engineers, in early June Army sappers were detailed to fill the craters. From 6 June, only four days without rain were needed to allow the completion of the levelling of the strip and mat laying. But to the bitter frustration of those labouring in the mud, there were only two rainless days from 6 to 25 June.[32] On 15 June, just as the strip dried from the previous week's downpours, 132 points (33 millimetres) of rain fell. By 21 June, the routes alongside the strip were so ruined by graders and bulldozers that drivers were allowed to drive over Marsden matting, causing subsidence and corrugations, especially on the fragile seaward end, which in turn needed repairs.[33] As Odgers observed, the continued wet weather 'had a depressing effect on the spirits of many of the men and they began to despair of ever completing the job'.[34]

The Japanese also did their best to slow the work. Hardly a night passed without infiltrators attempting to breach the perimeter. On the night of 31 May, for example, a large party of Japanese attempted to sneak through the Australian lines. During the resulting fight, a grenade killed an RAAF sergeant and wounded another, while the airfield construction engineers killed four Japanese. Work continued under floodlights throughout the night, in spite of the interruptions.[35]

Tarakan airfield finally received its first aircraft (aside from a handful of light Auster observation planes) on 28 June – seven weeks later than planned. Nevertheless, the diarist of 1 Airfield Construction Squadron wrote that the event 'caused a great uplift in spirits and to a man members showed great pleasure and pride in having at last mastered the weather and the conditions'.[36] Unfortunately, the strip remained too rough to handle the large twin-engine Beaufighters, and it could be used only by single-engine aircraft: the Kittyhawks and Spitfires of 78 (Fighter) Wing. Even then, the strip was perilous for the fighter pilots. Flying Officer Neville MacNamara (later Air Chief Marshal Sir Neville) commented that pilots could only take off to the west and land to the east. He also recalled the common folklore about the strip that 'it was one of the few airfields in the world where one end rose and fell with the tide'.[37] Later, Dakota transports were able to use the strip, but never safely.

The air commanders' lack of knowledge of the appalling state of the airfield was a major intelligence failure. Photographic reconnaissance on 20 February, and a pilot's report two weeks later, revealed that the bomb craters in the strip were filling with water. A I Corps intelligence review circulated on 20 March acknowledged that the strip would require 'considerable work', but it was not the engineers who were culpable, but rather it was 'the folly of the air planning staff officers who simultaneously planned the complete destruction of the airfield which they not only wished to use, but which formed the basis of the entire operation'.[38] A wing commander later admitted that 'had the correct information been available it is doubtful whether the project would have been attempted'.[39] When Scherger took over First TAF on 10 May, it was immediately apparent to him 'that a satisfactory strip could never be constructed'.[40]

As Tarakan could not be brought into operation in time for the Brunei Bay landings on 10 June, the Oboe 6 air plan had to be rapidly recast. The 77 Wing Beaufighters intended for Tarakan were moved temporarily to Sanga Sanga in the southern Philippines. Also flying out of Sanga Sanga was a squadron of Kittyhawks in the ground attack role. Meanwhile, the planned fighter cover from Tarakan was replaced by US long-range P-38 Lightnings, also flying from the Philippines.

The successful replacement of Tarakan by other existing bases has raised the question of whether it was necessary to seize the island in the first place. However, since the RAAF's planners were blind to the condition of the airfield, they simply carried on within the usual operational parameters. In particular, they had to deal with the problem that the RAAF's Kittyhawks and Spitfires were short-range fighters that had to be based as close as possible to the next objective (Brunei Bay) to have maximum patrol time over the area. The closest base to Brunei Bay in the Philippines was Sanga Sanga, some 560 kilometres distant, while Tarakan was only 320 kilometres away. Moreover, the RAAF's fighters could not cover Balikpapan from Sanga Sanga. Additionally, the RAAF's planners were aware that Kenney had already allocated Sanga Sanga and the other airfields in the southern Philippines to the Thirteenth Air Force. These bases were still being developed as the Borneo landings got underway and they simply could not accommodate both the Thirteenth Air Force and First TAF. Indeed, the RAAF had to vacate Sanga Sanga only three days after the Brunei Bay landings to make way for US Lightnings.[41]

These considerations meant that only Tarakan appeared to fit all the RAAF's operational requirements of an air base to support both Oboe 6 and Oboe 2. And with a 41-day period between the Tarakan assault on 1 May and the Brunei Bay Landing on 10 June, and two months until the Balikpapan landing on 1 July, it must have seemed a reasonable assumption that the airfield would be ready in time.

In the end, however, the delay in opening the Tarakan airstrip meant that the Brunei Bay landings had to be supported from the southern Philippines. It also meant that, as the Balikpapan operation drew closer, US Thirteenth Air Force Lightnings were called on to operate at extreme range from the Philippines to cover the assault area since the availability of the Tarakan airstrip remained in doubt. But, as will be explained, RAAF fighters based on Tarakan joined the fight just in time to support the landing.

RAAF Operations from Tarakan

After weeks of frustration, Tarakan airfield finally became an operational base to support the Borneo campaign, although with less capacity than originally intended. On 30 June, 78 (Fighter) Wing began flying combat missions from the strip. Despite the difficult flying conditions, the wing mounted a significant effort in support of the Balikpapan landing and the continuing operations in North Borneo. During July the four squadrons of the wing (75, 78, and 80 Kittyhawk and 452 Sptifire Squadrons) flew 858 operational sorties, during which they dropped 239,590 pounds of bombs and expended 337,442 rounds of ammunition. As a result, 78 Wing claimed to have destroyed or damaged 76 buildings and huts, seven watercraft, 14 vehicles, 12 fuel and ammunition dumps, two bridges and a railway engine.[42] 452 Squadron also shot down a Japanese bomber over Balikpapan (probably a Nakajima Helen).[43] The cost was the loss of three Kittyhawks and three Spitfires, with one pilot killed, one missing believed killed, two missing, and two who were uninjured following successful parachute descents.[44]

78 Wing's operations included providing close air support to the 7th Division at Balikpapan. The wing's official record underscored the

success of these operations by quoting a congratulatory message from the 7th Division: 'Strikes by Peters (fighters) this area over past three days highly successful. Bombing strafing excellent. Army personnel elated with support. Congratulations to aircrew ground staff responsible these actions.'[45]

Another focus of operations from Tarakan were airstrikes against Japanese troop concentrations in northeastern Borneo, including around Sandakan and Tawao. It appears that these strikes were intended, at least in part, to support the guerrilla operations coordinated and led by detachments of the Services Reconnaissance Department. As 78 Wing noted, the aim was to keep the Japanese units on the move, preventing them from gathering food supplies, 'and driving him into the jungle where friendly Dayaks could inflict casualties'.[46] In a letter dated 7 July to the Army Minister, Frank Forde, Blamey noted that while the capture of Tarakan, Labuan and Brunei Bay had gone ahead successfully, 'in the north the tasks of the capture of [the] JESSELTON and SANDAKAN areas lie ahead. It is believed that there are considerable enemy forces here . . .'[47] If the war had gone on as expected, 78 Wing at Tarakan airfield would probably have continued to provide air support over northern Borneo, even after the end of the Balikpapan operation.

For the first half of July, 78 Wing supported the 7th Division directly from Tarakan. The plan was to open a fighter strip on 7 July at Sepinggang, 5 kilometres along the coast from the Balikpapan beaches. But due mainly to the state of the road leading to the airfield, it did not become operational until 15 July.[48] From then on 78 Wing aircraft from Tarakan staged through Sepinggang allowing them to spend much more time over the battlefield and to respond to requests for air support at very short notice. It also allowed the wing's Kittyhawks and Spitfires to range as far as Banjermasin, 320 kilometres south of Balikpapan, and to cover US Patrol-Torpedo-boat operations along the west coast of Celebes. These operations involved round trips from Tarakan of up to 1800 kilometres.[49] So despite Odgers' assessment, the RAAF clearly did use Tarakan for strikes 'against other points in the Netherlands East Indies', although not on the scale intended.

As noted, the delay in opening Tarakan airfield caused despair among the RAAF engineers who struggled to repair it. Meanwhile, during the second half of May and through June morale in 78 Wing was also in a slump while its pilots waited impatiently on Morotai. The Operations Record Book of 80 Squadron noted that during May the 'morale of the whole squadron is lower than ever before, due to the continued inactivity'.[50] But once Tarakan airfield became operational at the end of June, morale rose accordingly. On 30 June, the Operations Record Book of 452 Squadron hit an optimistic note: 'all personnel are pleased to see our aircraft once more engaged against the enemy, all look to the future with keen anticipation'. By 19 July, after nearly three weeks of intense operations from Tarakan and Balikpapan, the squadron believed it was engaged in 'the most effective operations against the enemy in two years' and that its pilots 'thoroughly enjoyed' barge sweeps among the waterways and rivers around Balikpapan.[51]

JUDGEMENT ON TARAKAN

From an Army perspective, Oboe 1 resulted in bitter fighting and heavy casualties. As Gavin Long observed, 'Another reason why, in retrospect, the choice of Tarakan as an objective seems unfortunate is that it was an island from which the defenders had no means of withdrawal, and since they would not surrender, they sold their lives dearly.'[52] The result was that the 26th Brigade Group's casualties on Tarakan (225 killed and 669 wounded) were about the same as the much larger 7th Division at Balikpapan (229 killed and 634 wounded). This included the loss of outstanding veterans including Lieutenant Tom 'Diver' Derrick VC, who died of wounds from a burst of machine-gun fire during one of the many fights for the hills beyond the strip. This was a high price to pay for an airfield that did not meet the planners' expectations.

For the RAAF, Tarakan remained a deeply flawed operation. It threw the RAAF's internal divisions into sharp relief, and it revealed a number of problems with basic operational procedures, from the poor unloading of landing ships to the inability to provide continuous air cover for the assault convoy. These problems, however, would be largely overcome at Brunei Bay and Balikpapan, thanks to the hard lessons of Oboe 1. But it was poor intelligence about the state of Tarakan airfield that caused the overriding problem. The level of damage to the airfield, combined with appalling weather and enemy interference, meant that air support could not be provided from Tarakan to support the Brunei Bay landings, and the strip remained too rough to accommodate Beaufighters. Nevertheless, the RAAF's airfield construction engineers were able to overcome terrible conditions to make the strip suitable for fighter operations just ahead of the Balikpapan landing. This allowed 78 (Fighter) Wing to mount a creditable effort from Tarakan and to stage through Sepinggang in support of both the 7th Division and the wider Borneo campaign. Indeed, the airfield construction engineers and the men of 78 Wing rightly regarded their efforts as a job well done. Amid all the controversy, this positive side of the Tarakan leger should not be forgotten.

While acknowledging the flaws in the planning and execution of Oboe 1, it should be recalled that it contributed to the liberation of substantial areas of Japanese-occupied Borneo. Moreover, though coming into operation later than planned, and at a reduced capacity, Tarakan airstrip made a contribution to the success of Allied operations in Borneo, and, had the war continued (as all expected it would) it would probably have continued to play a useful role.

Further Reading

David Coombes, *Morshead: Hero of Tobruk and El Alamein*, Oxford University Press, Melbourne, 2001.

David Horner, *High Command: Australia and Allied Strategy 1939–1945*, Allen & Unwin, Sydney, 1982.

D. Clayton James, *The Years of MacArthur: Volume II 1941–1945*, Houghton Mifflin, Boston, 1975.

Mark Johnston, *Whispering Death: Australian Airmen in the Pacific War*, Allen & Unwin, Melbourne, 2011.

Tom O'Lincoln, *Australia's Pacific War: Challenging a National Myth*, Interventions, Melbourne, 2011.

Harry Rayner, *Scherger: A Biography of Air Chief Marshall Sir Frederick Scherger*, Australian War Memorial, Canberra, 1984.

Peter Stanley, *Tarakan: An Australian Tragedy*, Allen & Unwin, Sydney, 1997.

Gary Waters, *Oboe Air Operations over Borneo 1945*, Air Power Studies Centre, Canberra, 1995.

David Wilson, *Always First: RAAF Airfield Construction Squadrons 1942–1974*, Air Power Studies Centre, Canberra, 1998.

Notes

1 Gavin Long, *The Final Campaigns*, Australian War Memorial, Canberra, 1963, p. 406.

2 Tarakan has been treated by historians in detail only twice: by Gavin Long in his official history *The Final Campaigns*, in 1963, and by Peter Stanley in *Tarakan: An Australian Tragedy*, Allen & Unwin, Sydney, 1997. Various unit histories deal with the participation of army units, though few after the 1960s – the battalion histories of all the infantry involved had appeared by 1978. The higher direction of

the war in the Southwest Pacific in 1945 – the context of Oboe 1 – has attracted more attention from the American historian D. Clayton James in the second of his three volume biography, *The Years of MacArthur:* Volume II *1941–1945*, Houghton Mifflin, Boston, 1975; to John Robertson in *Australia at War 1939–1945*, Heinemann, Melbourne, 1981; and, magisterially in David Horner's *High Command*, Allen & Unwin, Sydney, 1982 (itself now over 30 years old and surely ready for reconsideration in the light of new evidence or fresh questions, if they are to be found). The controversial assertions (at least in Australia) of British historian Sir Max Hastings in *Nemesis: the Battle for Japan, 1944–45*, Harper Collins, London, 2007, also suggest that the argument deserves to be revisited. Chapter 14 of *Nemesis* is titled 'Australians: "Bludging" and "Mopping Up"'. For further discussion see Chapter 1.

3 Peter Charlton, *The Unnecessary War: Island Campaigns of the South-West Pacific 1944–45*, Macmillan, Melbourne, 1983.

4 Long, *The Final Campaigns*, pp. 451–2; George Odgers, *Air War Against Japan 1943–1945*, Australian War Memorial, Canberra 1957, reprinted 1968, p. 461. The official historians' view of Tarakan as a failure has been accepted in most Australian general histories of the Pacific War. For example, David Day, *Reluctant Nation: Australia and the Allied Defeat of Japan, 1942–45*, Oxford University Press, Melbourne, 1992; Peter Thompson, *Pacific Fury: How Australia and Her Allies Defeated the Japanese Scourge*, William Heineman, Sydney, 2008.

5 Peter Stanley, *Tarakan: An Australian Tragedy*, Allen & Unwin, Sydney, 1997.

6 Diary, George Kenney, 11 April 1945, USAF Historical Support Office, Bolling Air Force Base, Washington, DC.

7 Stanley, *Tarakan*, pp. 59–60 and Harry Rayner, *Scherger: A Biography of Air Chief Marshal Sir Frederick Scherger*, Australian War Memorial, Canberra, 1984, p. 88.

8 Stanley, *Tarakan*, pp. 220–22.

9 Stanley, *Tarakan*, p. 2.

10 Long, *The Final Campaigns*, pp. 451–2.

11 Odgers, *Air War Against Japan 1943–1945*, p. 461.

12 Ibid., p. 483.

13 Ibid., p. 437.

14 Ibid., pp. 438–9.

15 NAA A11093 320/5K4, RAAF units under Operational Command of US Air Forces. Bostock decided to change the name of 10 (Operational) Group to First TAF in 1944 to better reflect its role

and growing size and because in the US Air Force A Group was a unit of only three or four squadrons.

16 NAA A11225 224/8/Org, Organisation Memorandum – 1st TAF RAAF, 4 April 1945.

17 Odgers, *Air War Against Japan 1943–1945*, pp. 439, 477.

18 NAA 1966/5 383, RAAF Command Report of Oboe One Operation, p. 2.

19 Odgers, *Air War Against Japan 1943–1945*, p. 452.

20 AWM 3DRL 2632, Morshead Papers 7/6, *"Montclair" Basic Outline Plan for the Reoccupation of the Western Visayas-Mindanao-Borneo-NEI Area, 3rd Edition*, 25 February 1945.

21 Cobby originally allocated 81 (Fighter) Wing at Noemfoor for the task. However, it could not be brought forward in time so 78 Wing at Morotai was substituted, although it had only 10 days' notice. Odgers, p. 453.

22 Gary Waters, *Oboe Air Operations Over Borneo 1945*, Air Power Studies Centre, Canberra, 1995, p. 53.

23 Odgers, *Air War Against Japan 1943–1945*, p. 456.

24 NAA 1966/5 383, RAAF Command Report of Oboe One Operation, p. 2.

25 Waters, *Oboe Air Operations Over Borneo 1945*, p. 151.

26 David Coombes, *Morshead: Hero of Tobruk and El Alamein*, Oxford University Press, Melbourne 2001, p. 196.

27 Mark Johnston, *Whispering Death: Australian Airmen in the Pacific War*, Allen & Unwin, Melbourne, 2011, p. 413.

28 Odgers, *Air War Against Japan 1943–1945*, p. 458.

29 Stanley, *Tarakan*, pp. 133, 166.

30 David Wilson, *Always First: RAAF Airfield Construction Squadrons 1942–1974*, Air Power Studies Centre, Canberra, 1998, p. 84.

31 Stanley, *Tarakan*, p. 131.

32 Odgers, *Air War Against Japan 1943–1945*, p. 460.

33 Stanley, *Tarakan*, p. 165.

34 Odgers, *Air War Against Japan 1943–1945*, p. 460.

35 Ibid.

36 AWM64 15/2, Operations Record Book 1 Airfield Construction Squadron, 28 June 1945.

37 Waters, *Oboe Air Operations Over Borneo 1945*, p. 55.

38 Stanley, *Tarakan*, pp. 131–2.

39 Ibid.

40 Odgers, *Air War Against Japan 1943–1945*, p. 461.

41 Ibid p. 471.

42 NAA A9186 654, Operations Record Book No. 78 Wing Headquarters, Summary July 1945. These figures do not include another 401 non-operational sorties.

43 NAA A9186 137, Operations Record Book No. 452 Squadron, 24 July 1945.

44 NAA A9186 654, Operations Record Book No. 78 Wing Headquarters, Summary July 1945.

45 Ibid.

46 Ibid.

47 AWM 3DRL/6643 2/18, Blamey Papers, Letter Blamey to F. M. Forde Minister for the Army, 7 July 1945.

48 Odgers, *Air War Against Japan 1943–1945,* pp. 486, 488.

49 NAA A9186 654, Operations Record Book No. 78 Wing Headquarters, Summary July 1945.

50 NAA A9186 111 Operations Records Book No. 80 Squadron, Activities for the month of May 1945.

51 NAA A9186 137 Operations Record Book No. 452 Squadron, 30 June 1945 and 19 July 1945.

52 Long, *The Final Campaigns,* p. 452.

CHAPTER 14

'UNIQUE IN THE HISTORY OF THE AIF': OPERATIONS IN BRITISH BORNEO

Garth Pratten

Writing of the work of Australian medical units among the people of Sarawak, Australia's official historian of the Second World War, Gavin Long, observed that it was 'unique in the history of the AIF'.[1] This epithet can be readily applied to the broader campaign conducted in British Borneo between March 1945 and January 1946 – the most multi-faceted set of operations conducted under Australian command during the Second World War. Not only did the British Borneo campaign share the extensive joint cooperation of the operations at Tarakan and Balikpapan, it also featured special and military civil affairs operations unprecedented in scale and scope during Australia's contribution to the war. The integration of these elements suffered from inadequate command and control structures and poorly coordinated objectives, but their presence clearly demonstrates a level of operational maturity not glimpsed in earlier Australian campaigns.

The campaign was also the most politically complex of those waged by Australia, and some of the difficulties in operational, and sometimes tactical, level coordination stemmed from the politico-strategic agendas underlying its direction. The use of 'British Borneo' in this chapter follows British Colonial office practice and refers to four separate territories: the Crown Colony of Labuan, a small island off the east coast of northern Borneo, and the protectorates of Sarawak, Brunei and North Borneo. Prior to the Japanese occupation all three of the latter had different forms of government – Sarawak was ruled by the fourth of the Brooke family's paternalistic 'white rajahs', North Borneo was under control of a governor appointed by the directors of the British North Borneo

Company, and Brunei by its hereditary Sultan with advice from a British resident. The Colonial Office had plans for post-war administrative reform in the territories, and with the deeply wounded British economy needing their supplies of oil, rubber and minerals, regarded the United States' anti-colonial agenda with suspicion. Thus, at a time when the British Joint Chiefs questioned the military necessity of capturing Brunei Bay to secure a naval base they did not want – as discussed in Chapters 1 and 2 – other elements of the British government were keen for an early return.[2] For its part, Australia saw the liberation of British territory as a legitimate task for a member of the Commonwealth. Indeed, some individuals in its government may have seen an opportunity to subvert Britain's intentions. It was amid this 'tangled skein', as Long later wrote,[3] that operations in British Borneo were planned and executed.

'CHANGES OF PLAN ARE UNAVOIDABLE': MOUNTING OBOE 6

Planning for the Australian landings in British Borneo – codenamed Oboe 6 – was shaped by three major factors: the shifting higher-level plans for the Oboe series, the tight timetable imposed on its final revision, and a shortage of maritime resources – both transport shipping and amphibious assault craft. Headquarters 9th Division had already produced orders for Oboe 1 and its outline plan for Oboe 2 when, on 18 April, I Corps ordered it to cease work on the latter. It was instead to prepare for Oboe 6, originally a 7th Division task, with a target date of 23 May.[4] Major-General George Wootten, General Officer Commanding 9th Division, sensed the frustration of his staff, who had been working 'extremely long hours' to plan two operations simultaneously, and counselled on 20 May that 'changes of plan are unavoidable in operations and must be accepted, although at times staff may feel that a lot of work and time has been wasted unnecessarily, this feeling must be overcome'.[5] Their labours, however, were not necessarily wasted. The close working relationships with air force and, particularly, US Navy colleagues developed during Oboe planning thus far facilitated a relatively easy switch of objectives, and the work on Balikpapan was handed to the 7th Division to contribute to its planning.[6]

The concept of operations passed down to the 9th Division from General Headquarters (GHQ) via I Corps was for simultaneous brigade landings on Labuan and the Brunei peninsula, preceded by aerial and naval bombardment, and followed by operations to secure Brunei Bay and its environs, and the oil producing area around Miri and Lutong to the southwest.[7] The 24th Brigade under the command of Brigadier Selwyn Porter was tasked with Labuan, and the 20th Brigade, commanded by Brigadier Victor Windeyer, with Brunei. The division's third brigade, the 26th, was committed to Oboe 1. Ultimately, the divisional outline plan would feature four separate assault landings – one at Labuan, two on the Brunei peninsula, and one on Maura Island just inside the entrance to Brunei Bay – it was also quickly realised that subsequent operations would extend along nearly 300 kilometres of coastline and that the riverine environment offered much scope to out-manoeuvre the enemy.[8] The provision of amphibious shipping and, in particular, small craft was a constant concern for the planners. Continuing amendments to the order of battle to fit the available shipping were reported as being 'the most difficult part of the planning', and unit commanders had to reduce vehicles and stores to the 'bare essentials'.[9] Shipping allocations beyond the initial landings had to be juggled to facilitate both coastal operations and return trips to Morotai for follow-on troops; GHQ stipulated that most of the shipping allocated for Oboe 6 had to be released within 23 days of the landings.

Cargo shipping shortages and delays hampered the build-up of the Oboe 6 force at Morotai. On 3 May, it became apparent that two of the 20th Brigade's battalions and all of the field artillery would not arrive in time for the target date. GHQ was informed and responded that it was vital that the operation not be delayed – limited naval resources meant that a postponement of Oboe 6 would derail preparations for Oboe 2. Wootten and his staff found themselves recasting their plans to mount Oboe 6 on time despite the absence of a third of its combatants. It resulted in a plan to undertake the operation on what Lieutenant-General Frank Berryman, Chief of Staff of Advanced Land Headquarters (Adv LHQ), called 'a reduced half baked scale'. Fortunately, Adv LHQ's Brigadier General Staff, Brigadier Lindsay Barham, was able to convince GHQ to amend the Oboe schedule to allow the delayed units to arrive.[10] On 8 May, Oboe 6 was postponed until 10 June and Oboe 2 to 10 July.[11] Trusting in the work that had already been done, Wootten directed that the extra time not be wasted on detailed planning to maximise the time available for final preparations, loading, troop embarkation and rehearsals.[12]

The Oboe 6 landings were remarkable not for tales of human drama but rather their lack of it. They were models of joint force cooperation. The Royal Australian Air Force's First Tactical Air Force (First TAF) and the US Thirteenth Air Force had been striking a range of targets across northern Borneo since 3 May, and from 5 June had concentrated on the objective areas. Minesweepers had cleared the way for Rear Admiral Forest Royal's US Navy – Royal Australian Navy Task Force 78.1 on 7 May and it commenced its role in the preliminary bombardment the next day. No opposition was encountered at any of the landing beaches on 10 June. Of Labuan, Porter wrote:

> The timing of both the landing operations and the fire plan was as near to exact as could be expected – a tribute to the USA Navy, and a justification for their tiresome rehearsal at Morotai when troops were left wondering if there was any value in their being transported around the harbour under a blazing sun, for the benefit of the Navy ... The operation warranted General MacArthur's tribute – a 'A perfect landing'.[13]

'THE ENEMY HAS FOUGHT WITH HIS CHARACTERISTIC ZEAL': LABUAN

At Labuan the 24th Brigade landed at Brown Beach, the only viable site on the island, adjacent to its only town – Victoria. The main Japanese airfield was only 3 kilometres away; from the time the assault troops set foot ashore at 0915, they were fighting for their principal objective. Porter thus emphasised that speed and impetus must be maintained from the point the ramps dropped until the airfield was captured.[14] To assist the troops forward, a layered fire plan had been produced whereby a curtain of naval gunfire would move inland, reinforced by the fire of 4.2 inch mortars and 25-pounder field guns – brought ashore in LVT-4 amphibious personnel carriers in the first assault wave – came into action.[15] On the right of Porter's two-battalion front, the 2/43rd surged forward. Overrunning a number of ill-prepared Japanese outposts and skirmishing among the dispersal bays, it had secured the airfield by 1830.[16] Operating to the west of Victoria Harbour, the 2/11th Cavalry (Commando) Squadron encountered few Japanese.

In common with their practice on other small islands, the bulk of the Japanese force had holed up in well-sited defensive positions in rough country to the west of the airfield and to the east of the extensive mangrove swamp at the head of Victoria Harbour. After clearing Victoria, the 2/28th Battalion overcame several Japanese delaying positions at the edge of this area on the first day, but struggled among its ridges and heavy vegetation on 11 June. Captured documents informed Porter that the defended locality consisted of a main and rear position and revealed the Japanese intent to fight to the last at the latter if pushed from the former. He thus determined to destroy the forward position and contain the Japanese in the rear to allow the rapid clearance of the rest of island. On 12 June, in actions described as 'tedious' due to numerous Japanese road blocks, booby traps, and demolitions, the 2/43rd, from the east, and the 2/28th, from the south, pushed the Japanese back into an area that became known as 'The Pocket'. With the bulk of the enemy thus contained, the rest of the island was secured by nightfall on 14 June.[17]

Wootten's exhortations to avoid unnecessary risks guided Porter's decisions regarding the Pocket. After an attack on its northern approach by the 2/28th's A Company, supported by Matilda tanks, proved the strength of the position, he decided any further immediate action to capture it would only result in unnecessary casualties. For three days from 17 June, the position was pounded by artillery, naval gunfire and air attack. During this time the Pocket's defenders demonstrated they were of no mind to surrender when up to a 100 sallied forth under the cover of darkness on a suicide raid against the brigade's maintenance area and the airfield.[18] The fight for Labuan ended in a charnel house. On 21 June, after one last artillery barrage, two companies of the 2/28th and the ubiquitous Matildas, some equipped with flame-throwers, advanced. The surviving defenders were described as 'semi-demented' and the brigade report stated that 'any offensive spirit' the Japanese had left 'was quickly lost when the Frogs [Matilda variant] commenced projecting streams of flame'. One soldier described the Pocket as 'inferno', smashed 'to smithereens': 'everywhere was the smell of death and the stench of decaying rice'.[19] As a 9th Division intelligence summary noted, the 'enemy ... [had] ... fought with his characteristic zeal',[20] and had been destroyed. The brigade's 'thoughts turned to the next phase of the bigger picture – the operations on the mainland'.[21]

RAPID ADVANCES AGAINST INEFFECTUAL OPPOSITION: OPERATIONS ON THE MAINLAND

Operations on the Borneo mainland initially focused on securing Brunei Bay and the oil-producing area between Seria and Miri. They were characterised by a series of rapid advances against ineffectual opposition and further unopposed landings that exploited the littoral environment for manoeuvre. The 2/17th Battalion, which had been the first infantry battalion ashore, liberated Brunei town on 13 June after a series of section and platoon fights in preceding days. Two days later it commenced a motorised advance along the coast to the southwest that captured Seria and its oil wells – set aflame by the retreating Japanese – and Kuala Belait, on 21 and 24 June respectively. Meanwhile, Wootten had acted quickly to

Figure 14.1: Troops of the 2/32nd Battalion disembarking from an LVT-4 Alligator amphibious personnel carrier in the vicinity of Weston, 17 June 1945. (Australian War Memorial 018680)

establish a number of footholds around Brunei Bay: on 17 June the 2/32nd Battalion, a floating reserve until this point, landed, unopposed, at Weston on the northeastern corner of Brunei Bay; on 18 June the 2/15th Battalion occupied Limbang, near the southwestern corner of the bay, after moving up the river of the same name by landing craft; and on 19 June the 2/43rd Battalion and the 2/11th Cavalry (Commando) Squadron, shipped from Labuan, landed at Mempakul, on the bay's northern headland. One further amphibious landing completed the recapture of British Borneo's oilfields. On 20 June, the 2/13th Battalion, reinforced by two companies of the 2/15th, landed at Lutong, beyond Seria, and marched overland to Miri, which was entered three days later right on the heels of the retreating Japanese, who had again set the oil wells on fire.

Although the 9th Division's intelligence staff had assessed strong Japanese opposition on the beaches unlikely, it was expected that a more vigorous defence would be encountered inland.[22] The ease and speed of the division's advances were a surprise to many, but it was soon realised that the Japanese were weak, exhausted, disorganised and demoralised. Northwest Borneo had been only lightly garrisoned until early 1945, when the Japanese high command assessed Allied landings were likely there as a precursor to Allied operations against Malaya. Orders were given for the Thirty-Seventh Army, the Borneo garrison force, to move the bulk of its forces from the northeast and concentrate them in the west, in an area stretching from Brunei in the south to Jesselton in the north. Allied attacks precluded movement by sea and the redeployment was effected by torturous forced marches across northern Borneo.[23] It was this general movement that also resulted in the infamous Sandakan–Ranau death marches.

The 56th Independent Mixed Brigade was the principal combat formation in Brunei and southern North Borneo. The ravages of sickness, exhaustion and limited rations meant that less than half of its personnel completed the journey from the east, arriving between April and early June. Even at full strength, the 56th Independent Mixed Brigade was not a formidable force. Its battalions had only been raised in late 1944 and had seen no action. They had few heavy weapons and no artillery support.[24] A Japanese report later admitted 'their fighting strength was practically worthless'.[25] Even before the landings, a withdrawal to centres of resistance based on rice-producing areas inland – principally around Ukong, Ranau and Tenom (the first was made untenable by the speed of the Australian advance) – had commenced.[26] The troops the Australians encountered were largely rear guards, whose faltering morale was further undermined by the withdrawal of other Japanese units and Australian airpower and artillery.[27] The garrisons of the oil towns, a mix of infantry and service troops, were just as poorly equipped but less battered; the aggressiveness of their rear guards beyond Miri meant the Australians did not tangle with them lightly.[28]

The only major Japanese resistance encountered on the mainland was at Beaufort. In a landscape devoid of formed roads, Beaufort was an important communications hub. Both the Padas River and the North Borneo Railway linked the interior of northern Borneo to the shores of Brunei Bay via Beaufort, and the railway also ran north to Jesselton. For Wootten, control of Beaufort was critical to secure Brunei Bay against a Japanese counter-offensive, but his enemy was looking in the other direction. For them it was a key junction on their withdrawal routes, which had to be denied to the Australians. In a fine example of the manoeuvre potential offered by Brunei's rivers, Porter eschewed the obvious line of advance along the railway from Weston and used landing craft on the undefended river approaches to move much of the 20th Brigade, including its artillery, within striking distance of Beaufort. To maintain surprise to the last there was no preparatory artillery fire before the attack began on the afternoon of 27 June.

Attacking east along the south bank of the Padas, the 2/32nd Battalion quickly captured its objectives; on the north bank the 2/43rd met increasing resistance as it fought for high ground east of the town. After dark the Japanese launched a counterattack intended to 'grasp the enemy in confusion'.[29] Heavy fighting ensued throughout the night and into the next day, isolating one of 2/43rd's companies. The exploits of Private Leslie Starcevich during the effort to relive it provide an exemplar of the fighting. Advancing along a 'torturous, jungle flanked' foot pad, Starcevich's platoon encountered a string of Japanese machine-gun posts. Pushing through the forward scouts, Starcevich, the platoon Bren gunner, killed the occupants of two posts, with a magazine change in between. A comrade described his actions:

> Starcevich is possessive of a method of approach which in itself must be most disconcerting to the enemy. Firmly and confidently believing that he can never be hit, he walks in to an enemy post preceded by a single and unbroken stream of pellets. He is quite unmoved by returning fire and stops only when the enemy has been annihilated.

Several fox holes were dealt with by grenades, but a third, more strongly manned, machine-gun post required a section attack. In its final stages, Starcevich once again 'adopted his typically ruthless attitude and advanced on the luckless inhabitants of this last pit and eliminated them'.[30] Starcevich was awarded the Victoria Cross.

Despite such actions, the Japanese doggedly fought to regain their lost ground. Australian fire support resolved the battle in their favour. On the evening of 28 June the forward troops withdrew slightly and the Japanese were 'thrashed' throughout the night with mortars and artillery.[31] By the morning they were gone. Beaufort was cleared with the support of tanks, the landing of which the previous afternoon was later found to have influenced the Japanese decision to withdraw. The Japanese were pursued cautiously – airstrikes and artillery were directed onto any pockets of resistance – to a point about 7 kilometres east of Beaufort. There the 24th Brigade's advance stopped, frequent patrol clashes demonstrating Japanese intent to resist further movement towards Tenom.[32] With Beaufort secure, the 2/32nd Battalion set out along the railway to Papar, which it entered, opposed only by a lone light machine-gun team, a week later.[33]

With the 'occupation of all important centres from Papar to Miri, and control of routes leading in to the Brunei Bay area', the 9th Division's initial task was completed.[34] It now had to extend its control inland in order to facilitate the rehabilitation of oil and rubber resources and the re-establishment of civil administration. Wootten was concerned that the division's gains were lightly held and that there was potential for Japanese infiltration. Control would be consolidated, and security maintained, by an extensive patrolling program and the occupation of important tactical and administrative locations, within carefully limited areas of operation.[35] Some officers and men chafed under these restrictions, wanting to pursue and destroy the retreating enemy, but among the division's senior leadership there was a general sense that to do so would precipitate a Japanese reaction and result in avoidable Australian casualties.[36]

Thus, in the second half of July units settled into a patrolling routine from static locations that would last until the end of the war. Such operations where still arduous – one foot patrol from Lawas in the Brunei Bay hinterland covered 80 kilometres[37] – and could result in sudden, violent contacts, but superior Australian field skills and fire support meant most of the casualties were Japanese. Water transport continued to play a central role in these operations, shuttling patrols up to 50 kilometres inland and maintaining forward outposts. Wootten saluted the 'fighting qualities' of his men in the first phase of the operation, but now that they were widely dispersed and their war was 'not full time', he feared for a drop in standards. He enjoined his commanders to maintain discipline 'during this difficult time' and keep the troops fully occupied.[38]

Such concerns were not without foundation. As the time in static positions increased, contacts with the Japanese declined, and news of the repatriation of long-serving personnel signalled that 'Australia's role in the war ... [was] ... finished', commanders faced a variety of disciplinary issues including faltering standards of security, hygiene, dress and bearing; shirking, insubordination and refusal to join patrols; looting, the unauthorised use of weapons and explosives, prostitution and at least two cases of sexual assault involving civilian women.[39] The 9th Division essentially became a garrison force and soldiers not engaged upon patrols or other security duties were directed into organised sporting activities, camp improvements, education classes and relief programs for the civil population.

'WE KEPT CLEAR OF THEM AND THEY KEPT CLEAR OF US': SPECIAL OPERATIONS IN BORNEO

Among the chequered history of Australian special operations in the Second World War, those conducted in Borneo by Special Operations Australia (SOA), also known by its code name, the Services

Reconnaissance Department (SRD),[40] were both the most extensive and successful. These operations also represented the high point of cooperation and coordination between Australian conventional forces and SOA, although mistrust, ignorance and diverging objectives mitigated against the achievement of true synergy between their respective efforts.

SOA's first mission into North Borneo, codenamed Python, was deployed in October 1943 to establish an agent network and report on Japanese shipping movements through the Sibutu Passage and the Balabac Strait. Python was prematurely withdrawn in June 1944 due to compromise, but by this time Borneo featured in GHQ long-term planning and SOA proposed further operations there. The intent was to provide intelligence and establish guerrilla forces to facilitate the planning and execution of conventional operations. These operations were also influenced by Britain's political agenda in Borneo.[41] As the Secretary of State for Colonies reported to Churchill, with no conventional troops in the SWPA Britain relied on 'para-military forces to show the flag'[42] and was able to use the influence it wielded within SOA to ensure they did so. Two new SOA operations resulted: Agas and Semut. Malay for 'sand fly' and 'ant', respectively, the naming of these missions for small, irritating creatures that attack in swarms provided an inkling of their intended effect.

Agas focused on North Borneo and ultimately comprised five field parties inserted between March and July 1945. Agas 1 and 2 operated on the north coast, their agent networks, patrols and guerrillas covering the area between Sandakan and Kudat on Borneo's northwest tip. Agas 4 and 5 were both landed on the east coast but achieved little beyond recruitment and training by war's end. Agas 3 was a reconnaissance of the Ranau area directed by I Corps. Overall, Agas achieved its politico-strategic aims. Its parties established control of their areas of operation, mustered and disarmed neighbouring Japanese troops after the surrender, and handed over in good order to the British Borneo Civil Affairs Unit (BBCAU). Operationally and tactically, Agas achievements were patchier. Agas 1, in particular, provided considerable information about Japanese movements and dispositions, but it was often based on hearsay and gossip rather than direct observation. Tragically, it reported that all Allied prisoners of war had left Sandakan, contributing to the cancellation of a planned rescue mission, when in fact 800 remained. Agas' guerrillas were of disparate quality, and fear of Japanese reprisals undermined the commitment of many; the Japanese they killed amounted to less than 100.[43]

Agas was surpassed in both scale and impact by Semut, which saw over 100 British, New Zealand, Malay, but predominantly Australian, operatives inserted by air into the jungles of Sarawak from March 1945 onwards. The operation's objectives were to collect pre-invasion intelligence to assist the planning and execution of Oboe 6, to ascertain 'the attitudes of the natives of Sarawak to the return of British Control and Administration', and to train and recruit local guerrillas.[44] Semut's large area of operations and communications difficulties resulted initially in the establishment of three separate parties – Semut 1 to the east of Brunei, with outposts in British North Borneo and northern Dutch Borneo; Semut 2 to the south and south east of Brunei; and Semut 3 in southern Sarawak, ranged along the Rajang River. Semut 4 was later deployed to operate along the coast between Miri and the mouth of the Rajang.

The Semut parties found ready support among the peoples of the Sarawak interior, collectively known as Dayaks. Initial efforts were focused on recruitment and training, information gathering, and interdicting the movement of Japanese food supplies from the interior to the coast. Not until the eve of Oboe 6 – 9 June – did Semut's guerrillas launch their offensive. The Dayak peoples shared headhunting traditions and, as Corporal Roland Griffiths-March recorded, many took to the guerrilla war with relish:

> A few feet in front of me was a seething mass of alternately rising and falling parangs, around a circle of khaki bolsters. I could hear the thump of parangs, see bloody eddies and froth stain the water. A final victory howl terminated the slaughter and seven successful, pleased natives came to me: each carried the head of a Japanese, as one would carry a fish by the gills, fingers poked through the lower jaw.[45]

Although controlled by SOA's A Group Headquarters, first from Morotai and then Labuan, Semut operatives were essentially running private armies. As the commander of Semut 1, Major Tom Harrisson, recalled:

> For nearly everything I did in wartime Borneo I answered to no one ... That is not to say that I did not obey orders. I observed all I could, and explained when I could not. Those under my command conducted themselves in the same way towards me.[46]

Cooperation with the conventional forces was limited due to differences in outlook and experience. SOA reported that the 9th Division had 'little appreciation of the potentialities of Semut',[47] which viewed SOA primarily as an intelligence gathering organisation. In addition to Semut, a number of small SOA parties – codenamed Stallion – were employed at the division's behest to gather tactical intelligence before the Oboe 6 landings.[48] Problems with the accuracy and timeliness of SOA information, collected largely by Dayak agents moving on foot, passed on by operatives with limited Malay and no training in intelligence analysis, meant many 9th Division officers were sceptical of its utility. Post-operations reports are telling. The 20th Brigade admitted that cooperation was hampered 'by a lack of experience of working with SRD parties', while SOA noted 'the slightly unorthodox outlook of individualistic Semut junior leaders' could 'irritate the more orthodox type of battalion commander'.[49] In general, the commanding officer of A Group, Lieutenant-Colonel Godfrey Courtney reflected 'we kept clear of them and they kept clear of us'.[50]

When such difficulties were overcome, combined action could be productive, and demonstrated the complementarity of the two elements. For example, on 15 July D Company, 2/17th Battalion, in concert with Semut 2, seized the village of Marudi on the Baram River. The village had been occupied by Semut guerrillas to provide a line of communications to the coast and interfere with Japanese withdrawing from Miri, but they were unable to hold it against a Japanese counterattack. Once the commander of Semut 2 explained the significance of Miri to Windeyer he provided 'all help within his power' to recapture it. Marudi was retained as a 2/17th outpost and became Semut 2's headquarters, resulting in the establishment of a productive operating relationship between the two groups – the latter providing information, scouts and porters to facilitate action against the Japanese, and the former the troops and firepower to carry it out.[51]

The most glaring disjunction between the 9th Division and SOA in Sarawak was their respective missions. Whereas the 9th Division's operations were limited to securing the major population centres along the coast, Semut operatives believed they were a precursor to the liberation of the interior and told the Dayaks such in order to garner their support.[52] The result was a dangerous situation for the lightly armed Semut parties when large, organised groups of Japanese troops retreated inland, unmolested by the conventional forces. Semut's guerrillas harassed the retreating Japanese, and called in airstrikes by First TAF, with which SOA enjoyed a productive working relationship, but they had neither the firepower nor training to fight a positional battle. In some instances the persistence of the guerrilla attacks turned the Japanese back, in others the guerrillas had to withdraw ahead of the enemy leaving friendly areas to their depredations.

The end of the war brought most of the retreating Japanese to heel, none too soon in the assessment of an SOA report:

> Had the war continued it is certain, owing to the limitations imposed on 9 Div. operations, that the natives of Sarawak ... who had rendered Semut such loyal service, would have suffered increasing hardship and bewilderment.[53]

One Japanese party refused, despite repeated requests by leaflet and envoys, to surrender. On 25 October, over two months after the surrender it was engaged in a delaying action by Semut 2 guerrillas as it closed on their headquarters; the party surrendered four days later and only after the delivery by hand of a signed orders from the commander of the Thirty-Seventh Army.[54]

Although the Japanese withdrawal demonstrated the limitations of guerrilla operations, Semut had still been remarkably successful. Up until 15 August 1945, it killed 1622 Japanese troops and local auxiliaries. SOA claimed Semut's actions had prevented the Japanese from being able to counterattack the 9th Division, but given plans to retreat inland this assessment is overblown. Nevertheless, by the end of the war Semut controlled large sections of the Sarawak interior as well as parts of southern North Borneo and northern Dutch Borneo. In areas under SOA control, administrative structures had been re-established and were handed over to relieving officers from BBCAU and the Netherlands Indies Civil Administration. Weapons distributed to guerrillas had been carefully documented and were withdrawn without trouble.[55]

Much of Semut's success stemmed from the lessons learned on previous missions as well as the fact that its parties were leavened by British officers, like Harrisson, with pre-war experience in Borneo. The people whom Semut operated among were generally well-disposed to the British pre-war administration, and the limited penetration of the Japanese into the interior prior to June 1945 had spared them the worst aspects of the occupation inflicted on the coastal populations, meaning they did not share the latter's reticence to assist Allied forces.[56] While the military achievements of Semut can be debated, it accomplished its politico-strategic goal; Dennis White, a long-serving British official in Sarawak, observed to a Semut veteran in 1957 that 'regardless of grand strategy, the presence of SRD in Borneo was important to the local people'.[57]

'A CORDIAL ACT OF IMPERIAL CO-OPERATION': MILITARY CIVIL AFFAIRS IN BRITISH BORNEO

Although the Australian Military Forces (AMF) had gained some experience of military civil affairs in Papua and New Guinea, Blamey regarded the

military government role it was required to discharge in Borneo as a 'novelty'.-
[58] Indeed, civil affairs arrangements were found wanting due to the limited
scope of Australian experience, the extent of the depravation and destruction
inflicted both by the Japanese and Allied bombing and naval gunfire, and
simmering distrust between the Australian and British officers involved.

Suspicious of US intentions, and conscious of the value of British Borneo's
commodities, the British government insisted that any post-invasion military
administration be composed of British officers. The nucleus of a civil affairs
unit was therefore dispatched to Australia in April 1945, but the AMF was
dubious of both the officers provided and the unit's intended structure. The
AMF's Director of Research and Civil Affairs advised Berryman:

> It will be difficult if not impossible to use most of them in the
> operational phase. Their internal organization is inchoate and they
> resemble a section of the Colonial Office rather than a military unit.[59]

The advancement of Oboe 6 in MacArthur's operational timetable
overtook consultations with London and a civil affairs unit was required
urgently. Blamey ordered BBCAU to be raised as an Australian unit to
which some of the British officers were attached, although most were left
behind when the advanced parties deployed to Morotai.

Upon arrival in the Oboe 6 area of operations, BBCAU's advanced parties
struggled. On Labuan 'almost every building of size' had been destroyed in
the preliminary bombardment or subsequent fighting, and the Australians
encountered a dazed population, over 3000 without homes.[60]
Accommodation on the mainland was better, although the destruction of
public infrastructure and utilities was widespread, but the population in
liberated areas swelled as people emerged from hiding in the jungle. The
Japanese had not maintained drainage or sanitation systems and disease and
malnutrition were rife, particularly among Javanese forced labourers.[61]
BBCAU's medical resources were overwhelmed. Responsibility for civilian
medical care was taken over by the 9th Division's medical units that,
fortunately, had spare capacity due to the light Australian casualties; in
both Labuan and Brunei daily civilian hospital admissions in the third week
of June averaged 120, in the latter 500 people were treated as outpatients
each day.[62] Across the board, BBCAU would not have managed had it not
been able to draw upon 9th Division resources. But resources were not its
only problem. Most of its personnel had no experience with civil affairs,
spoke only rudimentary Malay and had no knowledge of Borneo.[63]

Writing to Morshead, Blamey observed that the British government
considered the Australian assumption of responsibility for civil affairs in

British Borneo as 'a cordial act of Imperial co-operation'.[64] With hindsight, it is an ironic description as the direction of civil affairs came to be characterised by disharmony and competing agendas. Several British officers believed that an Australian conspiracy to take control of British Borneo was delaying their deployment and reported such to London, requiring Blamey to have clarify Australia's position: 'I have ... made it as clear as possible to London that we have no interest in the matter except to ensure success of the operation and the restoration of the British territories to their proper control as soon as possible.'[65] There is some anecdotal evidence that Australian External Affairs officials may have coveted the territories, but it was never government policy.[66] Thus, when British officers began reinforcing BBCAU from late July they were already frustrated and dubious of Australian intentions.

In Borneo, Australian and British officers clashed over priorities and policy. The British saw their first priority to 'restore the general life of the community on pre-war lines' and perceived many Australian actions as

Figure 14.2: Personnel from the British Borneo Civil Affairs Unit issuing rations to displaced persons, Labuan, 11 June 1945. (Australian War Memorial 109065)

undermining this goal.[67] BBCAU's limited resources meant a great deal of rehabilitation work in local communities was done by the combatant units. Old Borneo hands in BBCAU felt that the free-and-easy way the 9th Division's troops mixed with local people, particularly the use of white troops for labouring tasks, undermined British prestige. They were also concerned by the medical treatment provided to prostitutes to reduce the incidence of sexually transmitted disease.[68] Australian commanding officers wilfully ignored direction that their units not trade with local people except through BBCAU – a measure intended to protect local traders from poor deals and limit inflation – and their men liberally distributed Army clothing and other supplies.[69]

Australians generally considered the British poor officers, unused to the conventions of staff duties and military etiquette, and were confused by their outlook; Long jotted sarcastically in his notebook: 'Perhaps the theory that you can rule natives only if you are rude to them has no more substance than . . . other myths.'[70] Many shared Wootten's assessment that they were impatient to re-establish a full civil administration in which they had been promised positions. Wootten and the Chief Civil Affairs Officer Brigadier Charles Macaskie, the former Chief Justice of British North Borneo, was BBCAU's commanding officer from 22 July, wrangled over the degree to which BBCAU would be subordinate to the 9th Division's control. Wootten was suspicious of Macaskie's loyalties, given that one of his roles was to communicate directly with London concerning 'long-term plans for reconstruction'.[71] Macaskie considered Wootten's approach to civil affairs to be that of a 'cautious parochial attorney'[72] and withheld policy documents from him. In late August, HQ I Corps had to intervene and clarify roles, responsibilities and lines of reporting.[73] This, however, could not remove the fact that Wootten and Macaskie had different agendas, and they clashed further in September as to whether it was the 9th Division's role to maintain an outpost at Kuching, beyond its objective area, for the purposes of re-establishing British administration.[74]

Despite ongoing infighting, BBCAU, with the continuing assistance of the 9th Division's brigades, managed to accomplish a great deal towards the restoration of functioning civil society in British Borneo. Its monthly progress reports reveal both the scope of its activities and the extent of its achievements. By the end of November, BBCAU estimated it had around 440,000 people under its direct control. Surveys had been conducted of agricultural land, forest reserves, rubber plantations, fishing resources and oil infrastructure, and remedial plans put in place. Crude oil was being shipped from Lutong and petrol produced at Miri was sold for local consumption. Ten hospitals and 63 dispensaries were operating and the health of the population overall was considered fair, although malaria remained a widespread problem. Over 100 schools were in operation, with 8000 pupils.[75] Progress on the reconstruction of public infrastructure varied but had benefitted greatly from the work of the 9th Division's engineers.[76] One particular example of this was the restoration of 132 kilometres of the North Borneo Railway, initially using jeeps as locomotives, between Jesselton and Weston.[77] Problems remained, however. Although over 1200 local police had been recruited, the force was blighted by poor morale and low standards, rates of petty crime were high, and the legal system struggled due to the frequent absence of appointed military magistrates on 'multifarious duties elsewhere'.[78]

On 5 January 1946, Windeyer, now administering command of the 9th Division after Wootten's return to Australia, handed over to Brigadier Edward Woodford, Commander of the 32nd Indian Brigade. BBCAU was disbanded and its British personnel transferred to the British Military Administration (British Borneo). Demonstrating that some Australians did enjoy productive working relationships with their British comrades, 57 opted to stay with the British Military Administration on secondment.[79] Five days later, overall control of operations in Borneo passed to Admiral Louis Mountbatten's Southeast Asia Command, thus ending the Australian campaign there.

'WE TAKE PRIDE IN OUR ACHIEVEMENT': ASSESSING BRITISH BORNEO

By the end of October 1945, the 9th Division had concentrated 21,000 Japanese soldiers, sailors and civilians from around British Borneo.[80] Given these numbers, Allied victory must be seen as having come at a relatively low cost. The 9th Division suffered 114 fatal and 221 non-fatal battle casualties; SOA lost no operatives and 35 guerrillas; but almost 3000 Japanese and local auxiliaries were killed.[81] After all the training and preparations for the operation, for some the 'discovery that the enemy would not fight' proved an anti-climax,[82] but for old soldiers like Staff Sergeant Fred Turner, who had fought with the 2/43rd Battalion through all of its campaigns, the lack of resistance was a relief. Concluding his account of British Borneo, Turner decided that kills and casualties were a flawed measure of the 'job "done"':

> This remarkable campaign proves beyond doubt that if you are
> properly led and you have confidence in your leaders, it is not necessary

... to sustain casualties to do a good job, and thus the merits of a body of men need not be gauged by its casualties.

Turner's reflections underscore the AMF's proficiency in the conduct of combat operations. His battalion's success in British Borneo, he wrote, was due to the troops 'at no time being committed to anything too hot to handle, without a constructive and unhurried appreciation and the necessary preparations having first been made'; these preparations including the employment of 'ample and devastating supporting arms'.[83] The experience of British Borneo, however, also reveals the AMF grappling with the transformation from an organisation that fought battles to one that conducted campaigns. Its efforts to integrate special operations and civil affairs with conventional forces were creditable but would have benefitted from more of Turner's constructive and unhurried appreciation and necessary preparation.

Beyond providing an insight into the origins of Australian success in British Borneo, Turner's reflections also serve as exemplar of what Australians thought they had achieved in British Borneo:

> We rest now ... in and around Beaufort ... rapidly returning to 'pre-war' Beaufort. We won the Town and the B[attalio]n have now won the hearts of the Town's people, who are thriving visibly under their new lease of life.

What is clear from both personal and official accounts is that Australian troops saw the value of their campaign not in the seizure of airfield too cratered by Allied air attacks to be easily repaired, or of the site for a naval base that would never be used, but in the liberation of a population from a harsh occupation: 'We take pride in our achievement and well might we do so.'[84]

FURTHER READING

Gavin Long, *The Final Campaigns*, Australian War Memorial, Canberra, 1963.

Keat Gin Ooi, *The Japanese Occupation of Borneo, 1941–1945*, Routledge, Abingdon, 2011.

Post-War Borneo, 1945–1950: Nationalism, Empire and State-buidling, Routledge, Abingdon, 2013.

Alan Powell, *War by Stealth: Australians and the Allied Intelligence Bureau 1942–1945*, Melbourne University Press, Melbourne, 1996.

Graeme Sligo, *The Backroom Boys: Alfred Conlon and the Army's Directorate of Research and Civil Affairs, 1942–46*, Big Sky Publishing, Newport, 2013.

Notes

1 Gavin Long, notebook, 2 September 45, AWM67, 2/100.

2 Graeme Sligo, *The Backroom Boys: Alfred Conlon and the Army's Directorate of Research and Civil Affairs, 1942–46*, Big Sky Publishing, Newport, 2013, pp. 187–8.

3 Long to Donninson, 9 July 53, cited in Sligo, *Backroom*, p. 186.

4 WD, 9 Div. GS, 12–18 April 1945, AWM52, 1/5/20/53.

5 WD, 9 Div. GS, 20 April 1945.

6 '9th Australian Division Report on Oboe 6' (9 Div RoO), p. 15, AWM54, 619/7/21 Part 2.

7 '1 Aust Corps Staff Study – Oboe Six', pp. 2–3, AWM54, 619/1/4.

8 'Notes on Corps Commander Conference', 26 April 1945, p. 2, AWM54, 619/3/16.

9 9 Div. RoO, p. 17; 'Notes on Divisional Commanders Conference' (GOC Conf.), 27 April 45, p. 1, AWM54, 619/3/16.

10 Frank Berryman, diary, 19 May 45, AWM PR84/370, 1/5.

11 '1 Aust. Corps Report on Operations Borneo Campaign' (I Corps RoO), p. 21, AWM52, 1/4/1/74.

12 GOC Conf., 9 May 45, p. 1.

13 Selwyn Porter, comments on draft of Chapter 19 of *The Final Campaigns*, p. 4, AWM93, 50/2/23/308.

14 '24 Australian Infantry Brigade Report on Operations Oboe Six' (24 Bde RoO), p. 7, AWM52, 8/2/24/36.

15 Porter, comments, p. 4.

16 24 Bde RoO, p. 14.

17 24 Bde RoO, pp. 16–23.

18 '9 Aust. Div. Intelligence Summary [Intsum] No. 1', p. 13, AWM52, 1/5/20/70.

19 Philip Masel, *The Second 28th: The Story of a Famous Battalion of the Ninth Australian Division*, 2/28th Battalion and 24th Anti-Tank Company Association, Perth, 1961, p. 174; 24 Bde RoO, p. 27.

20 9 Div. Intsum 1, p. 1.

21 Porter, comments, p. 4.

22 'Oboe Six Intelligence Review No. 1', p. 15, AWM52, 1/5/20/64.

23 Keat Gin Ooi, *The Japanese Occupation of Borneo, 1941–1945*, Routledge, Abingdon, 2001, pp. 38–9, 129–31.

24 9 Div. Intsum 1, p. 9; 9 Div. Intsum 4, pp. 3–4, AWM52 1/5/20/89; 'Int. Rep. 6', AWM 52, 8/3/15/40; 1 ACAEI interrogation reports, AWM52 1/4/1/76–79.

25 *Japanese Monograph No. 26: Borneo Operations 1941–1945*, Office of the Chief of Military History, Tokyo, 1957, pp. 41–2 cited in Ooi, *Occupation*, p. 131.

26 9 Div. Intsum 1, p. 10; 9 Div. Intsum 4, p. 5; 9 Div. Intsum 2, p. 1, AWM52, 1/5/20/87; 'Note on Jap Movement Behind Brunei Bay', AWM53, 8/3/15/40.

27 '2/15 Aust. Inf. Bn Report on Op Oboe Six', p. 4, AWM52 8/3/15/40; 1 ACAEI interrogation reports.

28 '20 Aust. Inf. Bde Report on Operation Oboe Six' (20 Bde RoO), p. 21, AWM54, 619/7/30.

29 'Enemy Counter Attack Plan – Beaufort', AWM52, 8/2/24/36.

30 Fred Turner, 'Summary of Ops – Labuan – NW Borneo', p. 7, AWM52, 8/3/35/48.

31 24 Bde RoO, p. 43.

32 24 Bde RoO, p. 44–5; I Corps RoO, p. 37.

33 9 Div. RoO, p. 36.

34 I Corps, RoO, p. 37.

35 WD HQ 9 Div. GS, 13 July 45, AWM52, 1/5/20/87; '9 Aust. Div. Operation Instruction [OI] 6', 15 July 45, pp. 1–3, AWM52, 1/5/2/88.

36 'Commander's Summary July 1945', p. 7, AWM52, 8/3/17/28; 9 Div. OI 6, p. 1.

37 'Comments and Impressions of 'B' Coy's Part in the Borneo (Oboe 6) Operation', p. 4; AWM54, 621/7/28.

38 'Special Order of the Day', 14 June 45, AWM52, 8/3/17/28; WD HQ 9 Div. GS, 16 July 45.

39 Survey of 20 and 24 Bde battalion WD for July–September 1945; Long, notebooks, AWM67, 2/100, pp. 36, 44, 47, 2/101, pp. 43–4, 76.

40 Special operations in Borneo are often incorrectly associated with Z Special Unit. Z Special was a holding unit established to recruit and administer the Australian personnel serving with SOA. Z Special Unit had no authorised war establishment or equipment table and did not conduct operations.

41 Alan Powell, *War by Stealth: Australians and the Allied Intelligence Bureau 1942–1945*, Melbourne University Press, Melbourne, 1996, p. 267.

42 Oliver Stanley to Churchill, 21 March 45, cited in Powell, *Stealth*, p. 267.

43 Powell, *Stealth*, pp. 279–80; Lynette Silver, *Sandakan: A Conspiracy of Silence* (3rd ed.), Sally Milner Publishing, Bowral, New South Wales,

2000, p. 232. The deliberations regarding a mission to rescue Allied prisoners of war at Sandakan and Ranau lie beyond the scope of this chapter. For discussion of the subject see: Athol Moffit, *Project Kingfisher*, ABC Books, Sydney, 1995; Silver, *Sandakan*; and Powell, *Stealth*, pp. 280–3.

44   'Special Operations Australia, Volume II: Operations', Part 3 (SOA RoO), p. 66, NAA A3269, O8/B.

45   Roland Griffiths-Marsh, *The Sixpenny Soldier*, Angus & Robertson, Sydney, 1990, p. 292.

46   Tom Harrisson, *World Within: A Borneo story*, The Crescent Press, London, 1959, p. 268.

47   SOA RoO, p. 70.

48   'SRD Requirements – Oboe Six', AWM54, 619/3/18.

49   20 Bde RoO, p. 23; 9 Div. RoO, p. 55; SOA RoO, p. 70; 'Note on Jap Movement Behind Brunei Bay'.

50   G. B. Courtney, interview with B. M. Armstrong in G. M. Pratten and G. J. Harper (ed.), *Still the Same: Reflections on Active Service from Bardia to Baidoa*, Army Doctrine Centre, Georges Heights, 1996, p. 139.

51   SOA RoO, pp. 41–3.

52   John Murray, interview with Long, 2 August 45, AWM67, 2/100, p. 22.

53   'Special Operations Australia, Volume II: Operations', Part 3, p. 44.

54   Powell, *Stealth*, p. 294.

55   SOA RoO, pp. 67–8, 72.

56   SOA RoO, pp. 1, 69.

57   Keith Barrie cited in Powell, *War by Stealth*, p. 301.

58   Thomas Blamey to Morshead, 20 July 1945, p. 1, AWM 3DRL 6643, 2/31.

59   Alfred Conlon to Berryman, 23 April 1945, p. 2, AWM 3DRL 6643, 2/31.

60   9 Div. RoO, pp. 62–3.

61   George Colvin, interview, 2 September 45, AWM67, 2/100, p. 33; 9 Div. RoO, p. 63.

62   'Reports on Civil Affairs' (RoCA), 23 June 45, AWM52, 1/10/8/2;

63   RoCA, 17 June 45, p. 2, 23 June 45, p. 3.

64   Blamey to Morshead, p. 1.

65   Graeme Sligo, *The Backroom Boys*, pp. 210–11; Blamey to Morshead, p. 1.

66   For a full discussion see Sligo, *Backroom*, pp. 208–19.

67   'CA Adm Instr. No. 9', p. 1, AWM52, 1/10/8/4.

68   William Refshauge and Victor Windeyer, interview, 2 September 45, AWM67, 2/100, pp. 48–9.

69   Long, notebook, AWM67, 2/101, p. 26; 'Wearing of Army Clothing and Equipment by Civilians', AWM52, 8/3/13/71.

70 Long, notebook, p. 51.
71 Sligo, *Backroom*, pp. 226–7; 'Civil Affairs Policy for British Borneo', p. 2, AWM54, 376/5/31.
72 Charles Macaskie to Dingle, 20 October 45, cited in Sligo, *Backroom*, p. 227.
73 'Policy – Civil Affairs – British Borneo', 27 August 45, AWM54, 376/5/31.
74 Sligo, *Backroom*, p. 226. Blamey had warned British authorities before the operation that providing relief and administration beyond the coastal fringe may not be possible – Blamey to Bovenschen, 1 June 45, AWM 3DRL6643, 2/31.
75 'Monthly Report – BBCAU', October and November 45, AWM52, 1/10/8/6, 1/10/8/7.
76 Long, *Final*, p. 497.
77 Garth Pratten, '"A triumph of ingenuity and devilry": The Australian Jeep Trains of British North Borneo', *Wartime*, 5 (1999), pp. 28–36.
78 BBCAU Report, November 45, pp. 7–9.
79 Sligo, *Backroom*, p. 232.
80 Long, *Final*, p. 565.
81 Powell, *Stealth*, p. 279; SOA RoO p. 68; Long, *Final*, p. 501.
82 'Comd's Summary – July', AWM52, 8/3/15/40.
83 Turner, 'Summary', pp. 8–9.
84 Turner, 'Summary', p. 9.

CHAPTER 15

'CALLING THE TUNE': AUSTRALIAN AND ALLIED OPERATIONS AT BALIKPAPAN

Garth Pratten

From 0715 on the morning of 1 July 1945, 126 LVT-4 'Alligators', lumbered down the ramps of the landing ships that had carried them from the island of Morotai and splashed into the sea offshore of the southeastern Borneo town of Balikpapan. Bobbing in the swell, the Alligators manoeuvred into two lines abreast. At 0834, the drivers of the first line gunned their engines, and, gurgling and belching exhaust fumes, the Alligators accelerated towards the shore; the second line followed three minutes later. Each Alligator carried around 25 troops from the 2/10th, 2/12th and 2/27th Australian Infantry Battalions – the assault waves of operation Oboe 2, the last Allied amphibious landing of the Second World War, and the largest ever under Australian command. The scene unfolding that clear morning along the beaches and ridgelines ahead provided an awe-inspiring demonstration of the way the Australians intended to fight. Captain Tom Kimber of the 2/27th Battalion recalled:

> As we approached the shore the warships stood off and bombarded the shore. Then the bombers came over and bombed the area and as we neared the landing . . . rocket ships which stood off . . . about 100 yards from the shore, and they fired these hundreds and hundreds of rockets . . . It was a magnificent display of fire power.[1]

By the time of the landings, there were few Australian senior officers who considered the operation necessary, and thus the manner in which it was conducted reflected their desire to protect the force while still attaining its stated objectives. The Australians would dictate the terms under which they fought to both their US partners and their Japanese enemy. That they were largely able to do so was testament to the high standard of training and leadership to be found in the Army by this stage in the war, and the overwhelming materiel superiority available to it. 1 July 1945, however, was not the first time the war had come to the east Borneo coast. Setting the broader series of air, naval and land operations mounted against Balikpapan in their strategic context reveals a disjointed relationship between Allied strategy, operations, and tactics there.

'THE FINEST AND MOST DECISIVE SET OF TARGETS': BALIKPAPAN, OIL, AND PACIFIC WAR STRATEGY

Balikpapan's strategic significance rested upon oil. In 1939, Balikpapan was the second most productive oil port in the Netherlands East Indies with an annual output of 1,800,000 tons.[2] The Netherlands East Indies' oil resources were one of the principal objectives of Japan's war, and troops from the 56th Mixed Infantry Group seized Balikpapan on 25 January 1942. Demolition efforts by Netherlands East Indies forces proved fruitless, and by 1943 Balikpapan's facilities were contributing various petroleum products, including aviation gasoline, to the Japanese war effort; fuel production in that year peaked at 3.9 million barrels.[3]

General George Kenney, the commander of Allied Air Forces in the Southwest Pacific Area (SWPA), believed that the destruction or neutralisation of Japan's oil infrastructure in the Netherlands East Indies was critical to Allied victory. The concentration of the Netherlands East Indies oil fields in the western half of the archipelago, however, placed most outside of the range of Kenney's aircraft. Balikpapan was the one exception; 1982 kilometres from Darwin, it stood on the very edge of the operational radius of B-24 Liberators operating from the Northern Territory. Intelligence reporting after three marathon 17-hour raids on Balikpapan seemed to confirm its significance in the Japanese fuel chain. Within a fortnight, the Japanese were said to be short of aviation fuel from Ambon to Wewak, and even as far afield as Palau and Truk. Writing to the Army Air Forces Commanding General 'Hap' Arnold on 20 October 1943, Kenney argued that Balikpapan's oil infrastructure constituted 'the finest and most decisive set of targets for bombing anywhere in the world'.[4]

Reports that the Japanese were strengthening the defences of Balikpapan, including constructing a fighter base, prompted another two

B-24 raids in December 1943 and January 1944, but throughout the first half of 1944 the burden of the campaign against Balikpapan's oil was carried by Catalinas of the Royal Australian Air Force's (RAAF) 11, 20 and 43 Squadrons, which laid mines in the harbour and its approaches in February, April and May. The mining operations not only had the direct effect of sinking Japanese vessels – 40 per cent of all vessels over 1000 tons that sailed into the area were sunk or damaged by mines – but also closed ports while sweeping operations were conducted, thus delaying the movement of cargo.[5]

Meanwhile, Balikpapan's strategic significance had continued to grow in Kenney's estimation. Having intelligence that estimated 70 per cent of Japanese aviation fuel originated from Balikpapan's refineries, Kenny believed their destruction would convince the Japanese to end the war. Between 30 September and 18 October 1944, Liberators operating from islands off the coast of northwest New Guinea mounted the most concerted attack on Balikpapan yet. Unescorted and poorly coordinated, the first two raids suffered heavily – the second was the most costly single air operation conducted under SWPA command – and did little damage. An operational pause to revise tactics and rally morale, in addition to the provision of escort fighters, allowed the final three raids to best their opposition, destroy the bulk of the Japanese fighters at Balikpapan, and inflict considerable damage on the refineries.[6]

Assessments of the extent of the damage inflicted on Balikpapan varied but were ultimately moot because the Allies' understanding of the Japanese fuel distribution system was flawed. Balikpapan's facilities concentrated on fuel oil for ships rather than aviation fuel, which constituted only 20 per cent of their production. Furthermore, Balikpapan's output had been reduced by 40 per cent between January and April 1944 in response to Allied attacks on shipping; the Japanese were no longer prepared to risk tankers on voyages to this outpost at the edge of their defensive perimeter. Production at the more secure Sumatran fields was increased to compensate. In place of Kenney's strategic shock, there was only a pragmatic cost–benefit analysis. No large tankers docked at Balikpapan after October 1944, and the limited facilities still functioning after the raids were sufficient to maintain local supply; it was decided not to repair those that had been destroyed.[7]

Balikpapan's oil facilities remained part of Allied strategic calculus even after their supposed destruction, suggesting poor planning and coordination inside General Headquarters (GHQ) SWPA. MacArthur considered Borneo oil to be of the 'utmost importance' to his operations against

Japan, although the US Army–Navy Petroleum Board estimated that the restoration of Borneo's oil facilities would take over a year.[8] When the GHQ Staff Study for Oboe 2 was issued on 21 March 1945, the Balikpapan oil facilities that Kenney had done his best to destroy were now to be protected and conserved. Additional tasks included the destruction of hostile garrisons, the establishment of air, naval and logistics facilities to support operations against Java, and to assist with the re-establishment of constituted government.[9]

The Joint Chiefs of Staff, however, were not convinced that operations in Borneo, or by extension the rest of the Netherlands East Indies, would make any contributions to Japan's defeat. On 3 April, they directed MacArthur to confine his operations to northern Borneo.[10] As was discussed in Chapters 1 and 2, MacArthur was not content with this decision and through duplicitous manipulation of both the Joint Chiefs of Staff and the Australian government gained approval to conduct Oboe 2. Historians have struggled to conclusively account for MacArthur's insistence on capturing Balikpapan. Sidelining Australia's forces seems just a little too Machiavellian, and with the landings on Java cancelled, and responsibility for the Netherlands East Indies due to be transferred to South East Asia Command, he had little use for the airfields. Given MacArthur's tendency to back his own judgement over intelligence reports to the contrary and his bloody-minded focus on an invasion of Japan, perhaps the decision to launch Oboe 2 was a continuation of the muddled thinking about Balikpapan's oil.[11]

'A METHODICAL PROGRESSION TO DESTROY HIM': PREPARING FOR OBOE 2

On 1 April 1945, Lieutenant General Frank Berryman noted in his diary that the US 10th Army's landing on Okinawa had effectively bypassed the SWPA theatre.[12] Although unaware of the immanence of victory over Japan, Australian senior officers shared the Joint Chiefs of Staff assessment that operations in Borneo, and particularly Balikpapan, lacked any strategic relevance. Brigadier Lindsay Barham reported that all commanders and staff he met at the staging area on Morotai felt Oboe 2 lacked 'any real object'.[13] A note of resignation is evident in the remarks made to the first Oboe 2 planning conference by Lieutenant-General Leslie Morshead, Commander I Australian Corps, on 27 May: 'the capture of airfield facilities at Balikpapan is consequently not so vital as it was originally, but Corps is still charged with their capture and development by the original target date'.[14] The concept of operations that evolved seems a product of assessments of the objective's low strategic worth, the preponderance of materiel support available, and the character and experience of the officer tasked to capture it: Major-General Edward 'Teddy' Milford, commander of the 7th Division. In further diary musings, Berryman presaged the approach that would be taken: 'the decisive battle was in the P.I. [Philippine Islands] and now it is a methodical progression to destroy him with the initiative and overwhelming force on our side'.[15]

Balikpapan presented a challenge for an invading force. The town, port and oil facilities were built on a relatively narrow coastal flat running north and east from Point Toekoeng, overlooked by steep hills. Along the coast to the northeast were Balikpapan's two airfields: Sepinggang, constructed by the Japanese 8 kilometres from the town, and the Dutch-built civilian strip at Manggar, another 8 kilometres further on. Balikpapan's oil flowed from the Sanga Sanga fields 120 kilometres to the northeast, which were accessed via Samarinda Road, later nicknamed Milford Highway by Australian planners. By June 1945, Allied intelligence had developed a good picture of the Japanese defences of Balikpapan. Seventy-nine guns ranging from 20- to 127-millimetre calibre, as well as 40 light anti-aircraft guns, had been identified, and the strength of the garrison was estimated at up to 5500 troops, with another 3000 civilians who could be impressed into military service.[16] The Japanese had many positions in the hills immediately behind the town, and a large tank farm on a ridge above the oil refineries led the Australians to fear that streams of burning oil would be used as a defensive measure. Other defended localities were established around the airfields and along the coastal road – nicknamed the Vasey Highway – that connected them with Balikpapan.

Oboe 2 was originally allocated to the 9th Australian Division, but changes to the scope and sequence of the Oboe operations meant that Milford, then located at Kairi in north Queensland, was warned out in late April. A career soldier and an artilleryman, Milford was well read, strong-willed, and had already proven himself as both an able divisional commander and staff officer in New Guinea. Milford's quiet demeanour, particularly in comparison to his charismatic predecessor George Vasey, raised the suspicions of some – Morshead regarded him as a misanthropist – but it also seems to have had a genuine quality that endeared him to his troops.[17]

The principle decision that Milford and his staff had to make was whether to land on the coast between Sepinggang and Manggar and advance west, thus avoiding the Japanese bastion at Balikpapan, at least initially, or to conduct an assault landing straight onto it. Having commanded the 5th Division as it winkled the Japanese out of bunkers and foxholes in the Lae-Salamaua hinterland in August–September 1943, Milford was determined that this fight would be conducted on his terms:

> Why land up the coast and have to fight through jungle which suits the enemy when you can go straight in under heavy supporting fire, which the enemy can't stand, in comparatively open and favourable country. (I was a gunner officer!)[18]

While a direct assault against Balikpapan, via the Dutch suburb of Klandasan, risked heavy casualties during the landing, and shallow water, coastal defence guns, and offshore mines presented difficulties for supporting naval forces, it was hoped that the shock of a vigorous attack against the centre of the Japanese defence would disorganise their command and control network and ultimately reduce casualties by avoiding a long, drawn out campaign. Landing on Klandasan beach would also allow 'the full power of the force to be quickly deployed as opposed to the narrow front imposed by a coastal advance', which would have confronted a series of river crossings and defences oriented to oppose such a drive. Capturing Balikpapan's port facilities quickly also reduced the risk inherent in having the force dependent on supply over the beach for a prolonged period.[19]

The Klandasan plan was dependent on overwhelming fire support from sea and air that would systematically destroy the Japanese defences. Milford's principal naval support was provided by Task Group 78.2, a US–Australian–Netherlands formation commanded by Rear Admiral Albert Noble, US Navy. Noble initially objected to landing at Klandasan for the reasons outlined above. He petitioned Morshead for a change to the landing area but was overruled and then supported the plan 'most loyally'.[20] Mine sweeping operations, conducted under fire from the Japanese coastal defence guns, began 16 days prior to the landings and were combined with the bombardment of positions ashore by both naval gunfire and air attack.

Preliminary air operations, commanded by Air Vice Marshal William Bostock's RAAF Command, had been underway since 28 May, and initially focused on Japanese airfields throughout the Netherlands East Indies that could be used to interfere with Allied operations, as well as the formidable anti-aircraft defences of Balikpapan. Attacks on Netherlands East Indies oil infrastructure without GHQ approval were initially forbidden, but concerns about burning oil defences and gun emplacements amid the Balikpapan facilities led to a removal of constraints there.[21] RAAF Command, however, seems to have misinterpreted this relaxation of targeting restrictions and was reprimanded by I Corps for attacks on oil infrastructure at Samarinda.[22] This targeting of oil facilities demonstrates a disjunction between Oboe 2's operational objectives and tactical means, making a mockery of the former.

Despite the negligible Japanese air strength around Balikpapan, air support for Oboe 2 was not without difficulties, poor weather foremost. Originally, air support was to have been provided predominantly by RAAF First Tactical Air Force squadrons operating from the newly captured and improved airstrip at Tarakan. Demonstrating the risks posed by the tight scheduling of the Oboe operations, this strip was not operational in time due to wet conditions. Bostock thus had to rely heavily on US and RAAF Liberators operating from Morotai and islands in the southern Philippines as well as tactical aircraft of the US Thirteenth Air Force, also based in the southern Philippines. The prevailing weather between the Philippines and Borneo, however, often prevented fighter aircraft taking up their assigned station to protect the mine sweeping operations, so Noble requested US Navy carrier air cover for the landings and was allocated three escort carriers.[23]

In the meantime, planning for the land component of Oboe 2 and the movement of troops to Morotai had continued. The short notice accorded to the 7th Division, in addition to prevailing shipping shortages, played havoc with established planning schedules and battle procedure. Shipping movements were confused and priorities poorly allocated. Troops and planning staffs arrived at Morotai late, or in the wrong order. Brigade headquarters had less than a week to prepare their orders, unit commanding officers (COs) had to prepare theirs without their staff, and US Navy planning procedures meant landing tables had to be estimated before tactical plans had been finalised.[24] Some troops had no more than a few days ashore at Morotai before having to re-embark, which the Commander of the 18th Brigade, Brigadier Frederick Chilton, considered insufficient for 'hardening and acclimatisation, or even adequately to carry out essential administration and briefing'.[25]

Milford's belt-and-braces approach to planning Oboe 2, informed by reports of stubborn Japanese resistance on Tarakan, led to further efforts to bolster his force. Only two of the 7th Division's brigades – the 18th and 21st – were initially assigned to Oboe 2, but concerns about having a sufficient reserve led Milford to request the third – the 25th.[26] He also sought a regiment of medium guns to reinforce his artillery. Shipping persisted as a major constraint. GHQ approved the use of only the 25th Brigade's combat elements, on the condition that no extra shipping was required to move them; Milford ditched 7000 RAAF support personnel from the assault convoy to make room. No shipping was available for the medium artillery.[27] Milford was clearly persistent in his requests for additional support; Morshead and Blamey confided to Berryman that they were fed up with his 'whinging'.[28] Milford, however, was reflecting the concerns of his subordinates. Among the 7th Division's senior officers, memories of the under-resourced Papua campaign of 1942 still ran deep.[29] Brigadier Ivan Dougherty, Commander of the 21st Brigade, asked to be paraded before Morshead when informed that supplies of some types of ammunition were limited, which he considered 'criminal': 'If we have to limit the fire support we give our troops . . . we can only make up for the deficiency . . . by the loss of men's lives.'[30]

The assault force commenced embarkation on 17 June and, after a successful landing rehearsal, set sail a week later. That the 7th Division was able to plan and mount the operation, including the coordination of its naval and air support, in spite of all its difficulties, owed much to the preliminary staff work and continuing support of Headquarters I Corps and Advanced Headquarters Allied Landing Force on Morotai, and also to the high levels of training and experience found among Milford's own staff and subordinates. Milford's three brigadiers had all commanded their formations in at least one previous campaign, and the command teams of the infantry battalions similarly represented a collection of experiences unprecedented during the war.[31] In the more junior ranks such experience was more thinly spread. In Australia the division had absorbed significant numbers of reinforcement soldiers and junior officers. This caused some disquiet, but a thorough round of briefings and the distribution of aerial photos down to section level meant that, as the CO of the 2/10th Battalion, Lieutenant Colonel Tom Daly reflected, 'when we hit the beach these fellows were better informed as to what they had to do than they had ever been before'.[32]

'WE GOT IN THERE PRONTO AND HELD THE HIGH GROUND': ESTABLISHING THE BEACHHEAD

The bombardment of Balikpapan reached its crescendo in the two hours following daylight on 1 July 1945. By the time the Alligators of the first assault wave rattled out of the surf, five minutes ahead of schedule at 0855, the Balikpapan area had been devastated by 3000 tons of bombs, 7361 rockets, 38,052 rounds of naval gunfire and 114,000 rounds of heavy automatic weapons fire.[33] The preparatory fire support saw to it that the greatest disorganisation caused to the landing force resulted from misdirected landings. A combination of the incomplete clearance of beach obstacles and difficulties identifying features ashore caused the assault waves to veer left and deposit their passengers up to 700 metres away from their intended landing points.[34] The resulting confusion could have had serious consequences if the assault troops had encountered serious opposition on the beaches, but they were subject only to desultory fire, which provided no obstacle to their reorientation and a rapid advance inland. Within 20 minutes an initial beachhead had been captured without a single landing-force casualty.[35]

In order to ensure his troops exploited Japanese disorganisation and seized the hills that dominated the landing area, Milford emphasised the 'need to push on and gain ground'. The fight that was most critical to the outcome of the first day at Balikpapan and thus epitomised Milford's exhortations to 'go hell for leather',[36] was the assault on 'Parramatta', the nickname given to a prominence on a ridgeline that ran perpendicular to the coast slightly to the northwest of the landing beaches. Topped by a gun position, denuded of vegetation by Japanese earthworks and Allied bombardment, Parramatta's excellent fields of observation and fire provided the ability to significantly interfere with the build-up of the 7th Division's force. Its capture was entrusted to Daly's 2/10th Battalion, which, in recognition of the significance of the task, had been allocated Matilda tanks, artillery, 4.2-inch mortars, a platoon of the division's medium machine guns and the fire of the USS *Cleveland* in direct support. But as C Company moved to its forming up place for the assault, Daly received a series of disconcerting reports: the USS *Cleveland* did not have a bombardment liaison officer embarked; the tanks were bogged on the beach; the artillery's radios were not working; the divisional machine gunners were not to be found; and the battalion's own mortars were not yet in action, having been landed in the wrong place.[37] Daly was faced with the dilemma of attacking without the planned fire support, or waiting until it was available but allowing the enemy to recover from the bombardment. He chose to follow the intent of his orders rather than the detail. At 1010, with the 4.2-inch mortars laying a smoke screen and the battalion's own machine guns providing limited supporting fire, Daly ordered the Officer Commanding C Company, Major Frank Cook, across the start line: 'Right, Frank, off you go.'[38]

Daly regarded Cook as an 'up and go, get at "em"' type and had specifically selected him and his company for the attack.[39] Utilising the tactics of fire and movement, the company raced up a spur towards Hill 87, the first knoll on the way to Parramatta. The leading platoon was ordered to bypass strong opposition to secure the summit of Hill 87 quickly; a 'mopping up' platoon followed to deal with the Japanese positions left behind. Opposition intensified as Cook's men climbed higher and the Japanese emerged from cover to reoccupy fighting positions. By 1130, the Australians were in a position just off the top of Hill 87 but pinned down by fire from neighbouring features. The attack was given fresh impetus by the arrival of the nonchalant Major Edward Ryrie of the 1 Armoured Regiment, leading his tanks forward on foot, eschewing a helmet for a slouch hat and puffing on his pipe. At 1240, Hill 87 was reported captured.[40]

Apart from the still missing divisional machine gunners, all of Daly's allocated fire support was now available. With the mortars, machine guns and artillery firing on Parramatta, and naval gunfire supressing any interference from Tank Plateau to the west, C Company reorganised and moved against Parramatta. Despite heavy Japanese mortar fire, the assault now developed a remorseless momentum as the tanks and infantry advanced along the ridgeline. Japanese were chased into tunnels and their entrances blown in by engineers; bunkers were blasted with flame-throwers; and the mopping up parties hunted down and killed those who managed to escape the onslaught. At 1412, the success signal was fired from the top of Parramatta.[41] Visiting Parramatta the next day, looking out over the landing beaches, Morshead remarked, 'Thank God for the 2/10th Battalion.'[42]

On those beaches, landing operations had continued unabated, bringing ashore more personnel and equipment to support and reinforce the enlargement of the beachhead. To the left of the 2/10th on Parramatta, the 2/9th Battalion advanced parallel to the coast through the rubble of Klandasan, while on the right the 2/12th secured a series of features along the Valley Road. In the 21st Brigade's area the 2/27th Battalion captured the high ground immediately overlooking the landing beaches to the northeast, providing a foothold for its sister battalions to strike forth: the 2/16th Battalion northeast onto Mount Malang, the highest feature in the Balikpapan area; and the 2/14th east across the Klandasan Besar River to the ridge, nicknamed 'Randwick', on the far bank. In turn, the 2/7th Cavalry (Commando) Regiment moved through the 2/14th to occupy the extension of Randwick to the north. Thus, by the end of the first day ashore the 7th Division had secured its bridgehead. Numerous defended localities had been overrun, and the Japanese were left with little observation of the landing beaches. The day's operations were summed up by one 2/27th veteran: 'we got in there pronto and held the high ground'.[43]

The first of July had not been without cost for the Australians – 22 were killed, and another 74 wounded[44] – but the Japanese suffered heavily, and continued to do so; by 3 July, Japanese dead exceeded 500.[45] Balikpapan was defended by 2 Garrison Force, a hodgepodge of marine infantry and gunners, base troops and civilians – Japanese, Formosan, Korean and Indonesian – pressed into military service, and a single Imperial Japanese Army unit: the 454th Independent Infantry Battalion. Levels of training and experience varied widely, and although the force was well-equipped with heavy calibre weapons, it was short of small arms, particular light machine guns, which tied it to fixed positions and limited its ability to counterattack.[46] The weeks of preliminary bombardment had already caused desertions, and the shock Milford sought to inflict is evident in reports of Japanese prisoners being dug out of collapsed bunkers, extracted from various hiding places, or being captured while wandering dazed and wounded.[47] Although the intent of the Japanese commander, Vice Admiral Yamada Michiaki, had been to prevent the establishment of a bridgehead, he had also made preparations to contain an attacking force further inland, drawing out the operations, and preventing it from being employed elsewhere. In the face of continuing Australian pressure, Yamada withdrew the remainder of his forces from the Balikpapan-Sepinggang area on 3 July.[48]

'PROBE IT – BLAST IT – OCCUPY IT': BEYOND THE BRIDGEHEAD

By the evening of 3 July, Balikpapan town and the remnants of its refineries had been cleared by the 18th Brigade; the 25th had landed and was pushing north along the axis of the Milford Highway; and the 18th, having captured Sepinggang without a fight, was poised to move on Manggar. 'Having got the essential ground', Milford later explained, 'time became of less importance so to save cas[ualties] the idea was to shell and manoeuvre him of position rather than direct assault.'[49] This message was not lost on Lieutenant Colonel Phil Rhoden, CO of the 2/14th Battalion, as he secured Manggar. Elements of the 454th Independent Infantry Battalion were well entrenched in hills overlooking the airfield, and, as a heavy barrage unleashed upon the Australians just before midday on 4 July demonstrated, they were well-equipped with mortars and artillery. Despite the destruction of three tanks landed to support the battalion the next afternoon by coastal defence guns, Rhoden advanced his operations with 'unhurried, calculated and deadly precision to pave the way for a final infantry assault'. He later recalled: 'there was no need to do it quickly ... I wasn't going to waste men's lives needlessly'.[50]

For two days the Japanese positions were pounded with mortars, artillery, naval gunfire and air strikes, and two 'sniping' guns – artillery used in a direct fire role – duelled with the enemy guns. In the meantime, observation posts identified individual positions and small patrols explored potential approaches to them. On the afternoon of 6 July, following an air strike with napalm and further bombardment, a 14-man fighting patrol from D Company was able to capture the coastal defence guns, driving off 50 Japanese. Firepower, however, did not remove the need for close-quarters fighting. The guns were captured in a rush, the attackers clambering over the bunkers and dropping grenades inside; two were killed, including Corporal Henry Waites, after whom the position was later named. The rest of D Company moved forward and, in heavy rain, with malfunctioning weapons, fought off four successive counterattacks that saw the Japanese leap out of the darkness into their water-filled weapon pits. The company report on the action recorded 'it was a company of very tired men who greeted the dawn'.[51] In ensuing days the bombardment was continued, allowing the remainder of the Japanese defences to be similarly captured by platoon-strength fighting patrols on 9 July.

Along the division's other axis of advance – the Milford Highway – the 25th Brigade operated in a similar fashion. The Japanese had prepared a non-continuous defensive line sited to prevent an advance up the highway, which was known by the unlikely name of the 'Muffle-Jam' position. The main defences were protected outposts situated on small features covered by heavy weapons to the rear. Between 4 and 8 July, Brigadier Ken Eather conducted a coordinated advance each day using two of his battalions, resting the third, to clear the outposts and concentrate the Japanese on Muffle-Jam. The tactics employed against each outpost were identical: 'patrolling to determine strength and dispositions ... softening up with supporting arms ... a co-ordinated attack by a co[mpan]y or less'; it was a technique a 2/33rd Battalion veteran summarised as 'probe it – blast it – then occupy it'.[52] In most instances the assaulting troops found their enemy gone. One prisoner told his interrogator that artillery and mortars were the Australians' most effective weapons; another, subjected to bombardment and without a personal weapon, deserted.[53] Once Muffle-Jam came under sustained bombardment and Eather's troops were in a position to turn its eastern flank, it too was abandoned on the night of 8 July.

Figure 15.1: Brigadier Kenneth Eather pointing out Japanese positions to Major General Edward Milford, 4 July 1945. (Australian War Memorial 111219)

Kamada, however, had not intended his troops to stand to the last at Muffle-Jam. He understood his enemy's strengths and his own, and was drawing the Australians into terrain that he hoped would allow him to start dictating the terms of the fight. The relatively open nature of the terrain thus far had been to the 25th Brigade's advantage, but beyond Muffle-Jam the jungle closed in, limiting manoeuvre and observation, and, as a result, the employment of supporting arms. Eather continued his advance on 9 July with just a single battalion – the 2/31st – moving astride the highway. Contacts were fleeting, but late in the day an ambush initiated by the detonation of a daisy-chain of five 500-kilogram bombs laid along the road, and continued with heavy machine guns, announced the character of the fight was changing.

After a night spent in a tight defensive perimeter, the 2/31st's advance began cautiously the next morning. A feature nicknamed 'Erode' was occupied without opposition, but as the battalion's lead elements reconnoitred the next feature along the highway – 'Cello' – a string of three 500-kilogram depth charges was detonated. Despite casualties, the

Australians rallied and Cello, lightly held, was quickly captured. The next position encountered, on an unnamed feature, was more stoutly defended and was captured after a preparatory bombardment by mortars and artillery and direct fire from Matilda tanks and a 6-pounder anti-tank gun. The assault itself took only 15 minutes – two bunkers were burnt out by a Matilda 'Frog' flame-throwing tank and the remainder cleared with bayonets, small arms and grenades.

Believing that the Japanese resistance had been broken, the 2/31st's CO, Lieutenant Colonel Murray Robson, ordered another assault on the next feature – 'Coke' – by A Company. After another preparatory bombardment, 18 Platoon, supported by three Matildas, would move out of the road cutting where the battalion's forward elements now held firm, traverse a slight dip in the road, and then seize the slopes of Coke beyond.[54] The plan sacrificed security to momentum – there was no patrolling through the thick scrub flanking the road – and was based on faith in Australian firepower and the assumption that the enemy was broken. They were not.

At 1700, the preparatory barrage ceased. As Bob Curtis, an attached journalist, reported, 'there was no movement on Coke Hill, nothing to disturb the low cloud of dust and smoke hanging over it'. The assaulting troops advanced: two engineers searching for mines, followed by 18 Platoon's sections interspersed with the tanks. They had moved barely 100 metres when, as Curtis continued, 'from both sides of the jungle screamed a cataract of lead'.[55] 18 Platoon rushed for their objective. Some made it to within 20 metres of a series of well-camouflaged positions dug under fallen trees, but many were shot down. Fire also fell on the battalion command post in the cutting. Edward Ryrie, the unflappable tank commander from the assault on Parramatta, fell dead beside where Robson stood. A Company's other two platoons were ordered into the scrub on both sides of the road but made little headway. The tanks fired until their ammunition was expended. At 1750, the order to withdraw was given; 18 men were dead, 11 of whom had to be left lying on the road, and 23 were wounded.[56]

After 2/31st's mauling, the 25th Brigade's operations reverted to patrolling and bombardment as it felt out the extent of the Japanese position; it was found to cover a frontage of around 500 metres with a depth three times that distance, and was estimated to be held by up to 800 troops. These actions developed into a gradual envelopment by the 2/25th Battalion to the west of the Milford Highway and the 2/33rd to the east. The enemy's reaction was largely confined to harassing fire from mortars and heavy calibre automatic weapons, and extensive night infiltration. Their only significant counterattack was launched in the early hours of 18

July after the occupation of a feature called 'Charm' threatened to cut the Milford Highway behind them. It failed. On the night of 21 July, the Japanese abandoned their positions, allowing the 25th Brigade to attain the junction of the Milford Highway and Pope's Track, approximately 11 kilometres from Balikpapan's outskirts.

By this stage in the war, the attitude underpinning Australian operations was one of casual brutality epitomised on Balikpapan by the unflinching use of flame-throwers wherever possible; one British Pathé newsreel shows a Japanese soldier stumbling, aflame, from a bunker, only to be given another 'squirt' for good measure.[57] Another insight to the character of the fighting is provided by an intelligence report of a Japanese soldier who survived being struck in the chest by Owen Gun fire thanks to a padded shirt. He was dropped by a non-fatal wound to the groin and then killed with a blow to the head with a pistol butt.[58] Somewhat incongruously the Japanese operations along the Milford Highway earned the respect of their enemy. The skill inherent in the Japanese withdrawals was recognised in the 7th Division's weekly intelligence review, and Robson described the troops he faced as '1st rate' and their defence of Cello and Coke as 'a classic'. The 25th Brigade report on operations similarly noted their 'determination, ability to maintain positions against bombardment, standard of personal camouflage' and the high standard of siting and concealment of their fighting positions.[59]

Milford's next order was in effect a recognition of Japanese skill in defence in jungle country. While the 25th Brigade had been edging north, Milford had been consolidating his position elsewhere. To the east, the 2/27th Battalion had advanced along the Vasey Highway as far as Sambodja, 29 kilometres from Manggar; and to the west, the 2/9th Battalion had cleared the far shore of Balikpapan Bay, having been landed there on 5 July. Off the main lines of advance, squadrons of the 2/7th Cavalry (Commando) Regiment and a company of Netherlands East Indies infantry collected information, harassed the enemy, and made contact with the more remote Indonesian settlements. Australian intelligence had correctly identified the next Japanese defence position along the Milford Highway, and Eather realised they would 'scrap like the very devil' if pushed, but his brigade would no longer need to.[60] Milford believed he had achieved his objectives and was content he could maintain security with an active patrolling program. Pushing on towards Samarinda would just incur more casualties. At I Corps, Morshead agreed.[61]

'EXERCISE BALIKPAPAN': ASSESSING OBOE 2

Advising his troops on 25 July that the 'first major task' in the Balikpapan campaign had now been achieved, Milford also recognised the contribution of the Navy and Air Force, stating that they 'paved the way so well, and answered every demand in such full measure' that that his division owed them 'deep gratitude' and shared 'with them the honour'.[62] Balikpapan was the most extensive and well-integrated joint and combined operation undertaken by Australian forces during the war. As Chilton later observed, the attacking force had benefitted from the 'accumulated experience and techniques of a long series of amphibious landings' – he doubted either the Australian or US forces would have been capable of such a complex operation in mid-1942 – and that what resulted was a 'real demonstration of allied power'.[63] The orchestration of this power, however, was still an evolving art. The I Corps post-operations report observed that throughout the Oboe series individual services' procedures had improved, as had their common 'appreciation of the problems to be solved'. Milford and Bostock shared a tetchy relationship, arguing over the Royal Australian Air Force's (RAAF) logistical requirements and the methods and control of close air support. Several attacks on Australian troops by Allied aircraft indicated that improvements were still required in tactical level ground–air communications and coordination.[64]

The extent to which Oboe 2's objectives, however ill-founded, were attained is questionable. Although Auster light observation aircraft were flying from Sepinggang by 3 July, the first fighter aircraft – Spitfire VIIIs from 452 Squadron RAAF – were not able to operate until 15 July, a week later than scheduled.[65] Neither Sepinggang nor Manggar proved suitable for heavy bombers; a new bomber strip was surveyed west of Manggar, but never built.[66] A combination of Allied bombing and Japanese demolition had wrecked Balikpapan's port facilities. Balikpapan's much vaunted oil infrastructure also lay in ruins, having been neither protected nor conserved; Milford's civil affairs report of 27 July stated bluntly that 'the oil refineries have been destroyed'.[67] The oilfields that supplied them remained in Japanese hands beyond the Australian patrol line. RAAF Command boasted over the scale of the destruction it had wrought, which it justified with reference to 'a successful assault landing involving negligible casualties ... carried out against an objective having the potentiality of extremely effective defence'.[68] There was no argument on this score from the army, but returning Netherlands East Indies officials were resentful of the extent of the damage – just one of several irritants in an increasingly tense relationship.[69] The Australian official historian Gavin Long visited Balikpapan in August 1945 and walked the ground with the likes of Milford, Daly and Robson. He would later write: 'the wreckage that had been Balikpapan was of no value to anybody except the scrap-metal traders'.[70]

The dubious objectives of Oboe 2 raises the question of the motivation of those required to fight and die for them. Although troops may have recognised the war was in its final stages and that Borneo was a long way from Japan, it would be wrong to presume a high level of strategic awareness among the rank and file and even junior officers. Security concerns dictated that knowledge of higher-level planning was limited; Brigadier Dougherty felt like he was being 'introduced to the mysterious and secret rites of some secret society' when he received his first briefing in a guarded room.[71] Some soldiers did not question the operation, relying upon faith in the judgement of their superiors, and others, in the absence of information, provided their own rationale – a stepping stone towards Singapore and the liberation of Australian prisoners of war was common.[72] The rationale was of little relevance to many: the veterans going forward once more out of loyalty to their unit and comrades; the untried recruits and new officers keen to prove themselves; others chafing at the boredom of I Corps' long training interregnum on the Atherton Tablelands;[73] and others that simply 'relished the prospect ... of killing "Japs"'.[74] Such sentiments were bolstered by the confidence bestowed by thorough training and tactical briefing, trusted leadership, and the preponderance of supporting arms.[75] Reflecting on his earlier experience in New Guinea, Corporal Roy Burbury of the 2/5th Cavalry (Commando) Squadron, observed that Balikpapan 'was a different campaign'; 'We had a different attitude because we felt we were more on top, we were calling the tune in Balikpapan.'[76] Which was just what Milford had intended.

Writing to his parents on 29 July, Eather remarked that the campaign had been a 'short, sharp little show beautifully planned & carried out with dash and speed'.[77] Dougherty similarly noted in his post operations report: 'I hope that all young men in this division will remember the demonstration of the use of fire power, and its effect, given to them in "Exercise Balikpapan".'[78] These assessments clearly had their origins in both men's experiences in the under-resourced and costly Papua campaign, but their benign nature belies the ruthless efficiency of high explosive, the shock of sudden ambush, or the 'quick and merciless melees' fought with Japanese infiltrators inside night harbours.[79] They also eschew the question as to whether the military skill exhibited at Balikpapan was employed in pursuit of worthy objectives.

At Balikpapan, the Australian Army killed 2032 Japanese it need not have, and lost 229 men who did not have to die doing so.

Further Reading

Jeffrey Grey, *A Soldier's Soldier: A Biography of Lieutenant-General Sir Thomas Daly*, Cambridge University Press, Melbourne, 2013.

T. E. Griffith, *MacArthur's Airman: General George C. Kenney and the Air War in the Southwest Pacific Theater in World War II*, University Press of Kansas, Kansas, 1998.

David Horner, *High Command: Australia's Struggle for an Independent War Strategy, 1939–45*, Allen & Unwin, Sydney, 1992.

Gavin Long, *The Final Campaigns*, Australian War Memorial, Canberra, 1963.

George Odgers, *Air War Against Japan, 1943–1944*, Australian War Memorial, Canberra, 1957.

Garth Pratten, *Australian Battalion Commanders in the Second World War*, Cambridge University Press, Melbourne, 2009.

Notes

1 Tom Kimber, interview, 28 March 1990, AWM S00921.

2 Gavin Long, *The Final Campaigns*, Australian War Memorial, Canberra, 1963, p. 502.

3 John Bunnell, 'Knockout Blow? The Army Air Force's operations against Ploesti and Balikpapan', MA thesis, School of Advanced Air and Space Studies, Air University, 2005, p. 54.

4 Kenney to Arnold, 29 October 1943, cited in Craven and Cate, *The Pacific: Matterhorn to Nagasaki, June 1944 to August 1945*, University of Chicago Press, Chicago, 1953, p. 316.

5 Odgers, *Air War Against Japan, 1943–1944*, Australian War Memorial, Canberra, 1957, pp. 120, 218–19, 230, 361–3.

6 Bunnell, 'Knockout Blow?', pp. 62–83; 1 ACAEI interrogation report (IR) 0081, p. 5, AWM52, 1/4/1/69.

7 Bunnell, 'Knockout Blow', pp. 54–5, 84–8; 1 ACAEI IR 0085, p. 2, AWM52, 1/4/1/69.

8 Richard Frank, *MacArthur*, Palgrave MacMillan, New York, 2007, p. 116.

9 GHQ SWPA, 'Staff Study Operation "Oboe-Two"', p. 1, AWM54, 621/3/7.

10 Forland to Landforces, 10 February 1945, AWM 3DRL 6643, 2/49 [4].

11 See Frank, *MacArthur*, pp. 118–20 for discussion of MacArthur's disregard of intelligence and dogged commitment to his plans for the invasion of Japan.

12 Frank Berryman, diary, 1 April 1945, AWM PR84/370, 1/5.

13 Lindsay Barham to Berryman, 2 June 1945, p. 1, AWM PR84/370, 3/51.

14 'Notes on Conference HQ 1 Aust. Corps – 1100 Hours – 27 May – Operation Oboe Two', AWM52, 1/4/1/63.

15 Berryman, diary, 3 April 1945.

16 '7 Aust. Div. Special Oboe Two Intelligence Review No. 2', pp. 4, 6, AWM52, 1/5/14/73.

17 Steve Gower, 'Milford, Edward James (1894–1972)', *Australian Dictionary of Biography*, http://adb.anu.edu.au/biography/milford-edward-james-11121/text19803, retrieved 15 November 2014; Berryman, diary, 10 July 1945; unnamed 2/10 Bn lieutenant, interview, 15 August 1945, AWM67, 2/89, p. 2.

18 Edward Milford to Long, 15 September 1956, p. 2, AWM 93, 50/2/23/445.

19 'Report on Operation Oboe Two' (7 Div RoO), pp. 6–7, AWM54, 621/7/1.

20 Milford to Long, 15 September 1956, p. 2.

21 Ivan Dougherty, notes on Oboe 2 planning, p. 12; AWM52 8/2/21/36.

22 WD HQ I Aust. Corps GS, 9 June 1945, AWM52, 1/4/1/65.

23 'RAAF Command, AAF, SWPA Report Oboe Two' (RAAF RoO), p. 2, AWM54 621/7/40.

24 7 Div. RoO, pp. 24–6.

25 '18 Aust Inf. – Bde Report on Operations "Oboe Two"' (18 Bde RoO), p. 2, AWM54, 621/7/1.

26 Dougherty, notes, p. 6; 7 Div. RoO, p. 3.

27 WD HQ I Corps GS, 2 June 1945; I Corps RoO, p. 40.

28 Berryman, diary, 26 June, 10 July 1945.

29 See, for example, '21 Aust. Inf. Bde Report Operation – Oboe Two' (21 Bde RoO), App. A, p. 1, AWM52, 8/2/21/34.

30 Ivan Dougherty to Milford, 14 June 1945, AWM52, 8/2/21/36.

31 Garth Pratten, *Australian Battalion Commanders in the Second World War*, Cambridge University Press, Melbourne, 2009, pp. 243–6.

32 Milford, interview, pp. 40–1; Thomas Daly, interview with Butler in Garth Pratten and Glyn Harper (ed.), *Still the Same: Reflections on Active Service from Bardia to Baidoa*, Army Doctrine Centre, Georges Heights, 1996, p. 24.

33 RAAF RoO, p. 7; 'Commander Task Group 78.2, Commander Amphibious Group Eight, Seventh Fleet, Action Report – Balikpapan Operation', pp. I–4, I–12, AWM54, 621/7/26.

34 'Report on Operation "Oboe Two" by Principal Beachmaster "B"', p. 2, Annex 2, p. 1, Annex 3, p. 1, Annex 4, p. 1, AWM54, 505/10/5.

35 7 Div. RoO, p. 12.

36 Milford, interview, p. 24.

37 '2/10 Aust. Inf. Bn Report on Operations – Oboe Two' (2/10 RoO), pp. 5–7, AWM54, 621/7/49.

38 Daly, interview with Butler, p. 28.

39 Daly, interview with Pratten, 26 October 2000.

40 Daly, Cook, Sullivan, interview, 18 August 1945, AWM67, 2/88, pp. 13–24.

41 Daly, Cook, Sullivan, interview, pp. 25–30.

42 Daly, interview with Pratten.

43 Charles Sims, interview, 31 January 1990, AWM S00789.

44 WD HQ 7 Div. GS, 1 July 1945, AWM52, 1/5/14/75.

45 '7 Aust. Div. Daily Intelligence Summary (7 Div. DIS) No. 1', p. 2, AWM52, 1/5/14/76.

46 '7 Aust. Div. Weekly Intelligence Review No. 1' (7 Div. WIR), p. 11, AWM52, 1/5/14/76.

47 Various IR in AWM52, 1/4/1/76, 1/5/14/76, 1/5/14/77.

48 'Japanese Military Operations – Interrogation of Japanese Commanders and Staffs', pp. 7–8, 18, AWM54, 424/4/6.

49 Milford, interview, p. 28.

50 Philip Rhoden, interview, October 2001.

51 D Coy, 2/14 Bn report in Long, *Final Campaigns*, pp. 528–9.

52 'Report on Operations 'Oboe Two' (25 Bde RoO), p. 1, AWM54, 621/6/1; William Crooks, *The Footsoldiers: The Story of the 2/33rd Australian Infantry Battalion, AIF*, Printcraft Press, Brookvale, 1971, p. 392.

53 7 Aust. Div. ATIS IR 10, p. 1, IR 25, p. 2, AWM52, 1/5/14/76.

54 WD 2/31 Bn, 10 July 1945, AWM52, 8/3/31/27.

55 Bob Curtis in John Laffin, *Forever Forward: The History of the 2/31st Australian Infantry Battalion*, Australian Military History Publications, Loftus, 2002, p. 166.

56 WD 2/31 Bn, 10 July 1945.

57 'Pacific Island Warfare', www.britishpathe.com/video/pacific-island-warfare, retrieved 28 November 2014.

58 7 Div. DIS No. 9, pp. 3–4, AWM52, 1/5/14/77.

59 7 Div. WIR, p. 12; Murray Robson, interview, 25 August 1945, AWM67, 2/88, p. 52; 25 Bde RoO, p. 2.

60 Steve Eather, *Desert Sands, Jungle Lands: A Biography of Major General Ken Eather*, Allen & Unwin, Sydney, 2003, p. 160.
61 Milford, interview, p. 33.
62 'To all ranks of 7 Aust. Div Task Force', 25 July 1945, AWM52, 1/5/14/75.
63 Frederick Chilton to Long, 23 October 1957, AWM93, 50/2/23/322.
64 Long, *Final Campaigns*, p. 546; Milford, interview, pp. 37–43; WD 2/10 Bn, 1 July 1945; WD 2/31 Bn, 9 July 1945; Gordon Dickens, *Never Late: The 2/9th Australian Infantry Battalion, 1939–1945*, Australian Military History Publications, Loftus, 2005, pp. 333–4.
65 'Operation Instruction No. 154/1945', p. 2, AWM54, 621/7/40; Odgers, *Air War*, p. 488.
66 Various folios, 12–20 July 1945, AWM54, 621/7/19.
67 'Reports on Civil Affairs', p. 2, AWM54, 376/7/1.
68 RAAF RoO, p. 14.
69 Long, notebook, 15 August 1945, AWM67, 2/89, pp. 11–12.
70 Long, review of *South-West Pacific 1941–45, Australian Army Journal*, No. 198, November 1965, p. 49.
71 Dougherty, notes, p. 1.
72 Alec Little, interview, 27 March 1990, AWM S00927; John Reddin, interview, 31 January 1990, AWM S00790; Robert Johns, interview, 22 February 1990, AWM S00799; Owen Curtis, interview, 3 March 1989, AWM S00541.
73 Curtis, interview; Johns, interview; '1 Aust. Field Censorship Report' (1 AFCR), Mar 45', p. 1, AWM54, 175/3/4.
74 Peter Stanley, 'An Oboe Concerto: Reflections on the Borneo Landings, 1945' in Wahlert, *Australian Army Amphibious Operations in the South-West Pacific: 1942–45*, Army Doctrine Centre, Georges Heights, 1995, p. 143.
75 Raymond Baldwin, interview, 23 March 1990, AWM S00926; Kimber, interview; Frank McClean, interview, 8 March 1990, AWM S00905.
76 Roy Burbury, interview, 15 March 1990, AWM S00919; 1 AFCR, June 45, pp. 1, 5, AWM54, 175/3/4; Milford, interview, p. 41.
77 Eather, *Desert Sands*, p. 160.
78 21 Bde RoO, App. A., p. 1.
79 Crooks, *Footsoldiers*, p. 392.

AFTERWORD: AND THEN CAME PEACE?

Michael McKernan

There was great public satisfaction and celebration in Australia when peace came on 15 August 1945, even though many Australians were unsettled by the devastation of the bombs at Hiroshima and Nagasaki that had brought the peace. Australians took pride and courage from the fact that they had faced up to their worst fear, invasion from Asia, that they had stared it down and fought it off. Australian sailors, airmen and soldiers had played crucial roles in the defeat of the Japanese, displaying professionalism, courage, ingenuity and endurance. They had defended their homeland and had protected their loved ones. Their victory was not for some abstract cause like 'empire', it was a victory for Australia and all its peoples. The fighting men and women of Australia had every reason to be satisfied and proud: Australians had defended their own.

Many of these men and women returned to their own homes exhausted and unwell. Much of the trauma that occurred in their homes went unreported and unremarked and much of it is only now being openly faced and discussed. In family histories and memoirs, and less directly in all sorts of general histories, we now read of difficulties in adapting to marriage again, of mental health issues that endured for years, and of troubles in the workplace and with alcohol. Family historians will tell, now, of the anger in many marriages after the war. For Australia's sake, many women had loyally accepted the absence of their husbands and had raised their children alone, they had managed the household and had taken all the decisions the home required. They had even worked outside the home where they could in paid employment or in the many 'good causes' war encouraged. Now these women were expected to accept, submissively, their husbands' resumption of all responsibility for family and household matters and were also expected to leave the workforce.

Returning servicemen, after long and difficult years in the jungle, on the seas, in the air and, crucially, in captivity were now expected to put on their overalls, pick up their kitbags or put on their suits and pick up their briefcases to settle down to life as it was before the war. They had to accept tedious and humdrum work, with long hours but little excitement; noisy and, to their minds, ill-disciplined children; and living in close confinement with wives who, for the most part, could not understand or empathise with the dangers, challenges, horrors and joys of life on active service. There was a flammable mix here that often ended in years of trouble, anger and resentment.

There has been too little written about this time of readjustment from war to peace post-1945 in the Australian story. Post-traumatic stress disorder at least is now known to many Australians, and its impact on service people returning from the Vietnam and later wars has been bravely and, in some cases, heroically documented. There has been almost no study, anywhere, of post-traumatic stress disorder in men and women returning from the Pacific War, except, guardedly, some study of the impact of captivity on its survivors. People of the immediate post-war generation will tell, now, of fathers who did not seem 'quite right', of teachers who seemed 'odd' and perhaps unbalanced, of neighbours seen in their backyards who relentlessly chopped wood, or sat in a shed alone for hours on end, or seemed intent on making their own children's lives miserable.

This is the hidden history of the immediate post-war years that will continue to be revealed as historians enlarge their horizons. The public history of the period is much better known and much easier to celebrate. Australia was an immediate and confident supporter of the concept and practice of the United Nations and an eager participant in its programs and solutions for a post-war world. The first great issue facing the victorious United Nations was the resettlement of upwards of 8 million Europeans made homeless and stateless by the war. Crowded into 'displaced persons' camps largely in Germany, peoples from many nations hoped for resettlement and the opportunity of starting again. Many of them were young and eager to start their families, but too many of them were older people who may not have had any realistic chance of a new start.

Australia, whose immigration program before this had looked almost exclusively to Britain for new settlers, understood, through the war, how gravely their security was threatened by too few people in too vast a territory.

With dynamic leadership from the Immigration Minister, Arthur Calwell, and carefully orchestrated programs designed to keep the home front onside, Australians slowly accepted that peoples from many nations might become 'new Australians'. The first displaced persons to reach Australia had been carefully selected. They were from the Baltic states (blonde hair and blue eyes), all were single (though some had become engaged on the ship over); they were young and all highly photogenic. Cameramen, newspapers and newsreels had a field day, as Calwell and selected Australian leaders celebrated the arrival of these high-quality immigrants. A series of sensible policy decisions around work and housing for the new arrivals meant that there was little area for conflict with older Australians and the resettlement process went off, over years, with few genuine complaints from either side.

The result of the displaced persons program and the consequent broader immigration program was to alter fundamentally and forever the nature and structure of Australian society. This was a direct consequence of the fright Australians experienced in 1942 and beyond. It was sensible that change was rendered slowly and that domestic institutions (complete abhorrence of the 'Continental Sunday', for example) withered only gradually. But the changing composition of the Australian community would inexorably alter Australian patterns of life and understandings of society. Returning Australian prisoners of war from the Asian camps vowed that they would never again eat rice, never drive a car made in Asia, or have any contact with Asian people. By the 1960s most of these vows were under threat, by the 1970s they were almost wholly abandoned as Australia embraced a truly multicultural society.

Australian society prospered after the war, although in the immediate post-war years life remained tough. Australia came out of the war with a disastrous housing shortage which meant that many returned men and their families had to 'bunk in' with parents or other family members. Building supplies were in great shortage and many of the incoming migrants put up the garage first, in which the family lived, while the father and some of his friends slowly built the family home. Rationing continued largely to assist the people of Britain to have reasonable food supplies. To some extent the 1949 Liberal federal election victory depended on Robert Menzies' seemingly improbable promise to end petrol rationing.

Gradually circumstances improved. Houses were built and whole new areas of the established cities were created. Schools were bursting at the seams, with the 'baby boomers' flooding into the junior grades, and it was not uncommon for 50–60 children to be crammed into the one classroom. New schools were built, community facilities created and new churches opened up. Roads and important amenities like power and sewerage followed later – in the case of sewerage in suburban Sydney and Brisbane, much later. Marriages gradually returned to a somewhat even keel, and if suburbia was deemed dull by later commentators it was a vast improvement on what people had lived through during the war and in its immediate aftermath.

Membership of the United Nations and commitment to the emerging American alliance gave Australia heavy responsibilities and obligations. With Australian troops housed in Japan, Australia was well placed to join the United Nations in resisting the North Korean invasion of South Korea in 1950. Indeed Australian pilots of Number 77 Squadron, then based in western Japan, were almost the first of the United Nations forces into action, and within five days of joining the fight the Squadron suffered its first battle casualty. Prime Minister Menzies also offered the United Nations two Australian ships, *Bataan* and *Shoalhaven*, and within weeks committed Australian ground forces. The Korean commitment set the pattern of subsequent Australian deployments in Southeast Asia, culminating in the expensive and often unpopular war in Vietnam. Those who led Australian forces in all these commitments had been junior officers and had learned their craft in the Pacific War.

The Korean War gave a considerable boost to the Australian economy, particularly to Australian woolgrowers, whose windfall profits fed into the wider economy. Thus began the 'long boom' in Australia, which saw full employment, rapidly expanding job opportunities, higher wages and much overtime. The 'Australian way of life' (an expression now heard for the first time) embraced home ownership for all, the purchase of a family car (pre-war, a luxury reserved for the wealthy), family entertainment, with the radio in every house and a weekly excursion to the 'pictures' common-place, and a growing emphasis on education and retention at school beyond the previous norm of departure at 14 years of age.

Victory in the Pacific, which came at great cost to Australia, as this book has shown, ushered in a period of unprecedented safety and comfort in a new Australia that had changed dramatically from the Australia of 1939 and earlier. The Pacific War was the pivotal moment in the story, and it shaped the nation in a way that no previous event in Australian history had done. Prime Minister 'Ben' Chifley hinted at this in his radio broadcast to the people announcing victory on 15 August 1945. His one regret, he said, was that John Curtin, the architect of it all, was not alive to celebrate the victory and, by implication, to guide Australia, with his calm and steady hand, into a new era.